INTENSIVE LATIN

FIRST YEAR & REVIEW

INTENSIVE LATIN
FIRST YEAR & REVIEW

A USER'S MANUAL

Carl A.P. Ruck

CAROLINA ACADEMIC PRESS
Durham, North Carolina

Library of Congress Cataloging-in-Publication Data

Ruck, Carl A. P.
Intensive Latin first year & review : a user's manual /
Carl A. P. Ruck.
p. cm.
ISBN 0-89089-912-6
1. Latin language—Grammar—Handbooks, manuals, etc.
I. Title.
PA2087.5.R78 1997
478.2'421—dc21 97-6301
CIP

CAROLINA ACADEMIC PRESS
700 Kent Street
Durham, NC 27701
Telephone (919) 489-7486
Fax (919) 493-5668

Printed in the United States of America

Cover Illustration: Piranesi, *Portico of the Pantheon*

CONTENTS

PREFACE

INTENSIVE LATIN: FIRST YEAR & REVIEW is intended primarily for the mature student, probably on the college level, although it would also be appropriate for younger students with strong motivation and high verbal aptitude. The course's concise nature and clear organization suits it for **intensive courses** and for **second year review,** as well as for the normal introductory course of about a semester in duration.

The material is subdivided into eleven segments or lessons of approximately equal length. Each segment is constructed according to the same general pattern: a concise grammatical introduction along structural principles is followed by ten or so exercises (**EXERCITATIONES**) of gradually increasing difficulty. The grammatical explanations deal with linguistic development of forms and, in so doing, are able to unify many different uses under a number of basic concepts, although the more traditional nomenclature is also introduced so that the course is compatible with other methods. The exercises prepare the student, not for the edited, simple texts often used in beginning courses, but for the complex and varying styles of the best Latin authors. To this end, the choice of quotations and readings is drawn from a variety of time periods and makes clear the vitality and range of use Latin enjoyed over the centuries. The sequence of topics is determined largely by the frequency of occurrence in Latin so that the most common structures will become the most familiar by the completion of the course. Thus **oratio obliqua** is introduced in the first lesson and the **subjunctive** in the third. Thus also the cases are introduced in accordance with their vitality and longevity in the evolution of the language as it progressed toward the Romance vernaculars: the opposition of nominative and accusative first, then the genitive, followed by the coalescing and moribund dative and ablative.

The exercises are of four types. In the first, the student is asked to **MATCH** one form to another. This replaces the more traditional recitation of declensional and conjugational paradigms, for the matching of forms directs the student's attention to the same problems of ambiguity encountered in reading the language and emphasizes the parity of meaning or structure in forms categorized into different paradigms. In a second type of exercise, the student is asked to **TRANSLATE** sentences and passages from Latin into English, first a section that uses the active vocabulary introduced in the **INDICES VERBORUM** and that presents multiple instances of the grammatical principles being learned; then a section of authentic Latin, with **reading notes** that gloss new words and suggest cognates, although the student is urged to guess the meaning from context before consulting the notes. The third type of exercise requires the student to **CHANGE** one mode of expression in Latin into another. These sentences drill the principles learned in the lesson and build upon structures previously taught. In addition to transformation, they offer another occasion for practice in translation from Latin to English. English-to-Latin composition is not emphasized, although the fourth type of exercise asks the student to **NOTE THE PATTERN** in a Latin quotation and to compose additional examples of the same pattern by translating English sentences into Latin. **ANSWERS** for all the exercises are provided at the back of the book, as well as a **REVIEW OF FORMS** to adapt its use for the second year level, to accompany the reading of selected Latin authors.

The computer tutorial **VADE MECUM** provides **FLASH CARDS** for each of the eleven INDICES VERBORUM (both Latin-English and English- Latin); and drills on all the **MATCH** exercises, with helps, if requested, offering the translation, the lexical entries, and the relevant paradigms, as well as the answers. A drill on **PRINCIPAL PARTS** is included for Lesson Six, to bring the previous Indices Verborum up to completion for the verbal entries.

Piranesi, The Roman Colosseum

THE LATIN LANGUAGE

About four thousand years ago, at the turn of the second millennium before the Christian era, a nomadic people, whose traditional homeland was later remembered as having once been the central Asiatic highlands, after numerous stages of migration and temporary relocation, began to show up at the frontiers of more settled peoples to their south and west. They brought with them their common language and aspects of their culture. When they finally emerge into history, they are found south of the Himalayas and westward into Europe and the British Isles, for which reason they are termed Indo-Europeans. With time, their language developed into various dialects in their new environments and their culture was modified through the influence of the various peoples whom they encountered or joined. In the valley of the Indus, their language developed into Sanskrit, the classical language of India and Hinduism. Another branch of these migrations moved down the Balkan peninsula toward the Aegean Sea, where their language evolved into classical Greek. Still others, a Celto-Italic branch, moved further west. One group that settled in the center of the Italian peninsula spoke a dialect that would eventually become Latin.

Latin was originally the language of the Latini, an Indo-European people inhabiting numerous small communities in the plain of Latium around the lower reaches of the river Tiber and who, between the sixth and fourth centuries before Christ, united into larger states, of which the greatest was Rome. With the expansion of Rome into an Empire, the language of the Latini was spread to most of the known ancient world.

Early in the course of this expansion, Rome slowly exerted dominance over the other Italic dialects of Umbrian, Oscan, and Sabellian, and the Celtic spoken in the north of the peninsula, and was, furthermore, profoundiy influenced by its Etruscan neighbors, a partially Hellenized people of apparently non-Indo-European descent, as well as by the numerous sophisticated colonial Greek settlements of southern Italy and Sicily, from all of whom Latin assimilated concepts and vocabulary.

Latin does not emerge as a literary, written language until the middle of the third century before Christ, although inscriptions and ritual formulae attest to earlier stages in the evolution of the language. This earliest literary language, under the influence of exotic Hellenic models, had already begun to diverge from the common spoken tongue. It underwent further refinement in the last years of the Republic and the reign of Augustus Caesar (70 B.C.–14 A.D.), a period generally considered its "Golden" or classical age, epitomized by the prose of Cicero and the poetry of Vergil and Horace. The writers of the early Empire (14 A.D.–180 A.D.), the so-called "Silver Age," display increasing artificial and rhetorical tendencies, although the prose of Petronius preserves a more natural vernacular speech. The Roman bureaucracy of Empire perpetuated a written language, so-called "Late Latin," that increasingly diverged from the spoken tongues that were meanwhile evolving in their separate ways into the Romance languages. These finally emerge with the dissolution of the Empire, although Latin persisted for over a millennium more as the language of the Church and of statesmen and scholars, as well as antiquarian poets and writers.

PRONUNCIATION. Given the long history of the Latin language, its numerous regional and class differences, and the lack of a living people for whom it is now a native tongue, there is understandably no generally accepted manner of pronouncing it.

Commonly today, Latin is pronounced as it is written, with consonants the same as in English and with a distinction made in the pronunciation of long and short vowels. The letter **v**, however, is usually pronounced as a **w**, a letter lacking in the Latin alphabet. Similarly lacking are the letters **j** and **u**. Latin is sometimes written with these two letters added. **U** is used in this book, (**servus** instead of

servvs) but not the **j**, (**Iānuārius** instead of **Jānuārius**). Latin originally used **i** for both the vowel and the consonant (pronounced like **y**), and **v** similarly did double duty as both the vowel (**u**) and consonant. Latin also had no **k**, but only a **c**, although **k** was sometimes used for transliterating the Greek **kappa** in Latin.

This manner of pronunciation is clearly not authentic. Native speakers apparently would commonly have elided adjacent vowels between words, as is required in reading Latin verse. In such elisions, a final **m** is also elided, indicating that the **m** was not consonantal, but marked a nasalization of the preceding vowel. An initial **h** is also elided in verse, suggesting that refined speakers at some periods suppressed the aspirate sound.

In **syllabification**, a Latin word has as many syllables as vowels or diphthongs (two vowels pronounced together). Each syllable ends with a vowel (a so-called **open syllable**), unless the vowel is followed by more than a single consonant (except those that can be pronounced together, such as **tr** or other examples of a stop plus a liquid), in which case the first of the consonants is pronounced with the preceding vowel (resulting in a so-called **closed syllable**). In verse, a rhythmical distinction is observed between long and short syllables. A syllable is long if it contains a long vowel or diphthong or if it is a closed syllable.

In **accentuation**, Latin early lost the pitch or tone accent characteristic of its parent Indo-European tongue and evolved a system of stress accentuation.

Each Latin word is accentuated. In words of multiple syllables, the accent falls only on the syllable third from the end (the **antepenultimate**) or the syllable second from the end (the **penultimate**). The latter, i.e., accent on the penultimate, occurs if the syllable is long (i.e., long vowel, diphthong, or a closed syllable).

LATIN ACCENTUATION

ALWAYS accent on antipenultimate	EXCEPT accent on penultimate	NEVER accent on ultimate
Ca-tu-lus **a**-ni-mal	**closed syllable** Ca-**tul**-lus	
	long vowel a-ni-**mā**-lis	

INTENSIVE LATIN
FIRST YEAR & REVIEW

Piranesi, Interior of the Pantheon

LESSON ONE

NOMINATIVE AND ACCUSATIVE

Vītam regit fortūna, nōn sapientia.

INFLECTION. Latin is an inflected language. This means that changes are made in the form of certain words (sometimes at the beginning or in the middle, but most commonly at the end) to indicate variations in meaning or grammatical function. The English word "inflection" is derived from a Latin word (**inflectere**) meaning to "turn or bend" something from one form to another.

To a large extent, English is not inflected, even though it evolved from the same Indo-European language group as Latin. In some instances, however, inflected forms have been retained in English, as in the change from **he** to **him**, or **sing** to **sang** and **sung**. To compensate for the loss of a full system of inflection,

English is dependent on the order and grouping of words to vary their meaning and grammatical function. For the most part, word order is not important in Latin, and Latin can express with a single word ideas which often require a whole group of words in English.

DECLENSION. The words of a language can be divided into eight categories of function. These are the so-called **"parts of speech."** One of these categories designates words that are **names of persons, places, or things**. They are called **nouns**, from the Latin word for "name" (**nōmen**). The simple naming of the person, place, or thing presents the noun in what was considered its basic form. According to ancient grammarians, it was thought to deviate or fall away from that basic form when it was inflected, and hence the **inflection of a noun is called its declension**, from the Latin word **dēclināre** meaning to "turn aside or fall away." The deviant forms into which it "falls" are called **cases**, from the Latin word **cāsus** meaning a "falling down."

NOMINATIVE CASE. The form from which a noun falls is called the **nominative**, the "name" case. It was thought of as the **upright case**, whereas the others are **oblique**. The nominative is the form used in simple lists of words, as in a lexicon or dictionary.

When a word or group of words makes a statement it is considered a **sentence**, from the Latin word **sententia** meaning an "expression of opinion." The nominative alone, without any other cases or inflected words, can be used to make a statement or sentence.

Homo deus. **"Man (is a) god."**

Such sentences are called **nominal sentences**. They simply name something or state an equation.

CONJUGATION. Another of the eight parts of speech is the **verb**. These are the words that make an assertion and express action or state of being.

Verbs also, in Latin, can be used alone to make a sentence.

Regit. **"(He, she, or it) rules."**

NOTE that the single word **regit** expresses not only the action of ruling, but also the additional information about who does the ruling, the so-called **subject of the verb**.

This subject in Latin is indicated by inflection.

Regit. **"(He, she, or it) rules."**

Regunt. **"They rule."**

In accordance with the ancient grammarians' terms, this inflection of a verb, as distinct from the declension of a noun, is called its **conjugation**, from the Latin word **conjugāre** meaning "to join together" the different elements that comprise the verb.

A sentence composed of a verb is called a **verbal sentence**.

The subject in such verbal sentences can be made more explicit by adding a nominative as further clarification.

Regit fortūna. **"(It, that is to say,) fortune rules."**

NOTE that the subject **fortūna** does not have to precede the verb as in English. **Regit** is already a complete sentence, and **fortūna** merely adds clarification to what was already ambiguously said about who does the ruling. That is to say that **fortūna** as subject is in apposition to the subject expressed in the conjugated verb.

The nominative is the case used for the subject in apposition to the subject suffix of the conjugated verb.

Declension and **conjugation** are the two forms of **inflection**. They are really just two terms for the same sort of thing. Not all of the eight parts of speech are inflected. Only verbs are conjugated, but later we will learn a few other kinds of words that are declined like nouns.

ACCUSATIVE CASE. The simple verb can also be made more explicit by further describing the action with an **adverb**. The adverb is another of the eight parts of speech. It is an indeclinable word that describes or modifies the action of the verb.

Semper regit fortūna. **"Fortune always rules."**

This same kind of adverbial modification can be supplied by a noun in one of its declensional cases.

Vītam regit fortūna. **"Fortune rules life."**

The noun **vītam** (declined from **vīta**) is in the accusative case. In the example given, it receives the action of the verb and can be called the **direct object of the verb.**

The accusative hence is often called the case of the direct object, although more exactly it should be thought of as the case that allows a noun to function as an adverb. Thus more than one accusative in certain situations can modify the verb, although in English they could not all be direct objects.

Virōs sapientiam docet fortūna. **"Fortune teaches men wisdom."**

NOMINATIVE AND ACCUSATIVE DECLENSION. As you can notice from the example above, the accusative case is characterized by a final [**-m**] for the singular and a final [**-s**] for the plural. Compare the final [**-m**] in English on **him** and **whom**. In Latin, the nouns onto which these accusative suffixes are added may end in any one of five different ways (**-ā-**, **-o-**, **consonant**, **-u-**, or **-ē-**). Hence in Latin there are five types of nouns or declensions.

The **noun stem** is the noun, ending in one of these five characteristic ways, without any declensional suffix. Since the suffix in some situations cannot be easily pronounced, it suffers euphonic alteration. For example, after a consonant, the [**-m**] suffix cannot be pronounced without being vocalized: **lēg-m** → **lēgem**. For this reason, it will be easier to learn the declensional forms as **case endings**, rather than as the actual declensional suffixes. **The case ending is the characteristic appearance of the suffix after euphonic alteration, or other changes, and joined with the final vowel of the stem, if there is one.**

The chart summarizes the case endings of both singular and plural for the nominative and accusative for all five declensions.

NOTE that in declensions II and III, the nominative singular can also occur with no distinctive ending.

PARADIGM 1
NOMINATIVE AND ACCUSATIVE ENDINGS FOR
THE FIVE DECLENSIONS

declension *stem*	Decl I ā-stem	Decl II o-stem	Decl III cons-stem	Decl IV u-stem	Decl V ē-stem
nom. sing.	-a	-us *sometimes no ending*	-s *sometimes no ending*	-us	-ēs
acc. sing.	-am	-um	-em	-um	-em
nom. plural	-ae	-ī	-ēs	-ūs	-ēs
acc. plural	-ās	-ōs	-ēs	-ūs	-ēs

EXAMPLES

	I	II		III		IV	V
nom.	fortūna	deus	vir	lex	homo	manus	diēs
acc.	fortūnam	deum	virum	lēgem	hominem	manum	diem
nom.	fortūnae	deī	virī	lēgēs	hominēs	manūs	diēs
acc.	fortūnās	deōs	virōs	lēgēs	hominēs	manūs	diēs

NOTE that because of the euphonic alterations, you cannot predict what declension a noun belongs to solely on the basis of the lexical entry (nominative singular). You must learn what declension a noun is as you learn each new word.

NOTE that you cannot always discover the noun's stem from the nominative singular (e.g., **vir / [virō]-s**, which is a declension II **o-stem**, or **homo / [homin]-em**, which is a declension III **consonant-stem** ending in **-n-**), but that it is easily discovered by removing the declensional suffix from any other case. Hence you will have to learn one of these declensional forms as part of what you commit to memory as you learn each new noun.

NOTE that the declensional forms are not always distinctive. The Romans, moreover, did not use long marks in writing. Long marks are used in this introductory book merely to make the forms less ambiguous and as an aid in pronunciation. You must always read words in their context and not attempt to translate each word as you come upon it since in isolation you often cannot tell what form it is.

NOTE that the [-s] suffix of the IIIrd declension can combine with the consonant that ends the stem. Thus, **leg-s → lex.**

NOTE that the vowels in the accusative plural of all five declensions are long. This is because the suffix for this form is actually [**-ms**]. The **-m-** is lost for euphony and the loss is compensated for by lengthening the preceding vowel, even in the o-stem and u-stem declensions, where the stem vowel was not long to begin with, and also in the consonant-stem declension, where the vowel was inserted in vocalizing the suffix.

NOTE that the declensional suffix for the nominative plural was originally [-i], but in classical Latin, it was no longer written as **-ai** in the first declension, and in the second declension, the **-o-** of the stem has been lost and the **-i-** lengthened. **In the other three declensions, the distinction between nominative and accusative has been lost in the plural, and the nominative imitates the accusative plural form. Such loss of distinctive declensional forms is typical of the evolution of Latin and the modern Indo-European languages.**

NOTE that most nouns in Latin belong to the IIIrd declension. The IVth and Vth declensions are relatively rare.

INFINITIVE AND THIRD PERSON CONJUGATION. From the contrast of **regit** ("he, she, or it rules") and **regunt** ("they rule"), you might suspect that the conjugation of the verb is characterized by the suffix [**-t**] for the singular and [**-nt**] for the plural.

Just as the nominative case is the basic form or zero-point for the declension of a noun, the basic form for the conjugation of a verb is the **infinitive,** so-called because it is "not limited" by a subject (or "personal") suffix, but is, as it were, "**infinite.**" This is the form of the verb that can be used like a noun to name the action, without making an assertion or sentence by itself. In English, the infinitive is characterized by the word "to," as, for example, "to rule," although there are other ways of translating the Latin infinitive into English. The infinitive is simply the action named and treated as a noun: for example, "(the act of) ruling."

As with nouns, the stem of a verb in Latin can end in different ways. There are four different stems and hence four conjugations: ā-stems, ē-stems, e-stems, and ī-stems. The stem is easily seen in the infinitive form.

PARADIGM 2
INFINITIVE

I ā-stem	II ē-stem	III e-stem	IV ī-stem
amā-re	docē-re	rege-re	audī-re

Since the subject or personal suffixes sometimes cause alterations in the stem, the following chart summarizes the conjugational **endings** (vowel plus suffix, after alteration). These are the endings for the so-called "third person" of the verb (i.e., "he, she, or it" or 3rd person singular and "they" or 3rd person plural).

PARADIGM 3
THIRD PERSON CONJUGATION

conjugation	I ā-stem	II ē-stem	III e-stem	IV ī-stem
3rd pers. sing.	**-at**	**-et**	**-it**	**-it**
3rd pers. pl.	**-ant**	**-ent**	**-unt**	**-iunt**

EXAMPLES

he, she, it	am**at**	doc**et**	reg**it**	aud**it**
they	am**ant**	doc**ent**	reg**unt**	aud**iunt**

ADVERBIAL MODIFICATION OF INFINITIVE. Since the infinitive is like a noun, it can be used in apposition to the subject suffix of a conjugated verb.

Oportet amāre. — **"To love (or loving) is proper and necessary."** Or, **"It behooves (one) to love."**

Because of the latter translation, this pattern is sometimes called an **impersonal construction,** but solely on the basis of the English translation with the impersonal third person "it." In Latin, the subject of **oportet** is the conjugational suffix with **amāre** in apposition to it.

Since the infinitive is a verb, it is modified by adverbs.

Oportet semper amāre. — **"It behooves (one) always to love."**

Hence it can also be modified by a noun in the accusative case functioning as its direct object.

Oportet deum semper amāre. — **"It behooves (one) always to love god."**

There can, of course, be more than one accusative modification. By context, one of these accusatives may function as the subject of the infinitive.

Oportet hominēs deum semper amāre. — **"It behooves men always to love god."** Or, **"Men ought always to love god."**

OBLIQUE STATEMENT. Although the infinitive cannot be declined, it is used like a noun. In the examples above, you saw that the infinitive could be used like the nominative case, in apposition to the subject suffix of a conjugated verb. Just like a noun, the infinitive can also be used like the accusative case, as adverbial modification (or direct object) of a conjugated verb.

Cupit amōrem. — **"He desires love."**

Cupit amāre. — **"He wants to love."**

Such infinitives as objects of a conjugated verb seem to complete the meaning of the verb and hence are called **complementary infinitives.** As you might expect, the infinitive in this structure too can be modified by an adverb or an adverbial accusative functioning as its direct object.

Cupit semper amāre. — **"He wants to love forever."**

Cupit deum amāre. — **"He wants to love god."**

In appropriate contexts, the accusative modification can also function as the subject of the infinitive.

Cupit hominēs deum amāre. — **"He wants men to love god."**

This is an extremely common structure in Latin. Because it often is found with verbs of perceiving, knowing, or saying, it is called **oblique statement (oratio obliqua)** or **indirect discourse,** but it is more common than merely a way to quote someone's words indirectly.

Dīcit hominēs deum amāre. **"He says (that) men love god."**

Videt hominēs deum amāre. **"He sees (that) men love god."**

Since the accusative case merely signals that the noun has an adverbial relationship with the infinitive, there is no way of telling whether the noun is functioning as the subject or object except from context.

Cupit deum amāre. This could also mean: **"He wants god to love."**

ARTICLE. Latin has neither a definite article ("the") nor an indefinite one ("a/an"). In translating into English, you must supply these according to the context.

Cupit hominēs deum amāre. **"He wants men (or the men) to love god (or a god or the god)."**

REMEMBER

Infinitives are not "limited" by subject suffixes and are modified by adverbs and nouns in their adverbial function as accusatives. Only by context can you determine which noun gives the kind of information that lets it function like its subject or its object. The structure is the same in English, except that word order can distinguish subject from object: *I want him to love her.* This is the structure called oratio obliqua, where the entire infinitive phrase is the object of the verb. Some verbs, in contrast, always have only infinitive phrases in apposition to the third person singular subject suffix, and are called impersonal verbs.

Actually, in English, the word "it" is not the subject in such sentences as "It is necessary to love." The subject, as in the Latin with *oportet* is the infinitive. "It" is an EXPLETIVE (or "filler"), which is a word that merely fills space without meaning, allowing the subject to be placed later, after the main verb "is."

INDEX VERBORUM / VOCABULARY LIST

NOUNS
(DECLINED WITH THE STEMS AND DECLENSIONS INDICATED)

amor, amōrem III	love
deus, deum II	god
diēs, diem V	day
fēmina, fēminam I	woman
fīlia, fīliam I	daughter
fīlius, fīlium II	son
fortūna, fortūnam I	fortune, luck
homo, hominem III	human being, man
lex, lēgem III	law
manus, manum IV	hand
mater, matrem III	mother
pater, patrem III	father
puella, puellam I	girl
puer, puerum II	boy
sapientia, sapientiam I	wisdom
vir, virum II	man
vīta, vītam I	life

VERBS
(CONJUGATED IN THE CONJUGATION INDICATED BY THE INFINITIVE)

amāre	love
audīre	hear
cupere	desire, want (Note: cupiunt)
dīcere	say, tell, speak
docēre	teach
oportēre	behoove, be necessary, be proper, ought
regere	rule
vidēre	see

ADVERBS
(UNINFLECTED)

nōn	not
semper	always, forever

CONJUNCTIONS
(UNINFLECTED)

et	**and**
-que	**and** (added onto the end of the word it connects; joins more closely than **et**)

EXERCITATIONES / EXERCISES

I. CHANGE each noun to the corresponding case in the plural. (**ANSWERS** for all exercises are found in the Appendix.)

1. fēminam
2. vir
3. fortūna
4. hominem
5. deum
6. diēs
7. diem
8. puerum
9. manus
10. lex
11. puer
12. fīlia
13. mater
14. puella
15. homo
16. amor
17. deus
18. virum
19. patrem
20. vīta

II. MATCH the second noun to the first by changing it into the same form (case and number).

1. hominem (vir)
2. amōrēs (deus)
3. diēs (homo)
4. fīliae (diēs)
5. manūs (vir)
6. fortūnam (mater)
7. diēs (manus)
8. patrēs (puer)
9. lēgēs (puella)
10. deum (diēs)
11. sapientiam (lex)
12. puellās (fēmina)
13. virī (amor)
14. diēs (sapientia)
15. amor (pater)
16. vītae (vir)
17. virōs (homo)
18. dī (diēs) **NOTE** that **dī** is sometimes contracted from **deī**.
19. fēminās (manus)
20. patrēs (vir)

III. MATCH the second noun to the first by changing it into the same form. (Long marks are not indicated in this exercise.)

1. dies (vir)
2. manus (amor)
3. leges (femina)
4. manus (filius)
5. dies (fortuna)

IV. MATCH the second verb to the first by changing it into the same form.

1. amat (audīre)
2. regunt (audīre)
3. videt (regere)
4. audiunt (amāre)
5. vident (docēre)
6. amant (regere)
7. docent (audīre)
8. docet (cupere)
9. regit (amāre)
10. audit (vidēre)

V. TRANSLATE.

1. Vītam fortūna semper regit, nōn sapientia. Oportet vītam regere. Fortūnam vītam regere nōn oportet. Sapientiam oportet vītam regere. Fēminae vītam regere cupiunt. Dīcunt hominēs fortūnam semper vītam regere. Virī fortūnam vītam regere vident. Dī vītam regunt, nōn fortūna. Dī vītam regunt, nōn fortūnam.

2. Amor deus, nōn fortūna.

3. Patrem matremque amant filiī filiaeque. Oportetque filiās filiōsque patrem matremque semper amāre. Mater filiam filium amāre videt. Pater matrem filiam amāre dīcit.

4. Lex hominēs regunt deusque. Puellae puerīque vident lēgem deumque semper hominēs regere. Fortūnam vītam regere nōn oportet. Deum oportet lēgemque.

5. Dī hominēs docent sapientiam amāre. Fēminae audiunt hominēs sapientiam nōn amāre.

VI. TRANSLATE. (Try to guess the meaning of unfamiliar words from context and cognates before consulting the adjacent **reading notes**. You are not required to commit the new words to memory unless they appear eventually in a **VOCABULARY LIST** in a later chapter.)

1. Manus manum **fricat**.

fricāre rub Cf. friction

2. **Pecūnia avārum irrītat,** nōn **satiat.**

pecūnia, pecūniam I money, wealth Cf. pecuniary, impecunious
avārus, avārum II greedy (person) Cf. avaricious
irrītāre provoke, exasperate Cf. irritate
satiāre satisfy Cf. satiate

3. Semper avārus **eget.**

egēre be in need

4. **Audācēs** fortūna **iuvat timidō**sque **repellit.**

audax, audācem III bold (person), Cf. audacious
iuvāre aid, help Cf. adjuvant
timidus, timidum II timid (person)
repellere repulse Cf. repel

5. Amor **gignit** amōrem.

gignere beget, produce Cf. genital

6. **Grātia grātiam parit.**

grātia, grātiam I favor Cf. gratitude
parere beget, produce Cf. parturition

7. **Lupus pilum mūtat,** nōn **mentem.**

lupus, lupum II wolf Cf. lupine
pilus, pilum II hair, fur Cf. pile, depilitate
mens, mentem III mind Cf. mental
mūtāre change Cf. mutate

8. **Līs lītem generat.**

līs, lītem III quarrel, law trial Cf. litigation
generāre (= **gignere, parere**) Cf. generate

9. Nōn generant **aquilae columbās.**

aquila, aquilam I eagle Cf. aquiline
columba, columbam I dove Cf. columbary

10. Lupus lupum **cognōscit** et **fūrem fūr.**

cognōscere recognize Cf. cognate, cognition
fūr, fūrem III thief Cf. furtive

VII. CHANGE each of the following statements to oblique statements (**oratio obliqua**) with the verbs **audit, dīcit,** or **videt.** (**REMEMBER** to make the verb an infinitive, with its subject in the accusative case; and the whole infinitive phrase becomes the direct object of the verb of saying or perceiving.)

1. Vītam fortūna regit.
2. Semper vident hominēs dī.

3. Cupit mater puellam docēre. (**REMEMBER** the main verb becomes the infinitive, not the complementary infinitive, which will still be complementary to the new infinitive.)
4. Virī lēgēs amant.
5. Fīliās docent matrēs fīliōsque patrēs.
6. Sapientiam vītam regere oportet.
7. Puer patrem amat.
8. Dī virōs fēmināsque regunt.
9. Amor deōs regit.
10. Pater fīlium lēgēs docet. (**REMEMBER** that here you will end up with three accusatives, and, as always, only context can help to distinguish which one is the subject of the infinitive.)

VIII. CHANGE each of the following statements into an infinitive phrase in apposition to the subject suffix of the impersonal verb **oportet**. (**REMEMBER** that this is like the previous exercise, but here the infinitive phrase is the subject of **oportet**.)

1. Mater puellam amat et pater puerum.
2. Dī hominēs regunt.
3. Sapientia vītam regit.
4. Cupit puer sapientiam amāre.
5. Semper vident dī fēminās virōsque.

IX. NOTE THE PATTERN in each of the following sentences and compose a translation of the English sentences into Latin using the same pattern.

1. **Amor gignit amōrem.**
   Man sees man.
   Fortune rules life.
   The mother loves (her) daughter.
2. **Vītam regit fortūna, nōn sapientia.**
   The father teaches (his) sons, not the mother.
   Law rules men, not the gods.
3. **Dīcit hominēs deum amāre.**
   He says (that) the mother loves her daughter.
   They see that the mother loves her sons.
   The woman hears that the man teaches his sons.

4. **Deum amāre oportet.**

It behooves (one) to rule (one's) life.

Men and women ought to teach their sons and daughters.

Piranesi, View of Three Temples

LESSON TWO

GENDER, ADJECTIVES, PRESENT CONJUGATION

Ars longa, vīta brevis.

GENDER. Nouns in Latin, as in English, are characterized as being one of three genders: masculine, feminine, or neuter. A noun's gender often corresponds to the "sex" of the person or thing named, but sometimes animate beings may be considered grammatically neuter and inanimate things as masculine or feminine. Thus in English a baby may be referred to as "it" or a ship as "she."

In Latin, quite a few inanimate things are classified grammatically as masculine or feminine, and quite often the sex does not determine whether an animate being is classified grammatically as masculine or feminine.

The three genders are not equally distributed amongst the five noun declensions.

Declension I	Declension II	Declension III	Declension IV	Declension V
F (but some M)	M, N (but some F)	M, F, N	M (but some F and N)	F (except for diēs)

NOTE that in Declension II, the exception is the **name of trees, countries, and small islands**, and a few other words which are Feminine; and in Declension V, **diēs** is Feminine when it means a special day or time.

The gender of a noun must be learned as part of the information that you commit to memory as you learn each new word. The following list presents the gender of the nouns you have already learned.

I	II	III	IV	V
fēmina F	deus M	amor M	manus F	diēs usually M
fīlia F	fīlius M	homo M		
fortūna F	puer M	pater M		
puella F	vir M	lex F		
sapientia F		mater F		
vīta F				

NEUTER NOMINATIVE AND ACCUSATIVE. As you can see from the list above, you have not yet learned any neuter nouns.

For all neuter nouns, the accusative case is always identical with the nominative (or lexical entry). The two cases can be distinguished only by context.

Perīculum videt vir. **"The man sees the danger."**

Perīculum docet virum. **"The danger teaches the man."**

The chart summarizes the declensional endings for the nominative-accusative singular and plural of neuter nouns.

PARADIGM 4
NEUTER NOMINATIVE-ACCUSATIVE DECLENSION

	I ā-stem	II o-stem	III con-stem	IV u-stem	V ē-stem
nom & acc sing		-um	lexical entry	-ū	
nom & acc pl		-a	-a	-ua	
		EXAMPLES			
		II	III	IV	
nom singular		perīcul**um**	**poēma**	cornū	
acc singular		perīcul**um**	**poēma**	cornū	
nom plural		perīcul**a**	poēmat**a**	corn**ua**	
acc plural		perīcul**a**	poēmat**a**	corn**ua**	

NOTE that you cannot tell the stem of declension III neuters from the accusative singular since it is identical with the lexical entry.

ADJECTIVE. An adjective is the part of speech that describes (or modifies) a noun. In Latin, adjectives are declined, and like nouns, they belong to different declensions depending upon the nature of their stem.

There are no adjectives of declensions IV and V. In declensions I, II, and III, adjectives are declined similarly to the nouns of the same declensional type.

AGREEMENT. Since an adjective describes a noun, the adjective must describe it as the same gender (or must "agree" with it). Obviously also it would not be sensible to describe the noun as a different number (singular or plural) or as performing a different grammatical function in the sentence (case). Hence, **an adjective must agree with its noun in gender, number, and case.**

Agreement, however, does not mean that the noun and adjective will always have the same endings, for both the noun and the adjective can only be declined in accordance each with its own declension.

Ars (III) longa (I), vīta (I) brevis (III). "**Art (is) long, life (is) short.**"

Hominem (III) videt avārum (II). "**He sees the greedy man.**"

NOTE that the order of words does not determine the meaning and that the adjective and noun do not have to be adjacent.

ADJECTIVES OF THE FIRST AND SECOND DECLENSIONS. One very common class of adjectives has a stem that varies between the **ā-stem** (I) and **o-**

stem (II) declensions. It has the endings of the first declension for feminine agreement and the endings of the second for masculine or neuter agreement.

The chart summarizes the endings for declension I/II adjectives.

PARADIGM 5
GENDER FOR I–II ADJECTIVES
NOMINATIVE & ACCUSATIVE

	I FEMININE	II MASCULINE	II NEUTER
nominative sing	**-a**	**-us** (or nothing)	**-um**
accusative sing	**-am**	**-um**	**-um**
nominative plur	**-ae**	**-ī**	**-a**
accusative plur	**-ās**	**-ōs**	**-a**

NOTE that adjectives of this type (combining the first and second declensions) are indicated in vocabulary lists in the following abbreviated form: **longus, -a, -um**. Or (if the masculine is declined like **puer** or **vir**): **miser, -era, -erum.**

NOTE in the examples given on the next page how the adjective often limits the ambiguity of the noun's case since it may belong to a declension that has more distinctive endings than the noun's declension.

NOTE that the order of words in a noun-adjective phrase is determined by emphasis, with the word that goes first receiving the greater emphasis:

longa vīta	**"a *long* life"**
vīta longa	**"a *life* that is long"**

ADJECTIVES OF THE THIRD DECLENSION. Another large class of adjectives is comprised of consonant-stems and hence they belong to declension III. Many of these adjectives have a separate form for the neuter (nominative-accusative), but the masculine and feminine have the same form. Others have a separate form for the feminine as well. Still others have a common form for all three genders. Whether an adjective is of **"three, two, or one termination"** must be learned as the lexical entry:

three terminations	*two terminations*	*one termination*
acer, acris, acre (M, F, N)	**brevis, breve** (M-F, N)	**atrox** (M-F-N)

Note that if an adjective is of one termination, an additional indication of the declensional stem must be learned; hence, **atrōcem.**

EXAMPLES: NOUN & ADJECTIVE DECLENSION

Declension I-II Adjectives **longus, -a, -um; miser, -era, -erum**

	with declension I noun		**with declension II noun**		**with declension III noun**		
	masculine **poēta**	*feminine* **vīta**	*masculine* **vir**	*neuter* **perīculum**	*masculine* **homo**	*feminine* **lex**	*neuter* **poēma**
	"unhappy tall poet"	"unhappy long life"	"unhappy tall man"	"miserable long danger"	"unhappy tall man"	"miserable long law"	"miserable long poem"
nom	**poēta miser longus**	**vīta misera longa**	**vir miser longus**	**perīculum miserum longum**	**homo miser longus**	**lex misera longa**	**poēma miserum longum**
acc	**poētam miserum longum**	**vītam miseram longam**	**virum miserum longum**	**perīculum miserum longum**	**hominem miserum longum**	**lēgem miseram longam**	**poēma miserum longum**
nom	**poētae miserī longī**	**vītae miserae longae**	**virī miserī longī**	**perīcula misera longa**	**hominēs miserī longī**	**lēgēs miserae longae**	**poēmata misera longa**
acc	**poētās miserōs longōs**	**vītās miserās longās**	**virōs miserōs longōs**	**perīcula misera longa**	**hominēs miserōs longōs**	**lēgēs miserās longās**	**poēmata misera longa**

	with declension IV noun			**with declension V noun**	
	masculine **lacus**	*feminine* **manus**	*neuter* **cornū**	*masculine* **diēs**	*feminine* **rēs**
	"unhappy long lake"	"miserable long hand"	"miserable long horn"	"miserable long day"	"miserable long thing"
nom	**lacus miser longus**	**manus misera longa**	**cornū miserum longum**	**diēs miser longus**	**rēs misera longa**
acc	**lacum miserum longum**	**manum miseram longam**	**cornū miserum longum**	**diem miserum longum**	**rem miseram longam**
nom	**lacūs miserī longī**	**manūs miserae longae**	**cornua misera longa**	**diēs miserī longī**	**rēs miserae longae**
acc	**lacūs miserōs longōs**	**manūs miserās longās**	**cornua misera longa**	**diēs miserōs longōs**	**rēs miserās longās**

The adjectives of two terminations, like **brevis, breve**, are the most common declension III adjectives.

The chart summarizes the endings for declension III adjectives.

PARADIGM 6
GENDER FOR DECLENSION III ADJECTIVES

	III MASCULINE	III FEMININE	III NEUTER
nominative sing	no ending	-is	-e
accusative sing	-em	-em	-e
nominative plur	-ēs	-ēs	-ia
accusative plur	-ēs	-ēs	-ia

NOTE that adjectives of three terminations have three distinct forms only in the nominative singular: **acer (M), acris (F), acre (N)**

NOTE that adjectives of one termination have only one form for each case except in the masculine-feminine and neuter accusative singular, and the nominative-accusative plural, where the neuter has a separate form: **atrōcēs, atrōcia.**

NOTE that it is only in the nominative singular (M, F, N) and the nominative and accusative singular and plural neuter that the distinction between one, two, or three terminations occurs.

ADJECTIVES AS NOUNS. Adjectives are often used without a noun if the implied noun is easily grasped from the context and the gender of the adjective.

Pecūnia avārum nōn satiat.	**"Money doesn't satisfy a greedy (person)." Cf. avārus, -a, -um.**
Varium et mūtābile semper fēmina.	**"Woman is always a changing and fickle (creature or thing)." Cf. varius, -a, -um. Varia et mūtābilis fēmina** would mean: **"A woman is changeable and fickle."**

PRESENT CONJUGATION. You have already learned the subject suffix or personal ending for the third person ("he, she, it / they") of the conjugated verb. The chart summarizes the other personal endings: first person ("I / we") and second person ("you," both singular and plural). Latin distinguishes between you (singular) and you (plural).

EXAMPLES: NOUN & ADJECTIVE DECLENSION

Declension III Adjectives: **acer, acris, acre** (three terminations); **brevis, breve** (two terminations); **atrox** (one termination)

	with declension I noun		**with declension II noun**		**with declension III noun**		
	masculine **poēta**	*feminine* **vīta**	*masculine* **vir**	*neuter* **perīculum**	*masculine* **homo**	*feminine* **lex**	*neuter* **poēma**
	"fierce short cruel poet"	"fierce short cruel life"	"fierce short cruel man"	"fierce short cruel danger"	"fierce short cruel man"	"bitter short cruel law"	"bitter short atrocious poem"
nom	**poēta acer brevis atrox**	**vīta acris brevis atrox**	**vir acer brevis atrox**	**perīculum acre breve atrox**	**homo acer brevis atrox**	**lex acris brevis atrox**	**poēma acre breve atrox**
acc	**poētam acrem brevem atrōcem**	**vītam acrem brevem atrōcem**	**virum acrem brevem atrōcem**	**perīculum acre breve atrox**	**hominem acrem brevem atrōcem**	**lēgem acrem brevem atrōcem**	**poēma acre breve atrox**
nom	**poētae acrēs brevēs atrōcēs**	**vītae acrēs brevēs atrōcēs**	**virī acrēs brevēs atrōcēs**	**perīcula acria brevia atrōcia**	**hominēs acrēs brevēs atrōcēs**	**lēgēs acrēs brevēs atrōcēs**	**poēmata acria brevia atrōcia**
acc	**poētās acrēs brevēs atrōcēs**	**vītās acrēs brevēs atrōcēs**	**virōs acrēs brevēs atrōcēs**	**perīcula acria brevia atrōcia**	**hominēs acrēs brevēs atrōcēs**	**lēgēs acrēs brevēs atrōcēs**	**poēmata acria brevia atrōcia**

	with declension IV noun			**with declension V noun**	
	masculine **lacus**	*feminine* **manus**	*neuter* **cornū**	*masculine* **diēs**	*feminine* **rēs**
	"bitter short cruel lake"	"fierce short cruel hand"	"fierce short cruel horn"	"bitter short cruel day"	"fierce short cruel thing"
nom	**lacus acer brevis atrox**	**manus acris brevis atrox**	**cornū acre breve atrox**	**diēs acer brevis atrox**	**rēs acris brevis atrox**
acc	**lacum acrem brevem atrōcem**	**manum acrem brevem atrōcem**	**cornū acre breve atrox**	**diem acrem brevem atrōcem**	**rem acrem brevem atrōcem**
nom	**lacūs acrēs brevēs atrōcēs**	**manūs acrēs brevēs atrōcēs**	**cornua acria brevia atrōcia**	**diēs acrēs brevēs atrōcēs**	**rēs acrēs brevēs atrōcēs**
acc	**lacūs acrēs brevēs atrōcēs**	**manūs acrēs brevēs atrōcēs**	**cornua acria brevia atrōcia**	**diēs acrēs brevēs atrōcēs**	**rēs acrēs brevēs atrōcēs**

NOTE that, as always, a nominative case can be used in apposition to the subject suffix of a conjugated verb.

Docēmus.	**"We teach."**
Docēmus fēminae.	**"We women teach."**

PARADIGM 7
PRESENT CONJUGATION: 1ST, 2ND, & 3RD PERSONS

	Conjug I ā-stem	Conjug II ē-stem	Conjug III e-stem	Conjug IV ī-stem
1st sg "I"	**-ō**	**-e-ō**	**-ō** **-i-ō**	**-i-ō**
2nd sg "you"	**-ā-s**	**-ē-s**	**-i-s**	**-ī-s**
3rd sg "he, she, it"	**-a-t**	**-e-t**	**-i-t**	**-i-t**
1st pl "we"	**-ā-mus**	**-ē-mus**	**-i-mus**	**-ī-mus**
2nd pl "you"	**-ā-tis**	**-ē-tis**	**-i-tis**	**-ī-tis**
3rd pl "they"	**-a-nt**	**-e-nt**	**-unt** **-i-unt**	**-i-unt**

NOTE that some verbs of conjugation III seem originally to have been **short i-stems**, which as a separate conjugation coalesced with **short e-stems** except in certain forms, where they resemble **long ī-stems** of conjugation IV. That is to say that there really are five conjugations, but **short i-stems** are usually classified as a special group in the conjugation III, the so-called **i-stems**, with a first person in [**-i-ō**] instead of simply [**-ō**]. These **short i-stems** of conjugation III are listed in vocabulary lists as follows: **incipiō, -ere.** Since the conjugational type of such verbs is not apparent from the infinitive alone (as it is for all other verbs), it is customary to list all verbs in the same manner: **I amō, -āre; II doceō, -ēre; III regō, -ere; incipiō, -ere; IV audiō, -īre.**

NOTE that in the 1st person singular of conjugations I and III (but not III i-stems), the suffix has contracted with the final stem vowel, which hence is lost. In conjugations II and IV, the vowel is retained, but shortened. It is similarly shortened (wherever originally long) in the 3rd person.

EXAMPLES

	Conj I ā-stem	Conj II ē-stem	Conj III e-stem	Conj III i-stem	Conj IV ī-stem
infinitive	am**āre**	doc**ēre**	reg**ere**	incip**ere**	aud**īre**
1st sing	am**ō**	doce**ō**	reg**ō**	incipi**ō**	audi**ō**
2nd sing	am**ās**	doc**ēs**	reg**is**	incip**is**	aud**īs**
3rd sing	am**at**	doc**et**	reg**it**	incip**it**	aud**it**
1st plur	am**āmus**	doc**ēmus**	reg**imus**	incip**imus**	aud**īmus**
2nd plur	am**ātis**	doc**ētis**	reg**itis**	incip**itis**	aud**ītis**
3rd plur	am**ant**	doc**ent**	reg**unt**	incip**iunt**	aud**iunt**

IRREGULAR VERBS. A few very common verbs in Latin do not conform to any of the four vowel-stem conjugations. Originally there were two types of verbs, those with a vowel before the personal suffixes (as in the four conjugations above) and those without a vowel. In Latin, most of these "**zero-stem**" verbs have been made to conform to one of the regular conjugations, but a few do not and must be learned as so-called "**irregular verbs**".

The verb "to be" (**esse**) is such a verb, formed from the stem [**es-**]. In the infinitive, the **r** has been assimilated to the final **s** of the stem (**es-re** → **es-se**) and the zero conjugation is obvious in some of the other forms: **es-t; es-tis.** In other forms, the initial **e** has been lost and other euphonic changes have occurred.

IRREGULAR CONJUGATION OF *ESSE*

INFINITIVE **esse**			
1st sing "I am"	**sum**	*1st plur "we are"*	**sumus**
2nd sing "you are"	**es**	*2nd plur "you are"*	**estis**
3rd sing "he-she-it is"	**est**	*3rd plur "they are"*	**sunt**

PREDICATE NOMINATIVE. When a nominative case (noun or adjective) in a verbal sentence is **not in apposition to the subject suffix**, it is said to belong to the "**predicate**" (or that which is said or predicated about the subject).

Videt prīmus. — **"He sees first."** Cf. ***Homo prīmus videt.*** **"The first man sees."** Often it is only context that can determine whether or not a nominative is predicate, for this could also mean: **"A man sees first."**

Such predicate nominatives are common with the verb **esse** since it (and verbs of similar meaning) often state an equation or 'coupling' (and hence are called **copulative verbs**).

Fēminae bonae sunt.	**"Women are good."** Cf. ***Sunt fēminae bonae.*** Not predicate: **"There are good women,** or **good women exist."**

The predicate nominative must agree with the subject.

Hominēs bonī sunt.	**"Men are good."**

When such copulative verbs are indirectly quoted (see page 8, oblique statement), the predicate nominative will have to change to accusative to agree with the accusative "subject" modification of the infinitive.

Dīcit fēminās esse bonās.	**"He says women are good."**
Dīcit hominēs esse bonōs.	**"He says men are good."**

REMEMBER

Adjectives must agree with the nouns they modify or describe in CASE, GENDER, and NUMBER, but they can only be declined in their own declension, which may or may not be the same as that of the noun.

INDEX VERBORUM

NOTE that the gender is indicated by the demonstrative adjective **ille (M)**, **illa (F)**, **illud (N)**. Although, as you already know, Latin does not have an indefinite article ("a/an") nor a definite article ("the"), the demonstrative is merely a more explicit or stronger article, pointing to the thing named ("that"). It is from this demonstrative that the article in modern Romance languages evolved, apparently because of its common use in colloquial or popular speech. In classical usage, it maintained its demonstrative force and was not used as a simple article, but it will be easier for you to memorize the gender of new nouns if you learn them with the appropriate demonstrative form.

Like all adjectives, the demonstrative must agree with its noun in number and case, as well as gender. For most of its forms, it is declined like a declension I-II adjective.

	MASCULINE	FEMININE	NEUTER
nominative singular	ille	illa	illud
accusative singular	illum	illam	illud
nominative plural	illī	illae	illa
accusative plural	illōs	illās	illa

(illa) ars, artem III	**skill, profession**
(illud) carmen, *nom. pl.* carmina III	**song, poem**
(illud) cornū, *nom. pl.* cornua IV	**horn (of an animal), (musical) horn**
(ille) daemon, daemonem III	**spirit, demon, god**
(ille) lacus, lacum IV	**tub, vat, lake, cistern**
(illa) pecūnia, pecūniam I	**property, money**
(illud) perīculum, *nom. pl.* perīcula II	**attempt, hazard, danger**
(illud) poēma, *nom. pl.* poēmata III	**poem**
(ille) poēta, poētam I	**poet**
(illa) rēs, rem V	**affair, thing, fact, property, cause, lawsuit, event**

acer, acris, acre	**sharp, acute, vehement, ardent, fierce**
amīcus, -a, -um	**friendly**
atrox (*accus.* atrōcem)	**savage, atrocious, cruel**
audax (*accus.* audācem)	**bold**
avārus, -a, -um	**covetous, avaricious, greedy**
brevis, -e	**short, small**
bonus, -a, -um	**(morally) good; *masc. pl..* bonī "upper-class people;" *neut. pl.* bona "goods"**
longus, -a, -um	**long, tall**
miser, -era, -erum	**miserable, wretched**
mūtābilis, -e	**changeable, mutable**
prīmus, -a, -um	**first, chief**
sōlus, -a, -um	**alone, only, lonely**
timidus, -a, -um	**afraid, cowardly, timid**
varius, -a, -um	**changing, various, diverse**

canō, -ere	**sing, celebrate by song, recite (poetry)**
incipiō, -ere	**begin**
scrībō, -ere	**write, draw, compose in writing**

satiō, -āre	**satisfy, satiate**
sum, esse	**be, exist**
neque (also **nec**)	**and not** (**neque** is commonly used instead of **et nōn**)

EXERCITATIONES

I. **IDENTIFY** the declensional type for each of the adjectives listed in the **index verborum.** (**ANSWERS** for all exercises are found in the Appendix.)

II. **MATCH** the adjective to the noun by changing it into the same form.

1. manūs (audax)
2. rēs (acer)
3. amīcī (mūtābilis)
4. poēta (miser)
5. patrēs (amīcus)
6. lex (atrox)
7. virōs (acer)
8. puellās (bonus)
9. pecūnia (miser)
10. carmina (brevis)
11. rem (miser)
12. poētās (bonus)
13. perīcula (atrox)
14. daemonēs (bonus)
15. vir (brevis)
16. cornua (acer)
17. lacūs (longus)
18. rēs (bonus)
19. puerōs (mūtābilis)
20. fīliī (miser)

III. **MATCH** the second phrase to the first by changing it into the same form.

1. virum acrem (fēmina acris)
2. amīcōs timidōs (mater timida)
3. diēs prīmōs (poēta bonus)
4. hominēs avārī (poēta audax)
5. diem brevem (carmen miserum)
6. fortūnam sōlam (cornū acre)
7. perīcula varia (daemon atrox)
8. avārī miserī (vīta brevis)
9. manūs audācēs (vir bonus)
10. lēgem prīmam (mūtābilis fēmina)
11. pecūniās miserās (mater audax)
12. rēs longae (poēma miserum)
13. cornua acria (ars prīma)
14. puēllās avārās (puer timidus)
15. carmina varia (timidus sōlus)
16. perīculum mūtābile (poēta miser)
17. lacum longum (rēs brevis)
18. dī audācēs (fīlius sōlus)
19. fīliae bonae (carmen breve)
20. amōrēs acrēs (rēs prīma)

IV. **MATCH** the second phrase to the first by changing it into the same form. (This time long marks are not marked.)

1. lacus (vir bonus)
2. res (lex atrox)

3. dies (amicus mutabilis)
4. pericula (pater avarus)
5. carmina (poeta timidus)

V. **MATCH** the second verb to the first by changing it into the same form.

1. oportet (incipiō)
2. scrībunt (canō)
3. vidēmus (satiō)
4. est (doceō)
5. cupitis (amō)
6. vident (incipiō)
7. canis (amō)
8. scrībimus (sum)
9. regunt (audiō)
10. dīcitis (satiō)
11. cupit (videō)
12. scrībis (sum)
13. docent (regō)
14. audītis (doceō)
15. amāmus (incipiō)
16. cupere (satiō)
17. docēs (audiō)
18. esse (incipiō)
19. estis (audiō)
20. satiant (doceō)

VI. TRANSLATE.

1. Poēta carmen canere incipit prīmus. Ille vir incipit prīmus, nōn illa fēmina. Ille incipit prīmus, nōn illa. Illa canit. Nōn incipit canere fēmina. Incipit ille. Prīmus est poēta et prīmus incipit canere. Nōn est illa prīma. Oportet poētam incipere prīmum. Fēminam incipere nōn oportet prīmam. Fēmina poēta est. Nōn est illa poēta prīma. Poēta fēminaque canunt.

2. Docent poētae hominēs vītam longam nōn amāre. Vīta brevis bona est, nōn longa. Timidī vītam longam amant, nōn bonī. Vīta mūtābilis est. Vītam brevem amant bonī. Vīta misera est. Vītam regit fortūna misera, nōn bona fortūna. Sapientiam oportet vītam regere, nōn fortūnam.

3. Avārōs oportet pecūniam semper nōn amāre. Miserī pecūniam amant, nōn bonī. Vir bonus nōn amat pecūniam. Sapientiam amat. Poētae bonī hominēs docent pecūniam nōn amāre. Avārī sōlī pecūniam amant.

4. Bonum est lēgēs scrībere. Virī bonī lēgēs scrībunt. Lex est prīma vītam longam nōn amāre.

5. Varium et mūtābile est semper illud perīculum. Miserum est. Vir miser perīculum nōn videt. Fēmina incipit perīculum vidēre prīma. Prīmum perīculum nōn videt fēmina misera.

6. Sunt hominēs bonī. Sunt fēminae bonae. Hominēs bonī sunt et fēminae miserae. Oportet hominēs fēmināsque bonōs esse. **NOTE** that masculine agreement dominates over the other genders.

7. Deōs oportet sōlōs semper vītam regere. Neque oportet hominēs mūtābilēs miserōsque vītam regere. Dī sōlī bonī sunt.

8. Fēminās docēmus poētae carmina canere prīmās neque virōs. Oportet fēminās incipere canere prīmās neque virōs. Fēminae canunt prīmae.

9. Scrībunt lēgēs bonī. Virī bonī lēgēs scrībunt bonās. Atrox lēgēs scrībit atrōcēs et bonus bonās.

10. Pecūniam cupiunt avārī semper. Nōn satiat pecūnia avārōs. Vītam bonam oportet hominēs satiāre, nōn pecūniam.

VII. TRANSLATE. (Try to guess the meaning of new words on the basis of context and cognates before consulting the adjacent **reading notes.**)

1. Varium et mūtābile semper fēmina. *VERGILIUS.* Cf. Varia et mūtābilis semper illa fēmina.

2. **Obsequium** amīcos, **vēritas odium parit.** *TERENTIUS.*

   (illud) **obsequium II** indulgence Cf. obsequious
   (illa) vēritas, vēritātem III truth Cf. verity
   (illud) odium II hatred Cf. odious
   pariō, -ere beget, produce Cf. parturition

3. **Dolēre malum** est. *CICERO.*

   doleō, -ēre feel pain, grieve Cf. dolorous
   malus, -a, -um bad

4. Fortūna nōn **mūtat genus.** *HORATIUS.*

   mūtō, -āre change Cf. mutation
   (illud) genus *nom. pl.* **genera III** birth, origin, class Cf. generic

5. **Errāre** est **hūmānum.** *CICERO.*

   errō, -āre wander, make a mistake, err
   hūmānus, -a, -um human

6. Homo sōlus aut deus aut daemon.

7. **Ambitiōsa** nōn est **fames.**

   ambitiōsus, -a, -um fawning, vain, willingly solicited, honored, admired Cf. ambition
   (illa) fames, famem III hunger Cf. famine

8. Aut amat aut **ōdit mulier. Nihil** est **tertium.**

ōdit he, she, it hates Cf. odious
(illa) mulier, mulierem III woman, female, wife Cf. muliebrity
(illud) nihil *indeclinable* nothing Cf. nihilism
tertius, -a, -um third Cf. tertiary

9. **Experientia** docet.

(illa) experientia, experientiam I experience

10. **Hōrās** nōn **numerō nisī serēnās.** *INSCRIPTION ON A SUNDIAL.*

(illa) hōra, hōram I hour Cf. horary
numerō, -āre count, number Cf. enumerate
nisī *conjunction* if not, unless
serēnus, -a, -um serene

11. Hūmānum errāre est, hūmānum **autem ignōscere** est. *PLAUTUS.*

autem *conjunction* however, on the other hand
ignōscō, -ere forgive

12. Ars est **cēlāre** artem. *VERGILIUS.*

cēlō, -āre hide, conceal

13. **Ignis aurum probat, miseria fortēs** virōs. *SENECA.*

(ille) ignis, ignem III fire Cf. ignite
(illud) aurum II gold Cf. aureate
probō, -āre prove, approve Cf. probe
(illa) miseria, miseriam I misfortune, misery
fortis, -e strong Cf. fortify

14. **Labōrāre** est **ōrāre.** *MONASTIC PUN.*

labōrō, -āre labor
ōrō, -āre pray Cf. oratorio

15. Manus manum **lavat.** *SENECA.*

lavō, -āre wash Cf. lavatory

16. Miserōs **prūdentia** prīma **relinquit.**

(illa) prūdentia, prūdentiam I prudence
relinquō, -ere leave Cf. relinquish

17. **Nātūra abhorret vacuum.** *RABELAIS.*

(illa) nātūra, nātūram I nature
abhorreō, -ēre abhor
vacuus, -a, -um empty Cf. vacuum

18. **Nōmen amīcitia** est, nōmen **ināne fidēs.** *OVIDIUS.*

(illud) nōmen *nom. pl.* **nōmina III** name, noun, word Cf. nomenclature
(illa) amīcitia, amīcitiam I friendship Cf. amicable
inānis, -e empty Cf. inane
(illa) fidēs, fidem V faith, trust Cf. fidelity

19. Rēs est **magna tacēre.** *SENECA.*

magnus, -a, -um big Cf. magnitude
taceō, -ēre be silent Cf. taciturn

20. **Virtūs** est **vitium fugere.** *HORATIUS.*

(illa) virtūs, virtūtem III manliness **(vir)**, virtue
(illud) vitium II fault, vice Cf. vitiate
fugiō, -ere flee Cf. fugitive

21. **Vīvere** est **cōgitāre.** *CICERO.*

vīvō, -ere live Cf. vivify
cōgitō, -āre think Cf. cogitate

22. Dī **lāneōs pedēs habent.** *MACROBIUS.*

lāneus, -a, -um woolen *(i.e., silent because covered with wool and hence not heard as they approach)* Cf. lanolin
(ille) pēs, pedem III foot Cf. pedestrian
habeō, -ēre have Cf. habitude

VIII. CHANGE each of the following statements into indirectly quoted material (**oratio obliqua** or "oblique statement," see page 8) with one of the following verbs: **audit, canit, docet, dīcit, scrībit, videt. REMEMBER** that the verb becomes an infinitive with accusative modification (for both its subject and its object or predicate) and that the whole infinitive phrase becomes the object of the verb of perceiving or saying.

1. Diēs semper aut longī sunt aut brevēs.

2. Pecūnia avārōs satiat sōla.

3. Mūtābile et varium semper est fēmina. Mūtābilis et varia semper illa fēmina. **REMEMBER** to express the infinitive if it is only implied in the original statement.

4. Puellae et puerī semper mūtābilēs variīque sunt.

5. Carmina audācia poēta miser scrībit.

6. Prīmus incipit poēta canere poēma longum.

7. Cornua acria audiunt timidī.

8. Sapientiam oportet semper vītam bonam regere.

9. Homo sōlus aut deus aut daemon.

10. Vīta brevis est arsque longa.

IX. NOTE THE PATTERN in each of the following sentences and compose a translation of the English sentences using the same pattern.

1. **Varium et mūtābile semper fēmina.**
   Man is always an unhappy and avaricious creature.
   Gods are always good.

2. **Dolēre malum est.**
   To sing is a good thing.
   Loving (one's) friends is the chief thing.

3. **Hōrās nōn numerō nisī serēnās.**
   I don't sing songs unless (they are) good (ones).
   He doesn't see friends unless they are wretched.
   The gods don't love men unless they are good.

Piranesi, Portico of the Temple of Hercules

LESSON THREE

GENITIVE AND SUBJUNCTIVE

Vītae brevis cursus, glōriae sempiternus.

GENITIVE CASE. You have already learned (Lesson Two) that adjectives modify nouns. Just as nouns (in the accusative case, Lesson One) can be made to function as adverbs (adverbially modifying a verb), so also can nouns be made to modify other nouns or to function adjectivally. To signal this adjectival function for a noun, Latin has a separate declensional case, the **genitive**. In the following examples, notice that the noun in the genitive case provides the same kind of modification as an adjective.

Vītae brevis cursus. "**The life course is short,** or **life's course is short.**" **Vītae** is in the genitive case.

Vītālis cursus brevis. "**The vital course is short.**" (*adjective* **vītālis, -e**)

Glōriae cursus sempiternus. "**The glory course is eternal,** or **the course of glory is eternal.**" **Glōriae** is similarly in the genitive case.

Glōriōsus cursus sempiternus. "**The course full of glory is eternal,** or **the glorious course is eternal.**" (*adjective* **glōriōsus, -a, -um**)

The genitive case was named in Latin as the case of origin (**genus**), and one very common example of the adjectival function of the genitive case is its use to express origin and possession. It is often translated, therefore, as an English possessive (i.e., "**glory's**") or with the preposition **of** (e.g., "**of glory**"). Sometimes, mere word order in English conveys the noun's adjectival function (**vītae cursus** "**the life course**").

Patris vīta glōriōsa. "**A father's life is glorious,** or **the life of a father is glorious,** or **the father life is glorious.**" **Patris** is in the genitive case. Compare the equivalent expression with an adjective: **Paterna vīta glōriōsa.** (*adjective* **paternus, -a, -um**)

Remember that adjectives must agree with the noun they modify (see page 17): **paterna vīta,** the adjective **paterna** agrees in gender (**feminine, like vīta,** even though a father is male), number, and case. This is not so when a noun in the genitive case modifies another noun: **patris vīta,** the noun must be in the genitive case, obviously, regardless of the case of the noun it modifies, and it will have its own number and gender.

The so-called **possessive genitive** is merely one common instance of a noun's possible adjectival functions. Another possible meaning is common in contexts of evaluation, and yields the so-called **genitive of price.**

Magnī aestimō sapientiam. "**I value wisdom (as something) of great (value).**" **Magnī** is in the genitive case. It is an adjective (**magnus, -a, -um**) used in the neuter alone as the equivalent of a noun (see page 20). Compare the similar expression with an adjective of value: **Pretiōsam aestimō sapientiam. "I value wisdom as precious."** (*adjective* **pretiōsus, -a, -um**)

Domum habeō magnī pretiī. **"I have a house of great price."**

In these examples of the genitive of price, it is only the context (words of evaluation like **aestimō** or **pretium**) that indicates that the possessive idea is inappropriate as a translation of the genitive. In contexts where the evaluation is negative, this same adjectival function yields what grammarians call the **genitive of the charge or the penalty.**

Homo capitis reus est. **"The man is liable (at the price) of his head,** i.e., **the man is a capital offender." Capitis** is in the genitive case. (*adjective* **reus, -a, -um**)

Hominem pecūniae damnō. **"I sentence (or condemn) the man (at the price or fine) of money,** i.e., **I sentence the man to pay a fine." Pecūniae** is in the genitive case.

Hominem furtī damnō. **"I sentence the man for (at the assessed charge of) theft." Furtī** is in the genitive case.

In these examples, the negative assessment is established by words like the adjective **reus, -a, -um** ("guilty") and the verb **damnō** ("condemn").

In appropriate contexts (namely, words of material), this same adjectival function of the noun in the genitive case can express the **material** of which something is composed.

Domum lignī habeō. **"I have a house (made) of wood." Lignī** is in the genitive case. Compare the similar expression with an adjective of material: **Domum ligneam habeō.** (*adjective* **ligneus, -a, -um**)

Similarly, the **quality** of something can be described with this same genitive structure.

Vir magnae sapientiae est. — **"He is a man of great wisdom." Sapientiae** is in the genitive case. Compare the similar expression with an adjective: **Vir sapiens est.** (*adjective* **sapiens, sapientem**) This genitive of quality is common only when the noun is modified, as in the example (**magnae**).

Differing only on the basis of context is the so-called **partitive genitive**. Here, the genitive states the whole from which a part is taken.

Lacum vīnī habeō. — **"I have a vat of wine." Vīnī** is in the genitive case.

Pars prīma sapientiae est deōs amāre. — **"The first part of wisdom is to love the gods." Sapientiae** is in the genitive case.

The so-called **genitive of remembering or forgetting** is still the same structure in a different context (words of remembering or forgetting).

Memoriam repetit glōriae. — **"He recollects (or seeks again) the memory of glory." Glōriae** is in the genitive case.

Glōriae dēpōnit memoriam. — **"He puts aside (or forgets) the memory of glory."**

When the verb alone implies this context of remembering or forgetting, the word **memoriam** is commonly not expressed.

Virum admoneō glōriae. — **"I remind the man of glory."**

In contexts of **pity** and other feelings, this same structure occurs without the expression of the word for the feeling itself.

Miserescō virī. — **"I pity the (pitiableness, *miseriam,* of the) man." Virī** is in the genitive case.

Miseret fēminam virī. — **"(The pitiableness of) the man makes the woman feel sorry,** or **the woman feels pity for the man."** Notice that the subject of the verb (**miseria**) is not expressed.

All of the above examples of the genitive differ only in context, but all demonstrate the adjectival function of the genitive. Their various names, as classified by grammarians, simply indicate the different contexts:

genitive of possession
genitive of the charge or the penalty
genitive of material
genitive of quality
genitive of the whole or partitive genitive
genitive of remembering or forgetting
genitive of pity or other feelings

Clearly you cannot read Latin word by word, but must read enough to establish the context. This is doubly true since, as you will have noticed, the genitive declension has forms that sometimes resemble the cases you have already learned and thus are ambiguous outside of context. Nor can you think of the genitive as always translatable by the English "of" since often it is word order that correctly conveys the meaning of the Latin genitive.

SUBJECTIVE AND OBJECTIVE GENITIVES. There are two basic ways that the genitive can modify a noun when the noun is one that names an action or verbal activity. It can be the doer of that activity (**subjective genitive**) or the receiver of that activity (**objective genitive**). Only context can indicate which is intended.

amor deī — This can mean either **"god's love,"** subjective genitive with god doing the loving, or **"the love of god,"** objective genitive with someone else loving god. The same ambiguity is conveyed in the English phrase **"god love."**

PREDICATE GENITIVE. Just as an adjective can be used in predicate function (see pages 23–24), a genitive too can belong to the predicate.

Domus magna est virī. — **"The big house is the man's."** Only from context can you know that this does not mean: **"The man's house is big"** or **"The man's big house exists."**

Virī est deōs amāre. — **"To love the gods is a man's (task)."**

GENITIVE DECLENSION. The chart summarizes the endings for the genitive case, singular and plural, of the five declensions.

PARADIGM 8
GENITIVE CASE

	Decl I ā-stem	Decl II o-stem	Decl III con-stem	Decl IV u-stem	Decl V ē-stem
singular	-ae	-ī	-is	-ūs	-eī
plural	-ārum	-ōrum	-um -ium	-uum	-ērum

NOTE that the **genitive singular** of all five declensions is distinctive. For this reason it is customary to indicate the declension of a noun by showing its genitive singular in lexica and vocabulary lists:

decl I	decl II	decl III	decl IV	decl V
vīta, -ae	**vir, -ī**	**lex, lēgis**	**manus, -ūs**	**rēs, -eī**

EXAMPLES

	I	II	III	IV	V
nom sing	vīta	**vir** deus	lex	manus	rēs
acc sing	vīt**am**	vir**um**	lēg**em**	man**um**	r**em**
gen sing	vīt**ae**	vir**ī**	lēg**is**	man**ūs**	r**eī**
nom pl	vīt**ae**	vir**ī**	lēg**ēs**	man**ūs**	r**ēs**
acc pl	vit**ās**	vir**ōs**	lēg**ēs**	man**ūs**	r**ēs**
gen pl	vīt**ārum**	vir**ōrum**	lēg**um** ign**ium**	man**uum**	r**ērum**

NOTE that several of the new forms are ambiguous or resemble forms of nouns of other declensions, especially if long marks are not indicated.

NOTE that there is a variant ending for the genitive plural of declension III. Amongst the consonant-stem nouns are those that end in **-i**, a letter that actually is a "semi-consonant" since its consonantal value (**j**) can shift to vocalic **i**. In case endings that have an **i**, this semi-consonant is not doubled. Hence, **ignium** (from **ignis, -is** "fire"), whereas the **i** in the genitive singular is lost in the **-is** ending: **ignis.** These **i-stem nouns** sometimes also have an **i** (as one would expect) in the accusatives: **turrim** "tower;" and in the plural, **ignīs** (instead of **ignēs**). In addition to **true i-stems**, certain other declension III nouns (the so-called **mixed i-stems**) have either lost their distinctive i-stem forms in the singular or have anomalously assumed i-stem forms in the plural. These mixed i-stems never have **-im** for the accusative singular, but they do have the genitive plural in **-ium**

and have the accusative plural in either **-īs** or **-ēs**. Which nouns were declined as i-stems was confusing even to the Romans, and usage changed with time. Lexica and vocabulary lists record i-stems with an additional indication of the genitive plural:

ignis, -is, -ium

Of the nouns you have already learned, **ars** is an i-stem (**ars, artis, artium**). Also, **all declension III adjectives are i-stems.**

EXAMPLES: DECLENSION III I-STEMS

ars brevis
artem brevem
artis brevis
artēs brevēs
artēs brevēs
artium brevium

NOTE that i-stems should be learned as part of the vocabulary entry, but there are three rules that are helpful in determining if a noun is an i-stem:

(1) **neuter nouns ending in -e, -al, or -ar in the nominative singular** (**animal, animālis, -ium**);

(2) **most, but not all, nouns that have the same number of syllables in the singular nominative and genitive** (**ignis, ignis, -ium, but not pater, patris, etc.**);

(3) **nouns whose stem ends in two consonants (but not if the second consonant is i or r)** (**ars, artis, -ium, but not pater, patris, because the second consonant is r**).

The chart on the following pages shows the complete declension of the five noun declensions with the two types of adjective declensions (I-II and III).

SUBJUNCTIVE MOOD. In the verbal conjugation you have already learned, the verb states or "**indicates**" something factual. The attitude of the speaker is one of detached observation, without any input of personal feelings. This "**mode**" of viewing the action or state of being is called the **Indicative Mood.** This same mode is appropriate for questioning something factual.

Vītam regit fortūna.

EXAMPLES: NOUN & ADJECTIVE DECLENSION

Declension I-II Adjectives **longus, -a, -um; miser, -era, -erum**

	with declension I noun		with declension II noun		with declension III noun		
	masculine **poēta**	*feminine* **vīta**	*masculine* **vir**	*neuter* **perīculum**	*masculine* **homo**	*feminine* **lex**	*neuter* **poēma**
	"tall unhappy poet"	"long unhappy life"	"tall unhappy man"	"long miserable danger"	"tall unhappy man"	"long miserable law"	"long miserable poem"
nom	**poēta miser longus**	**vīta misera longa**	**vir miser longus**	**perīculum miserum longum**	**homo miser longus**	**lex misera longa**	**poēma miserum longum**
acc	**poētam miserum longum**	**vītam miseram longam**	**virum miserum longum**	**perīculum miserum longum**	**hominem miserum longum**	**lēgem miseram longam**	**poēma miserum longum**
gen	**poētae miserī longī**	**vītae miserae longae**	**virī miserī longī**	**perīculī miserī longī**	**hominis miserī longī**	**lēgis miserae longae**	**poēmatis miserī longī**
nom	**poētae miserī longī**	**vītae miserae longae**	**virī miserī longī**	**perīcula misera longa**	**hominēs miserī longī**	**lēgēs miserae longae**	**poēmata misera longa**
acc	**poētās miserōs longōs**	**vītās miserās longās**	**virōs miserōs longōs**	**perīcula misera longa**	**hominēs miserōs longōs**	**lēgēs miserās longās**	**poēmata misera longa**
gen	**poētārum miserōrum longōrum**	**vītārum miserārum longārum**	**virōrum miserōrum longōrum**	**perīculōrum miserōrum longōrum**	**hominum miserōrum longōrum**	**lēgum miserārum longārum**	**poēmatum miserōrum longōrum**

EXAMPLES: NOUN & ADJECTIVE DECLENSION

Declension I-II Adjectives **longus, -a, -um; miser, -era, -erum**

	with declension III i-stem noun	**with declension IV noun**			**with declension V noun**	
	"long miserable fire"	"long miserable lake"	"long unhappy hand"	"long miserable horn"	"long unhappy day"	"long miserable affair"
	masculine **ignis**	*masculine* **lacus**	*feminine* **manus**	*neuter* **cornū**	*masculine* **diēs**	*feminine* **rēs**
nom	**ignis miser longus**	**lacus miser longus**	**manus misera longa**	**cornū miserum longum**	**diēs miser longus**	**rēs misera longa**
acc	**ignem miserum longum**	**lacum miserum longum**	**manum miseram longam**	**cornū miserum longum**	**diem miserum longum**	**rem miseram longam**
gen	**ignis miserī longī**	**lacūs miserī longī**	**manūs miserae longae**	**cornūs miserī longī**	**diēī miserī longī**	**reī miserae longae**
nom	**ignēs miserī longī**	**lacūs miserī longī**	**manūs miserae longae**	**cornua misera longa**	**diēs miserī longī**	**rēs miserae longae**
acc	**ignēs miserōs longōs**	**lacūs miserōs longōs**	**manūs miserās longās**	**cornua misera longa**	**diēs miserōs longōs**	**rēs miserās longās**
gen	**ignium miserōrum longōrum**	**lacuum miserōrum longōrum**	**manuum miserārum longārum**	**cornuum miserōrum longōrum**	**diērum miserōrum longōrum**	**rērum miserārum longārum**

EXAMPLES: NOUN & ADJECTIVE DECLENSION

Declension III Adjectives: **acer, acris, acre** (three terminations); **brevis, breve** (two terminations); **atrox** (one termination)

	with declension I noun		**with declension II noun**		**with declension III noun**		
	masculine **poēta**	*feminine* **vīta**	*masculine* **vir**	*neuter* **perīculum**	*masculine* **homo**	*feminine* **lex**	*neuter* **poēma**
	"fierce short cruel poet"	"fierce short cruel life"	"fierce short cruel man"	"fierce short cruel danger"	"fierce short cruel man"	"bitter short cruel law"	"bitter short atrocious poem"
nom	**poēta acer brevis atrox**	**vīta acris brevis atrox**	**vir acer brevis atrox**	**perīculum acre breve atrox**	**homo acer brevis atrox**	**lex acris brevis atrox**	**poēma acre breve atrox**
acc	**poētam acrem brevem atrōcem**	**vītam acrem brevem atrōcem**	**virum acrem brevem atrōcem**	**perīculum acre breve atrox**	**hominem acrem brevem atrōcem**	**lēgem acrem brevem atrōcem**	**poēma acre breve atrox**
gen	**poētae acris brevis atrōcis**	**vītae acris brevis atrōcis**	**virī acris brevis atrōcis**	**perīculī acris brevis atrōcis**	**hominis acris brevis atrōcis**	**lēgis acris brevis atrōcis**	**poēmatis acris brevis atrōcis**
nom	**poētae acrēs brevēs atrōcēs**	**vītae acrēs brevēs atrōcēs**	**virī acrēs brevēs atrōcēs**	**perīcula acria brevia atrōcia**	**hominēs acrēs brevēs atrōcēs**	**lēgēs acrēs brevēs atrōcēs**	**poēmata acria brevia atrōcia**
acc	**poētās acrēs brevēs atrōcēs**	**vītās acrēs brevēs atrōcēs**	**virōs acrēs brevēs atrōcēs**	**perīcula acria brevia atrōcia**	**hominēs acrēs brevēs atrōcēs**	**lēgēs acrēs brevēs atrōcēs**	**poēmata acria brevia atrōcia**
gen	**poētārum acrium brevium atrōcium**	**vītārum acrium brevium atrōcium**	**virōrum acrium brevium atrōcium**	**perīculōrum acrium brevium atrōcium**	**hominum acrium brevium atrōcium**	**lēgum acrium brevium atrōcium**	**poēmatum acrium brevium atrōcium**

EXAMPLES: NOUN & ADJECTIVE DECLENSION

Declension III Adjectives: **acer, acris, acre** (three terminations); **brevis, breve** (two terminations); **atrox** (one termination)

	with declension III i-stem noun	**with declension IV noun**			**with declension V noun**	
	masculine **ignis**	*masculine* **lacus**	*feminine* **manus**	*neuter* **cornū**	*masculine* **diēs**	*feminine* **rēs**
	"fierce brief atrocious fire"	"bitter short cruel lake"	"fierce short cruel hand"	"fierce short cruel horn"	"bitter short cruel day"	"fierce short cruel thing"
nom	**ignis acer brevis atrox**	**lacus acer brevis atrox**	**manus acris brevis atrox**	**cornū acre breve atrox**	**diēs acer brevis atrox**	**rēs acris brevis atrox**
acc	**ignem acrem brevem atrōcem**	**lacum acrem brevem atrōcem**	**manum acrem brevem atrōcem**	**cornū acre breve atrox**	**diem acrem brevem atrōcem**	**rem acrem brevem atrōcem**
gen	**ignis acris brevis atrōcis**	**lacūs acris brevis atrōcis**	**manūs acris brevis atrōcis**	**cornūs acris brevis atrōcis**	**diēī acris brevis atrōcis**	**reī acris brevis atrōcis**
nom	**ignēs acrēs brevēs atrōcēs**	**lacūs acrēs brevēs atrōcēs**	**manūs acrēs brevēs atrōcēs**	**cornua acria brevia atrōcia**	**diēs acrēs brevēs atrōcēs**	**rēs acrēs brevēs atrōcēs**
acc	**ignēs acrēs brevēs atrōcēs**	**lacūs acrēs brevēs atrōcēs**	**manūs acrēs brevēs atrōcēs**	**cornua acria brevia atrōcia**	**diēs acrēs brevēs atrōcēs**	**rēs acrēs brevēs atrōcēs**
gen	**ignium acrium brevium atrōcium**	**lacuum acrium brevium atrōcium**	**manuum acrium brevium atrōcium**	**cornuum acrium brevium atrōcium**	**diērum acrium brevium atrōcium**	**rērum acrium brevium atrōcium**

Fortūnane vītam regit? — **"Does fortune rule life?"** The interrogative suffix **-ne** indicates that a question is about to be asked and it emphasizes the item questioned: "Is it *fortune* that rules life?" Although **-ne** is commonly used for questions, it is not essential if the context makes clear that a question is being asked.

The Indicative Mood is only one of several "modes" of viewing the action or state of being. In the **Subjunctive Mood,** the action or state of being is not indicated as fact, but as **something that does not yet exist, except as a possibility or as something willed or wished for** by the speaker. English, for the most part, does not have a subjunctive mood, but expresses such ideas with the so-called "**modal" auxiliary verbs,** for example, *can, may, will, ought,* etc. Latin already also could replace the subjunctive mood with such modal auxiliaries, as, for example **oportet** and others that you will eventually learn, but in addition, Latin has a complete separate conjugation to express such ideas.

POTENTIAL SUBJUNCTIVE. The subjunctive can express an action, not as factually occurring, but merely as a **possibility or potential.** Whether or not the action actually occurs cannot be factually determined until some later time. English uses the modal auxiliaries **may** and **can** to express such possibilities.

Vītam regit fortūna.

(Forsitan) vītam regat fortūna. — **"(Perhaps) fortune may rule life."** The word **forsitan ("perhaps")** is itself not essential, but generally something in the context should suggest that the action is merely possible.

A possibility, just like an actual occurrence, can be negated.

(Forsitan) vītam nōn regat fortūna.

JUSSIVE (HORTATORY) SUBJUNCTIVE. The subjunctive mood can also express an action, not as something that factually occurs, but merely as something **willed, an exhortation or command.** Again, whether or not the action actually takes place cannot be factually determined until some later time. English uses the modal auxiliaries **let** and **may** placed before the verb to express this modality.

Amāmus sapientiam.

Amēmus sapientiam. — **"Let's love wisdom."**

Amat sapientiam.

Amet sapientiam. — **"Let him love wisdom,** or **May he love wisdom."** Compare the potential: **(Forsitan) amet sapientiam. "He may love wisdom."**

If an exhortation or polite command is expressed as a question, the speaker is actually questioning his own will or essentially asking for his own advice, and hence is deliberating. This interrogative jussive is what grammarians have called the **deliberative subjunctive.** English uses the modal auxiliaries **should** and **ought** to express such deliberative modalities.

Amō(ne) sapientiam?

Amem(ne) sapientiam? — **"Should I love wisdom** or **Ought I love wisdom?"**

Jussive or hortatory subjunctives can also be negated, but since they are emotive expressions of will, the plain factual negative **nōn** is not used, but instead, an emotive negative, **nē**, is employed. In the deliberative subjunctive, however, the negative is usually **nōn,** since the emotive willfulness has been toned down by context to a questioning essentially about duty. The occurrence of **nōn** with a subjunctive is the context that will determine that the subjunctive is a potential or (if a question) deliberative.

Nē amēmus sapientiam. — **"Let's not love wisdom."**

Nōn amēmus sapientiam? — **"Should we not love wisdom?"**

OPTATIVE SUBJUNCTIVE. The subjunctive mood can also express an action, not as actually occurring, but merely as a **wish or hope.** Whether or not the wish comes true cannot be factually determined until some later time. English does not easily distinguish between the jussive and optative modality, although the optative is named for the Latin verb "to hope" (**optāre**) and optatives are like prayers, rather than jussive commands.

(Utinam) amēmus sapientiam. — **"(O that) we may love wisdom!"** The word **utinam ("O that, if only")** is itself not necessary, but generally something in the context should suggest that the action is merely a wish.

Wishes can also be negative. Since a wish, like an exhortation or will, is emotive, the negative, here too, is usually **nē.**

(Utinam) nē amēmus sapientiam. **"(If only) we may not love wisdom!"**

NOTE that in translating a Latin subjunctive into English, one generally does not use the English subjunctive (which exists in only a few forms, e.g., "So **be** it!"), but instead, various modal auxiliary verbs. Hence, you must grasp the concept **(possibility or will or hope)** and then find some suitable way of expressing the same idea in English. Until you become more familiar with the Latin subjunctive, however, you can use, as a rule of thumb, **let** for jussives, **may** or **can** for potentials, and **may** before the verb for optatives.

SUBJUNCTIVE CONJUGATION. The subjunctive generally uses the same personal subject suffixes as the indicative, but **is marked by a change in the preceding vowel.** The chart on the next page summarizes the endings for the subjunctive and shows examples of the subjunctive conjugation, with the indicative juxtaposed for comparison.

REMEMBER

that you must look for the context before you can translate: words like *aestimō, damnō, reus,* should trigger the genitive of price or penalty or charge; words like *miseret, miserescō* should trigger the genitive of pity and other feelings; words of material should trigger the genitive of material; words of memory or forgetting or of quality should trigger the corresponding genitive.

There are three basic meanings for the subjunctive that you can distinguish only from context:

POTENTIAL (translate as *may, can*),
JUSSIVE (translate as *let*);
OPTATIVE (translate as *may* before the verb).

Distinguishing context are words like *utinam, forsitan,* and the use of *nōn* instead of *nē.*

PARADIGM 9
SUBJUNCTIVE CONJUGATION

	Conj I ā-stem	Conj II ē-stem	Conj III e-stem	Conj III ī-stem	Conj IV ī-stem
1	**-em**	**-eam**	**-am**	**-iam**	**-iām**
2	**-ēs**	**-eās**	**-ās**	**-iās**	**-iās**
3	**-et**	**-eat**	**-at**	**-iat**	**-iat**
1	**-ēmus**	**-eāmus**	**-āmus**	**-iāmus**	**-iāmus**
2	**-ētis**	**-eātis**	**-ātis**	**-iātis**	**-iātis**
3	**-ent**	**-eant**	**-ant**	**-iant**	**-iant**

NOTE that the subjunctive of **esse** is irregular.

	indicative	subjunctive
1	**sum**	**sim**
2	**es**	**sīs**
3	**est**	**sit**
1	**sumus**	**sīmus**
2	**estis**	**sītis**
3	**sunt**	**sint**

EXAMPLES
(with indicative juxtaposed for comparison)

	Conj I ā-stem		Conj II ē-stem		Conj III e-stem		Conj III ī-stem		Conj IV ī-stem	
	subj	*ind*	*subj*	*ind*	*subj*	*ind*	*subj*	*ind*	*subj*	*ind*
1	amem	amō	doceam	doceō	regam	regō	incipiam	incipiō	audiam	audiō
2	amēs	amās	doceās	docēs	regās	regis	incipiās	incipis	audiās	audīs
3	amet	amat	doceat	docet	regat	regit	incipiat	incipit	audiat	audit
1	amēmus	amāmus	doceāmus	docēmus	regāmus	regimus	incipiāmus	incipimus	audiāmus	audīmus
2	amētis	amātis	doceātis	docētis	regātis	regitis	incipiātis	incipitis	audiātis	audītis
3	ament	amant	doceant	docent	regant	regunt	incipiant	incipiunt	audiant	audiunt

NOTE that:

Conjugation III subjunctives can resemble conjugation I indicatives.
Conjugation I subjunctives can resemble conjugation II indicatives.
Conjugation III i-stems and conjugation IV are identical in the subjunctive.

INDEX VERBORUM

(illud) animal, -ālis, -ium	animate creature, animal, beast
(illud) caput, -itis	head
(ille) cursus, -ūs	course, way
(illa) domus, -ūs (*also* -ī)	house
(illud) furtum, -ī	theft
(illud) genus, generis	descent, origin, race, class
(illa) glōria, -ae	glory
(ille) ignis, -is, -ium	fire
(illud) lignum, -ī	wood
(illa) memoria, -ae	memory, remembrance
(illa) miseria, -ae	wretchedness, misery
(illa) pars, partis, -ium	part
(illud) pretium, -ī	price
(illud) vīnum, -ī	wine

glōriōsus, -a, -um	glorious
ligneus, -a, -um	wooden
magnus, -a, -um	big, great
paternus, -a, -um	paternal
pretiōsus, -a, -um	expensive
reus, -a, -um	guilty
sapiens, -ientis, -ium	wise
sempiternus, -a, -um	eternal
stultus, -a, -um	stupid

ad-moneō, -ēre	remind, admonish
aestimō, -āre	value, appraise
damnō, -āre	sentence, condemn
dēbeō, -ēre	owe, be bound in duty (for use, see EXERCITATIO VII)
dē-pōnō, -ere	put aside
habeō, -ēre	have
misereō, -ēre	feel pity (for use, see EXERCITATIO X)
possum, posse	be able (for use, see EXERCITATIO VIII)
re-petō, -ere	seek again

forsitan	perhaps (potential adverb)
tamen	nevertheless
-ne	(interrogative suffix, for use, see page 44)

nē	**not** (emotive negative, cf. factual negative **nōn**)
utinam	**O that, if only, may** (optative adverb)

NOTE that verbs that are compounded of a basic verb and an adverb are listed in the **INDEX VERBORUM** as follows: **ad-moneō**, etc. Such verbs can often be compounded with other adverbs: **re-moneō "warn again."**

EXERCITATIONES

I. IDENTIFY the declension for each of the nouns and adjectives listed in the **INDEX VERBORUM.**

II. MATCH the second phrase to the first by changing it into the same form. Some items may require more than one answer.

1. poēmatis miserī (poēta stultus)
2. lēgum bonārum (amor avārus)
3. virōs magnōs (prīma fēmina)
4. cornua longa (puer reus)
5. amīcōrum sapientium (ignis sempiternus)
6. domūs ligneae (animal timidum)
7. furta stulta (glōria sempiterna)
8. generum variōrum (ars paterna)
9. hominem sōlum (perīculum prīmum)
10. rērum bonārum (lacus magnus)
11. mūtābilium fēminārum (acer puer)
12. carminum brevium (daemon atrox)
13. amōrum audācium (diēs glōriōsus)
14. patris stultī (manus atrox)
15. vītās brevēs (sapiens mater)
16. lēgēs miserae (caput stultum)
17. fīliae sapientis (cornū acre)
18. puellārum avārārum (pars prīma)
19. bonōrum poētārum (animal atrox)
20. pretia magna (reus audax)

III. MATCH the second verb to the first by changing it into the same form.

1. dēbeat (amō)
2. dīcunt (incipiō)
3. satiēs (admoneō)
4. canātis (sum)
5. aestimāmus (videō)
6. regāmus (damnō)
7. incipiās (cupiō)
8. habēmus (satiō)
9. dēpōnere (satiō)
10. dēpōnit (dīcō)
11. sīmus (incipiō)
12. repetat (audiō)

13. estis (dēbeō)
14. scrībant (habeō)
15. dīcās (sum)
16. audiātis (satiō)
17. esse (doceō)
18. videt (amō)
19. canis (cupiō)
20. incipiunt (regō)

IV. TRANSLATE.

1. Illum poētam sapientem audīmus domum habēre magnī pretiī.

2. Magnī aestimēmus semper amīcōs sapientēs habēre.

3. Forsitan damnet vir sapiens fēminam stultam furtī.

4. Hominēs atrōcēs audācēsque dīcās reōs esse semper aut capitis aut pecūniae. (**NOTE** that the potential subjunctive in the second person singular of a verb for indirect quotation often designates not a specific "you," but an unspecified "you" or "someone." **"You, i.e., someone or anyone, may say. . . ."** The same is true of the jussive subjunctive, although it is not limited to verbs of indirect quotation. **"May you, i.e., anyone or someone, say. . . ."** This is called a **generalized second person.**)

5. Estne sapientis carmina canere brevia?

6. Matrum patrumque vītārum nōn dēpōnunt memoriam virī sapientēs.

7. Utinam aestiment stultī sapientiam glōriamque semper magnī!

8. Habetne avārus lacūs vīnī ligneōs aut domum lignī pretiōsam?

9. Sit poēta magnae sapientiae. Scrībit tamen poēmata misera longaque. (**NOTE** that the jussive subjunctive, in certain contexts, can indicate a **concession** made for argument. **"Let him be, i.e., granted that he is. . . . Nevertheless, he is. . . ."**)

10. Admoneāmus bonōs glōriae?

V. TRANSLATE. (Try to guess the meaning of new words on the basis of cognates and context before consulting the adjacent **reading notes.**)

1. **Caveat emptor!**

caveō, -ēre beware, be on one's guard Cf. English caveat
(ille) emptor, -ōris buyer Cf. emporium

2. **Infīnītus** est **numerus** stultōrum. *ECCLESIASTES.*

infīnītus, -a, -um boundless, unlimitied, infinite
(ille) numerus, -ī number

3. **Vīvāmus, mea Lesbia,** atque amēmus. *CATULLUS.*

vīvō, -ere live Cf. vivacious, vivid
meus, -a, -um my
(illa) Lesbia, -ae a woman's name, as someone from the Greek island of Lesbos (The form, although identical with the nominative, is not nominative, but the case used for direct address, the so-called vocative case.)

4. **Parens nec** habeat **vitia** nec **toleret.** *QUINTILIANUS.*

(ille) parens, -entis parent
nec (= neque) shortened form for **nē + que**
tolerō, -āre tolerate

5. Est **nātūra** hominum **novitātis avida.** *PLAUTUS.*

(illa) nātūra, -ae nature
(illa) novitas, -ātis novelty
avidus, -a, -um avid, greedy

6. **Nūlla cōpia** pecūniae avārum virum satiat. *SENECA.*

nūllus, -a, -um no, none Cf. null
(illa) cōpia, -ae abundance Cf. copious

7. **Ratio mē dūcat,** nōn fortūna. *LIVIUS.*

(illa) ratio, -iōnis reason, calculation Cf. rationale
mē me
dūcō, -ere lead Cf. duke, conduct

8. Amīcōrum sunt **commūnia omnia.** *CICERO.*

commūnis, -e common Cf. communism
omnis, -e all, every Cf. omniscient

9. **Gravis īra rēgum** est semper. *SENECA.*

gravis, -e heavy, grave Cf. gravid
(illa) īra, -ae anger Cf. irate
(ille) rex, rēgis king Cf. regal

10. Amor **laudis** hominēs **trahit.** *CICERO.*

(illa) laus, laudis praise Cf. laud
trahō, -ere draw, drag Cf. tractor

VI. **CHANGE** each of the following sentences into indirectly quoted material (**oratio obliqua,** see page 8). **REMEMBER** that the entire sentence becomes an infinitive phrase as the object of the main verb of saying or perceiving; the subject and object of the infinitive must be accusatives; genitives are not affected by this change.

1. Ille prīmus est poētārum magnōrum.
2. Partem sōlam vītae regunt dī.
3. Sapientis est deōs amāre.

4. Poētae virōs admonent vītae glōriōsae.
5. Ille poēta vir est magnae sapientiae.

VII. **CHANGE** each of the following sentences into equivalent expressions using the jussive (hortatory, deliberative) subjunctive. (**NOTE** that, as in English, Latin can state ideas similar to the subjunctive mood by the use of modal auxiliaries ("should, ought"). The verbs **dēbeō** and **oportet** convey the idea of "**duty;**" the indicative with these modal auxiliaries states the factual opinion that such a duty or obligation exists, whereas the subjunctive alone (without these auxiliaries) gives direct expression to the volition, implying that such a duty exists. Modal auxiliaries can also be expressed in the subjunctive mode: **dēbeat, oporteat**, but your task here is to **replace the modal auxiliary** by changing the infinitive to a subjunctive with any former accusative subject changed into the nominative in apposition to the subjunctive's personal suffix.)

Dēbēmus aestimāre sapientiam magnī. — **"We ought to value wisdom highly."**

Aestimēmus sapientiam magnī. — **"Let's value wisdom highly!"**

Sapientiam oportet vītam regere. — **"Wisdom ought to rule life,** or **It behooves wisdom to rule life."**

Sapientia vītam regat. — **"Let wisdom rule life!"**

1. Virī dēbent semper sapientēs esse.
2. Dēbēmusne stultum damnāre furtī?
3. Glōriae memoriam nōn dēbēs dēpōnere.
4. Nōnne dēbēmus sapientiam magnī aestimāre?
5. Ille poēta dēbet scrībere aut bona aut brevia carmina.
6. Puerōs oportet patrēs matrēsque aestimāre magnī.
7. Oportet domum pretiōsam lignī esse.
8. Fēmināsne reās dēbēmus capitis damnāre?
9. Stultōs dēbēmus deōrum admonēre sempiternōrum.
10. Pecūnia avārōs nōn dēbet satiāre.

VIII. **CHANGE** each of the following sentences into equivalent expressions using the potential subjunctive. (**NOTE** that, as in English, Latin can state ideas similar to the subjunctive mood by the use of modal auxiliaries ("can, may"). The verb **posse** conveys the idea of "**possibility;**" the indicative with this modal auxiliary states the factual opinion that such a possibility exists, whereas the subjunctive alone (without this auxiliary verb) gives direct emotive expression to the doubt or possibility.)

Potest sapientia vītam regere.	**"Wisdom can (or is able to) rule life."**
Forsitan sapientia vītam regat.	**"(Perhaps) wisdom may rule life."**

Possum is a compound of **sum** (= **potis sum,** literally, "I am able or have the possibility to"):

PARADIGM 10
CONJUGATION OF *POSSUM*

	INDICATIVE			SUBJUNCTIVE	
	singular	*plural*		*singular*	*plural*
1	possum	possumus	1	possim	possīmus
2	potes	potestis	2	possīs	possītis
3	potest	possunt	3	possit	possint

NOTE that the **t** (of **pot-**) is retained before vowels, but assimilated to **s** before **s**.

1. Possum fēmina magnae sapientiae esse. **REMEMBER** that your task is to replace the modal auxiliary, not to change it into a subjunctive.
2. Poētās admonēre possumus miseriae hominum.
3. Rea potest esse puella capitis.
4. Nōn potest sapientia sapientium sempiterna esse.
5. Poēta potest carmina brevia canere.
6. Lignī potes domum habēre.
7. Potestis magnī aestimāre sapientiam fēminārum.
8. Lēgēs vītam hominum stultōrum regere nōn possunt.
9. Ille timidus memoriam ignis magnī nōn potest dēpōnere.
10. Mūtābile et varium potest homo esse.

IX. CHANGE each of the following sentences into equivalent expressions using the optative subjunctive. **NOTE** that, as in English, Latin can state ideas similar to the subjunctive mood by the use of modal auxiliaries ("may"). The verb **optāre** conveys the idea of "**hope**" or "**wish;**" the indicative with this modal auxiliary states the factual opinion that such a hope exists, whereas the subjunctive alone (without this verb) gives direct emotive expression to the hope. (**optō, -āre "hope"**)

Fortūnam vītam regere optō.	**"I hope fortune rules life."**
Utinam fortūna vītam regat.	**"If only fortune may rule life,** or **May fortune rule life."**

1. Vītam avārī brevem miseramque esse optō. **REMEMBER** that your task is to replace the modal auxiliary.

2. Cursum glōriae sempiternum esse optō.

3. Optō hominem daemonem nōn esse.

4. Prīmus poētārum optō esse.

5. Lacūs ligneōs optāmus habēre vīnī.

6. Artem sapientium longam esse optō.

7. Amīcōrum esse lēgēs scrībere optō.

8. Atrōcēs stultōsque vītam longam habēre nōn optō.

9. Timidōs admonēre perīculī optō.

10. Cornua acria audīre nōn optō.

X. **NOTE THE PATTERN** in each of the following sentences and compose a translation of the English sentences using the same pattern.

1. **Miseret fēminam virī.**

(**NOTE** that **miseret** is a so-called "impersonal verb" (see page 7) because it appears to have "it" for its subject, with the person affected in the accusative and the recipient of the pity in the genitive. Actually, the subject of **miseret** is **miseria** understood from the context of the verb, and the genitive modifies this subject (see page 36).

The gods pity mankind.
The father pities his son.
The wise pity the stupid.
Friends pity friends.

2. **Caveat emptor.**

Let the wise teach.
Let money satisfy the greedy.
Let the mother love her daughter.

3. **Vīvāmus atque amēmus.**

Let's listen and speak.

Piranesi, The Portico of Octavia

LESSON FOUR

PASSIVE, PURPOSE CLAUSES, INDIRECT QUESTIONS

Quaeritur num mors malum sit.

PASSIVE VOICE. "Voice" is a grammatical term that describes the nature of the relationship between the verbal stem and the personal subject suffix. In the conjugation you have already learned, the subject suffix designates the doer or "enactor" of the action: this is termed the **active voice.** Latin, like English, also has a **passive voice;** in this conjugation, the subject suffix designates the receiver or "sufferer" of the action. In the active voice, this receiver of the action is often the direct object, which, as you have seen, is merely one of the functions of the adverbial accusative. In the passive voice, the doer of the action is either not known or not of primary interest. Something is being said about the receiver of the action, rather than about the doer.

Fābulam narrat. **"He (she, or it) tells a story."**

Fābula narrātur. **"(He, she, or it, i.e.,) a story is told."**

PASSIVE CONJUGATION. The passive voice is signaled by a separate set of suffixes. As with the active voice, these suffixes are added to the various verbal stems, hence producing four (or actually five, i.e., the III i-stems) conjugations.

PASSIVE ENDINGS

	SINGULAR	PLURAL
1	**-r**	**-mur**
2	**-ris (re)**	**-minī**
3	**-tur**	**-ntur**

INFINITIVE

conj I	conj II	conj III	conj IV
-rī	**-rī**	**-ī**	**-rī**

NOTE that there is an alternative form for the 2nd person singular. This form looks like the infinitive of the active voice; only context can distinguish which is intended. **NOTE** also the distinctive ending for the IIIrd conjugation infinitive. The chart on the following pages presents examples of the passive conjugation.

NOTE that in the passive the subjunctive is signaled by the same vowels as in the active.

NOTE that in conjugation III (both e-stem and i-stem), the **i** of the indicative's 2nd person singular is replaced by an **e**.

DEPONENT VERBS. The Latin language sometimes conceives of an action as inherently passive, even though English may express it as active. For such actions, the Latin verb was thought by grammarians to have "put aside" (**dē-pōnō**) its active conjugation, and such verbs are thus called deponent. Even though they are passive in Latin, they will have to be translated as active in English. Such deponent verbs are listed in vocabulary lists and lexica only in the passive forms: **sequor, -ī "follow."**

Ovis ovem sequitur. **"A sheep follows a sheep."**

PARADIGM 11
PASSIVE CONJUGATION
(with Active for Comparison)

	FIRST **ā-stem**	SECOND **ē-stem**	THIRD **e-stem**	THIRD **i-stem**	FOURTH **ī-stem**
			PRESENT ACTIVE INDICATIVE		
1	amō	doceō	regō	incipiō	audiō
2	amās	docēs	regis	incipis	audīs
3	amat	docet	regit	incipit	audit
1	amāmus	docēmus	regimus	incipimus	audīmus
2	amātis	docētis	regitis	incipitis	audītis
3	amant	docent	regunt	incipiunt	audiunt
			PRESENT PASSIVE INDICATIVE		
1	amor	doceor	regor	incipior	audior
2	amāris amāre	docēris docēre	regeris regere	inciperis incipere	audīris audīre
3	amātur	docētur	regitur	incipitur	audītur
1	amāmur	docēmur	regimur	incipimur	audīmur
2	amāminī	docēminī	regiminī	incipiminī	audīminī
3	amantur	docentur	reguntur	incipiuntur	audiuntur

PARADIGM 11 *continued*
PASSIVE CONJUGATION
(with Active for Comparison)

	FIRST **ā-stem**	SECOND **ē-stem**	THIRD **e-stem**	THIRD **i-stem**	FOURTH **ī-stem**
			PRESENT ACTIVE SUBJUNCTIVE		
1	amem	doceam	regam	incipiam	audiam
2	amēs	doceās	regās	incipiās	audiās
3	amet	doceat	regat	incipiat	audiat
1	amēmus	doceāmus	regāmus	incipiāmus	audiāmus
2	amētis	doceātis	regātis	incipiātis	audiātis
3	ament	doceant	regant	incipiant	audiant
			PRESENT PASSIVE SUBJUNCTIVE		
1	amer	docear	regar	incipiar	audiar
2	amēris amēre	doceāris doceāre	regāris regāre	incipiāris incipiāre	audiāris audiāre
3	amētur	doceātur	regātur	incipiātur	audiātur
1	amēmur	doceāmur	regāmur	incipiāmur	audiāmur
2	amēminī	doceāminī	regāminī	incipiāminī	audiāminī
3	amentur	doceantur	regantur	incipiantur	audiantur
			INFINITIVE active		
	amāre	docēre	regere	incipere	audīre
			passive		
	amārī	docērī	regī	incipī	audīrī

DEPENDENT SUBJUNCTIVE CLAUSES (PURPOSE, INDIRECT QUESTION). In addition to the independent uses of the subjunctive mood (potential, jussive, optative), the subjunctive also occurs in dependent clauses of various kinds. This is actually the more common use of the subjunctive, which was so named as the "subjoined" mood or the mood of subordination. Latin, like English, tended to replace the independent subjunctive with equivalent modal auxiliaries. The dependent subjunctive uses are usually clear extensions of the subjunctive's independent usages, and occur actually more frequently than the indicative.

The jussive subjunctive, as you have seen (see page 44), expresses an action or state of being as something willed. In a subordinate or dependent clause, this jussive subjunctive expresses the will or intention, not of the subject of the subjunctive verb itself, but of the subject of the verb that introduces the dependent subjunctive clause. It therefore expresses the **purpose** that is intended by the subject of the main verb.

Carmen canit poēta ut sapientiam amēmus. — **"The poet sings his poem so that we may love wisdom."** (Or, **"in order that we love wisdom."**)

Since the volition is an emotive expression, the negative is **nē**.

Carmen canit poēta nē sapientiam amēmus. — **"The poet sings his poem so that we not love wisdom."**

NOTE that purpose is often expressed by an infinitive in English, but rarely is an infinitive used in Latin. Instead, this structure of the dependent jussive subjunctive is the ordinary pattern.

Scrībit ut virōs artem doceat. — **"He writes to teach men art."** (Or, **"so that he teach,** or **in order to teach."**)

The will when questioned, as you have seen, produces the independent (jussive) deliberative subjunctive (see page 45). When subordinated, this interrogatory subjunctive is retained and becomes the ordinary way of expressing an **indirectly quoted question.**

Sapientiam amēmus?

Rogat num sapientiam amēmus. — **"He asks whether we love wisdom."**

Quaeritur num mors malum sit. — **"It is questioned whether death is (or be) something bad."**

NOTE that English also can use the subjunctive for both purpose and indirect question, although English has other possibilities as well.

He writes so that he teach. Compare the indicative "he teaches."

It is questioned whether death be something bad. Compare the indicative "death is."

NOTE that indirect questions do not use the same structure as other indirectly quoted material (see **oratio obliqua**, page 8).

Dīcit mortem malum esse.	**"He says that death is something bad."**

REMEMBER

that purpose is not expressed by an infinitive, but by a subjunctive clause introduced by *ut* or *nē.*

Indirect questions are always subjunctive.

Oratio obliqua is expressed by an infinitive phrase with the subject in the accusative.

INDEX VERBORUM

(illa) aqua, -ae	**water**
(illa) amīcitia, -ae	**friendship**
(illud) dōnum, -ī	**gift**
(illa) fābula, -ae	**story**
(illa) grātia, -ae	**favor, friendship, grace, loveliness**
(illa) mors, mortis, -ium	**death**
(illud) odium, -ī	**hatred**
(illud) ōtium, -ī	**leisure**
(illa) ovis, -is, -ium	**sheep**
(ille) philosophus, -ī	**philosopher**
(ille) rex, rēgis	**king**
(illa) vēritas, -ātis	**truth**
(illa) virtūs, -ūtis	**virtue, manliness, courage**
(illud) vitium, -ī	**vice, fault**
caecus, -a, -um	**blind**
malus, -a, -um	**bad, evil**
omnis, -e	**every, all**
pulcher, -chra, -chrum	**beautiful**
pār, paris	**equal**
parvus, -a, -um	**small**
dō, dare	**give** (In most forms **dō** has a short **a.**)
faciō, -ere	**do, make**
morior, morī	**die**
narrō, -āre	**narrate, tell**

negō, -āre	**deny** (for use, see EXERCITATIO VI)
oblīviscor, oblīviscī	**forget**
proficiscor, proficiscī	**set forth, travel, start out**
quaerō, -ere	**seek to learn, investigate, question**
rogō, -āre	**ask**
sequor, sequī	**follow**
vīvō, -ere	**live**
num	**whether**
sed	**but**
ut	**(in order) that**

EXERCITATIONES

I. **MATCH** the second phrase to the first by changing it into the same form. Some items will require more than one answer.

1. animālia pulchra (pār pars)
2. odiī malī (vitium pār)
3. sapientium daemonum (ovis caeca)
4. diērum parium (dōnum parvum)
5. fābulam omnem (atrox vir)
6. mūtābilium amīcōrum (grātia omnis)
7. domūs omnēs (vēritas sōla)
8. rēgum acrium (philosophus sapiens)
9. rēs pretiōsa (virtūs prīma)
10. longa poēmata (amīcus omnis)
11. cornua pulchra (aqua bona)
12. capita stulta (mater caeca)
13. cursuum brevium (parvum vitium)
14. ōtiī malī (magnus ignis)
15. carmina varia (ars omnis)
16. generum sempiternōrum (lacus parvus)
17. partēs parēs (puer miser)
18. hominum omnium (vīta brevis)
19. lignī pretiōsī (rēs magna)
20. fīlia pulchra (omne animal)

II. **MATCH** the second verb to the first by changing it into the same form.

1. amēmur (proficiscor)
2. satiantur (quaerō)
3. repetātur (rogō)
4. canunt (doceō)
5. negārī (morior)
6. possīs (negō)
7. incipiās (dō)
8. oblīvisceris (amō)
9. regī (audiō)
10. rogāminī (canō)
11. dīcere (scrībō)
12. incipiātis (vīvō)
13. facis (rogō)
14. doceāminī (regō)
15. morere (quaerō)
16. dīcāris (aestimō)
17. habentur (damnō)
18. videor (audiō)
19. regāre (amō)
20. moriāmur (damnō)

III. CHANGE each of the following verbs to the opposite voice. Some items will require more than one answer.

1. incipī
2. det
3. quaeruntur
4. scrīberis
5. rogāre
6. doceāmur
7. audīrī
8. videāminī
9. canunt
10. vīvunt
11. videar
12. audīre
13. regat
14. audiam
15. daris
16. admoneō
17. damnēminī
18. habētur
19. repetere
20. satiem

IV. TRANSLATE.

1. Quaeritur num rēgēs semper atrōcēs sint. Forsitan ille rex atrox nōn sit. Utinam nē sit atrox. Nē sit ille rex atrox. Bonus sit. Omnēs rēgēs atrōcēs semper damnentur aut pecūniae aut capitis. Negāsne omnēs atrōcēs dēbēre capitis damnārī? Dīcō sapientis esse omnēs atrōcēs damnāre.

2. Magnī aestimētur carmina scrībere. Ille poēta tamen semper canit et longa et glōriōsa poēmata. Dīcit omnēs posse vītam bonam regere. Dēbēmus omnēs vītam regere. Nē sit fortūna rex omnium rērum. Quaerit ille poēta num mors sempiterna sit. Negat mortem malum esse.

3. Misereat omnēs virī caecī. Damnātur capitis sed reus nōn est furtī. Magnī aestimēmus illum virum et dīcāmus bonum esse. Negēmus virum reum esse. Utinam quaerātur num dēbeat capitis damnārī ille vir caecus. Nōn oportet virum morī. Nē moriātur. Vītam longam vīvat. Nē oblīviscāmur virī miserī. Semper vīvat. Nē miser sit.

4. Sit fēmina magnae sapientiae. Rea tamen est furtī. Nōn dēbet illa fēmina sapiens lēgum omnium oblīviscī. Oportet semper lēgēs vītam hominum regere. Rogātur num illa sapiens dēbeat aut pecūniae damnārī aut capitis.

5. Dīcās cursum vītae glōriōsum esse. Oportet vītam glōriōsam esse, sed nōn est semper glōriōsa. Dīcitur fortūnam caecam esse et vītam hominum regere. Omnēs vīrī nōn sunt sapientēs. Pars magna hominum stulta est. Utinam omnēs philosophī sint ut vītam regant bonam. Nē sit fortūna rex hominum, sed virtūs. Regāmus omnēs nē regāmur.

V. TRANSLATE. (Try to guess the meaning of new words on the basis of context and cognates before consulting the adjacent **reading notes.**)

1. **Ēsse** oportet ut vīvās, nōn vīvere ut **edās**. *SOCRATES (translated from the Greek).*	**edō, -ere** (or **ēsse**) eat Cf. edible
2. Aqua vītae **fons**. *PROVERB*	**(ille) fons, fontis** spring, fountain, well
3. **Dominus pascit mē**. *PSALMUS 23 (translated from the Hebrew by Sanctus Hieronymus).*	**(ille) dominus, -ī** lord Cf. dominate **pascō, -ere** drive to pasture, shepherd **mē** me
4. **Caelī ēnarrant** glōriam Deī, et **opus** manūs **adnuntiat firmāmentum**. *PSALMUS 18 (translated from the Hebrew).*	**(ille) caelus, -ī** sky, heavens Cf. caerulian, celestial **ē-narrō, -āre** explain in detail Cf. narrate **ad-nuntiō, -āre** announce **(illud) firmāmentum, -ī** a strengthening support, the heavens fixed above the earth, the firmament

VI. CHANGE each of the following sentences into indirectly quoted material (statement or question) using the verb in parentheses.

NOTE that **negō** is usually used instead of **dīcō nōn** to introduce negated statements.

1. Omnēs sapientēs dēbent magnī aestimārī. (quaeritur)
2. Pars hominum sōla memoriam repetit grātiae. (rogō)
3. Philosophus sapiens virtūtis oblīviscitur. (negāmus)
4. Fēmina furtī rea dēbet pecūniae damnārī. (quaeritur)
5. Miseret matrem filiae caecae. (rogās)
6. Ōtium habent semper stultī. (scrībit sapiens)
7. Fēminae virōrum parēs possunt esse. (dīcit philosophus)
8. Moritur grātia et odium vīvit. (negant)
9. Ovis ovem sequitur et caecus caecum. (vidēmus semper)
10. Vir magnae sapientiae vitia nōn dēbet habēre. (audīmus)

VII. CHANGE each of the following sentences into a single sentence with a purpose clause replacing the second sentence.

Scrībit philosophus. Prōpōnit virtūtem docēre. — **"The philosopher writes. He proposes to teach virtue."**

Scrībit philosophus ut virtūtem doceat. — **"The philosopher writes to teach virtue. Or, so that he teach virtue."** (prō-pōnō, -ere)

1. Vēritātem dīcō. Prōpōnō damnāre illum virum capitis.
2. Poēta incipit canere. Prōpōnit hominēs virtūtem docēre.
3. Dōnum pecūniae das. Prōpōnis avārum satiāre.
4. Semper admonet hominēs glōriae. Prōpōnit magnī aestimārī.
5. Proficisciminī. Prōpōnitis poētam magnum audīre.
6. Omnēs amat illa fēmina stulta. Prōpōnit semper amārī.
7. Philosophum sapientem sequimur. Prōpōnimus virtūtis nōn oblīviscī.
8. Rēgem sapientem sequor. Prōpōnō vitia nōn habēre.
9. Ovēs ovēs semper sequuntur. Prōpōnunt nōn morī sōlae.
10. Sapiens cupiō esse. Prōpōnō vītam bonam regere.

VIII. NOTE THE PATTERN in each of the following sentences and compose a translation of the English sentences using the same pattern.

1. **Ēsse oportet ut vīvās, nōn vīvere ut edās.**
   You ought to love so that you are loved, not be loved so that you love.
   We ought to give gifts so that we are esteemed highly.
   I ought not forget the truth so that I seem wise. (**NOTE** that the passive of **videō** means "**be seen or seem.**")

NOTE that the pattern sentence could say almost the same thing differently: **Ēsse dēbēs ut vīvās, nōn vīvere ut edās.** Or: **Edās ut vīvās, nē vīvās ut edās.** Try composing translations of the English sentences using these patterns instead.

2. **Quaeritur num mors malum sit.**
   It is questioned whether life is a good thing.
   We are asked whether a greedy person can be satisfied.
   They question whether sheep follow sheep.

Piranesi, The Temple of Neptune

LESSON FIVE

ABLATIVE AND DATIVE

Ōtium sine litterīs mors est.

ABLATIVE AND DATIVE CASES. The language from which Latin evolved had more declensional cases than are preserved in Latin, just as Latin itself has more than survive into English. This general process of declensional simplification has meant that the surviving cases have had to assume the burden of the lost cases, in addition to their own true functions, with word order or other auxiliary words added to clarify ambiguities. In English, these lost cases have all been assumed into the accusative, and to avoid confusion between their various original meanings, the particular function intended is clarified by so-called "prepositions" (from **prae-pōnō, "place in front"**); these are really adverbs, usually placed in front or in close proximity to the declensional form, which is said to be the "object." In Latin, an earlier stage in this process of declensional simplification is preserved. In addition to the accusative case, which sometimes will require particular clarification with an adverb-preposition, one other case, the **ablative,** survives to share the burden of the lost cases. It too will often require an adverb-preposition for clarification, especially since in most of its declensional forms it is indistinguishable from yet another case, the **dative.** The ablative and dative were well on their way to coalescing into one, although the dative retains only its true function and never requires an adverb preposition for clarification.

TRUE ABLATIVE (SEPARATION). The basic meaning of the ablative case is the idea of separation or movement **away** from something, and hence its name, which means literally **"carried away" (ab-ferō).** Because the ablative has also assumed the burden of two lost cases that expressed the ideas of **association** (**"with"**) and **place** (**"in"**), the ablative, even in its true function, will usually be clarified by a preposition expressing separation ("away, from"). Such prepositions in Latin are: **ā** (**ab**, before vowels) **"away from," ex** (**ē**, sometimes before consonants) **"out from,"** and **dē "down from,"** as well as **"concerning,"** for the Romans did not necessarily conceive of the ablatival idea simply as a spacial separation, but extended it often to metaphoric contexts which often differ from our way of thinking. Such clarifying prepositions are said "to take the ablative" as their object. The preposition is sometimes omitted in poetic diction or metaphoric usage.

Ab urbe proficiscor.	**"I set out (away) from the city."**
Ōtium sine litterīs mors est.	**"Leisure without (i.e., away from) literature is death."**

NOTE that the adverbial function of the accusative case can similarly be clarified by a preposition, but the accusative indicates the **goal** rather than the origin or separation.

Ad urbem proficiscor.	**"I set out toward the city."**

The true ablatival idea of **separation** (or source) can also be used to express the **agent** (as the source) **of an action in the passive voice.**

Ā poētā fābula narrātur.	**"The story is told by the poet (i.e., a story from the poet is told.)"**

This is the so-called **ablative of agent,** but again it is merely a true ablative in a passive context.

NOTE that this ablative of agent allows the same thing to be said in the passive voice as in the active voice, although with a different emphasis. In the passive voice, of course, the agent does not have to be expressed if the speaker prefers to omit it, as, for example, when the doer of the action is unknown or immaterial to the context.

Poēta fābulam narrat. **Ā poētā fābula narrātur.**

The true ablatival idea of separation (or source) can also be made to express the **material** out of which something is made.

Domum ex lignō habeō. **"I have a house (made out) of wood."**

This is the so-called **ablative of material,** but again it is merely a true ablative in a particular context (of constructive material).

NOTE that this ablative of material gives the same kind of information that you have already learned to express by the adjectival function of the genitive (see page 35).

Domum lignī habeō. **"I have a house of wood (i.e., wooden)."**

COMITATIVE ABLATIVE ("WITH"). In addition to the true ablatival idea, the ablative case assumed the burden of a lost **comitative case**, which expressed the idea of **association** with something.

An example of this comitative ablative is the so-called **ablative of accompaniment,** which expresses the person or thing in company with which something is done.

Cum amīcīs proficiscor. **"I set out with friends."**

The preposition **cum** is regularly required for clarification; consider, for example, the possible confusion with the true ablative, which would mean exactly the opposite: **Sine amīcīs proficiscor. "Without friends, I set out."** But since an opposite is a related meaning, one can see why the burden of the lost comitative case was assumed by the true ablative.

The associative idea can be expressed with a thing as well as with a person. Idiomatically, the preposition is often omitted if the ablative noun is modified by an adjective.

Cum perīculō proficiscor. **"I set out with danger."**

Magnō perīculō proficiscor. **"I set out with great danger."**

NOTE that this comitative ablative, in certain contexts, gives the same kind of information that you have already learned to express by the adjectival function of the genitive (of quality, see page 36).

Vir magnā sapientiā proficiscitur. **"A man with great wisdom sets out."**

This same associative idea of the comitative ablative can indicate the manner in which the action is done. This is the so-called **ablative of manner,** but it is merely another context for the comitative ablative.

Cum sapientiā regit. — **"He rules with wisdom."**

Magnā sapientiā regit. — **"He rules with great wisdom."**

This same associative idea can indicate the instrument with which the action is done. This is the so-called **ablative of means,** but it is merely another context for the comitative ablative.

Arte fābula narrātur. — **"With art the story is told (or by means of art)."**

NOTE that this ablative of means is similar to the ablative of agent, but the ablative of agent is the true ablative (source) and is always clarified by an ablatival preposition (such as **ab**), whereas the ablative of means is a comitative ablative and it is never clarified by a preposition (such as **cum**), for it then would not express the "means or instrument," but rather the "manner."

Cum arte fābula narrātur. — **"With art (i.e., artfully, but not through the instrumentality of art) the story is told."**

NOTE that both means and agent are common with passive verbs.

Arte ā poētā fābula narrātur. — **"With art (as means) the story is told by (or from) the poet (as source)."**

This same associative idea of the ablative of means, in contexts of evaluation, can indicate the **price or value** as the means with which the action is done.

Magnō pretiō sapientia aestimātur. — **"Wisdom is valued with a high price."**

NOTE that this so-called **ablative of price** gives the same kind of information that you have already learned to express by the adjectival function of the genitive (of price, see page 34).

Magnī sapientia aestimātur. — **"Wisdom is valued of great (value)."**

LOCATIVE ABLATIVE ("IN"). In addition to the true ablatival idea, the ablative case has assumed, not only the comitative idea, but also the burden of a lost **locative case,** which expressed the idea of position or location, either in space or time. In this meaning, the ablative is usually clarified by a preposition only for spacial location, but not for temporal, probably because words for time gave a sufficiently unambiguous context for this locative idea.

In urbe est. — **"He is in the city."**

Nocte proficiscitur. **"He sets out at night."**

NOTE that the adverbial function of the accusative can also be used to indicate time, but this so-called **accusative of duration** indicates not the locative idea of "**when,**" but rather "**how long,**" like the accusative of the goal (see page 66), "from here all the way **toward** there."

Tōtam noctem narrātur fābula. **"All night long a story is told."**

DATIVE CASE. Although the dative case is only rarely distinguishable as a declensional form distinct from the ablative, with which it too is in the process of coalescence, it retains always only its own distinct idea and **never is clarified by a preposition**. The dative case indicates the idea of the person or thing receiving **either some benefit** or **some disadvantage** from the action of the verb. In some contexts, this idea is equivalent to what is called the indirect object, and the case was termed dative by example of such use with the verb "to give" (**dare**).

Carmen hominī dō. **"I give a poem to the man."**

The example above really means that the action of giving a poem was performed for the man's benefit (in that he received it). As with the other cases you have learned, it is important to grasp the basic functional idea of the dative, for in other contexts, the dative can mean something other than what would be termed an indirect object.

For example, the so-called **dative of possession** is this same idea of benefit in contexts with the verb **esse.**

Domus hominī est. **"The man has a house." (Or, "There is a house for the man, who is benefited by being its owner or recipient.")**

NOTE that you have already learned to express equivalent ideas, although with a different emphasis, by using the verb **habēre.**

Domum homo habet. **"The man has a house."**

In contexts with certain verbs, the dative is the ordinary completion, indicating, as the Latin language viewed the action, the person or thing benefited or disadvantaged by the verb. Such verbs are said "to take the dative."

Hominī homo nocet. **"Man hurts man." (Or, "Man is harmful to man.")**

Hominī homo placet. **"Man pleases man." (Or, "Man is pleasing to man.")**

The so-called **double dative** is this same idea of advantage or disadvantage in contexts with **both a person and a thing** as datives.

Hominī perīculō est sapientia. "**Wisdom exists as a danger for man.**" (Or, "**Wisdom exists for man's disadvantage as a danger.**")

In the above example, the "thing" (as distinct from the "person") benefited is actually equivalent to an indication of the goal or use intended for the thing, and hence this same basic idea, in other contexts, produces the so-called **dative of the goal.**

Dōnō domus datur (hominī). "**The house is given (to the man) as a gift (or, to be a gift.)**"

ABLATIVE AND DATIVE DECLENSION. The chart summarizes the endings for the dative and ablative in the five declensions of nouns.

ABLATIVE AND DATIVE DECLENSIONAL ENDINGS

	decl I ā-stem	decl II o-stem	decl III cons-stem	 i-stem	decl IV masc-fem	 neuter	decl V ē-stem
dat sing	**-ae**	**-ō**	**-ī**		**-uī**	**-ū**	**-eī / -ē**
abl sing	**-ā**	**-ō**	**-e**	**-ī**	**-ū**		**-ē**
dat pl	**-īs**	**-īs**	**-ibus**		**-ibus / -ubus**		**-ēbus**
abl pl	**-īs**	**-īs**	**-ibus**		**-ibus / -ubus**		**-ēbus**

EXAMPLES

	I	II		III		IV		V
nom	vīta	vir	servus	lex	ignis	manus	cornū	rēs
acc	vītam	virum	servum	lēgem	ignem	manum	cornū	rem
gen	vītae	virī	servī	lēgis	ignis	manūs	cornūs	reī
dat	**vītae**	**virō**	**servō**	**lēgī**	**ignī**	**manuī**	**cornū**	**reī**
abl	**vītā**	**virō**	**servō**	**lēge**	**ignī -e**	**manū**	**cornū**	**rē**
nom	vītae	virī	servī	lēgēs	ignēs	manūs	cornua	rēs
acc	vitās	virōs	servōs	lēgēs	ignēs	manūs	cornua	rēs
gen	vītārum	virōrum	servōrum	lēgum	ignium	manuum	cornuum	rērum
dat	**vītīs**	**virīs**	**servīs**	**lēgibus**	**ignibus**	**manibus** **lacubus**	**cornibus**	**rēbus**
abl	**vītīs**	**virīs**	**servīs**	**lēgibus**	**ignibus**	**manibus** **lacubus**	**cornibus**	**rēbus**

NOTE that the dative and ablative are always identical in the plural. **NOTE** that in the singular, the distinctive **-i** of the dative is lost in declension II and sometimes in declensions IV and V, and is changed to **-ae** in declension I.

NOTE that several of the new forms are ambiguous. As usual, you must distinguish them from context

NOTE that declension III i-stems (see pages 38–39) usually have **-e** in the **ablative singular** (like **igne**), but sometimes have **-ī**, especially **neuter i-stems** (like **animālī**) and **declension III adjectives**, and always for adjectives of three or two terminations (like three-termination **acrī** and two termination **brevī**, but one-termination **sapiens** and **atrox** may be **sapiente atrōce**, although **sapientī atrōcī** is also possible). **NOTE** that the **-ū** alternative for declension IV dative singular always occurs with neuter nouns, like **cornū**. **NOTE** that some declension IV nouns have **-ubus** for the dative-ablative plural: **lacubus**. This is something characteristic of the particular word and is unpredictable.

NOTE that the dative-ablative of declension II neuter nouns and adjectives is not distinct from the masculine(-feminine): **perīculō magnō** and **perīculīs magnīs**. Similarly for the plural of declension III neuters: **animālibus acribus brevibus atrōcibus**.

NOTE that in declension V **diēs** sometimes is identical with the ablative in the dative singular: **diēī** can also be **diē**.

Consult the chart on the next pages for examples of the full declensions of nouns and adjectives.

REMEMBER

that the dative is only rarely distinguishable from the ablative as a form, but it retains its true function and meaning and is never clarified by a preposition, although context can allow 'advantage-disadvantage' to mean possession, goal, and the special 'double dative' structure. In contrast, the true ablative of separation (agent, material) has absorbed comitative (togetherness: means, manner, quality, price-evaluation) and locative (temporal-spacial placement) functions and is often clarified by a preposition, unless otherwise obvious from particular contexts or idioms.

INDEX VERBORUM

(ille) **gladius, gladiī**	**sword**
(illa) **lingua, -ae**	**tongue, language, dialect**
(illa) **littera, -ae**	**letter** (of the alphabet), **mark**; in pl., **epistle, letters** (as scholarship), **literature**
(illud) **nōmen, -inis**	**name, noun, renown**
(illa) **nox, noctis, -ctium**	**night**
(illud) **saxum, -ī**	**rock, stone**
(ille) **stilus, -ī**	**stake, style** (pointed iron pen used for writing on wax tablets)

PARADIGM 12: ABLATIVE AND DATIVE DECLENSION

	FIRST	SECOND		THIRD					FOURTH		FIFTH
	(masc)-fem	*masc-(fem)*	*neuter*	*masc-(fem)*	*i-stem*	*true i-stem*	*neuter*	*neuter i-stem*	*masc-(fem)*	*neuter*	*fem-(masc)*
						SINGULAR					
nom	vīta	servus	bellum	rex	urbs	ignis	nōmen	animal	lacus	cornū	rēs
acc	vītam	servum	bellum	rēgem	urbem	ignem	nōmen	animal	lacum	cornū	rem
gen	vītae	servī	bellī	rēgis	urbis	ignis	nōminis	animālis	lacūs	cornūs	reī
dat	vītae	servō	bellō	rēgī	urbī	ignī	nōminī	animālī	lacuī/ū	cornū	reī
abl	vītā	servō	bellō	rēge	urbe	ignī/e	nōmine	animālī	lacū	cornū	rē
						PLURAL					
nom	vītae	servī	bella	rēgēs	urbēs	ignēs	nōmina	animālia	lacūs	cornua	rēs
acc	vītās	servōs	bella	rēgēs	urbēs	ignīs/ēs	nōmina	animālia	lacūs	cornua	rēs
gen	vītārum	servōrum	bellōrum	rēgum	urbium	ignium	nōminum	animālium	lacuum	cornuum	rērum
dat	vītīs	servīs	bellīs	rēgibus	urbibus	ignibus	nōminibus	animālibus	lacubus manibus	cornibus	rēbus
abl	vītīs	servīs	bellīs	rēgibus	urbibus	ignibus	nōminibus	animālibus	lacubus manibus	cornibus	rēbus

PARADIGM 12: ABLATIVE AND DATIVE DECLENSION *continued*

	ADJECTIVE I and II			ADJECTIVE III		
	masc. II	fem. I	neut. II	masc. III	fem. III	neut. III
				SINGULAR		
nom	magnus	magna	magnum	**acer brevis atrox**	**acris brevis atrox**	**acre breve atrox**
acc	magnum	magnam	magnum	acrem	acrem	acre
gen	magnī	magnae	magnī	acris	acris	acris
dat	magnō	magnae	magnō	acrī	acrī	acrī
abl	magnō	magnā	magnō	acrī brevī atrōcī (-e)	acrī brevī atrōcī (-e)	acrī brevī atrōcī (-e)
				PLURAL		
nom	magnī	magnae	magna	acrēs	acrēs	acria brevia atrōcia
acc	magnōs	magnās	magna	acrēs	acrēs	acria brevia atrōcia
gen	magnōrum	magnārum	magnōrum	acrium	acrium	acrium
dat	magnīs	magnīs	magnīs	acribus	acribus	acribus
abl	magnīs	magnīs	magnīs	acribus	acribus	acribus

brevis, breve & **atrox** same as **acer, acris, acre** unless indicated

(illa) toga, -ae	**toga** (outer garment of male clothing, usually worn in times of peace and to conduct public affairs)
(illa) urbs, -rbis, -rbium	**city**
(ille) vultus, -ūs	**visage, countenance, face**
dēformis, -e	**ugly, misshapen**
difficilis, -e	**difficult**
dulcis, -e	**sweet, pleasant**
fortis, -e	**strong, courageous**
tōtus, -a, -um	**all, whole** (for use see EXERCITATIO VI)
agō, -ere	**do, drive, conduct, impel:** *grātiās agere*: **thank**
appellō, -āre	**accost, speak to, address**
cōgitō, -āre	**pursue something in the mind, reflect, think**
cognōscō, -ere	**learn** (by inquiring), **recognize, know**
crēdō, -ere	**entrust** (as a loan), **confide to, believe** (+ dat.)
cupiō, -ere	**desire, want**
interficiō, -ere	**kill, murder**
loquor, -ī	**speak, talk, say**
nāscor, -ī	**be born**
noceō, -ēre	**hurt, be harmful**
perdō, -ere	**destroy, lose**
placeō, -ēre	**please, be pleasing**
ego	**I** (for use, see EXERCITATIO VI)
ille, illa, illud	**he/ she/ it** (for use, see EXERCITATIO VI)
tū	**you** (for use, see EXERCITATIO VI)
ā, ab	**(away) from** (+ abl.)
ad	**toward, to** (+ acc.)
cum	**with** (+ abl.)
dē	**(down) from, concerning** (+ abl.)
ē, ex	**(out) from** (+ abl.)
sine	**without** (+ abl.)
sub	**(toward) under** (+ acc.); **(within) under** (+ abl.); **near (below)** (+ abl.)
autem	**however, moreover** (placed second in its clause)
satis	**enough** (indeclinable, both adverb and adjective)
nihil	**nothing** (indeclinable noun)

EXERCITATIONES

I. MATCH the second phrase to the first by changing it into the same form. Some items will require more than one answer.

1. carmine pulchrō (dēformis fīlia)
2. diēbus longīs (nox brevis)
3. fābulārum omnium (mors mala)
4. poētae timidō (rex sapiens)
5. ignium pulchrōrum (urbs fortis)
6. amōrī glōriōsō (rēs difficilis)
7. vēritāte paternā (vultus audax)
8. dōnō pretiōsō (ovis stulta)
9. domibus ligneīs (pars dēformis)
10. furtō omnī (nōmen dulce)
11. omnia animālia (atrox reus)
12. ove timidā (vēritas sempiterna)
13. cursūs omnēs (vir fortis)
14. generibus variīs (mūtābilis fēmina)
15. dī paternī (pulcher poēta)
16. grātiae magnae (vīnum forte)
17. rēbus malīs (stilus longus)
18. virō sapientī (fābula dulcis)
19. fīliī bonī (mater pulchra)
20. lēgum atrōcium (mors misera)

II. MATCH the second verb to the first by changing it into the same form. Some items will require more than one answer.

1. docentur (amō)
2. noceam (interficiō)
3. scrībere (satiō)
4. dīcitur (habeō)
5. amēminī (audiō)
6. nāscī (amō)
7. vidēre (perdō)
8. vīvat (cōgitō)
9. possim (placeō)
10. cupiāmur (canō)
11. quaereris (crēdō)
12. oblīviscuntur (dō)
13. facis (audiō)
14. neget (cognōscō)
15. moriāris (dō)
16. nocētis (vīvō)
17. nāscar (amō)
18. esse (loquor)
19. crēdam (interficiō)
20. satiēre (rogō)

III. TRANSLATE.

1. In urbe magnus est poēta. Poētae magnō domus lignī est. Vir est ille magnae virtūtis et sapiens. Poētae placet canere et semper magnā sapientiā canit. Semper canat magnā cum arte. Dīcitur ab omnibus sapiens esse et vir dulcī linguā. Quaeritur in poēmātibus ā poētā num fortūna vītam hominum regat. Nē regātur vīta hominum ā fortūnā sed omnibus ā sempiternīs deīs. Fortūna semper mūtābilis est, neque hominēs oportet fortūnae crēdere mūtābilī. Bonīs crēdāmus dīs. (**NOTE** that **dīs** is a contraction for **deīs**.) Omnēs oportet illum poētam audīre. Magnī ab omnibus sapientibus aestimātur ille poēta. Omnēs dēbent poētae crēdere. Crēdant omnēs poētae sapientī. Poētae carmina sapientia sunt.

Utinam stultī poētae crēdant. Forsitan stultī incipiant dē dīs sempiternīs cōgitāre. Vēritātem dē omnibus rēbus cognōscant omnēs stultī. Diem tōtum et tōtam noctem poēmata scrībit et cum amīcīs loquitur. Semper nocte scrībit. Dīcitur ab amīcīs nocte scrībere magnā cum arte ille vir magnae virtūtis. Omnibus cum amīcīs proficiscāmur ad urbem poētae ut poētam videāmus. Cum poētā cupimus loquī.

2. Rex rogat num atrox in illā urbe damnētur ab omnibus bonīs semper aut pecūniae aut capitis. Dīcit rex omnem atrōcem dēbēre damnārī ab omnibus sapientibus. Sapientis est semper atrōcēs damnāre aut pecūniae aut capitis. Rex est vir magnae virtūtis. Magnā virtūte regit. Semper regat ille rex. Grātiās rēgī agunt omnēs bonī. Omnēs oportet rēgī grātiās agere. Aut saxō aut gladiō dēbet atrox reus interficī. Reum interficiant omnēs bonī aut saxō aut gladiō.

3. Sit rex. Vir tamen est magnae virtūtis. Vir fortis est et cum virtūte urbs regitur ā rēge fortī. Omnēs bonī dīcunt urbem regī lēgibus ā rēge sapientī.

4. Utinam sit sapientia omnibus hominibus nē homo semper hominī noceat neque stulta atrōcia faciat. Nē noceant hominēs hominibus. Nōn oportet hominem hominī nocēre. Hominī placet hominī nocēre. Utinam crēdat homo hominī. Cognōscimus hominem hominī nocēre. Homo ab homine interficitur. Homo saxō aut gladiō hominem interficit. Nōn miseret hominem hominis.

5. Forsitan nōn possīmus sine perīculō vīvere sed omnēs nōn oportet semper timidōs esse. Ā fortūna regimur, nōn ā dīs sempiternīs. Ē poētā magnō dēbēmus quaerere num mors malum sit. Ā poētā in carminibus dulcibus quaeritur num vir magnae sapientiae possit sine perīculō vīvere.

6. Nōn oblīviscimur deōrum. Nē oblīviscāmur deōrum. Hominibus placet deōrum nōn oblīviscī. Utinam deōrum nē oblīviscāmur. Deōrum nōn oportet hominēs oblīviscī.

7. Vīta longa hominibus bonīs dōnō ā dīs datur ut magnā virtūte vīvant. Vītae dōnum hominibus dī dant. Vītam hominibus dōnō dant. Nē vītam brevem dī hominibus dōnō dent. Hominibus vīta brevis est ē dīs. Hominum est vītam brevem ē dīs habēre.

8. Tōtam noctem ā poētā cum amīcīs quaeritur num oporteat poētās carmina brevia scrībere aut longa. Nocte rogat num poēma breve bonum sit. Bonum est poēmata scrībere dē hominum virtūte. Dē homine fortī carmen canitur ā poētā. Stilō poēma scrībitur ā poētā magnā cum arte. Amīcīs poēma dōnō dat.

9. Dēbēmus omnium artium oblīviscī et sine litterīs vīvere. Possumusne sine artibus vīvere? Rogō num vīta sine litterīs mors sit. Stilō scrībō vītam sine litterīs mortem esse. Bonum est ōtium cum litterīs habēre. Sapientis est cum litterīs vīvere. Parvī aestimātur vīta sine litterīs ab omnibus sapientibus. Sapientēs miseret stultōrum.

10. Sapientia hominī perīculō datur ā dīs. Sapientiam hominibus perīculō dī semper dant. Philosophī cognōscunt sapientiam hominibus perīculō darī. Quaerunt num sapientia hominibus noceat.

IV. TRANSLATE. (Try to guess the meaning of new words on the basis of context and cognates before consulting the adjacent **reading notes.**)

1. Difficile est **crīmen** nōn **prōdere** vultū. *OVIDIUS.*

(illud) **crīmen, -inis** crime
prōdō, -ere give over, betray Cf. prodition

2. Homo hominī **lupus.**

(ille) **lupus, -ī** wolf Cf. lupine

3. **Dictum** sapientī **sat** est. *TERENTIUS.*

(illud) **dictum, -ī** word, thing said (**dīcere**) Cf. diction
sat = satis

4. Cēdant **arma** togae, **concēdat laurea** linguae. *CICERO.*

cēdō, -ere go away from, yield Cf. cede
(illud) **armum, -ī** armament, weapon (used only in the plural **arma,** like *arms)*
con-cēdō, -ere yield along with, go away together with Cf. concede
(illa) **laurea, -ae** laurel branch carried as sign of triumph

5. Dē **mortuīs nihil nisī** bonum dīcāmus. *DIOGENES LAERTIUS (translated from the Greek).*

mortuus, -a, -um dead Cf. mortify
nihil *(indeclinable neuter)* nothing Cf. nihilism
nisī unless, except, if not

6. Cēdant carminibus rēgēs rēgumque **triumphī.** *OVIDIUS.*

(ille) **triumphus, -ī** triumphal procession

7. Ars varia **vulpī, ast ūna echīnō maxima.** *ARCHILOCHOS (translated from the Greek).*

(illa) **vulpes, -is, -ium** fox Cf. vulpine
ast (or **at**) but, moreover
ūnus, -a, -um one Cf. unify
(ille) **echīnus, -ī** hedgehog, sea urchin Cf. echinate

8. Ōtium sine litterīs mors est. *CICERO.*

9. Virtūs est vitia **fugere.** *HORATIUS.*

fugiō, -ere flee, shun Cf. fugitive, fugue

10. **Comedunt pānem impietātis** et vīnum **inīquitātis bibunt.** *LIBER PROVERBIŌRUM SALOMŌNIS Ē BIBLIĪS SACRĪS VULGĀTĒĪS (translated from the Hebrew).*

com-edō, -ere eat entirely up, consume Cf. comestible
(ille) **pānis, -is, -ium** bread
(illa) **impietas, -ātis** impiety
(illa) **inīquitas, -ātis** iniquity
bibō, -ere drink Cf. imbibe

11. **Principium** sapientiae **timor Dominī** et **scientia sanctōrum prūdentia.** *Ibīdem.*

(illud) **principium, -ī** beginning, first element Cf. principle
(ille) **timor, -oris** fear Cf. timorous
(ille) **dominus, -ī** lord Cf. dominate
(illa) **scientia, -ae** knowledge Cf. science
sanctus, -a, -um holy, sacred Cf. sanctify
(illa) **prūdentia, -ae** intelligence, prudence
ibīdem in that very same place

12. Sapientēs **abscondunt** scientiam, **ōs** autem stultī **confūsiōnī proximum** est. *Ibīdem.*

abs-condō, -ere conceal, hide Cf. abscond
(illud) **ōs, ōris** mouth Cf. oral
(illa) **confūsio, -ōnis** confusion
proximus, -a, -um (+ *dat.*) nearest to Cf. proximity

13. Lex sapientis **fons** vītae ut **dēclīnet** ā **ruīnā** mortis. *Ibīdem.*

(ille) **fons, fontis, -ium** fountain
dē-clīnō, -āre turn away Cf. declension
(illa) **ruīna, -ae** downfall, ruin

14. In **multitūdine populī dīgnitas** rēgis et in **paucitāte plebis ignōminia principis.** *Ibīdem.*

(illa) **multitūdo, -inis** multitude
(ille) **populus, -ī** people Cf. populace
(illa) **dīgnitas, -ātis** dignity, worth, merit
(illa) **paucitas, -ātis** paucity, scarcity
(illa) **plebs, -bis** common people, plebians
(illa) **ignōminia, -ae** dishonor, ignominy
princeps, -cipis first, prince

15. **Ingrediātur** ad **doctrīnam cor tuum** et **aurēs** tuae ad verba scientiae. *Ibīdem.*

in-gredior, -ī enter in
(illa) doctrīna, -ae learning Cf. doctrine (**doceō**)
(illud) cor, cordis, -ium heart Cf. coronary
tuus, -a, -um your (singular)
(illa) auris, -is, -ium ear Cf. aural

V. **CHANGE** each of the following sentences into equivalent expressions using (1) the genitive of possession and (2) the dative of possession.

Habet rex urbem. — **"The king has a city."**

(1) **Rēgis est urbs.** — **"The city is the *king's*."** (Emphasizes the possessor.)

(2) **Rēgī est urbs.** — **"The king *has* a city (amongst other things)."** (Emphasizes the fact of possession.)

1. Pecūniam nōn habet avārus acer.
2. Mater dēformis dēformēs habet fīliōs fīliāsque.
3. Poēmata difficilia sapiens habet poēta.
4. Amīcus rēgum atrox habet ovēs.
5. Cornua longa acriaque animal habet.
6. Urbs rēgis bonās habet lēgēs.
7. Nē habeant stultī sapientiam.
8. Forsitan habeat puer dēformis vītam longam.
9. Potestne fēmina magnae sapientiae domum lignī habēre?
10. Omnēs rēs nōmina varia habent.

VI. **CHANGE** each of the following sentences into equivalent expressions using the dative of possession. This exercise is like the second part of the previous, but it allows you to practice the new vocabulary items for the personal pronouns.

Habeō domum pulchram. — **Mihi est domus pulchra.**

The chart summarizes the pronominal declension. When new material is introduced, as here, in the EXERCITATIONES, it is presented primarily as a peculiarity of vocabulary, in order not to distract from the main items of grammar. Practicing it in the exercises will facilitate familiarity, although often complete retention will not come until further exposure through review and more extensive reading.

PARADIGM 13
PRONOMINAL DECLENSION

	1st person	*2nd person*	*3rd person lacking: use demonstrative* *masc.*	*fem.*	*neuter*	*pronominal adjective* *sōlus, -a, -um*	*tōtus, -a, -um*
nom	**ego**	**tū**	**ille**	**illa**	**illud**	**sōlus -a -um**	**tōtus -a -um**
acc	**mē**	**tē**	**illum**	**illam**	**illud**	**sōlum -am -um**	**tōtum -am -um**
gen	**meī**	**tuī**	**illīus**	**illīus**	**illīus**	**sōlīus**	**tōtīus**
dat	**mihi**	**tibi**	**illī**	**illī**	**illī**	**sōlī**	**tōtī**
abl	**mē**	**tē**	**illō**	**illā**	**illō**	**sōlō -ā -ō**	**tōtō -ā -ō**
nom	**nōs**	**vōs**	**illī**	**illae**	**illa**	**sōlī -ae -a**	**tōtī -ae -a**
acc	**nōs**	**vōs**	**illōs**	**illās**	**illa**	**sōlōs -ās -a**	**tōtōs -ās -a**
gen	**nostrum**	**vestrum**	**illōrum**	**illārum**	**illōrum**	**sōlōrum**	**tōtōrum**
	nostrī	**vestrī**				**-ārum -ōrum**	**-ārum -ōrum**
dat	**nōbīs**	**vōbīs**	**illīs**	**illīs**	**illīs**	**sōlīs**	**tōtīs**
abl	**nōbīs**	**vōbīs**	**illīs**	**illīs**	**illīs**	**sōlīs**	**tōtīs**

NOTE that the personal pronouns for the first and second persons are declined as in the chart above. Latin does not have a pronoun for the third person, but demonstratives (like **ille** "he there") often function as the missing pronoun. It too is declined, with separate forms for the three genders. **NOTE** in particular the forms for the **genitive and dative singular.** Apart from these two forms (which are the same for all three genders, **ille** is declined like adjectives of declensions I and II **(bonus, -a, -um)**. **THIS PECULIARITY IS COMMON FOR ALL OTHER PRONOUNS.** Thus **sōlus, -a, -um** ("only one") and **tōtus, -a, -um** ("entire one") are similarly declined in this so-called **pronominal declension.** Unfortunately, there is no way to predict which adjectives will be declined in the pronominal manner; so this must be learned as part of the lexical entry.

The nominative forms of the first and second persons give the same information as the personal conjugational suffix, and hence are used only for emphasis or without a verb expressed.

Proficisceris, nōn ego. **"You set forth, not I."**

Tū proficisceris. **"*You* set forth."**

The genitive is not used for possession, but in the other functions of the genitive (partitive genitive, objective genitive, etc.).

Oblīvisceris meī. **"You forget me."**

In the plural there are two forms for the genitive. The forms ending in **-trum** are used as partitive genitives (see page 36), and the forms in **-trī** are objective genitives (see page 37).

Pars nostrum sōla moritur. **"Part of us only dies."**

Amor nostrī magnus est. **"Love for us is great."**

1. Pecūniam nōn habeō.

2. Neque fīliōs neque fīliās habēmus. (**neque . . . neque "neither . . . nor"**)

3. Illa magnam partem domūs habet sōla.

4. Forsitan cum omnibus bonīs habeātis mortem glōriōsam.

5. Utinam in illā urbe habeās omnibus cum amīcīs illīus rēgis magnam ex lignō domum.

6. Illud animal cornua illīus generis habet.

7. Ille tēcum nōn habet cursum vītae glōriōsum. (**Cum** follows and is joined to the ablative of the first and second person pronouns: **mēcum, tēcum, nōbīscum, vōbīscum.**)

8. Lacum neque vīnī neque aquae habēs.

9. Utinam amīcōs stultōs avārōsque nē habeātis in illā urbe atrōcī.

10. Illa puella sapiens sōla ex omnibus fēminīs vītam miseram nōn habet.

VII. CHANGE each of the following sentences into equivalent expressions using the passive voice. (For practice, keep the same word order.) REMEMBER that the agent is clarified by a preposition of source (**ā, ab, ē, ex**), but the instrument or means is never clarified; if it were clarified by **cum** it would mean manner, instead of means.

Poēta fābulam narrat. **Ā poētā fābula narrātur.**

Stilō fābulam scrībit. **Stilō fābula scrībitur (ab illō).**

1. Nōn regunt vītam hominēs stultī, sed sapientēs sōlī.

2. Capitis damnat rex in illā urbe omnēs reōs et interficit gladiō.

3. Animal pulchrum illīus generis mater puerīs dōnō dat.

4. Magnī aestimās amīcōs sapientēs tēcum semper habēre, sed nōn ego.

5. Nōbīscum videātis in urbe virum magnae sapientiae.

6. Poēmata brevia sed magnā arte canat ille poēta sapiens.

7. Vēritātis sempiternae admoneat philosophus sapiens rēgem omnem atrōcem stultumque.

8. Forsitan omnēs virī bonī damnent illum hominem audācem furtī.

9. Poētae quaerunt num mors malum sit.

10. Pecūniam avārīs dōnō nōn cupiō dare.

VIII. CHANGE each of the following sentences into indirectly quoted material (statement or question) using the verb in parentheses.

1. Varium et mūtābile est semper homo stultus. (quaeritur ab illō)

2. Illud vēritas est. (negant dēformēs fēminae)

3. Illī ex urbe nōbīscum nocte ad rēgem magnae virtūtis proficiscuntur. (nōs rogātis)

4. Mater rēgis, fēmina dēformis sed magnae sapientiae, nostrī nōn oblīviscitur. (vidēmus)

5. Interficiuntur gladiō omnēs reī furtī in illā urbe. (ē rēge quaeris)

6. Semper bona faciunt hominēs sapientēs. (negātur)

7. Possunt rēgēs atrōcēs cum perīculō omnibus cum amīcīs regere et urbem perdere. (illās rogō)

8. Aqua mors ignī, hominī vīta. (dīcō)

9. Dē tē fābula narrātur. (audiō)

10. Tēcum nōn possum ego vīvere neque sine tē. (dīcō)

IX. CHANGE each of the following pairs of sentences into a single sentence with a purpose clause replacing the second sentence.

Ab urbe proficiscor. Prōpōnō tē vidēre. — **"I set out from the city. I propose to see you."**

Ab urbe proficiscor ut tē videam. — **"I set out from the city to see you."**

1. Amīcus tibi pecūniam dōnō dat. Prōpōnit tibi placēre.

2. Mihi placēs. Prōpōnis mēcum semper vīvere.

3. Ad illam urbem nocte omnibus cum amīcīs proficisciminī. Prōpōnitis nōs vidēre.

4. Pecūniam nōbīs dōnō das. Prōpōnis nōbīs grātiās agere.

5. Vidēris amīcus rēgis atrōcis esse. Prōpōnis nōn morī neque ab illō interficī.

6. Sub urbe mihi domus est magna. Prōpōnō sine perīculō cum amīcīs vītam agere.

7. Amōris grātiā ad tē litterās dē illā rē difficilī scrībō. Prōpōnō nōn tibi nocēre.

8. Lēgēs scrībunt hominēs sapientēs. Prōpōnunt sub manū rēgis sine perīculō vīvere et ab illō sapientiā regī.

9. Dē dīs sempiternīs vēritas sōla ā poētā scrībitur. Prōpōnit hominēs docēre.

10. Cupiō morī. Prōpōnō tuī oblīviscī.

X. NOTE THE PATTERN in each of the following sentences and compose a translation of the English sentences using the same pattern.

1. **Homo hominī lupus.**
   Woman to woman is friend.
   Men to men are devils.

2. **Dē mortuīs nihil dīcāmus.**
   Concerning the affairs of the gods let us not write.
   Concerning friends let us think only good.

3. **Cēdant carminibus rēgēs, rēgumque triumphī.**
   Let not men nor the sons of men be harmful to men.

4. **Difficile est crīmen nōn prōdere vultū.**
   It is good to write poems with art.
   Bad is it not to be ruled by laws.

Piranesi, The Colosseum and the Arch of Constantine

LESSON SIX

IMPERFECT, PRESENT PERFECT, PAST PERFECT

Ōtium et rēgēs prius et beātās perdidit urbēs.

TENSE. You have already used the indicative mood to make statements of fact in the present time, but it is, of course, possible to state an event that occurred at earlier or previous times. The time of the verbal action is called its tense. In this lesson, you will learn to say things in three different past tenses.

IMPERFECT TENSE. The imperfect tense of the indicative states an action or state of being as **in progress or habitual in past time and "not completed"** (or **imperfect), either during that past time or by the time of the present.**

Amābat. — **"He used to love, or he was loving."** (The action may have ceased later, but the speaker is not interested in making a statement about the completion of the action.)

PRESENT PERFECT. The present perfect tense views the action or state of being from the vantage of the present, as **either completed at some point before the present time or as having yielded some situation in the present.**

Amāvit. — **"He has loved (and the loving is over by now)."** Thus: *Vīxit.* **"He has lived."** This could announce that his living is over and he is, in fact, now dead!

Amāvit. — **"He loved (and presumably that experience makes him a certain kind of person by now)."**

NOTE that since the form is identical, the distinction between the two meanings can be determined only from context. In the second meaning, the present perfect differs from the imperfect by viewing the action not as being in progress. You have seen that the present tense does not make this distinction since **amat** means either "he loves" or "he is loving." **NOTE** also that every action probably has some duration to it, but it is not the reality of the situation that matters, but the way the speaker chooses to view it.

PAST PERFECT (OR PLUPERFECT). The past perfect tense views the action or state of being from the vantage of some time in the past, as **either completed by that past time or as having yielded some situation by that time in the past.**

Amāverat. — **"He had loved (by that time and was finished loving by then)."**

Amāverat. — **"He had loved (by that time and presumably that experience had made him a certain kind of person then)."**

IMPERFECT INDICATIVE CONJUGATION. The imperfect indicative is indicated by the suffix {-**ba**-}, before the final personal subject suffix. The chart presents examples of the four conjugations.

PARADIGM 14
IMPERFECT INDICATIVE CONJUGATION

	Conj I ā-stem	Conj II ē-stem	Conj III e-stem	Conj III i-stem	Conj IV ī-stem
			ACTIVE VOICE		
1	amā**bam**	docē**bam**	regē**bam**	incipiē**bam**	audiē**bam**
2	amā**bās**	docē**bās**	regē**bās**	incipiē**bās**	audiē**bās**
3	amā**bat**	docē**bat**	regē**bat**	incipiē**bat**	audiē**bat**
1	amā**bāmus**	docē**bāmus**	regē**bāmus**	incipiē**bāmus**	audiē**bāmus**
2	amā**bātis**	docē**bātis**	regē**bātis**	incipiē**bātis**	audiē**bātis**
3	amā**bant**	docē**bant**	regē**bant**	incipiē**bant**	audiē**bant**
			PASSIVE VOICE		
1	amā**bar**	docē**bar**	regē**bar**	incipiē**bar**	audiē**bar**
2	amā**bāris**	docē**bāris**	regē**bāris**	incipiē**bāris**	audiē**bāris**
	amā**bāre**	docē**bāre**	regē**bāre**	incipiē**bāre**	audiē**bāre**
3	amā**bātur**	docē**bātur**	regē**bātur**	incipiē**bātur**	audiē**bātur**
1	amā**bāmur**	docē**bāmur**	regē**bāmur**	incipiē**bāmur**	audiē**bāmur**
2	amā**bāminī**	docē**bāminī**	regē**bāminī**	incipiē**bāminī**	audiē**bāminī**
3	amā**bantur**	docē**bantur**	regē**bantur**	incipiē**bantur**	audiē**bantur**

NOTE that in conjugations I and II, the {-**ba**-} suffix is added directly onto the stem. In conjugation III e-stem, the stem -**e**- is lengthened (and not changed to -**i**- as in the present: **regit / regēbat**). In conjugations III i-stem and IV, a long -**ē**- is inserted between the stem and the {-**ba**-} suffix.

NOTE that the second person singular passive has the same alternate suffix as in the present: -**ris** / -**re** (**amābāris / amābāre**, etc.).

PRESENT PERFECT AND PAST PERFECT CONJUGATION. The perfect active conjugation is indicated either by the suffix {-**v**-} (or {-**u**-}) added onto the stem or by a modification of the stem itself (such as doubling or **reduplication** of the initial syllable) or by the suffix {-**s**-} or, in some instances, by an entirely different verb that simply functions as the perfect for the verb of the lexical entry. Since these changes cannot be predicted with certainty, you must learn the **1st person present perfect active of the indicative** as part of the basic information you commit to memory for each verb that you learn.

The perfect passive is formed from another unpredictable verbal form, a passive verbal adjective ("**perfect passive participle**"), in agreement with the appropriate form of the verb **esse.** This participial form also must be committed to memory. There are thus **four principal parts** of a Latin verb, which means four unpredictable basic forms necessary to conjugate the verb through all its forms; these four forms comprise its lexical entry.

All verbs are conjugated in the same way in the perfect (regardless of the conjugation to which they belong in the present system); the endings are added onto the verb's third principal part or combined with **esse** and the fourth principal part.

PARADIGM 15
PRESENT PERFECT & PAST PERFECT INDICATIVE CONJUGATION

PRESENT PERFECT ACTIVE
(formed from the 3rd principal part)

	amō, -āre, -**āvī**, -ātus	doceō, -ēre, -**cuī**, doctus	regō, -ere, **rēxī**, rectus both e- & i-stems	audiō, -īre, **audīvī**, audītus
1	amā**vī**	docu**ī**	rēx**ī**	audī**vī**
2	amā**vistī**	docu**istī**	rēx**istī**	audī**vistī**
3	amā**vit**	docu**it**	rēx**it**	audī**vit**
1	amā**vimus**	docu**imus**	rēx**imus**	audī**vimus**
2	amā**vistis**	docu**istis**	rēx**istis**	audī**vistis**
3	amā**vērunt**	docu**ērunt**	rēx**ērunt**	audī**vērunt**
	amā**vēre**	docu**ēre**	rēx**ēre**	audī**vēre**

NOTE that the 3rd person plural active of the present perfect has an alternate ending: **amāvērunt / amāvēre,** etc. **NOTE** that the -**v**- between vowels can sometimes be lost and the resulting adjacent vowels then contracted: **amāvīstis** → **amāstis,** etc.

PAST PERFECT ACTIVE
(formed from the 3rd principal part)

	amō, -āre, -**āvī**, -ātus	doceō, -ēre, -**cuī**, doctus	regō, -ere, **rēxī**, rectus	audiō, -īre, **audīvī**, audītus
1	amā**veram**	docu**eram**	rēx**eram**	audī**veram**
2	amā**verās**	docu**erās**	rēx**erās**	audī**verās**
3	amā**verat**	docu**erat**	rēx**erat**	audī**verat**
1	amā**verāmus**	docu**erāmus**	rēx**erāmus**	audī**verāmus**
2	amā**verātis**	docu**erātis**	rēx**erātis**	audī**verātis**
3	amā**verant**	docu**erant**	rēx**erant**	audī**verant**

PRESENT PERFECT PASSIVE
(formed from the 4th principal part with present of *esse*)

	amō, -āre, -āvī, -**ātus**	doceō, -ēre, -cuī, **doctus**	regō, -ere, rēxī, **rectus**	audiō, -īre, audīvī, **audītus**
1	**amātus -a -um sum**	**doctus -a -um sum**	**rectus -a -um sum**	**audītus -a -um sum**
2	**amātus -a -um es**	**doctus -a -um es**	**rectus -a -um es**	**audītus -a -um es**
3	**amātus -a -um est**	**doctus -a -um est**	**rectus -a -um est**	**audītus -a -um est**
1	**amātī -ae -a sumus**	**doctī -ae -a sumus**	**rectī -ae -a sumus**	**audītī -ae -a sumus**
2	**amātī -ae -a estis**	**doctī -ae -a estis**	**rectī -ae -a estis**	**audītī -ae -a estis**
3	**amātī -ae -a sunt**	**doctī -ae -a sunt**	**rectī -ae -a sunt**	**audītī -ae -a sunt**

PAST PERFECT PASSIVE
(formed from the 4th principal part with imperfect of *esse*)

	amō, -āre, -āvī, -**ātus**	doceō, -ēre, -cuī, **doctus**	regō, -ere, rēxī, **rectus**	audiō, -īre, audīvī, **audītus**
1	**amātus -a -um eram**	**doctus -a -um eram**	**rectus -a -um eram**	**audītus -a -um eram**
2	**amātus -a -um erās**	**doctus -a -um erās**	**rectus -a -um erās**	**audītus -a -um erās**
3	**amātus -a -um erat**	**doctus -a -um erat**	**rectus -a -um erat**	**audītus -a -um erat**
1	**amātī -ae -a erāmus**	**doctī -ae -a erāmus**	**rectī -ae -a erāmus**	**audītī -ae -a erāmus**
2	**amātī -ae -a erātis**	**doctī -ae -a erātis**	**rectī -ae -a erātis**	**audītī -ae -a erātis**
3	**amātī -ae -a erant**	**doctī -ae -a erant**	**rectī -ae -a erant**	**audītī -ae -a erant**

NOTE the irregular imperfect indicative of **esse: eram, erās, erat, erāmus, erātis, erant.**

The two possibilities of meaning for the perfect are more clearly sensed in the passive.

Beāta est.	**"She has been blessed (it's over and done with now)."** Or: **"She is blessed."**

NOTE that the adjectival form (or past participle, 4th principal part) must agree with the personal subject suffix in number and gender. **beō, -āre, beāvī, beātus (-a, -um) "bless, make happy"**

Beātī sunt.	**"They have been blessed."**
Amātae sumus.	**"We (females) have been loved."**

TENSE IN THE SUBJUNCTIVE. In the subjunctive mood, as you have already seen, tense does not have the same meaning as in the indicative.

Amet. — **"Let him love."** The so-called **"present subjunctive,"** but, although I am expressing my volition now, obviously my will is directed toward some future action on the part of the subject.

Forsitan amet. — **"Perhaps he may love (in a little while)."** Or, **"Perhaps he is loving (right now)."**

Utinam amet. — **"If only he would love (right now or in a little while)."**

Amēmus? — **"Should we love (right now or in a little while)?"**

Amēmus. — **"Let's love (as soon as we can)."**

In moods other than the indicative, tense is somewhat relative and determined in certain ways by the context.

IMPERFECT SUBJUNCTIVE. When a volition, possibility, or wish is viewed from the vantage of the past, there is a strong suspicion implied that the event, in fact, never occurred; otherwise the speaker, from the vantage of the present, would not have refrained from a simple factual statement.

The **jussive subjunctive in the imperfect** expresses what was to have been done, and probably wasn't. It is still an emotive expression, and thus the negative is usually **nē**, but since the speaker can express someone else's opinion, instead of his own, about what was to have been done, the more factual **nōn** can sometimes be used.

Amāret. — **"He ought to have loved (but probably didn't)."**

Nē amāret. — **"He ought not have loved (but probably did)—that's what I wanted."**

Nōn amāret. — **"He ought not have loved (but probably did)—that's what someone else wanted."**

The **potential subjunctive in the imperfect** expresses what might have happened in the past, but probably didn't. Since it was a possibility for an actual event, the factual negative **nōn** can negate it.

Forsitan amāret. — **"He might have loved (but probably didn't)."**

Forsitan nōn amāret. — **"He might not have loved (but probably did)."**

The **optative subjunctive in the imperfect** expresses what was wished for in the past, but probably wasn't fulfilled. This pessimistic attitude toward the wish allowed the imperfect subjunctive also to express what is wished for now in the present, although the wish probably can never be fulfilled. The emotive negative **nē** is usually used.

Utinam amāret. — **"If only he had loved (but he probably didn't)."** Or, **"If only he would love (but he probably won't)."**

Utinam nē amāret. — **"If only he had not loved (but he probably did)."** Or, **"If only he wouldn't love (but he probably will)."**

IMPERFECT SUBJUNCTIVE CONJUGATION. All verbs are conjugated similarly in the imperfect subjunctive. **Personal suffixes are added to the present active infinitive.** The chart presents examples of the imperfect subjunctive conjugation.

PARADIGM 16
IMPERFECT SUBJUNCTIVE CONJUGATION

	Conj I ā-stem amāre	Conj II ē-stem docēre	Conj III e-stem regere	Conj III i-stem incipere	Conj IV ī-stem audīre
			ACTIVE VOICE		
1	amā**rem**	docē**rem**	rege**rem**	incipe**rem**	audī**rem**
2	amā**rēs**	docē**rēs**	rege**rēs**	incipe**rēs**	audī**rēs**
3	amā**ret**	docē**ret**	rege**ret**	incipe**ret**	audī**ret**
1	amā**rēmus**	docē**rēmus**	rege**rēmus**	incipe**rēmus**	audī**rēmus**
2	amā**rētis**	docē**rētis**	rege**rētis**	incipe**rētis**	audī**rētis**
3	amā**rent**	docē**rent**	rege**rent**	incipe**rent**	audī**rent**
			PASSIVE VOICE		
1	amā**rer**	docē**rer**	rege**rer**	incipe**rer**	audī**rer**
2	amā**rēris**	docē**rēris**	rege**rēris**	incipe**rēris**	audī**rēris**
	amā**rēre**	docē**rēre**	rege**rēre**	incipe**rēre**	audī**rēre**
3	amā**rētur**	docē**rētur**	rege**rētur**	incipe**rētur**	audī**rētur**
1	amā**rēmur**	docē**rēmur**	rege**rēmur**	incipe**rēmur**	audī**rēmur**
2	amā**rēminī**	docē**rēminī**	rege**rēminī**	incipe**rēminī**	audī**rēminī**
3	amā**rentur**	docē**rentur**	rege**rentur**	incipe**rentur**	audī**rentur**

PRESENT PERFECT AND PAST PERFECT SUBJUNCTIVE. The present and imperfect subjunctive pretty well handle the necessary range of meanings, and the perfect tenses are redundant for independent usage. The present perfect easily can lose its past time reference and thus double for a present, and the past perfect can either double for the imperfect or intensify the past time reference, as is needed, for example, to clarify whether the imperfect subjunctive expresses a wish unfulfilled in the past or unfulfillable in the future.

Of these uses, the only one that requires special notice is the common use of the **present perfect in the second person** to express a jussive subjunctive as a **negative command or prohibition.**

Nē amāveris. "Don't love!"

PRESENT AND PAST PERFECT SUBJUNCTIVE CONJUGATION. All verbs are conjugated the same way in the perfect. To form the active of the present perfect subjunctive, the suffix {**-eri-**} is added to the perfect active stem (**3rd principal part**) before the personal subject suffixes. To form the active of the past perfect subjunctive, the personal subject suffixes are added to the **perfect infinitive** (which is formed by adding **-isse** to the perfect active stem).

To form the passive of the present and past perfect subjunctive, the present and imperfect subjunctives of **esse** are conjugated with the past participle (**4th principal part**).

PARADIGM 17
PRESENT & PAST PERFECT SUBJUNCTIVE CONJUGATION

PRESENT PERFECT ACTIVE
(formed from the 3rd principal part with suffix *-eri-*)

	amō, -āre, -āvī, -ātus	doceō, -ēre, -cuī, doctus	regō, -ere, rēxī, rectus	audiō, -īre, audīvī, audītus
1	amāverim	docuerim	rēxerim	audīverim
2	amāveris	docueris	rēxeris	audīveris
3	amāverit	docuerit	rēxerit	audīverit
1	amāverimus	docuerimus	rēxerimus	audīverimus
2	amāveritis	docueritis	rēxeritis	audīveritis
3	amāverint	docuerint	rēxerint	audīverint

PRESENT PERFECT PASSIVE
(formed from the 4th principal part with present subjunctive of *esse*)

	amō, -āre, -āvī, **-ātus**	doceō, -ēre, -cuī, **doctus**	regō, -ere, rēxī, **rectus**	audiō, -īre, audīvī, **audītus**
1	**amātus -a -um sim**	**doctus -a -um sim**	**rectus -a -um sim**	**audītus -a -um sim**
2	**amātus -a -um sīs**	**doctus -a -um sīs**	**rectus -a -um sīs**	**audītus -a -um sīs**
3	**amātus -a -um sit**	**doctus -a -um sit**	**rectus -a -um sit**	**audītus -a -um sit**
1	**amātī -ae -a sīmus**	**doctī -ae -a sīmus**	**rectī -ae -a sīmus**	**audītī -ae -a sīmus**
2	**amātī -ae -a sītis**	**doctī -ae -a sītis**	**rectī -ae -a sītis**	**audītī -ae -a sītis**
3	**amātī -ae -a sint**	**doctī -ae -a sint**	**rectī -ae -a sint**	**audītī -ae -a sint**

PAST PERFECT ACTIVE
(formed from the 3rd principal part with suffix *-isse-*)

	amō, -āre, **-āvī**, -ātus perf. active infinitive **amāvisse**	doceō, -ēre, **-cuī**, doctus perf. active infinitive **docuisse**	regō, -ere, **rēxī**, rectus perf. active infinitive **rēxisse**	audiō, -īre, **audīvī**, audītus perf. active infinitive **audīvisse**
1	**amāvissem**	**docuissem**	**rēxissem**	**audīvissem**
2	**amāvissēs**	**docuissēs**	**rēxissēs**	**audīvissēs**
3	**amāvisset**	**docuisset**	**rēxisset**	**audīvisset**
1	**amāvissēmus**	**docuissēmus**	**rēxissēmus**	**audīvissēmus**
2	**amāvissētis**	**docuissētis**	**rēxissētis**	**audīvissētis**
3	**amāvissent**	**docuissent**	**rēxissent**	**audīvissent**

PAST PERFECT PASSIVE
(formed from the 4th principal part with imperfect subjunctive of *esse*)

	amō, -āre, -āvī, **-ātus**	doceō, -ēre, -cuī, **doctus**	regō, -ere, rēxī, **rectus**	audiō, -īre, audīvī, **audītus**
1	**amātus -a -um essem**	**doctus -a -um essem**	**rectus -a -um essem**	**audītus -a -um essem**
2	**amātus -a -um essēs**	**doctus -a -um essēs**	**rectus -a -um essēs**	**audītus -a -um essēs**
3	**amātus -a -um esset**	**doctus -a -um esset**	**rectus -a -um esset**	**audītus -a -um esset**
1	**amātī -ae -a essēmus**	**doctī -ae -a essēmus**	**rectī -ae -a essēmus**	**audītī -ae -a essēmus**
2	**amātī -ae -a essētis**	**doctī -ae -a essētis**	**rectī -ae -a essētis**	**audītī -ae -a essētis**
3	**amātī -ae -a essent**	**doctī -ae -a essent**	**rectī -ae -a essent**	**audītī -ae -a essent**

The synchronous chart on the following pages summarizes the past conjugations, indicative and subjunctive, active and passive.

SYNCHRONOUS CHART: PAST TENSES OF FOUR VERB CONJUGATIONS
INDICATIVE MOOD (MODE)

	FIRST **ā-stem**	SECOND **ē-stem**	THIRD **e-stem**	THIRD **i-stem**	FOURTH **ī-stem**
	IMPERFECT ACTIVE INDICATIVE				
1	amābam	docēbam	regēbam	incipiēbam	audiēbam
2	amābās	docēbās	regēbās	incipiēbās	audiēbās
3	amābat	docēbat	regēbat	incipiēbat	audiēbat
1	amābāmus	docēbāmus	regēbāmus	incipiēbāmus	audiēbāmus
2	amābātis	docēbātis	regēbātis	incipiēbātis	audiēbātis
3	amābant	docēbant	regēbant	incipiēbant	audiēbant
	IMPERFECT PASSIVE INDICATIVE				
1	amābar	docēbar	regēbar	incipiēbar	audiēbar
2	amābāris amābāre	docēbāris docēbāre	regēbāris regēbāre	incipiēbāris incipiēbāre	audiēbāris audiēbāre
3	amābātur	docēbātur	regēbātur	incipiēbātur	audiēbātur
1	amābāmur	docēbāmur	regēbāmur	incipiēbāmur	audiēbāmur
2	amābāminī	docēbāminī	regēbāminī	incipiēbāminī	audiēbāminī
3	amābantur	docēbantur	regēbantur	incipiēbantur	audiēbantur
	PRESENT PERFECT ACTIVE INDICATIVE				
1	amāvī	docuī	rēxī	incēpī	audīvī
2	amāvistī	docuistī	rēxistī	incēpistī	audīvistī
3	amāvit	docuit	rēxit	incēpit	audīvit
1	amāvimus	docuimus	rēximus	incēpimus	audīvimus
2	amāvistis	docuistis	rēxistis	incēpistis	audīvistis
3	amāvērunt amāvēre	docuērunt docuēre	rēxērunt rēxēre	incēpērunt incēpēre	audīvērunt audīvēre

SYNCHRONOUS CHART: PAST TENSES OF FOUR VERB CONJUGATIONS
INDICATIVE MOOD (MODE) *continued*

	FIRST **ā-stem**	SECOND **ē-stem**	THIRD **e-stem**	THIRD **i-stem**	FOURTH **ī-stem**
			PRESENT PERFECT PASSIVE INDICATIVE		
1	amātus -a -um sum	doctus -a -um sum	rectus -a -um sum	inceptus -a -um sum	audītus -a -um sum
2	amātus -a -um es	doctus -a -um es	rectus -a -um es	inceptus -a -um es	audītus -a -um es
3	amātus -a -um est	doctus -a -um est	rectus -a -um est	inceptus -a -um est	audītus -a -um est
1	amātī -ae -a sumus	doctī -ae -a sumus	rectī -ae -a sumus	inceptī -ae -a sumus	audītī -ae -a sumus
2	amātī -ae -a estis	doctī -ae -a estis	rectī -ae -a estis	inceptī -ae -a estis	audītī -ae -a estis
3	amātī -ae -a sunt	doctī -ae -a sunt	rectī -ae -a sunt	inceptī -ae -a sunt	audītī -ae -a sunt
			PAST PERFECT ACTIVE INDICATIVE		
1	am**āveram**	doc**ueram**	r**ēxeram**	inc**ēperam**	aud**īveram**
2	am**āverās**	doc**uerās**	r**ēxerās**	inc**ēperās**	aud**īverās**
3	am**āverat**	doc**uerat**	r**ēxerat**	inc**ēperat**	aud**īverāt**
1	am**āverāmus**	doc**uerāmus**	r**ēxerāmus**	inc**ēperāmus**	aud**īverāmus**
2	am**āverātis**	doc**uerātis**	r**ēxerātis**	inc**ēperātis**	aud**īverātis**
3	am**āverant**	doc**uerant**	r**ēxerant**	inc**ēperant**	aud**īverant**
			PAST PERFECT PASSIVE INDICATIVE		
1	amātus -a -um eram	doctus -a -um eram	rectus -a -um eram	inceptus -a -um eram	audītus -a -um eram
2	amātus -a -um erās	doctus -a -um erās	rectus -a -um erās	inceptus -a -um erās	audītus -a -um erās
3	amātus -a -um erat	doctus -a -um erat	rectus -a -um erat	inceptus -a -um erat	audītus -a -um erat
1	amātī -ae -a erāmus	doctī -ae -a erāmus	rectī -ae -a erāmus	inceptī -ae -a erāmus	audītī -ae -a erāmus
2	amātī -ae -a erātis	doctī -ae -a erātis	rectī -ae -a erātis	inceptī -ae -a erātis	audītī -ae -a erātis
3	amātī -ae -a erant	doctī -ae -a erant	rectī -ae -a erant	inceptī -ae -a erant	audītī -ae -a erant

SYNCHRONOUS CHART: PAST TENSES OF FOUR VERB CONJUGATIONS *continued*

INFINITIVE MOOD (MODE)

	FIRST **ā-stem**	SECOND **ē-stem**	THIRD **e-stem**	THIRD **i-stem**	FOURTH **ī-stem**
pres act	amāre	docēre	regere	incipere	audīre
pres pass	amārī	docērī	regī	incipī	audīrī
perf act	amāvisse	docuisse	rēxisse	incēpisse	audīvisse
perf pass	amātum -am -um / -ōs -ās -a esse	doctum -am -um / -ōs -ās -a esse	rectum -am -um / -ōs -ās -a esse	inceptum -am -um / -ōs -ās -a esse	audītum -am -um / -ōs -ās -a esse

SYNCHRONOUS CHART: PAST TENSES OF FOUR VERB CONJUGATIONS *continued*

SUBJUNCTIVE MOOD (MODE)

	FIRST **ā-stem**	SECOND **ē-stem**	THIRD **e-stem**	THIRD **i-stem**	FOURTH **ī-stem**
			IMPERFECT ACTIVE SUBJUNCTIVE		
1	amārem	docērem	regerem	inciperem	audīrem
2	amārēs	docērēs	regerēs	inciperēs	audīrēs
3	amāret	docēret	regeret	inciperet	audīret
1	amārēmus	docērēmus	regerēmus	inciperēmus	audīrēmus
2	amārētis	docērētis	regerētis	inciperētis	audīrētis
3	amārent	docērent	regerent	inciperent	audīrent
			IMPERFECT PASSIVE SUBJUNCTIVE		
1	amārer	docērer	regerer	inciperer	audīrer
2	amārēris amārēre	docērēris docērēre	regerēris regerēre	inciperēris inciperēre	audīrēris audīrēre
3	amārētur	docērētur	regerētur	inciperētur	audīrētur
1	amārēmur	docērēmur	regerēmur	inciperēmur	audīrēmur
2	amārēminī	docērēminī	regerēminī	inciperēminī	audīrēminī
3	amārentur	docērentur	regerentur	inciperentur	audīrentur
			PRESENT PERFECT ACTIVE SUBJUNCTIVE		
1	amāverim	docuerim	rēxerim	incēperim	audīverim
2	amāveris	docueris	rēxeris	incēperis	audīveris
3	amāverit	docuerit	rēxerit	incēperit	audīverit
1	amāverimus	docuerimus	rēxerimus	incēperimus	audīverimus
2	amāveritis	docueritis	rēxeritis	incēperitis	audīveritis
3	amāverint	docuerint	rēxerint	incēperint	audīverint

SYNCHRONOUS CHART: PAST TENSES OF FOUR VERB CONJUGATIONS
SUBJUNCTIVE MOOD (**MODE**) *continued*

	FIRST **ā-stem**	SECOND **ē-stem**	THIRD **e-stem**	THIRD **i-stem**	FOURTH **ī-stem**
			PRESENT PERFECT PASSIVE SUBJUNCTIVE		
1	amātus -a -um sim	doctus -a -um sim	rectus -a -um sim	inceptus -a -um sim	audītus -a -um sim
2	amātus -a -um sīs	doctus -a -um sīs	rectus -a -um sīs	inceptus -a -um sīs	audītus -a -um sīs
3	amātus -a -um sit	doctus -a -um sit	rectus -a -um sit	inceptus -a -um sit	audītus -a -um sit
1	amātī -ae -a sīmus	doctī -ae -a sīmus	rectī -ae -a sīmus	inceptī -ae -a sīmus	audītī -ae -a sīmus
2	amātī -ae -a sītis	doctī -ae -a sītis	rectī -ae -a sītis	inceptī -ae -a sītis	audītī -ae -a sītis
3	amātī -ae -a sint	doctī -ae -a sint	rectī -ae -a sint	inceptī -ae -a sint	audītī -ae -a sint
			PAST PERFECT ACTIVE SUBJUNCTIVE		
1	am**āvissem**	doc**uissem**	**rēxissem**	incē**pissem**	aud**īvissem**
2	am**āvissēs**	doc**uissēs**	**rēxissēs**	incē**pissēs**	aud**īvissēs**
3	am**āvisset**	doc**uisset**	**rēxisset**	incē**pisset**	aud**īvisset**
1	am**āvissēmus**	doc**uissēmus**	**rēxissēmus**	incē**pissēmus**	aud**īvissēmus**
2	am**āvissētis**	doc**uissētis**	**rēxissētis**	incē**pissētis**	aud**īvissētis**
3	am**āvissent**	doc**uissent**	**rēxissent**	incē**pissent**	aud**īvissent**
			PAST PERFECT PASSIVE SUBJUNCTIVE		
1	amātus -a -um essem	doctus a -um essem	rectus -a -um essem	inceptus -a -um essem	audītus -a -um essem
2	amātus -a -um essēs	doctus -a -um essēs	rectus -a -um essēs	inceptus -a -um essēs	audītus -a -um essēs
3	amātus -a -um esset	doctus -a -um esset	rectus -a -um esset	inceptus -a -um esset	audītus -a -um esset
1	amātī -ae -a essēmus	doctī -ae -a essēmus	rectī -ae -a essēmus	inceptī -ae -a essēmus	audītī -ae -a essēmus
2	amātī -ae -a essētis	doctī -ae -a essētis	rectī -ae -a essētis	inceptī -ae -a essētis	audītī -ae -a essētis
3	amātī -ae -a essent	doctī -ae -a essent	rectī -ae -a essent	inceptī -ae -a essent	audītī -ae -a essent

TENSE IN DEPENDENT USES OF THE SUBJUNCTIVE. In dependent uses of the subjunctive, tense is relative to the tense of the main verb. The present perfect indicates a time that is past with reference to a present indicative, whereas, as you have seen, a present subjunctive indicates a time present or future to the present indicative.

If the main indicative verb is a past tense, the imperfect subjunctive indicates a time that is the same or future to that of the main verb, and the past perfect indicates a past time with reference to the main verb.

Since the present perfect indicative, as you have seen, can indicate either a past completed action or a resultant present situation (i.e., "he has been educated vs. he is an educated person now" or "it has been questioned vs. it is now something questioned"), the present perfect indicative as a main verb can be used with either the so-called **primary sequence** (present / present perfect subjunctives) or the **secondary sequence** (imperfect / past perfect subjunctives), depending upon which meaning is dominant in the main verb.

PRIMARY SEQUENCE:

Quaeritur num mors malum sit.	**"It is questioned whether death is an evil."**
Quaeritur num mors malum fuerit.	**"It is questioned whether death was an evil."**
Quaesītum est num mors malum sit (fuerit).	**"It is a question whether death is (was) an evil."**

SECONDARY SEQUENCE:

Quaerēbātur num mors malum esset.	**"It was questioned whether death was (or is) an evil."**
Quaerēbātur num mors malum fuisset.	**"It was questioned whether death had been an evil."**
Quaesītum est num mors malum esset (fuisset).	**"It has been questioned whether death was (had been) an evil."**
Quaesītum erat num mors malum esset (fuisset).	**"It had been questioned whether death was (had been) an evil."**

PRIMARY SEQUENCE:

Magnī aestimō vēritātem ut tibi placeam.	**"I value truth at a high price in order to please you."**
Magnī aestimāvī vēritātem ut tibi placeam.	**"I'm a high appraiser of truth in order to please you."**

SECONDARY SEQUENCE:

Magnī aestimābam vēritātem ut tibi placērem.	**"I used to value truth highly in order to please you."**
Magnī aestimāvī vēritātem ut tibi placērem.	**"I have valued truth highly in order to please you."**
Magnī aestimāveram vēritātem ut tibi placērem.	**"I had valued truth highly in order to please you."**

TENSE IN INFINITIVES. You now know two tenses of the infinitive: the present (**amāre, amārī**) and the perfect (**amāvisse, amātum esse**). Like the subjunctive, infinitives have only relative tense. They conform to the same pattern of primary and secondary sequences: the present infinitive indicates the same time as the main verb; the perfect infinitive indicates a time before the time of the main verb.

Dīcit fortūnam vītam regere.	**"He says that fortune rules life."**
Dīcit fortūnam vītam rēxisse.	**"He says that fortune used to rule life."**
Dīcēbat fortūnam vītam regere.	**"He used to say that fortune ruled life."**
Dīcēbat fortūnam vītam rēxisse.	**"He used to say that fortune once used to rule life."**
Dīxit fortūnam vītam regere.	**"He has said that fortune ruled life."**
Dīxit fortūnam vītam rēxisse.	**"He has said that fortune once used to rule life."**
Dīxerat fortūnam vītam regere.	**"He had said that fortune ruled life."**
Dīxerat fortūnam vītam rēxisse.	**"He had said that fortune once used to rule life."**

VERBS WITH NO PRESENT. Some verbs in Latin conceive of an action as appropriate only in the perfect sense. Such verbs have no present or imperfect, and the perfect tenses indicate what in English would be expressed as a simple present or imperfect. Verbs of this kind are listed in lexica and vocabulary lists with only their perfect parts: **ōdī, -isse**.

REMEMBER

form:	*from:*
imperfect indicative	pres. stem + -**bā**- + personal endings
imperfect subjunctive	pres. act. inf. conjugated
present perfect active indicative	3rd prin. part conjugated
pres. perf. pass. indicative	4th prin. part + pres. indic. of ***esse***
pres. perf. act. subjunctive	3rd prin. part + ***-eri-*** + personal endings
pres. perf. pass. subjunctive	4th prin. part + pres. subj. of ***esse***
past perf. act. indicative	3rd prin. part + ***-era-*** + personal endings
past perf. pass. indicative	4th prin. part + imperf. indic. of ***esse***
past. perf. act. subjunctive	perf. act. infinitive conjugated
past. perf. pass. subjunctive	4th prin. part. + imperf. subj. of ***esse***

SEQUENCE OF TENSES

indicative	subjunctive
primary	
present, present perfect (resultant condition)	present for contemporaneous present perfect for prior
secondary	
imperfect, present perfect (perfected action), past perfect	imperfect for contemporaneous past perfect for prior

INDEX VERBORUM

principal parts of verbs from previous INDICES VERBORUM

agō, -ere, ēgī, actus
aestimō, -āre, -āvī, -ātus
amō, -āre, -āvī, -ātus
appellō, -āre, -āvī, -ātus
audiō, -īre, -īvī, -ītus
canō, -ere, cecinī, cantus
cōgitō, -āre, -āvī, -ātus
cognōscō, -ere, cognōvī, cognitus
crēdō, -ere, crēdidī, crēditus
cupiō, -ere, -īvī, -itus
damnō, -āre, -āvī, -ātus
dēbeō, -ēre, dēbuī, dēbitus
dīcō, -ere, dīxī, dictus
dō, -are, dedī, datus
doceō, -ēre, docuī, doctus
faciō, -ere, fēcī, factus
habeō, -ēre, habuī, habitus
incipiō, -ere, -cēpī, -ceptus
interficiō, -ere, -fēcī, -fectus
loquor, -ī, locūtus
misereō, -ēre, miseruī, -itus
(*also* **misereor, -ērī**)
(ad)-moneō, -ēre, -monuī, -itus
morior, -ī, mortuus
narrō, -āre, -āvī, -ātus
noceō, -ēre, nocuī, nocitus
nascor, -ī, nātus
negō, -āre, -āvī, -ātus
oblīviscor, -ī, oblītus
oportet, -ēre, oportuit

perdō, -ere, perdidī, perditus
(re)-petō, -ere, -īvī, -ītus
placeō, -ēre, placuī, placitus
(dē)-pōnō, -ere, -posuī, -positus
possum, posse, potuī
proficiscor, -ī, profectus
quaerō, -ere, quaesīvī, quaesītus
regō, -ere, rēxī, rectus
rogō, -āre, -āvī, -ātus
satiō, -āre, -āvī, -ātus
scrībō, -ere, scrīpsī, scrīptus
sequor, -ī, secūtus
sum, esse, fuī (futūrus, see Lesson 8)
videō, -ēre, vīdī, vīsus
vīvō, -ere, vīxī, victus

NOTE that **amō, doceō,** and **audiō** form the 3rd principal part with the {-v-/-u-} suffix, **regō** with the {-s-} suffix (**reg-s** → **rēx-**), and **incipiō** with the modification of its stem (**-cip-** → **-cēp-**). An example of reduplication is **perdō, -ere, perdidī, perditus.** Of an entirely different verb is **sum, esse, fuī.**

(illa) arbor, -oris	**tree**
(illa) avis, -is, -ium	**bird**
(illud) corpus, -oris	**body**
(illa) invidia, -ae	**envy, ill will**
(ille) modus, -ī	**a measure, mode, manner**
(illud) speculum, -ī	**mirror**
(illud) tempus, -oris	**time**

dīgnus, -a, -um	**deserving, worthy** (+ *abl.*)
hīc, haec, hōc	**this** (for use, see EXERCITATIO VII)
is, ea, id	**this / that** (for use, see EXERCITATIO VII)
meus, -a, -um	**my** (for use, see EXERCITATIO IX)
noster, -stra, -strum	**our** (for use, see EXERCITATIO IX)
nūllus, -a, -um	**none, no** (for use, see EXERCITATIO IX)
similis, -e	**similar** (+ *gen.* or *dat.*)
tuus, -a, -um	**your (singular)** (for use, see EXERCITATIO IX)
vester, -stra, -strum	**your (plural)** (for use, see EXERCITATIO IX)

beō, -āre, -āvī, -ātus	**make happy, bless**
con-spiciō, -ere, -spexī, -spectus	**look at attentively, catch sight of, perceive**
laudō, -āre, -āvī, -ātus	**praise**
meminī, -isse	**remember, be mindful of**
ōdī, -isse	**hate**

dum	**while** (for use, see EXERCITATIO X)
numquam (nōn / nē umquam)	**never, (not ever)**

EXERCITATIONES

I. MATCH the second phrase to the first by changing it into the same form. Some items will require more than one answer.

1. vīrīs dīgnīs (animal forte)
2. invidiae omnī (speculum dēforme)
3. avium timidārum (arbor similis)
4. gladiō longō (corpus parvum)
5. perīculī sōlīus (poēta sapiens)
6. nōmina prīma (rēs magna)
7. bonae artēs (cornū acre)
8. avibus miserīs (fēmina fortis)
9. tempus breve (homo laudātus)
10. ōtiō beātō (invidia similis)
11. avārōs omnēs (arbor pulchra)
12. lacuum similium (puella omnis)
13. poētae magnī (sōla avis)
14. amīcō acrī (atrox rex)
15. dī omnēs (speculum malum)
16. audācis poētae (illud corpus)
17. rēbus mortuīs (urbs perdita)
18. virum laudātum (carmen scrīptum)
19. ignium sempiternōrum (fēmina docta)
20. omnia dicta (domus aestimāta)

II. MATCH the second verb to the first by changing it into the same form. Some items will require more than one answer.

1. incēpisset (noceō)
2. damnābat (morior)
3. monitae sint (conspiciō)
4. nāscī (amō)
5. placeam (satiō)
6. petīvērunt (possum)
7. vīxeris (laudō)
8. aestimēre (morior)
9. dictum erat (perdō)
10. cecinistī (appellō)
11. quaerēbās (audiō)
12. ēgit (sum)
13. habēbāminī (dīcō)
14. oblīviscēbāre (loquor)
15. fēcēre (dō)
16. meminerimus (beō)
17. possint (damnō)
18. essent (petō)
19. negāre (loquor)
20. rēxerātis (doceō)

III. TRANSLATE.

1. Ille mihi semper cum sapientiā loquī dē omnibus rēbus vidēbātur. Amīcīs meīs semper dīcēbam illum doctum esse et philosophum sapientem et patribus nostrīs dīgnum similemque. Vir magnae virtūtis erat. Mē sine invidiā amāvit et sōlus ex amīcīs meīs semper faciēbat nē umquam rex mihi nocēret. Utinam omnēs amīcī meī illīus generis essent. Illum oportēret semper ā mē laudārī. Illī grātiās agerem, sed numquam illud fēcī. Nihil dē illō bonum dīxī. Capitis damnātus est ā rēge, et nihil dē illīus virtūte dīxī. Forsitan nōn cognōsceret mē amīcum esse. Utinam ille nē morerētur. Utinam nē ab illō rēge atrōcī interficerētur. Sed mortuus est. Interfectus est. Illum interficī gladiō illīus rēgis acris vīdī, et nihil dīxī. Mē nōn illīus miseret sed meī. Numquam mē nātum esse oportuit. Utinam morerer, sed dī mihi vītam longam dedērunt, et semper illīus meminisse dēbeō.

2. Nē meī oblīta sīs. Dēformis sim et tū pulchra; tē tamen semper amāvī et tēcum vīvere cupiēbam. Utinam caeca essēs. Forsitan mē amārēs. Utinam mē nē vīdissēs. Semper dē tē cum amīcīs loquēbar, semper tuī memineram et semper mēcum quaerēbam num tibi placēre possem. Tē magnī aestimāvī, sed numquam mē amāvistī. Nē mē amāveris, sed nē meī oblīta sīs. Nē dīcerēs matrī tuae tē ā mē nōn amārī neque ā mē semper amātam esse, sed illud illī dīxistī. Pecūniam habēbam. Domus sub urbe mihi erat. Prīmus ex amīcīs rēgis eram. Omnia mea tibi dedissem ut tibi placērem. Mater tua mihi grātiās ageret. Mē magnī aestimāret.

3. Dum ab urbe cum amīcīs meīs proficiscēbar ut amātam meam, puellam pulchram et magnae sapientiae, vidērem, in arbore conspexī avem timidam. Canēbat illa avis parva, et meō dē amōre illa mihi vidēbātur canere. Beātam illud animal mihi vidēbātur vītam agere. Utinam illī animālī similis essem. Utinam similem vītam agerem, et dē meā puellā tōtam noctem tōtumque diem in arbore canerem. Sub illā arbore canerem. Sub illā arbore stilō meō incēpī carmen breve scrībere meae amātae puellae ut dīcerem mē illam amāre. Illam rogāvī num mē amāret. Tē sōlam mē amāre dīxī, tē oportēre ā mē sōlō amārī. Forsitan mē nōn oportuisset illud dīcere. Utinam nē dīxissem illam oportēre ā mē sōlō amārī. Nē memineris mē illud dīcere. Amōris sim avārus; sine tē nē possim vīvere; dīcō tamen tē omnēs hominēs amāre posse. Nē mē sōlum amāveris. Forsitan omnēs puellās amem ego.

4. Parvī semper mihi erat amor. Numquam amōris eram avārus, sed pecūniae sōlīus. Omnēs hominēs ōdī et omnium oblītus sum, et patris matrisque meae et meae fēminae et omnium nātōrum, ut sōlus meā cum pecūniā vītam agam. Hominem hominī daemonem esse malum dīcō. Mihi placeat pecūnia sōla. Utinam omnēs meae similem vītam agerent. Utinam omnēs meī oblīviscerentur. Mihi vīta illīus generis beāta vidētur esse. Pecūniā avārus sōlā satiātur, nōn ab amīcīs.

IV. TRANSLATE. (Try to guess the meaning of new words on the basis of context and cognates before consulting the adjacent **reading notes.**)

1. MARTIALIS

Difficilis facilis, iūcundus acerbus, es **īdem**:
nec tēcum possum vīvere nec sine tē.

difficilis, -e difficult
facilis, -e easy Cf. facile
iūcundus, -a, -um pleasant, agreeable Cf. jocund, joke
acerbus, -a, -um bitter, disagreeable Cf. acerbic
īdem, eadem, idem the same (*adjective declined with* ***-dem*** *as an unchanging suffix:* **is-dem**, etc., from **is, ea, id**)
nec = neque

2. PSEUDO-AUSONIUS

Dum **dubitat nātūra marem** faceret**ne** puellam,
factus es, **O pulcher, paene puella,** puer.

Paraphrase: **Dum dubitat (aut rogat) nātūra maremne faceretne puellam, factus es puer, sed pulcher et paene puella.**

dubitō, -āre, -āvī, -ātus be in doubt, be uncertain Cf. doubt
(illa) nātūra, -ae nature
mās, maris, -ium male Cf. masculine
-ne In double questions, the interrogative particle (**-ne**) is often omitted in the first of the alternatives.
O pulcher, . . . puella These forms, which are identical with the nominative case, are actually the vocative case, the form used for direct address; see Lesson 7.
paene *adverb* almost Cf. Latin **paeninsula** peninsula

3. PHAEDRUS (adapted)

In **prātō quondam rāna** conspexit **bovem**, et **tacta** invidiā **tantae magnitūdinis, rūgōsam inflāvit pellem: tum** nātōs **suōs interrogāvit,**

(illud) prātum, -ī meadow Cf. prairie, pratincolous
quondam *adverb* formerly, once upon a time Cf. a phrase like *my quondam lover*
(illa) rāna, -ae frog Cf. **ranidae**
(ille, illa) bōs, bovis bull, cow Cf. bovine
tangō, -ere, tetigī, tactus touch, impress, affect Cf. tactile, tango
tantus, -a, -um so great Cf. tantamount
(illa) magnitūdo, -dinis magnitude
rūgōsus, -a, -um wrinkled Cf. rugose
in-flō, -āre, -āvī, -ātus inflate
(illa) pellis, -is, -ium skin, hide Cf. pelt
tum *adverb* then, thereupon
suus, -a, -um his (her, its) own Cf. **suī generis**
inter-rogō, -āre, -āvī, -ātus ask Cf. interrogate

an esset **latior quam** bōs. Illī **negārunt. Rursus intendit cutem maiōre nīsū** et similī quaesīvit modō, **quis** maior esset. Illī dīxērunt bovem. **Novissimē indignāta**, dum cupit **validius** inflāre **sēsē**, **ruptō iacuit** corpore.

an = num
latior, latius (*genitive* **latiōris**) broader Cf. latitude
quam *adverb* than
negārunt = negā(vē)runt
rursus *adverb* again
in-tendō, -ere, -tendī, -tensus stretch out Cf. intense
(illa) cutis, -is, -ium = pellis Cf. cuticle
maior, maius (*genitive* **maiōris**) greater Cf. major
(ille) nīsus, -ūs exertion, effort Cf. nisus
quis, quid who (what)?
novissimē *adverb* finally (i.e., newest, looking backward) Cf. novelty
indignor, -ārī, -ātus be angry, be displeased Cf. indignation
validius *adverb* more strongly Cf. valid
sēsē = sē him- (her-, its)self
rumpō, -ere, rūpī, ruptus burst Cf. rupture
iaceō, -ēre, -uī be cast down, lie ill or dead Cf. adjacent

4. ANNIUS FLORUS

Omnis **mulier intrā pectus cēlat**
vīrus pestilens:

(illa) mulier, -eris woman (**Mulier** is a woman, either married or unmarried, but essentially a grown woman, whereas **fēmina** refers to sex, as opposed to being a **vir**, while **puella** is a girl or young woman.) Cf. muliebrity
intrā *adverb & prep.* inside Cf. intramural
(illud) pectus, -oris breast Cf. pectoral
cēlō, -āre, -āvī, -ātus hide Cf. conceal
(illud) vīrus, -ī poisonous liquid Cf. virus

dulce dē **labrīs** loquuntur, **corde** vīvunt **noxiō**.

pestilens, -entis pestilential
dulcis, -e sweet **dulce** *adverb* sweetly Cf. dulcet
(illud) **labrum, -ī** lip Cf. labial
(illud) **cor, cordis** heart Cf. cordial
noxius, -a, -um harmful (**nocēre**) Cf. noxious

5. AESOPUS (translated from the Greek)

Corvus alicunde cāseum rapuerat et cum illō in **altam** arborem **subvolāverat. Vulpēcula** illum cāseum **appetēbat** et corvum **blandīs verbīs adoritur**. Prīmum corvī **formam pennārum**que **nitōrem** laudāvit. "**Pol**," **inquit**, "tē avium rēgem esse dīcerem sed **cantus pulchritūdinī** tuae nōn **rēspondet**." Tum ille **laudibus** vulpis inflātus, pulchritūdinem cantūs **dēmonstrāre** cupīvit.

(ille) **corvus, -ī** raven Cf. corvine
alicunde *adverb* from somewhere
(ille) **cāseus, -ī** cheese Cf. casein
rapiō, -ere, -puī, -ptus seize Cf. rape, rapture
altus, -a, -um high Cf. altitude
sub-volō, -āre, -āvī fly up (from beneath) Cf. volatile
(illa) **vulpēcula, -ae** (diminutive of **vulpes, -is**) little fox
ap-petō, -ere, -īvī, -ītus strive after, try to get Cf. appetite
blandus, -a, -um flattering, fawning Cf. blandishment
(illud) **verbum, -ī** word Cf. verbal
ad-orior, -īrī, -ortus rise up to address, accost Cf. orientation
(illa) **forma, -ae** figure, shape, appearance Cf. form
(illa) **penna, -ae** feather Cf. pennate
(ille) **nitor, -ōris** lustre, sheen, sleekness Cf. nitor
pol *interjection* shortened name of the god Pollux
inquit "says he (she, it)" *used for direct quotation*
(ille) **cantus, -ūs** singing Cf. chant
(illa) **pulchritūdo, -inis** beauty (**pulcher**) Cf. pulchritude
rē-spondeō, -ēre, -spondī, -sponsus answer, correspond
(illa) **laus, laudis** praise Cf. laud, laudatory
dē-monstrō, -āre, -āvī, -ātus show,

Ita vērō ē **rōstrō apertō** cāseus **dēlapsus** est et vulpes illum **arripuit dēvorāvit**que.

demonstrate
ita *adverb* thus
vērō (with) truth, truthfully
(illud) rōstrum, -ī beak, snout, muzzle, prow of a ship Cf. **rōstrum,** from the speaker's platform originally made from the prow of a ship
aperiō, -īre, -eruī, -ertus open Cf. aperture
dē-labor, -ī, -lapsus fall down Cf. collapse
arripiō, -ere, -ripuī, -reptus snatch
dē-vorō, -āre, -āvī, -ātus swallow, devour

6. AUSONIUS

Lais anus Venerī speculum dīcō:
dīgnum habeat **sē**
aeterna aeternum **forma ministerium.**

At mihi nūllus in hōc **ūsus, quia cernere tālem**
quālis sum **nōlō,** quālis eram **nequeō.**

The first sentence is a parody of the formula for a votive offering. **Dīcō** here means *dedicate as an offering.*
(illa) Lais, Laidis a woman's name
(illa) anus, -ūs old woman Cf. ancestor
(illa) Venus, -neris the goddess of love Cf. venereal
sē him-(her-, its) self *ablative case with* **dīgnum**
aeternus, -a, -um = sempiternus, -a, -um Cf. eternal
(illa) forma, -ae figure, shape, appearance
(illud) ministerium, -ī attendance, ministry, employment
at = sed
(ille) ūsus, -ūs use, employment
quia because
cernō, -ere, crēvī, crētus = videō, conspiciō Cf. discern
tālis, -e such, of such a nature (*usually with the corresponding* **quālis, -e** as, of such a nature) Cf. quality
nōlō = nōn cupiō
nequeō = nōn possum

7. CATULLUS

Ōtium, **Catulle**, tibi **molestum** est:
Ōtiō **exsultās nimium**que **gestis**:
Ōtium et rēgēs **prius** et beātas
perdidit urbēs.

Catulle *vocative*
molestus, -a, -um troublesome Cf. molest
exsultō, -āre, -āvī, -ātus leap up, exult
nimium *adverb* too much
gestiō, -īre, -īvī, -ītus gesticulate, exult
prius *adverb* before Cf. previous, prior

8. CARMEN (sine auctōris nōmine)

Marmoreō Licīnus tumulō iacet, at **Cato** nūllō,
Pompeius parvō: crēdimus esse deōs?

marmoreus, -a, -um marble Cf. marmoreal
(ille) Licīnus, -ī a man's name, (presumably somebody of little importance)
(ille) tumulus, -ī sepulchral mound Cf. tumulary
(ille) Cato, -ōnis Cato, the great Roman writer and politician, 234-149 BC
(ille) Pompeius, -ī Pompey, the great Roman general, 106-48 BC

9. PACUVIUS

Fortūnam **insānam** esse et caecam et **brūtam perhibent** philosophī,

saxōque **instāre** in **globōsō praedicant volūbilī**.

insānus. -a, -um insane, sick
brūtus, -a, -um irrational Cf. brute
per-hibeō, -ēre, -buī, -itus call, name = **appellō**
in-stō, -āre, -stetī, -stātus stand upon Cf. instant
globōsus, -a, -um spherical Cf. globular
prae-dicō, -āre, -āvī, -ātus proclaim Cf. predicate
volūbilis, -e rolling Cf. voluble

10. ACCIUS

Virtūtī sīs pār, **dispār** fortūnīs patris.

dispār, -paris = nōn pār Cf. disparate

V. CHANGE each of the following sentences into equivalent expressions using the jussive subjunctive. REMEMBER to replace the modal auxiliaries **dēbēre** and **oportēre**.

Illīus generis carmen mihi placēre (placuisse) dēbēbat, sed nōn placuit. — **"A poem of that sort ought to have pleased me at that time (before that time) but it didn't."**

Illīus generis carmen mihi placēret, sed nōn placuit. — **"A poem of that sort should have pleased me, but it didn't."**

1. Patris similis dēbēbās esse, sed nōn erās.
2. Tē oportēbat parem esse patrī in omnibus rēbus, sed nōn erās.
3. Patre vestrō dīgnī dēbēbātis esse, sed nōn erātis.
4. Nōn mē oportuit carmen illīus generis similī modō canere. Illud tamen cecinī.
5. Capitis damnārī ab omnibus bonīs illī reī dēbēbant, sed nōn damnātī sunt.
6. Magnī oportuit illam domum aestimārī, sed parvī aestimābātur.
7. Tibi dēbēbat illud speculum dēforme datum esse dōnō, sed nōn datum est.
8. Nōn vōs oportēbat meī oblīviscī, sed meī nōn meministis.
9. Matris vidērī similis illa puella pulchra dēbēbat, sed nōn vidēbātur.
10. Mē amāvisse tē oportuit, sed semper mē ōderās.

VI. CHANGE each of the following sentences into equivalent expressions using the potential subjunctive. (**Possum** is a compound of **sum (potis sum)**, literally "I am able or possible"); the [t] of **pot** is retained before vowels, but assimilated to [s] before [s].)

	present				imperfect			
	indic.	*subj.*	*indic.*	*subj.*	*indic.*	*subj.*	*indic.*	*subj.*
1	**possum**	**possim**	sum	sim	eram	essem	**poteram**	**possem**
2	**potes**	**possīs**	es	sīs	erās	essēs	**poterās**	**possēs**
3	**potest**	**possit**	est	sit	erat	esset	**poterat**	**posset**
1	**possumus**	**possīmus**	sumus	sīmus	erāmus	essēmus	**poterāmus**	**possēmus**
2	**potestis**	**possītis**	estis	sītis	erātis	essētis	**poterātis**	**possētis**
3	**possunt**	**possint**	sunt	sint	erant	essent	**poterant**	**possent**

The perfect is regular, as always, formed from the perfect stem, **potuī**.

Illīus generis carmen mihi placēre poterat, sed nōn placuit. — **"A poem of that sort could have pleased me, but it didn't."**

Forsitan illīus generis carmen mihi placēret, sed nōn placuit. — **"Perhaps a poem of that sort might have pleased me but it didn't."**

1. Illīus generis animālia hominibus nocēre poterant, sed nōn nocuērunt.

2. Illud animal rex avium potuit esse, sed nōn erat.
3. Ille poterat vidērī stultus, sed sapiens erat.
4. Illa fēmina dēformis, invidiā recta, potuit amīcīs nocēre, sed numquam illīs nocuit.
5. Ille puer morī poterat, sed longam vītam ēgit neque mortuus est puer.
6. Tē in speculō poterās conspicere, sed stulta erās neque vīdistī tē in illō speculō.
7. Meī potuistis meminisse, sed oblītī estis et similī modō vestrī oblīviscī cupiō.
8. Magnā invidiā poteram ad tē scrībere dē omnibus rēbus, sed cupīvī amīcus tuus vidērī et tēcum sub urbe vīvere.
9. Mihi speculum potuit esse, sed nōn cupīvī mē in speculō vidēre.
10. Urbem illam beātam potuēre perdere, sed ab omnibus bonīs laudārī illīs placuit.

VII. CHANGE each of the following sentences into equivalent expressions using the optative subjunctive. Distinguish between unfulfilled and unfulfillable wishes or hopes.

NOTE that a wish that can still be fulfilled is expressed by the present subjunctive, whereas an unfulfilled wish is expressed by a past tense subjunctive; to emphasize that a wish is impossible of fulfillment, rather than merely unfulfilled, a past perfect subjunctive may be used.

Tē illīus generis carmen cecinisse optāvī, sed nōn illud cecinistī.	**"I wished you had sung a song of that kind, but you haven't sung it."**
Utinam illīus generis carmen cecinissēs, sed nōn illud cecinistī.	**"If only you had sung a song of that kind, but you haven't sung it."** The imperfect subjunctive could also be used: **Utinam illīus generis carmen canerēs. "If only you sang a song of that kind."** This second version, however, could also express an unfulfilled, but not necessarily unfulfillable wish: **"If only you'd sing a song of that kind (but you probably won't.)"** (See page 92.)
Tē illīus generis carmen canere optō.	**"I hope you sing a song of that kind."**
Utinam illīus generis carmen canās.	**"O that you sing a song of that kind."**

1. Vōs matris patrisque similēs fuisse optāvī, sed dissimilēs erātis.
2. Tē nostrī nōn oblītam esse optāvī, sed nostrī nōn meministī.
3. Capitis illum reum nōn ab omnibus damnātum esse optāvī, sed omnēs illum damnāvērunt.
4. Bonum amīcum ab omnī sapientī magnī aestimārī optō (et illud potest esse).
5. Speculum mihi dōnō ā tē datum esse optāvī, sed mihi illud nōn dedistī.

VIII. CHANGE the main verb to an appropriate past tense in each of the following sentences and adjust the sequence of tenses.

NOTE that the demonstrative adjective-pronouns **hīc** and **is** conform to the pronominal declension (see page 80). The genitive singular ends in **-ius**, as with **ille**, and the dative singular is characterized by **-i** for all three genders. The final **-c** in certain forms of **hīc** is an inflexible intensive suffix (dative singular: **hui-c**) and causes euphonic change in the accusative singular (**hum-c → hun-c**). Like **ille**, **hīc** and **is** can be used to indicate the missing third person pronoun in Latin. **Is** points without specifying "here" or "there" and thus is similar to the article "the." It is more common than **ille** and **hīc** as a substitute for the third person pronoun.

PARADIGM 18
PRONOMINAL DECLENSION OF *hīc, ille, is*

	hīc			**ille**			**is**		
	masc	*fem*	*neut*	*masc*	*fem*	*neut*	*masc*	*fem*	*neut*
					singular				
n	hīc	haec	hōc	ille	illa	illud	is	ea	id
ac	hunc	hanc	hōc	illum	illam	illud	eum	eam	id
ge	huius	huius	huius	illīus	illīus	illīus	eius	eius	eius
da	huic	huic	huic	illī	illī	illī	eī	eī	eī
ab	hōc	hāc	hōc	illō	illā	illō	eō	eā	eō
					plural				
n	hī	hae	haec	illī	illae	illa	eī iī ī	eae	ea
ac	hōs	hās	haec	illōs	illās	illa	eōs	eās	ea
ge	hōrum	hārum	hōrum	illōrum	illārum	illōrum	eōrum	eārum	eōrum
da	hīs	hīs	hīs	illīs	illīs	illīs	eīs iīs īs	eīs iīs īs	eīs iīs īs
ab	hīs	hīs	hīs	illīs	illīs	illīs	eīs iīs īs	eīs iīs īs	eīs iīs īs

NOTE that there are variants for **is, ea, id** in the nominitive masculine plural and for the dative and ablative plural.

Nūllus (like **sōlus** and **tōtus**, see page 80) also conforms to the pronominal declension. It is declined like a regular I-II adjective (e.g., **bonus, -a, -um**) in all cases except the genitive and dative singular.

	masculine	*feminine*	*neuter*
genitive singular	**nūllīus**	**nūllīus**	**nūllīus**
dative singular	**nūllī**	**nūllī**	**nūllī**

This exercise will give you an opportunity to familiarize yourself with these additional pronominal declensions, while practicing the principle of **sequence of tenses.**

Hōc eīs dicō ut ab eīs lauder.	**"I say this to them so that I be praised by them."**
Hōc eīs dīcēbam (dīxī) ut ab eīs laudārer.	**"I used to say (said) this to them so that I'd be praised by them."**

1. Pecūniam eī dōnō damus ut ab eā amēmur.
2. Quaesītum est num haec fēmina sine eō et eius pecūniā potuerit agere hanc vītam beātam.
3. Is mēcum loquitur ut amīcus mihi videātur.
4. Ā nūllō avārī hominēs cupiunt laudārī nē videantur beātī esse.
5. Eam rogāmus num vēritātem dē vītā eius hominis nōbīs dīcere possit.
6. Nūllī vōbīs dīcere cupiunt eum capitis dāmnātum esse.
7. Nūllīus amīcus sum ut omnēs ōdisse possim.
8. Scrībis tē ā nūllīs laudārī.
9. Cum eīs proficiscimur ut domum eōrum videāmus.
10. Similī modō semper ab eīs quaeritur num dī hominibus noceant aut nocuerint.

IX. CHANGE each of the following sentences into indirectly quoted material using the verb indicated in parentheses. Be careful to express whether the quoted material is contemporaneous or antecedent to the tense of the main verb.

1. Id aut est aut erat huius generis. (dīcō)
2. Is carminibus ā poētīs aut laudābātur aut laudātur. (dīcēbat)
3. Sapientiam eius vēritātemque ab omnibus bonīs laudārī oportet aut oportuit. (scrīpsēre)
4. Haec matre dīgna erat et ille similī modō patris pār est. (vidēbāmus)
5. Mēcum vīvere cum ōtiō magnōque amōre ea aut cupiēbat aut cupit. (negāverant)
6. Huius generis vīnum eī placuit aut placet. (dīxī)
7. Magnā invidiā speculum eī fēminae dēformī ab eō aut dabātur aut datur. (audīmus)
8. Ā nūllō cum vēritāte aut poterat aut potest hīc laudārī. (dīcis)

9. Eīs fortis vidērī is aut cupit aut nōn cupit. (audiēbam)
10. Ea huius oblīviscitur et meī meminit. (dictum est)

X. CHANGE each of the following sentences so that it is dependent upon the main clause indicated in parentheses. Be careful to conform to the principle of the sequence of tenses.

NOTE that the genitive of the personal pronouns (**meī, tuī,** etc.) is not used to indicate possession (see page 80), although the genitive of **is, ille,** and **hīc** does. For possession for the first and second persons, either the dative of possession is used (see page 69) or the adjectives **meus, tuus, noster,** or **vester.**

Domus mihi est. (*dative of possession*)	**"I have a house."**
Domus mea est. (*possessive adjective*)	**"The house is mine."**
Amor meī magnus est. (*personal pronoun—objective genitive*)	**"Great is the love (other people have) for me."**

1. Magnus est meus amor tuī tuōrumque amīcōrum. (negāvī)
2. Magna pars vestrum nostrī oblīviscitur. (hōc fēcimus ut)
3. Nōbīs erat domus vestra. (quaeritur ā vōbīs num)
4. Meus pater tuaque mater nūllōs vestrum ōderant. (dīcēbam)
5. Patrī nostrō huius generis vīta semper placēbat. (quaesītum est ab eīs num)
6. Ā deō nostrō vester rex nāscitur. (nōbīs dīxistis)
7. Tua magna invidia meī vītam meam perdidit. (quaesīvī num)
8. Nostrī dī nūllōs vestrum vītā longā beāvēre. (ad amīcum meum scrībō)
9. Nūllī eōrum ā nostrō poētā possunt laudārī. (hōc fēcī ut)
10. Sine invidiā vestrī loquēbar vōbīscum dē magnō amōre meō urbis vestrae beātae. (dīxī)

XI. NOTE THE PATTERN in each of the following sentences and compose a translation of the English sentences using the same pattern.

1. **Tē avium rēgem esse dīcerem sed cantus pulchritūdinī tuae nōn rēspondet.**
   You would see that I am ugly, but your love for me has made you blind.
   I would have been your king, but my love for you destroyed me.

2. **Dum dubitat nātūra, factus es puer.**

Note that **dum** commonly (although not always) expresses a past contemporaneous action as a present indicative (instead of an imperfect indicative). This is an example of the so-called **historical present**, that is to say, the use of a present tense as a vivid way of narrating a past event as though you were actually reliving it as an ongoing event.

Dum hōc narrat, audīvī. **"While he's there saying this, I heard it."**

While we were saying these things about the gods, that blessed city was destroyed.
While this man of great wisdom was being condemned to death, his friends did not speak the truth about his life.
While she was beginning to speak, I gave her my poem as a gift.

Piranesi, Portico of the Pantheon

LESSON SEVEN

RELATIVE-INTERROGATIVE PRONOUNS, VOCATIVE

Crās amet quī numquam amāvit quīque amāvit crās amet.

RELATIVE-INTERROGATIVE PRONOUN-ADJECTIVES. A pronoun is a word that can be substituted for a noun. You have already learned the personal pronouns **ego / nōs, tū / vōs** and the demonstratives **ille, is,** and **hīc** that can be used to supply the missing pronouns for the third person. You have also learned that any adjective can be used without a noun explicitly expressed, as for example, **bonī** "**good (men)**" or **avārus** "**a greedy (man).**" You have also seen that certain adjectives, such as **nūllus, tōtus,** and **sōlus,** can be used alone as pronouns and like **ille, is,** and **hīc** have a distinctive pronominal declension in the genitive and dative singular (**-ius, -i**).

A relative pronoun is a pronoun that refers back (or **relates**) to its antecedent (a noun, usually earlier, that expresses more explicitly the same person or thing).

Fēmina quam amābam pulchra erat. **"The woman *whom* I loved was beautiful."** The relative **quam** relates back to its antecedent **fēmina.** It allows the two ideas (namely, *Fēmina pulchra erat.* and *Eam amābam.*) to be combined into a single sentence by subordinating the relative clause to the main clause.

Since the relative means the same thing as its antecedent, it must agree with it in gender and number, but since it introduces its own clause, it generally will be in whatever case is required by its use in its own clause.

Vir quem amābam bonus erat. **"The man whom I loved was good."** **Quem** is masculine singular like **vir**, but accusative instead of nominative because it is the object of **amābam.**

Virum quī dīcēbat amābam. **"I loved the man who was speaking."** **Quī** is singular and masculine like **virum,** but nominative because it is subject of **dīcēbat.**

The relative pronoun can also be used as an adjective to ask a question (**interrogative adjective**).

Quī vir dīcēbat? **"What man was speaking?"** Here it agrees with its noun **vir** like any other adjective. It is in the same case as **vir** since it has the same grammatical function and does not introduce its own clause.

Quem virum amābas? **"What man did you love?"**

You can also ask a question simply with the pronoun, with no noun expressed. In most forms, this **interrogative pronoun** is identical with the relative pronoun-adjective and interrogative adjective. (In the singular, but not in the plural, it has only one form for both masculine and feminine, and it has a slightly different form for the singular nominative and nominative-accusative neuter.)

Quis dīcēbat?	**"Who was speaking?"**
Quem amābās?	**"Whom did you love?"**

RELATIVE-INTERROGATIVE DECLENSION. The chart summarizes the forms for the relative pronoun-adjective, interrogative adjective, and interrogative pronoun. All of them have the distinctive pronominal declension in the genitive and dative singular (**cu-** is a variant of the **qu-** stem and occurs only in these forms: **cuius, cui**).

PARADIGM 19

	RELATIVE PRONOUN "(the man) **who**"			INTERROGATIVE PRONOUN "**who, what?**" INDEFINITE PRONOUN "**anybody, somebody**"		
	masc	*fem*	*neuter*	*masc-fem*		*neuter*
nom	**quī**	**quae**	**quod**	**quis**		**quid**
acc	**quem**	**quam**	**quod**	**quem**		**quid**
gen	**cuius**	**cuius**	**cuius**	**cuius**		**cuius**
dat	**cui**	**cui**	**cui**	**cui**		**cui**
abl	**quō**	**quā**	**quō**	**quō**		**quō**
				masc	*fem*	*neuter*
nom	**quī**	**quae**	**quae**	**quī**	**quae**	**quae**
acc	**quōs**	**quās**	**quae**	**quōs**	**quās**	**quae**
gen	**quōrum**	**quārum**	**quōrum**	**quōrum**	**quārum**	**quōrum**
dat	**quibus**	**quibus**	**quibus**	**quibus**	**quibus**	**quibus**
abl	**quibus**	**quibus**	**quibus**	**quibus**	**quibus**	**quibus**
	INTERROGATIVE ADJECTIVE "**what** (man)?"			INDEFINITE ADJECTIVE "**any** (man)"		
	masc	*fem*	*neuter*	*masc*	*fem*	*neuter*
nom	**quī**	**quae**	**quod**	**quī**	**qua**	**quod**
acc	**quem**	**quam**	**quod**	**quem**	**quam**	**quod**
gen	**cuius**	**cuius**	**cuius**	**cuius**	**cuius**	**cuius**
dat	**cui**	**cui**	**cui**	**cui**	**cui**	**cui**
abl	**quō**	**quā**	**quō**	**quō**	**quā**	**quō**
nom	**quī**	**quae**	**quae**	**quī**	**quae**	**qua**
acc	**quōs**	**quās**	**quae**	**quōs**	**quās**	**qua**
gen	**quōrum**	**quārum**	**quōrum**	**quōrum**	**quārum**	**quōrum**
dat	**quibus**	**quibus**	**quibus**	**quibus**	**quibus**	**quibus**
abl	**quibus**	**quibus**	**quibus**	**quibus**	**quibus**	**quibus**

NOTE that the forms of the interrogative pronoun are identical with the forms for the indefinite pronoun (**quis "anyone"**), and the interrogative adjective is identical with the indefinite adjective (**quī "any"**) except that **qua** usually replaces **quae.**

Rogō num quis amet. — **"I ask whether anyone loves."**

Rogō num qua fēmina amet. — **"I ask whether any woman loves."** Usually, however, **quae** is retained in the feminine plural: **Rogō num quae fēminae ament.**

RELATIVE CLAUSE IN INDIRECT DISCOURSE. Relative clauses in indirectly quoted material (**oratio obliqua**, see page 8) commonly have their verb in the subjunctive as an indication of subordination. This is common for all relative clauses in indirect discourse, but it probably evolved from situations where the subject of the main verb is presenting the opinion of someone else in the indirectly quoted material and the use of the subjunctive for clauses within that quoted material is a way of indicating that the speaker does not vouch for the factual validity of that other person's opinion.

Dīcit fēminam quam amem pulchram esse. — **"He says that the woman whom (according to me) I love is beautiful."**

Thus, even if there is no formal structure for indirect discourse (i.e., infinitive with accusative subject), the subjunctive in a relative clause implies that the speaker is presenting someone else's opinion.

Fēminam quam amēs videō. — **"I see the woman whom (according to you) you love."**

Normally, if the relative clause in indirect discourse has its verb in the indicative, instead of the subjunctive, the speaker is emphasizing that it is in fact his own opinion.

Dīcit fēminam quam amō pulchram esse. — **"He says that the woman whom (according to him) I love is beautiful."**

NOTE the regular pattern for sequence of tenses (see pages 99–101). **Primary sequence:** present or present perfect with emphasis on present result = present subjunctive for action contemporaneous with (or subsequent to) the main indicative verb; and present perfect subjunctive for action prior to the main indicative verb. **Secondary sequence:** imperfect or present perfect with emphasis on perfected action or past perfect = imperfect subjunctive for action contemporaneous with (or subsequent to) the main verb, and past perfect subjunctive for action prior to the main indicative verb.

PRIMARY SEQUENCE:

present indicative: present subjunctive or present perfect subjunctive

Dīcit fēminam quam amem (amāverim) pulchram esse.	**"He says that the woman whom I love (loved) is beautiful."**

present perfect indicative (present result): present subjunctive or present perfect subjunctive

Dictum est fēminam quam amem (amāverim) pulchram esse.	**"It is said that the woman whom I love (loved) is beautiful."**

SECONDARY SEQUENCE:

imperfect indicative: imperfect subjunctive or past perfect subjunctive

Dīcēbat fēminam quam amārem (amāvissem) pulchram esse.	**"He used to say that the woman whom I loved at that time or love now (loved before that time) was or is beautiful."**

present perfect indicative (perfected action): imperfect subjunctive or past perfect subjunctive

Dīxit fēminam quam amārem (amāvissem) pulchram esse.	**"He said or has said that the woman whom I loved at that time or love now (loved before that time) was or is beautiful."**

past perfect indicative (past result or perfected action): imperfect subjunctive or past perfect subjunctive

Dīxerat fēminam quam amārem (amāvissem) pulchram esse.	**"He had said that the woman whom I loved at that time or love now (loved before that time) was or is beautiful."**

RELATIVE CLAUSES OF PURPOSE. In addition to clauses introduced by **ut / nē** (see pages 59–60), purpose can be expressed by a relative clause indicating the use or purpose to which the subject of the main verb intends to put the antecedent of the relative. This is a subordinated use of the jussive subjunctive expressing will, obligation, or duty.

Poētam mittō quī carmen canat.	**"I send a poet to sing a song."**
Scrībēbat carmen quod ille poēta caneret.	**"He was writing a poem which that poet was to recite."**

RELATIVE CLAUSES OF GENERIC CHARACTERISTIC. The potential subjunctive, as you have seen (see page 44), expresses, not what actually occurs, but what is likely or apt to occur. In a relative clause, this subjunctive expresses the **generic characteristic of the antecedent**, the sort of thing the antecedent can be expected to do. This kind of relative clause is particularly common when the antecedent is in some way indefinite, requiring the ensuing relative clause to be more specific about its potential.

Vir est quī carmen canat.	**"He is a man (of the sort) who would sing a song."**
Nēmō est quī carmen canat.	**"Nobody is there who would sing a song."**
Sunt quī carmen canant.	**"There are people who would sing a song."**
Quis est quī carmen canat?	**"Who is there who would sing a song?"**
Dīgnus est quī carmen canat.	**"He is a man (of the sort) worthy of singing a song."**

VOCATIVE CASE. In addition to the five declensional cases you have already learned, there is one more case, the vocative, which has lost its distinctive ending in all declensions **except the singular of declension II masculine nouns (and adjectives) ending in -us.** In all other instances, it is identical with the nominative, which it resembles in function. Whereas the nominative is the naming case, the vocative is the case for using the name for directly addressing or speaking to the person or thing.

Poēta, quid canis?	**"(Hey you) poet, what are you singing?"**

For declension II masculine nouns (and adjectives) ending in -us, the vocative ending is **-e.**

Philosophe, quid dīcis?	**"(Hey you) philosopher, what are you saying?"**

Proper names (and only proper names) of declension II ending in **-ius** have a vocative ending in a single **-ī.**

Vergilī, quid scrībis?	**"(Hey you) Vergilius, what are you writing?"**

In addition to proper nouns the phrase **meus fīlius** follows the same pattern.

Mī fīlī, quid agis?	**"(Hey you) my son, what are you doing?"**

CONDITIONS CONTRARY TO FACT. You have already seen that when a subjunctive of volition, possibility, or wish is viewed from the vantage of the past, there is a strong suspicion implied that the event, in fact, never occurred (see pages 90–91). That suspicion is intensified when a hypothesis ("if") is explicitly expressed.

Sī poēta essem, canerem. **"If I were a poet, I would sing, (but I'm not and I won't)."**

Such a hypothesis is called a **condition contrary to fact.** It states a hypothesis that in fact is not true, and hence a conclusion that similarly is untrue. Compare a similar **possible hypothesis** in the indicative.

Sī poēta sum, canō. **"If I am a poet, I sing. (I may or may not be a poet, but if I am, I sing."**

The imperfect subjunctive in both clauses hypothesizes something untrue at the present time. The past perfect subjunctive in both clauses hypothesizes something untrue in the past.

Sī poēta fuissem, cecinissem. **"If I had been a poet, I would have sung, (but wasn't and I didn't)."**

> REMEMBER
>
> a relative pronoun is normally in the case required for its use in its own clause, but agrees with its antecedent in gender and number.

INDEX VERBORUM

(illud) **bellum, -ī**	**war**
(illa) **cēna, -ae**	**dinner**
(ille) **liber, -brī**	**book, scroll**
(ille) **servus, -ī**	**slave, servant**
līber, -bera, -berum	**free**
multus, -a, -um	**much, many**
paucus, -a, -um	**few, little**
suus, -a, -um	**his (her, its, their) own** (for use, see EXERCITATIO V)
alius, alia, aliud	**other, another** (pronominal declension, see pages 80 and 112–13)
īdem, eadem, idem	**same** (contraction of **is-dem, ea-dem, id-dem,** pronominal declension: **eiusdem** but **n** for **m: eundem)**
ipse, ipsa, ipsum	**very self** (intensive) pronominal declension

nēmō, (-minis)/ nūllīus	**no one** (commonly not used in the genitive and ablative singular; instead the corresponding cases of **nūllus, -a, -um** are substituted)
quī, quae, quod	**who, what** (relative pronoun-adjective, interrogative adjective, indefinite adjective (with **qua** for **quae**, except in feminine plural)
quis, quid	**who/ what/ anyone** (interrogative pronoun, indefinite pronoun)
sē (suī, sibi, sē)	**himself, herself, itself** (reflexive pronoun) (for use, see EXERCITATIO V)
ferō, ferre, tulī, lātus	**bring, carry, endure** (for use, see EXERCITATIO VII)
gerō, -ere, gessī, gestus	**conduct, wage (war), wear**
mittō, -ere, mīsī, missus	**send**
nōlō, nōlle, nōluī	**be unwilling** (for use, see EXERCITATIO VII)
volō, velle, voluī	**be willing** (for use, see EXERCITATIO VII)
apud	**at, near, at the house of** (conceived as goal directed action, hence + acc.)
inter	**between, among** (conceived as goal directed action, hence + acc.)
propter	**on account of, because of** (+ acc.)
an	**whether** (used like **num** to introduce an indirect question; also in both direct and indirect questions to indicate second or more alternative questions)
bene	**well**
crās	**tomorrow**
enim	**indeed, of course** (placed after the first word of the sentence)
herī	**yesterday**
hodiē	**today** (contracted from **hōc diē**)
nam	**for, because**
nōnne	negative adverb in direct questions, anticipates the answer "yes"
num	negative adverb in direct questions, anticipates the answer "no"
sī	**if**

EXERCITATIONES

I. MATCH the second phrase to the first by changing it into the same form. Some items will require more than one answer.

1. cuius bellī (cēna ipsa)
2. serve stulte (meus fīlius)
3. librī multī (līber homo)
4. huius fēminae (īdem puer)
5. paucīs rēbus (manus atrox)
6. fīlia mea (sapiens Lucilius)
7. aliī cēnae (nēmō caecus)
8. corporī mortuō (quod speculum)
9. alīus manūs (diēs beātus)
10. quod bellum (cēna pretiōsa)
11. Horātī sapiens (vir līber)
12. modō similī (noster rex)
13. tempora mala (quod saxum)
14. quārum mortium (vultus dēformis)
15. vīta dulcis (philosophus magnus)
16. noctium oblītārum (eadem toga)
17. patrēs acrēs (quī vir)
18. saxī magnī (sōlum carmen)
19. nōmen idem (lingua docta)
20. alīus gladiī (nūllus fortis)

II. MATCH the second verb to the first by changing it into the same form. Some items will require more than one answer.

1. ēgissent (cōgitō)
2. gesta sint (canō)
3. mittar (damnō)
4. dēbent (cupiō)
5. crēdidimus (audiō)
6. laudāre (sequor)
7. mittī (negō)
8. scrībās (dō)
9. vidērētur (nāscor)
10. interficiāminī (rogō)
11. conspicimur (doceō)
12. aestimāveris (dēbeō)
13. appellātae erant (cognōscō)
14. crēderem (gerō)
15. videantur (vīvō)
16. scrīpsēre (faciō)
17. ōdērunt (laudō)
18. placuit (conspiciō)
19. dīcant (possum)
20. quaeritis (pōnō)

III. TRANSLATE.

1. Nihil habēbam quod ad tē scrīberem dē rēbus quae in urbe gestae erant. Nam nūllī hīs diēbus in urbe sunt quī dē rē publicā agant. Omnēs cum rēge ad bellum profectī sunt. Nihil enim scrīpsissem sī nēmō ad tē proficiscī posset, sed dē aliīs rēbus tēcum loquī cupiēbam propter meum tuī magnum amōrem. Quem propter amōrem hās litterās servō meō dedī quem ad tē mīsī. Eum cognōscis, virum omnibus meīs rēbus doctum, cui omnia semper dīcō. Is sōlus est cui in hīs malīs temporibus crēdam. Dīgnus est quī līber sit. Sunt aliī quī amīcī videantur, sed is sōlus est quī numquam mihi noceat. Utinam omnēs eius similēs essent. Sed quid agis? Quō modō, mī fīlī, vīvis? Sī tēcum apud tē essem, dīcerem alia quae hīs in litterīs nōn possem scrībere.

2. Ab amīcō tuō, quem herī in urbe vīdī, tē audīvī, mī amīce, fābulās scrīpsisse quae dē vitiīs animālium narrārent ut eadem vitia in nostrā vītā ipsī cognōcerēmus. Tē semper dīxī virum magnae sapientiae esse. Fābulās magnā sapientiā scrīpsistī. Dīgnus es quī ab omnibus laudēris et magnī aestimēris. Sī animālia similī modō librōs scrībere possent, dē hominum vitiīs fābulās narrārent quae dē eīsdem rēbus in suā vītā docērent. Sī vītae animālium hominumque nōn similēs essent, nōn possēmus nōs et nostra vitia cognōscere in illō speculō quod appellātur fābula dē animālibus scrīpta. Sed sunt quī nōn sē cognōscant in illīs fābulīs quae dē animālibus narrantur. Quā rē illī sē nōn cognōscunt? Quaerō quā rē sē nōn cognōscant. Quō modō sē nōn cognōscere possunt? Nōnne stultī sunt? Stultī sunt. Nōnne caecī ad sua vitia? Caecī sunt. Num sapientēs sunt? Nōn sunt sapientēs. Utinam omnēs vidērent dē sē et suīs vitiīs narrārī, sed nōn vident.

3. Nēmō est quī mē amet. Sī quis esset quī mē amāret, mē amāret. Rogō num quis sit quī mē amet. Num est quī mē amet? Nōn, nēmō est. Et nēmō est quem amem. Sī quis esset quem amārem, eum amārem.

4. Nūllī sunt quōs laudem. Nūllī sunt quī ā mē laudārī possint. Sī quī essent quōs laudārem, eōs laudārem. Quaerō num quī sint quōs laudem. Quōs laudārem? Num sunt quōs laudem? Nōn sunt.

5. Dīgnus est cui crēdam. Dīgnī sunt quibus grātiās agam. Dīgna est quācum loquar. Nōnne dīgnae sunt? Dīgnae sunt. Quis dīgna est? Quae fēmina dīgna est? Illa est. Quaerō num quis dīgna sit. Quaerō num qua fēmina dīgna sit.

IV. TRANSLATE. (Try to guess the meaning of new words on the basis of context and cognates before consulting the adjacent reading notes.)

1. IULIUS CAESAR (dē Bellō Gallicō Commentārius Liber Prīmus)

C. IŪLIĪ CAESARIS DĒ BELLŌ GALLICŌ COMMENTĀRIUS PRĪMUS. **Gallia** est omnis **dīvīsa** in partēs **trēs**, quārum **ūnam incolunt Belgae**, aliam **Aquītānī**, **tertiam** quī ipsōrum linguā **Celtae**, nostrā **Gallī** appellantur.

(illa) Gallia, -ae Gaul, France
dīvidō, -ere, -vīsī, -vīsus divide
trēs, tria three Cf. triad
ūnus, -a, -um (pronominal declension) one Cf. unify
incolō, -ere, -uī inhabit Cf. colonize
(illī) Belgae, -ārum Belgians
(illī) Aquītānī, -ōrum Aquitanians (in southern France, between the Loire and the Pyrenees)
tertius, -a, -um third Cf. tertiary
(illī) Celtae, -ārum Celts
(illī) Gallī, -ōrum Gauls

Hī omnēs linguā, **institūtīs**, lēgibus **inter** sē **dīfferunt.** Gallōs ab Aquītānīs **Garumna flūmen**, ā Belgīs **Mātrona** et **Sēquana** dīvidit. Hōrum omnium **fortissimī** sunt Belgae, **propterea quod** ā **cultū atque hūmanitāte prōvinciae longissimē absunt, proximī**que sunt **Germānīs,** quī **trans Rhēnum** incolunt quibuscum **continenter** bellum gerunt. Quā dē causā **Helvētiī quoque reliquōs** aliōs virtūte **praecēdunt cum** aut suīs **finibus** eōs **prohibent** aut ipsī in eōrum finibus bellum gerunt.

(illud) institūtum, -ī institution
inter amongst Cf. intermural
dīf-ferrō, -fferre, -stulī, -lātus differ
(illa) Garumna, -ae Garonne River
(illud) flūmen, -minis river, flowing water Cf. fluid
(illa) Mātrona, -ae Marne River
(illa) Sēquana, -ae Seine River
fortissimus, -a, -um most brave, strongest, most powerful (from **fortis, -e**) Cf. fortissimo
propterea quod because of which (= **propter quod**)
(ille) cultus, -ūs culture
atque = et, -que
(illa) hūmanitas, -ātis humanity, civilization
(illa) prōvinia, -ae province, a territory outside of Italy that was conquered and brought under Roman rule
longissimē *adverb* farthest (from **longus, -a, -um)**
ab-sum, -esse, -fuī be away Cf. absent
proximus, -a, -um closest Cf. proximate
(illī) Germānī, -ōrum Germans
trans (+ *acc*) beyond, across Cf. transport
(ille) Rhēnus, -ī Rhine River
continenter continually
(illī) Helvetiī, -ōrum Swiss
quoque also
reliquus, -a, -um remaining, that which is left
prae-cēdō, -ere, -cessī, -cessus go before, precede, surpass
cum when (*not the same word as the preposition*)
(illa) finis, -is (-ium) boundary; *in plural:* territory, country Cf. finite
prohibeō, -ēre, -uī, -itus hold back Cf. prohibit

2. CARMEN SINE NŌMINE AUCTŌRIS (Pervigilium Veneris)

Crās amet quī numquam amāvit
quīque amāvit crās amet:
Vēr novum, vēr **iam canōrum**, vēr
renātus orbis est;
Vēre **concordant** amōrēs, vēre **nūbunt**
ālitēs,
Et **nemus comam resolvit** dē **maritīs**
imbribus.
Crās amet quī numquam amāvit
quīque amāvit crās amet.

(illud) **vēr, vēris** Spring Cf. vernal
novus, -a, -um new, fresh, young Cf. novelty, novel
iam now, already
canōrus, -a, -um melodious, harmonious (from **canō, -ere**)
re-nāscor, -ī, -nātus be born again Cf. renascent
(ille) **orbis, -is, -ium** orb (of the earth)
concordō, -āre, -āvī, -ātus agree together, become concordant
nūbō, -ere, nūpsī, nuptus veil oneself for the bridegroom, marry Cf. nuptial
ālēs, ālitis winged (= **avis**)
(illud) **nemus, nemōris** grove, glade, meadow
(illa) **coma, -ae** hair of the head, foliage
re-solvō, -ere, -solvī, -solūtus untie, loosen Cf. resolve
maritus, -a, -um nuptial, conjugal, marital
(ille) **imber, -bris** rain, rainstorm

3. PHAEDRUS (adapted)

Ad **rīvum** eundem **lupus** et **agnus**
vēnerant sitī compulsī: superior
stābat lupus, **longēque inferior**

(ille) **rīvus, ī** stream, brook Cf. river
(ille) **lupus, -ī** wolf Cf. lupine
(ille) **agnus, -ī** lamb
veniō, -īre, vēnī, ventus come Cf. advent
(illa) **sitis, -is, -ium** thirst
com-pellō, -ere, -pulī, -pulsus drive together, compel
superior, -ōris higher up Cf. superior
stō, -āre, stetī, status stand
longē *adverb* far, long, at a distance (from **longus, -a, -um**)
inferior, -ōris lower down Cf. inferior

agnus. **Tunc fauce improbā latro incitātus iurgiī causam intulit.** "**Cur,**" **inquit,** "**turbulentam** fēcistī mihi aquam quam **bibō?**" **Lāniger contrā** timidus: "Quō modō possum, quaerō, facere quod **quereris,** lupe? Ā tē **dēcurrit** ad meōs **haustūs liquor.**" **Rēpulsus** ille vēritātis **vīribus:** "**Ante** hōs **sex mensēs male,**" **ait,** "dīxistī mihi." **Rēspondit** agnus: "**Equidem** nātus nōn eram."

tunc then
(**illa**) **faux** *usually only in the plural:* **faucēs, -ium** throat, gullet Cf. faucet
improbus, -a, -um wicked, bad, violent Cf. improbity
(**ille**) **latro, -ōnis** thief
in-citō, -āre, -āvī, -ātus set in rapid motion, incite
(**illud**) **iurgium, -ī** quarrel
(**illa**) **causa, -ae** cause, reason
in-ferō, -ferre, -tulī, -lātus carry in, introduce Cf. infer
cur why?
inquit *used only for direct quotation* = **dīcit**
turbulentus, -a, -um turbulent, turbid, muddy
bibō, -ere, bibī, bibitus drink Cf. imbibe
lāniger, -gera, -gerum wool-bearing, wooly, fleecy = **agnus** Cf. lanolin
contrā in opposition Cf. contrary
queror, -ī, questus complain Cf. querulous
dē-currō, -ere, -cucurrī run down, flow down Cf. current
(**ille**) **haustus, -ūs** drinking, swallowing Cf. exhaust
(**ille**) **liquor, -ōris** liquid = **aqua**
rē-pellō, -ere, -ppulī, -pulsus drive back, repulse
(**illa**) **vīs, vīs** *plural* **vīrēs, -ium** force, strength Cf. virial
ante (+ *acc*) before Cf. antecedent
sex six
(**ille**) **mensis, -is, -ium** month
male *adverb* badly (from **malus, -a, -um**) Cf. malediction
ait = **inquit** (**dīcit**)
rē-spondeō, -ēre, -sponsī, -sponsus respond, present in return
equidem truly, indeed

"Pater, **hercle**, tuus **ibi**" inquit, "male dīxit mihi," atque **ita** agnum **correptum lacerat iniustā nece.** Haec propter illōs scrīpta est hominēs fābula, qui **fictīs** causīs **innocentēs opprimunt.**

hercle an oath on the name of Hercules
ibi there, in that case
ita thus
cor-ripiō, -ere, -ripuī, -reptus seize upon, snatch up
lacerō, -āre, -āvī, -ātus tear to pieces, lacerate
in-iustus, -a, -um unjust
(illa) nex, necis violent death, murder Cf. internecine
fingō, -ere, finxī, fictus form, fashion **fictus, -a, -um** fictitious Cf. fiction
in-nocens, -entis innocent (from **noceō, -ēre**)
opprimō, -ere, -pressī, -pressus overpower, oppress

V. **CHANGE** each of the following sentences by substituting the reflexive pronoun (**suī**, etc.) or the reflexive adjective (**suus, -a, -um**) for the weak demonstrative **is, ea, id.** Translate both versions of each sentence.

NOTE that although Latin does not have a true third person pronoun corresponding to the first person **ego** and the second person **tū** (see page 80), it does have a third person reflexive pronoun. **A reflexive refers back to the same person as the subject of the main verb**, whereas the ordinary pronoun (or demonstrative substitute) would **refer to anyone other than the subject**. In Latin, the first and second person pronouns are used for both the ordinary and the reflexive functions, but a distinction is made in the third person. Since the reflexive is never the subject, but always refers back to the subject from some other function in the sentence, there is no nominative form. The declensional forms for the third person reflexive are identical for both singular and plural.

PARADIGM 20
REFLEXIVE PRONOUN

	singular	*plural*
nominative	—	—
accusative	**sē**	**sē**
genitive	**suī**	**suī**
dative	**sibi**	**sibi**
ablative	**sē**	**sē**

Amābat sē. "**He loved himself.**" Contrast: **Amābat eum.** "**He loved him (i.e., someone else).**"

Amābam mē. "**I loved myself.**" The same form is also not reflexive: **Amābat mē.** "**He loved me.**"

As with the pronouns for the first and second persons, the genitive is not used for possession (see page 80); instead, the reflexive possessive adjective is used (**suus, -a, -um,** like the adjectives **meus, tuus, noster,** and **vester**).

Amābat suum fīlium. "**He loved his own son.**" Contrast: **Amābat fīlium eius.** "**He loved his (i.e., someone else's) son.**"

Amābās tuum fīlium. "**You loved your own son.**" The same form is also not reflexive: **Amābam tuum fīlium.** "**I loved your son.**"

The emphatic demonstrative **ipse, ipsa, ipsum** often is translated into English by the same words used to translate the reflexive, but it should not be confused with the reflexive. It is purely emphatic in function.

Tē ipse amābam. "**I loved you myself.**"

1. Multōs librōs servō eius dōnō dedit ut fīliōs eōrum docēret linguam Graecam.
2. Sī librōs scrībere possent, dē eīs animālia fābulās narrārent ut vitia eōrum vidērent.
3. Paucī sunt quī nātōs eōrum cognōscant.
4. Dīxērunt eās vītam sub urbe apud eum ēgisse.
5. Īdem erat quem ipse dīxī eī nocēre.
6. Semper eōrum oblīviscuntur et urbis eōrum.
7. Eum rogat num quis litterās dē eius vītā ad eum mīserit.
8. Nūllus erat in eius urbe poēta quī eī pār esset aut patre eius dīgnus.
9. Bonam magnamque cēnam eī apud eum dedit ut ab eō laudārētur et eī beātus vidērētur esse.
10. Propter eius magnam virtūtem semper omnibus in rēbus eum bene dīcat.

VI. CHANGE each of the following sentences so that the same idea is expressed by a single sentence with a relative clause.

Poēma breve erat. Id scrīpserat hīc sapiens poēta. "**The poem was short. This wise poet had written it.**"

Poēma breve erat quod hīc sapiens poēta scrīpserat. "**The poem was short that this wise poet had written.**"

1. Nēmō poēta omnium poētārum eius similis erat. Cum eō dī sempiternī loquēbantur. (**NOTE** that, as with the personal pronouns, the relative is joined to the preposition **cum: quōcum, quibuscum, tēcum, vōbīscum, mēcum, nōbīscum, sēcum.**)
2. Nēmō eam ōdit. Dīxit sē omnēs amāre.
3. Nēminī omnium amīcōrum suōrum apud sē cēnam dedit. Eī nocuerant.
4. Nēmō tē amābat. Stultus erās et semper vir nūllīus sapientiae.
5. Fābulās dē sē narrābant hominēs nūllīus sapientiae. Eās illī scrīpserant ipsī.
6. Dī vōs amant. Vōbīs omnia bona in vestrā vītā dedērunt.
7. Tuī oblītus sum. Matre dīgna numquam erās neque fēmina magnae virtūtis.
8. Eum cum eīs ad eam mīsī. Eī togam pulchram dōnō dedī.
9. Domus sub urbe eīs erat. In eā vītam beātam agēbant.
10. Capitis damnātae erant. Eae propter suum amōrem suī suam urbem perdiderant.

VII. CHANGE each of the following sentences into equivalent expressions using the jussive subjunctive.

NOTE that a few Latin verbs do not conform to the pattern of the four conjugations. The parent language (Indo-European) from which Latin developed had two kinds of conjugation, one in which the subject personal suffixes were joined to the verbal stem by various vowels and one in which the suffixes were added directly without connecting vowels. Latin simplified this system by regularizing most verbs into the four vowel conjugations that you have learned, but a few verbs maintained characteristics of the vowel-less conjugation. These are the so-called **irregular verbs** in Latin. You have already learned one of them: **sum, esse, fuī**. The stem is [**es-**], and thus you have forms like **es-t**, or the infinitive **esse** (from **es-re**, with the **r** assimilated to the preceding consonant). In forms like **s-um**, the initial **e** has been lost and personal suffix [**-m**] has been vocalized so that it can be pronounced.

Three other verbs show similar irregular characteristics in some of their forms:

volō, velle, voluī
nōlō (from **nōn volō**), **nōlle, nōluī**
ferō, ferre, tulī, lātus

Other forms are predictable, as though the verbs belonged to the third conjugation. The imperfect subjunctive uses the vowel-less infinitive as its stem: **vellem / nōllem / ferrem**, etc.

This exercise will famliarize you with these irregular verbs, while practicing the jussive subjunctive as a replacement for the modal auxiliaries **volō** and **nōlō**.

Patris similem sē vult esse.	**"He wants to be similar to his father."**

Patris similis sit. **"May he be like his father."**

PARADIGM 21
CONJUGATION OF *volō, nōlō,* and *ferō*
PRESENT

	volō		*nōlō*		*ferō*			
	indic.	*subj.*	*indic.*	*subj.*	*indic. active*	*indic. passive*	*subj. active*	*subj. passive*
1	volō	velim	nōlō	nōlim	ferō	feror	feram	ferar
2	vīs	velīs	nōn vīs	nōlīs	fers	ferris (-re)	ferās	ferāris -re
3	vult (volt)	velit	nōn vult	nōlit	fert	fertur	ferat	ferātur
1	volumus	velīmus	nōlumus	nōlīmus	ferimus	ferimur	ferāmus	ferāmur
2	vultis	velītis	nōn vultis	nōlītis	fertis	feriminī	ferātis	ferāminī
3	volunt	velint	nōlunt	nōlint	ferunt	feruntur	ferant	ferantur

1. Matre dīgnam volō illam esse.
2. Virum magnae sapientiae tē volēbam esse, sed nōn erās.
3. Nōlō tē illam fēminam amāre. (**REMEMBER** that negative commands or prohibitions commonly are expressed in the present perfect; see page 92).
4. Beātam vītam inter amīcōs nostrōs volumus agere.
5. Tibi nōlēbam nocēre, sed nocēbam.
6. Speculum ad tē ferrī volō ut tē videās.
7. Nōlō tē carmen illīus generis canere.
8. Tē nostrī meminisse volēbam, sed nostrī oblīta es.
9. Pecūniam tibi darī volō ut ad rēgem ferās.
10. Speculum sibi esse vult ut sē in speculō videat.

VIII. CHANGE each of the following sentences to indirectly quoted material introduced by the phrase in parentheses.

Nēmō cognōscēbat servum quī missus erat. (scrībunt)

Scrībunt nēminem cognōvisse servum quī missus sit. **"They write that nobody recognized the slave who had been sent."**

NOTE that **an** is used just like **num** to introduce indirect questions. It can also be used in both direct and indirect questions to indicate suggested alternative questions.

Quaeritur an mors malum sit.

Estne mors malum an bonum? **"Is death an evil or something good?"**

Quaeritur sitne mors malum an bonum. — **"It is questioned whether death be an evil or something good."** The first interrogative particle can also be omitted: **Quaeritur mors sit malum an bonum.**

1. Vīta mala fuit quam ēgit servus miser. (dīxit)
2. Vītamne regit fortūna an sapientia? (quaesītum est)
3. Aliī mihi dedērunt pecūniam quae propter mea bene facta dēbēbātur. (dīcō)
4. Cum invidiā semper ab omnibus vidētur poēta magnae virtūtis quī vītam beātam inter suōs amīcōs agit. (scrīpsit)
5. Magnam bonamque cēnam dederat suō amīcō quī carmen dē suā virtūte voluit scrībere. (dīxit)
6. Togam nōlumus gerere quī vītam sine perīculō hāc in urbe volumus agere. (scrībimus)
7. Avem timidam quae dē amōre suō cecinit vīdit in arbore. (dīcō)
8. Nōs oportuit togam gerere quam līberī sōlī dēbent gerere. (dīcimus)
9. Magnō perīculō ab eō scrīptum erat illud poēma in quō dē eius vītā narrat. (dīcit) (**REMEMBER** that reflexives refer back to the same person as the main verb.)
10. Hodiē nōn est īdem quī herī erat. (scrīpsit)

IX. CHANGE each of the following sentences so that the hypothesis and result are contrary to fact.

Sī reus erat, capitis damnātus est. — **"If he was guilty, he has been condemned to death."**

Sī reus esset, capitis damnātus esset. — **"If he were guilty, he would have been condemned to death."**

1. Sī qua fēminam bene dīxit, nēmō crēdidit eam cum vēritāte dē aliā dīcere.
2. Sī qua dōna pecūniae ab hōc avārō dēformī aliīs dabantur, ā nōbīs omnibus laudābātur.
3. Si quis mihi crēdidit, stultus fuit.
4. Sī quae rēs dē bellō cum illīs atrōcibus gerēbantur, omnēs cōgitābant quid sē oportēret agere.
5. Sī quibuscum voluī loquī, semper quaesīvī num quī essent sapientēs in hāc urbe quī linguam Graecam mē possent docēre.
6. Sī magnum vīnī lacum ad meam cēnam ferēbās, mihi vidēbāre sōlus dīgnus quī meus amīcus appellārēre.
7. Sī quid bellum gerēbat, semper ā stultīs laudābātur.
8. Sī mihi nocēbat, aliīs semper dīcēbat sibi ā mē nocērī.
9. Sī mē amāvistī, semper dīxistī tē mē amāre.
10. Sī fābulam audīvistis, vōs cognōvistis.

X. NOTE THE PATTERN in each of the following sentences and compose a translation of the English sentences using the same pattern.

1. **Crās amet quī numquam amāvit.**
   Let her speak who never has spoken.
   Let it be what never has been.

2. **Mī fīlī, quid agis?**
   My friend, who are you?
   Philosopher, whom do you praise?
   Vergil, what poem are you writing?

Piranesi, Temple of the Sibyl, Tivoli

LESSON EIGHT

FUTURE, FUTURE PERFECT

Cēnābīs bene, mī Fabulle, apud mē sī tēcum attuleris bonam cēnam.

FUTURE TENSE. The future tense states an action or state of being that will occur some time after the present.

Cēnābis. — **"You will dine."**

In addition to the **simple future**, Latin can express an action or state of being as something completed in the future, the **future perfect tense**.

Cēnāveris. — **"You will have dined (by some time in the future.)"**

There is no subjunctive of the future. In English, the use of the modal auxiliary "will" expresses the volitional nature of the future, which makes it similar in certain respects to a subjunctive; and in Latin, some of the future endings developed originally from subjunctives. The future, however, is an indicative mode or Mood, making a statement of fact, although the fact, of course, can only be presumed in reality since it has not yet taken place.

You have already seen that there is a certain futurity implied by the subjunctive. The present subjunctive projects the speaker's will upon the future.

Crās amet. **"Let him love tomorrow."**

The imperfect subjunctive does the same thing from the vantage of the past upon a future that has come before the present.

Herī amāret. **"He should have loved yesterday (but he probably hasn't)."**

FUTURE INDICATIVE CONJUGATION. In **conjugations I and II**, the future is formed by adding the suffix [-**b**-] to the present stem: **amābō, amābis,** etc./ **docēbō, docēbis,** etc.; **and the resulting verb is conjugated like the indicative of the Third Conjugation e-stems.** In **conjugations III and IV**, the future is formed by adding the endings **-am, -ēs,** etc. These were originally subjunctive endings, and thus the future of conjugations III and IV resembles some forms of the present subjunctive of conjugations I and II, as well as that of conjugations III and IV.

The future perfect is formed from the perfect stem by adding the suffix [-**er**-] for the **active** voice: **amāverō, amāveris,** etc. The **passive** is compounded from the fourth principal part (perfect passive participle) with the future of **esse.**

The charts on the following pages summarize the future conjugations. The present subjunctive is shown in juxtaposition for comparison.

NOTE that despite the similarity of forms, the only ones that are ambiguous are the first person singular of conjugations III and IV, both active and passive. The future changes from **-a-** to **-e-**, whereas the present subjunctive maintains **-a-** throughout. The future forms with **-e-** do resemble the present subjunctive of conjugation I, but that conjugation is the only one that has -e- in the subjunctive. (If it had **-a-** like the other conjugations, it would be indistinguishable from the present indicative.)

NOTE that the passive second person singular of **conjugation III** has a short **-e-** in the present indicative, but a long **-ē-** in the future; and that **conjugation III i-stems** have **-iē-** for this form in the future, instead of just a short **-e-**.

NOTE that the present perfect active subjunctive is identical with the future perfect active indicative except in the first person singular (**-eri-** was originally a subjunctive suffix).

COMPARISON: FUTURE INDICATIVE AND PRESENT SUBJUNCTIVE

	conj. I ā-stem		conj. II ē-stem		conj. III e-stem		conj. III i-stem		conj. IV ī-stem	
	fut. indic.	*pres. subj.*	*fut. indic.*	*pres. subj.*	*fut. indic.*	*pres. subj.*	*fut. indic.*	*pres. subj.*	*fut. indic.*	*pres. subj.*
ACTIVE VOICE										
1	amābō	amem	docēbō	doceam	regam	regam	incipiam	incipiam	audiam	audiam
2	amābis	amēs	docēbis	doceās	regēs	regās	incipiēs	incipiās	audiēs	audiās
3	amābit	amet	docēbit	doceāt	reget	regat	incipiet	incipiat	audiet	audiat
1	amābimus	amēmus	docēbimus	doceāmus	regēmus	regāmus	incipiēmus	incipiāmus	audiēmus	audiāmus
2	amābitis	amētis	docēbitis	doceātis	regētis	regātis	incipiētis	incipiātis	audiētis	audiātis
3	amābunt	ament	docēbunt	doceant	regent	regant	incipient	incipiant	audient	audiant
PASSIVE VOICE										
1	amābor	amer	docēbor	docear	regar	regar	incipiar	incipiar	audiar	audiar
2	amāberis	amēris	docēberis	doceāris	regēris	regāris	incipiēris	incipiāris	audiēris	audiāris
	amābere	amēre	docēbere	doceāre	regēre	regāre	incipiēre	incipiāre	audiēre	audiāre
3	amābitur	amētur	docēbitur	doceātur	regētur	regātur	incipiētur	incipiātur	audiētur	audiātur
1	amābimur	amēmur	docēbimur	doceāmur	regēmur	regāmur	incipiēmur	incipiāmur	audiēmur	audiāmur
2	amābiminī	amēminī	docēbiminī	doceāminī	regēminī	regāminī	incipiēminī	incipiāminī	audiēminī	audiāminī
3	amābuntur	amentur	docēbuntur	doceantur	regentur	regantur	incipientur	incipiantur	audientur	audiantur

COMPARISONS

pres. perf. act. subj. & fut. perf. act. indic.		fut. indic. **sum** & fut. perf. pass. indic.	
present perfect subjunc	future perfect indicative	future indicative of sum	fut. perf. passive indic.
amāverim	amāverō	erō	amātus -a -um erō
amāveris	amāveris	eris	amātus -a -um eris
amāverit	amāverit	erit	amātus -a -um erit
amāverimus	amāverimus	erimus	amātī -ae -a erimus
amāveritis	amāveritis	eritis	amātī -ae -a eritis
amāverint	amāverint	erunt	amātī -ae -a erunt

PARADIGM 22

	conj I ā-stem	conj II ē-stem	conj III e-stem	conj III i-stem	conj IV ī-stem
	FUTURE ACTIVE INDICATIVE CONJUGATION				
1	amābō	docēbō	regam	incipiam	audiam
2	amābis	docēbis	regēs	incipiēs	audiēs
3	amābit	docēbit	reget	incipiet	audiet
1	amābimus	docēbimus	regēmus	incipiēmus	audiēmus
2	amābitis	docēbitis	regētis	incipiētis	audiētis
3	amābunt	docēbunt	regent	incipient	audient
	FUTURE PASSIVE INDICATIVE CONJUGATION				
1	amābor	docēbor	regar	incipiar	audiar
2	amāberis amābere	docēberis docēbere	regēris regēre	incipiēris incipiēre	audiēris audiēre
3	amābitur	docēbitur	regētur	incipiētur	audiētur
1	amābimur	docēbimur	regēmur	incipiēmur	audiēmur
2	amābiminī	docēbiminī	regēminī	incipiēminī	audiēminī
3	amābuntur	docēbuntur	regentur	incipientur	audientur
	FUTURE PERFECT ACTIVE INDICATIVE CONJUGATION				
1	amāverō	docuerō	rēxerō	incēperō	audīverō
2	amāveris	docueris	rēxeris	incēperis	audīveris
3	amāverit	docuerit	rēxerit	incēperit	audīverit
1	amāverimus	docuerimus	rēxerimus	incēperimus	audīverimus
2	amāveritis	docueritis	rēxeritis	incēperitis	audīveritis
3	amāverint	docuerint	rēxerint	incēperint	audīverint

PARADIGM 22 *continued*

	FUTURE PERFECT PASSIVE INDICATIVE CONJUGATION				
	conj I ā-stem	conj II ē-stem	conj III e-stem	conj III i-stem	conj IV ī-stem
1	amātus -a -um erō	doctus -a -um erō	rectus -a -um erō	inceptus -a -um erō	audītus -a -um erō
2	amātus -a -um eris	doctus -a -um eris	rectus -a -um eris	inceptus -a -um eris	audītus -a -um eris
3	amātus -a -um erit	doctus -a -um erit	rectus -a -um erit	inceptus -a -um erit	audītus -a -um erit
1	amātī -ae -a erimus	doctī -ae -a erimus	rectī -ae -a erimus	inceptī -ae -a erimus	audītī -ae -a erimus
2	amātī -ae -a eritis	doctī -ae -a eritis	rectī -ae -a eritis	inceptī -ae -a eritis	audītī -ae -a eritis
3	amātī -ae -a erunt	doctī -ae -a erunt	rectī -ae -a erunt	inceptī -ae -a erunt	audītī -ae -a erunt
	FUTURE ACTIVE INFINITIVE CONJUGATION				
	amātūrum esse	doctūrum esse	rectūrum esse	inceptūrum esse	audītūrum esse
	FUTURE PASSIVE INFINITIVE CONJUGATION				
	amātum īrī	doctum īrī	rectum īrī	inceptum īrī	audītum īrī
	FUTURE ACTIVE PARTICIPLE				
	amātūrus -a -um	doctūrus -a -um	rectūrus -a -um	inceptūrus -a -um	audītūrus -a -um

NOTE that the future of **esse** is identical with the ending of the future perfect except in the third person plural, where **esse** has **erunt** instead of **-erint.**

FUTURE INFINITIVE. In addition to the two tenses of the infinitive that you already know (present: **amāre / amārī**; and perfect: **amāvisse / amātus, -a, -um esse**, or since the subject must always be accusative: **amātum (-am, -um) esse** and **amātōs (-ās, -a) esse**), the infinitive can also be expressed in the future. Both the active and the passive future infinitives are compound forms. The **future active infinitive** is formed from a future verbal adjective (or participle) with the infinitive **esse.** This future participle is formed by adding **-ūrus (-a, -um)** to the stem of the perfect passive participle (fourth principal part of the verb).

amātūrum (-am, -um) esse — **"to be about to love"**

The **future passive infinitive** is formed from a word that is identical with the neuter singular of the perfect passive participle (fourth principal part of the verb) plus the passive infinitive of a verb meaning "to go": **īrī.**

amātum īrī — **"to be going to be loved" (or literally, "to be gone to love")**

For all the infinitives that are compounded with participles (i.e., verbal adjectives), the participle will agree with the noun or pronoun that functions as its subject; since infinitives are modified by accusatives, which in certain contexts function as their subject (see page 7), the participle component of these compounded infinitives will always be accusative.

Dīcit puellam pulchram futūram esse. — **"He says that the girl is going to be beautiful."**

Dīcit puellam amātūram esse. — **"He says that the girl is going to love."**

The **future passive infinitive**, however, is not compounded with a participle.

Dīcit puellam amātum īrī. — **"He says that the girl is going to be loved." Amātum** is actually a Fourth Declension masculine noun in the accusative, modifying **īrī** (see Lesson 11).

SEQUENCE OF TENSES. You have already seen that Latin tenses in the indicative belong either to a primary group (associated with present tenses) or a secondary group (associated with past tenses). Infinitives in oratio obliqua and subjunctives in subordinate clauses express time relative to the main verb; subjunctives, furthermore, can be used only with one or the other of the two groupings: primary indicatives can be followed only by subjunctives belonging to the primary sequence, and secondary indicatives can be followed only by subjunctives of the secondary sequence.

The future is a primary tense, grouped together with the present and the present perfect (when the emphasis is upon a present result of the completed action). The future, therefore, never will introduce an imperfect subjunctive or a past perfect subjunctive. It will occur only with a present subjunctive (for an action contemporaneous or later) or a present perfect subjunctive (for action completed previously).

Quaerētur num mors malum sit.	**"It will be questioned whether death be (i.e., is or will be) something bad."**
Quaerētur num mors malum fuerit.	**"It will be questioned whether death was something bad."**
Quaesītum erit num mors malum sit.	**"It will have been questioned whether death be (at that time or later) something bad."**
Quaesītum erit num mors malum fuerit.	**"It will have been questioned whether death was something bad."**

SUMMARY OF SEQUENCE OF TENSES

INDICATIVE TENSE	SUBORDINATED SUBJUNCTIVE
PRIMARY SEQUENCE	
Present Future Present Perfect (with present emphasis)	Present (for contemporaneous action or later) Present Perfect (for previous action)
SECONDARY SEQUENCE	
Imperfect Present Perfect (with past emphasis) Past Perfect	Imperfect (for contemporaneous action or later) Past Perfect (for previous action)
INFINITIVES (IN ORATIO OBLIQUA)	
Any tense of Indicative or independent Subjunctive	Present infinitive (for contemporaneous action) Perfect infinitive (for previous action) Future infinitive (for later action)

In indirect discourse, the future infinitive indicates time after the time of the main verb.

EXPLICITNESS OF TIME RELATIONSHIP. Latin is usually more explicit than English in viewing the previous completion of related actions.

Sī carmen scrīpserit, id canēs. **"If he will have written a poem, you will recite it."** English would be apt to say: **"If he writes a poem, you will recite it."**

Carmen canam quod scrīpserit. **"I'll sing a song that he will have written."**

FUTURE CONDITIONS. You have already seen that a hypothesized potential and its potential result in the past produces a **contrary-to-fact condition,** i.e., potentials (or "futures") in the past for which subjunctives of the secondary group are used (see pages 122–23).

A present or future potential can also be hypothesized, with its potential result. As you would expect, subjunctives of the primary group express such potentials, and since the potential is viewed from the vantage not of the past (which implies that by now the speaker suspects that the actions have not in fact taken place), but from the vantage of the present, these primary group subjunctive potentials allow the possibility that the actions will in fact occur in reality.

Sī poēta sim, canam. **"If I should (ever) be a poet, I would sing."**

Sī poēta fuerim, cecinerim. **"If I should (ever) turn out being a poet, I should turn out having sung."** The emphasis is upon potential completed actions; the situation is not common, and for practical purposes, the present subjunctive in both clauses adequately expresses such hypothesized possible potentials.

Since such possible hypothesized potentials can be translated into English by the modal auxiliaries "should/ would," grammarians have termed these conditions **future-less-vivid,** in contrast to conditions that are **future-more-vivid,** translated by "shall/ will."

These grammatical terms, however, are somewhat unfortunate, for they describe an English translation, rather than the Latin structures. The latter example is merely a simple future indicative hypothesized, whereas the true contrast is between hypothesized past potentials (condition contrary to fact) and a hypothesized present-future potential. Both are expectable uses of the independent potential subjunctive.

CUM CLAUSES. In addition to the preposition **cum** which you have already learned, there is another **cum** (originally **quom**), which is an entirely unrelated word and that is used to introduce subordinate clauses. From its original spelling you can see that the subordinating conjunction is related to the relative pronouns, etc. The basic meaning of **cum** (**quom**) is temporal: "when."

Cum eam vīdī, pulchra erat. **"When I saw her, she was beautiful."**

Just as other relatives, however, can be used to introduce potential subjunctives (relative clauses of characteristic, see pages 121–22), **cum** also can introduce a similar subjunctive, with the temporal meaning generalized into the idea of attendant circumstances: "since, because, although, while." So also **ubi** when its meaning is generalized to "whenever."

Cum bene nōn canat, pulchra est. **"Although she doesn't sing well, she is beautiful."**

Cum eam vidērem, mēcum loquēbātur. **"Since I saw her, she spoke with me."**

As for all subordinating subjunctive clauses, the normal pattern of sequence of tenses is observed.

REMEMBER

TO FORM THE FUTURE INDICATIVE

Conj. I & II: add the suffix [-**b**-] to the verbal stem with its final vowel not shortened; conjugate like a Conj. III e-stem Present Indicative.

Conj. III & IV: conjugate like the Present Indicative of Conj. II, except in the first person singular, which is identical with the Present Subjunctive.

TO FORM THE FUTURE PERFECT INDICATIVE ACTIVE VOICE

For all conjugations: identical with the Present Perfect Subjunctive, except in the first person singular, which has an ending like the future of *sum* (*erō*).

TO FORM THE FUTURE PERFECT PASSIVE VOICE

For all conjugations: use the perfect passive participle (fourth principal part of the verb) with the future of *sum*.

INDEX VERBORUM

(ille aut illa) dux, ducis	**leader, commander-in-chief**
(ille) nāsus, -ī	**nose**
(ille) pānis, -is, (-ium, -um)	**bread**
(ille) sāl, salis	**salt, wit, sarcasm**

candidus, -a, -um	**dazzling white, beautiful, clear**
ēgregius, -a, -um	**distinguished, eminent, excellent**
plēnus , -a, -um	**full, filled (+ *abl. of means:* "filled with;" *or* + *gen. adjectival:* "full of")**
tantus, -a, -um	**so great, so much** (correlative with **quantus, -a, -um "how great, how much"** Example: ***Tantus sum quantus es.*** **"I am as great as you."**
tālis, -e	**such, of such a quality** (correlative with **quālis, -e "as which quality"**) Example: ***Tālis sum quālis es.*** **"I am (a person) of such quality as you."**
aliquis, aliquid (indefinite pronoun) **aliquī, aliqua, aliquod** (indefinite adjective)	**someone, anyone** (like **quis, quid** and **quī, qua, quod**: see pages 119–20), pronominal declension, see page 80. The forms without **ali-** are used only after **num, sī, nisī,** and **nē.** Example: ***Aliquem rogō num quis loquātur.*** **"I ask someone whether anyone is speaking."**
ūllus, -a, -um	**any** (pronominal declension, see page 80). Usually used in negative sentences, whereas **aliquis (aliquī)** is used in affirmative sentences. Example: ***Nōn erat in urbe ūllus servus, sed aliquis erat sub urbe.*** **"There wasn't any servant in the city, but someone was in the suburbs."** Compare: ***Nūllus in urbe erat.*** **"There was none in the city."** ***Nēmō in urbe erat.*** **"No one was in the city."**

bibō, -ere, bibī, bibitus	**drink**
cēnō, -āre, -āvī, -ātus	**take a meal, dine, eat**
discō, -ere, didicī, (discitūrus)	**learn**

edō, -ere, ēdī, ēsus	**eat** (although **edō** has a regular conjugation, it also has some forms without the vowel connecting the personal suffixes: see pages 132–33. In particular: **ēs** (from ***ed-s,*** note the different vowel length from **es** "**you are,**"), **ēst,** and **ēstis;** also imperfect subjunctive: **ēssēs** (from ***ed-re-s***), **ēsset, ēssēmus, ēssētis, ēssent.**
fīō, fierī, factus	**be made, become** (functions as the passive equivalent of **faciō**). Regular conjugation III, but note the unusual passive infinitive and hence the imperfect subjunctives: **fierem, fierēs,** etc.
iungō, -ere, iūnxī, iūnctus	**join**
mereō, -ēre, -uī, -itus also deponent: **mereor, -ērī, meritus**	**deserve, merit, be worthy of**
nesciō, -īre, -īvī, -ītus	**not know, be ignorant of**
sciō, -īre, -īvī, -ītus	**know**
timeō, -ēre, -uī	**fear, be afraid of**
tollō, -ere, sustulī, sublātus	**lift, take up**
veniō, -īre, vēnī, ventus	**come**
pro	**in front of, on behalf of, instead of** (+ *abl.*)
autem	**however, moreover** (placed after beginning of clause)
cum (quom)	**when** (or generalized to "**since, because, although, while**")
cur	**why?**
quārē (quā rē)	**why? for which reason** (*an abl. of manner*)
nisī	**unless, if not**
ubi	**where, when**
umquam	**ever** (compare **numquam** "**never**")

EXERCITATIONES

I. MATCH the second phrase to the first by changing it into the same form. Some items will require more than one answer.

1. nāsō longō (sāl candidus)
2. tantīs ducibus (aliqua aqua)

3. cēnae quantae (dux ēgregius)
4. pānēs magnī (aliqua avis)
5. ūllīus corporis (quae arbor)
6. similium bellōrum (tālis homo)
7. mī serve (homo stultus)
8. liber brevis (īdem līber)
9. aliō modō (puella lībera)
10. nūllī ipsī (qua cēna)
11. sōlō pāne (haec rēs)
12. alicui invidiae (pars pār)
13. vultuī dēformī (hōc speculum)
14. hanc togam (aliqua domus)
15. animālia nūlla (vester dux)
16. cēnīs ēsīs (quī dux)
17. aqua bibita (ūllum caput)
18. duce ventō (fābula narrāta)
19. dōnīs meritīs (sal tantus)
20. tālī fīliō (noster pater)

II. MATCH the second verb to the first by changing it into the same form. Some items will require more than one answer.

1. bibētis (cēnō)
2. fīat (volō)
3. discam (cēnō)
4. missae erunt (edō)
5. timēbimus (fīō)
6. sustulerō (iungō)
7. nesciam (cōgitō)
8. ēst (agō)
9. fierēs (nōlō)
10. gerent (aestimō)
11. mereantur (faciō)
12. timēbam (incipiō)
13. venīre (appellō)
14. conspexerint (bibō)
15. satiāre (sequor)
16. futūrās (videō)
17. ēssēmus (fīō)
18. habitum īrī (perdō)
19. interficiēminī (dō)
20. scrībam (rogō)

III. TRANSLATE

1. Sī sibi nōn placeat nāsus suus quī omnibus videātur dēformis esse et longus, numquam dēbeat ille sē in speculō conspicere. Cur nam eum oportet scīre quālis aliīs semper videātur ubi eum conspiciant? Tālem sē videat quālis velit vidērī. Sī umquam scīverit quālis aliīs videātur, quō modō poterit inter aliōs vītam agere? Tollātur illud speculum atrox quod eī vēritātem dīcet. Ab eō perdātur. Nēmō est quī sē velit vidēre. Nesciat quālis cum vēritāte sit. Sit quālis velit esse. Sed forsitan hunc nāsum dēformem habeat ā patre suō et ab illīus patre. Hī erant virī dīgnī quōs omnēs laudārent. Dīgnī erant quī ab omnibus laudārentur. Ēgregiās ēgerant vītās suās. Omnēs eōs semper bene dīxerant. Nisī similis eōrum esset, quō modō posset ipse vir ēgregius esse? Similī modō aget et ipse vītam ēgregiam. Sī vītam glōriae plēnam ēgerit, omnēs eius sapientiam virtūtemque laudābunt. Vir erit magnae sapientiae magnaeque virtūtis, īdemque nāsō longō. Vir tantae glōriae erit ipse quantae erant patrēs suī. Utinam esset vir tantus quantī patrēs suī. Nāsum habet tantum quantum patrēs suī habēbant. Sī similis voluerit esse suōrum patrum, deōs rogābit tōtum ut sē faciant nāsum. Appellētur nōmine Nāsus. Sī tōtus fieret nāsus, nēmō posset negāre eum patrum eius similem esse. Nūllī erunt quī negent eum fīlium fuisse eius patris.

2. Alicui cēnam magnam bonamque apud mē darem sī quid mihi esset quod ēssēmus aut biberēmus, sed, ut tēcum cum vēritāte loquar, nihil mihi est dīgnum quod dem. Sī tuleris tēcum, mī amīce, cēnam quam edāmus, cēnābis bene apud mē. Nē sōlus vēneris, sed tēcum veniat aliqua candida puella quam amem. Nē vēneris sine aliquā puellā. Edāmus et bibāmus et amēmus. Pānem edēmus vīnumque bibēmus et illam candidam puellam amābimus. Hōc modō tē ad cēnam apud mē invītō. Nam pecūnia mihi nōn est multa, sed tē ex omnibus quōs cognōscō bene amō neque est ūllus quōcum velim loquī. Tū sōlus dīgnus es quem nōmine amīcum appellem. Magnō cum sale semper mēcum loqueris, et pro nostrō amōre tibi cēnam dare vellem sī possem. Sī ad cēnam vēneris, amīce sapiens, tibi dīcam quantus mihi sit meus amor tuī. Quantus est tuus meī amor? Quaerō an quantus sit tuus amor meī tantus meus tuī. Cum ad cēnam vēneris nōn sine vīnō et pāne et illā candidā puellā, poēma canam dē nostrō amōre, quod, cum audīveris, dīcēs ab aliquō ēgregiō poētā scrīptum esse. Cum amīcī sīmus, cur hōc modō nōn bene cēnābimus? Cum tēcum loquī mihi placeat, nōnne oportet tē ad cēnam venīre? Num mē ōdistī? Nisī meus amor tuī esset tantus quantus tuus meī, hōc modō nōn cēnārēmus. Nōn est ūllus quem hōc modō ad cēnam invītāverim. Nūllus est dē quō idem poēma scrīpserim. Hōc modō bene cēnēmus. Et mea ipsīus puella, quam bene hīs diēbus amō, quae mihi sōla est vīta mea ipsa, ad hanc cēnam veniet. Eī dī ipsī aliquid vīnī dedērunt, quod, cum biberimus deōs rogābimus ut nōs tōtōs faciant linguam. Tāle nōn est aliud quāle hōc quod eī ā dīs ipsīs datum est.

IV. TRANSLATE. (Try to guess the meaning of new words on the basis of context and cognates before consulting the adjacent **reading notes.**)

1. CATULLUS 13

Cēnābis bene, mī Fabulle, apud mē
paucīs, sī tibi dī **favent**, diēbus,
sī tēcum **attuleris** bonam **atque** magnam
cēnam, nōn sine candidā puellā
et vīnō et sale et omnibus **cachinnīs.**
Haec sī, **inquam,** attuleris, **venuste** noster,
cēnābis bene; nam tuī Catullī
plēnus **sacculus** est **arāneārum.**

faveō, -ēre, fāvī, fautus favor, be favorable to (+ *dat.*)
af-ferō, (ad-ferō), af-ferre, at-tulī, al-lātus bring to a place
atque = et
(ille) cachinnus, -ī loud laughter Cf. cachinnation
inquam = dīcō
venustus, -a -um lovely, graceful, elegant Cf. Venus, the goddess of Love
(ille) sacculus, -ī little sack, purse
(illa) arānea, -ae spider Cf. araneid
contrā in return, opposite
ac-cipiō, -ere, -cēpī, -ceptus receive, take, accept

Sed **contrā accipiēs merōs** amōrēs
seu quid **suāvius ēlegantiusve** est:
nam **unguentum** dabō, quod meae puellae
dōnārunt Venerēs Cupīdinēsque,
quod tū cum **olfaciēs,** deōs rogābis
tōtum ut tē faciant, Fabulle, nāsum.

merus, -a, -um undiluted, pure (of wine not mixed with water)
seu = aut
suāvior, -ius (gen. **-iōris**) more delightful, more agreeable Cf. suave
ēlegantior, -ius (gen. **-iōris**) more elegant
-ve = aut
(illud) unguentum, -ī perfume, perfumed unguent (for anointing oneself at dinner)
dōnō, -āre, -āvī, -ātus = dōnō dō for form, see note, page 88
(illa) Venus, -neris
(ille) Cupīdo, -dinis
olfaciō, -ere, -fēcī, -factus smell Cf. olfactory

2. CATULLUS 85

Ōdī et amō. Quārē id faciam, **fortasse requīris?**
Nesciō, sed fierī **sentiō** et **excrucior.**

fortasse = forsitan (but usually not with potential subjunctive)
requīrō, -ere, -quīsī(v)ī, -quīsitus seek to know, ask Cf. require
sentiō, -īre, sensī, sensus perceive, sense
ex-cruciō, -āre, -āvī, -ātus torment Cf. excruciating

3. CATULLUS 87

Nūlla potest **mulier tantum** sē dīcere amātam
  vērē, quantum ā mē Lesbia amāta mea est.
Nūlla **fidēs** ūllo fuit umquam **foedere** tanta,
  quantā in amōre tuō ex parte **reperta** meā est.

(illa) mulier, -eris woman Cf. muliebrity
tantum (accusative of adjectives are adverbs, cf. adverbial function of the accusative) so much
vērē truthfully
quantum (see **tantum**)
(illa) fidēs, -eī trust, fidelity
(illud) foedus, -eris treaty
reperiō, -īre, -pperī, -pertus find again

4. PHAEDRUS (adapted)

Societātem iunxerant **leo, iuvenca, capra,** ovis. **Praeda** autem, quam **cēperant,** in **quattuor** partēs **aequālēs dīvīsa** erat. **Tum deinde** leo, "**Prīma,**" **ait,** "mea est; dēbētur enim haec **praestantiae** meae. Tollam et **secundam,** quam merētur **rōbur** meum. **Tertiam vindicat** sibi ēgregius labor meus. **Quartam** quī sibi **arrogāre** voluerit, is sciat sē habitūrum mē **inimīcum** sibi."

(illa) **societas, -ātis** society, association, corporation, union
(ille) **leo, -ōnis** lion Cf. leonine
(illa) **iuvenca, -ae** cow
(illa) **capra, -ae** she-goat Cf. caprine
(illa) **praeda, -ae** booty, plunder
capiō, -ere, cēpī, captus take, capture
quattuor four Cf. quartet
aequālis, -e equal
tum deinde then, next, thereupon
dī-vidō, -ere, -vīsī, -vīsus divide
prīmus, -a, -um first Cf. prime
ait = dīcit
(illa) **praestantia, -ae** preeminence, superiority
secundus, -a, -um second
(illud) **rōbur, -ōris** strength Cf. robust
tertius, -a, -um third Cf. tertiary
vindicō, -āre, -āvī, -ātus lay legal claim to as one's own Cf. vindicate
quartus, -a, -um fourth
ar-rogō, -āre, -āvī, -ātus claim as one's own, arrogate
in-imīcus, -a, -um inimical, enemy

5. L. ANNAEUS SENECA

Omnia tempus **edax dēpascitur,** omnia **carpit,**
Omnia **sēde movet, nil sinit** esse **diū.**

edax, -ācis voracious (**edō**)
dē-pascō, -ere, -pāvī, -pastus (also **dē-pascor**) = **edō** Cf. pasture
carpō, -ere, carpsī, carptus pluck, snatch
(illa) **sēdes, -is** seat, foundation
moveō, -ēre, mōvī, mōtus move
nil = nihil
sinō, -ere, sīvī, situs allow
diū for a long time (from adverbial accusative of duration of **diēs**)

Flūmina dēficiunt, profugum mare
lītora siccant,
Subsīdunt montēs et **iuga celsa**
ruunt.
Quid tam parva loquar? **Mōles pul-**
cherrima caelī
Ardēbit flammīs tōta **repentē** suīs.
Omnia mors **poscit.** Lex est, nōn
poena, perīre:
Hīc aliquō **mundus** tempore
nūllus erit.

(illud) flūmen, -minis river, flood
dē-ficiō, -ere, -fēcī, -fectus fail, cease Cf. deficit
profugus, -a, -um fugitive
(illud) mare, -ris, -ium (-um) sea Cf. maritime
(illud) lītus, -toris seashore, beach Cf. litoral
siccō, -āre, -āvī, -ātus dry up Cf. desiccate
sub-sīdō, -ere, -sēdī, -sessus sink down, subside
(ille) mons, montis, -ium mountain
(illud) iugum, -ī yoke, ridge of a mountain
celsus, -a, -um lofty, high Cf. excel
ruō, -ere, -uī, -utus fall down, go to ruin Cf. ruin
quid = cur aut quārē?
tam so (with respect to quantity)
(illa) mōles, -is, -ium shapeless, huge, heavy mass (related to **magnus**)
pulcherrimus, -a, -um most beautiful (**pulcher**)
(illud) caelum, -ī sky, heavens
ardeō, -ēre, arsī, arsus be on fire, burn Cf. ardent
(illa) flamma, -ae flame
repentē suddenly
poscō, -ere, poposcī demand, desire, beg for
per-eō, -īre, -ī(v)ī pass away, Cf. perish
(ille) mundus, -ī world Cf. mundane

V. CHANGE each of the following sentences from present-future potentials (**future-less-vivid**) to simple futures (**future-more-vivid**).

1. Sī tantum glōriae mihi sit quantum tibi et patribus tuīs, vir ēgregius sim.
2. Sī quid vīnī nōbīs fuerit, aliquid aliī dēmus ut nōbīscum bibat.
3. Nisī quam cēnam vōbīscum attuleritis, nihil habeāmus apud mē ut edāmus.
4. Nisī meruerim ut mē bene amēs, īdem nōn sim quem semper cognōveris.

5. Nisī apud eum litterās didicerim, magnā sapientiā dē omnibus rēbus loquī nōn possim.

6. Sī mortem timeant, mēcum nōn veniant ut ducī nostrō vēritātem dē eius amīcīs dīcam.

7. Sī nesciās id quod pro tē fēcī, alius, nōn ego, id tibi dīcat.

8. Nisī cui sē in amōre iunxerint, sōlī moriantur sine ūllō amīcō quī scrībat quid in vītā suā ēgerint aut quantum meritī sint.

9. Sī umquam tē rogāverim num quis mē bene dīxerit, discam quantī ab eō pro meō eī bene factō aestimer.

10. Sī qua avis discat linguā hominum loquī, rex avium fīat.

VI. CHANGE each of the above sentences into **contrary-to-fact conditions.** Be careful to adjust the sequence of tenses where necessary in dependent clauses. Translate each conditional sentence.

VII. CHANGE each of the following temporal clauses (**cum, ubi**) to more generalized **circumstantial clauses of characteristic.** Translate both versions.

1. Cum ad tē cum perīculō vēnerō, tibi dīcam id quod hīs in litterīs dē illō atrōcī duce timēbam scrībere.

2. Cum cēnam et aliquid vīnī tēcum attulerās, bene apud mē cēnāvistī.

3. Cum tē tuīs cum amīcīs vīdērunt, scīvistī quantum tibi esset perīculum.

4. Cum hās litterās meā manū scrīptās ad tē ipse mittēbam, volēbam ā tē discere an aliquī esset tibi amīcus cui crēderem.

5. Cum tālis est quālis sua mater, haec est fēmina quae ab omnibus laudētur.

6. Cum sē in speculō conspicit, videt sē quālem aliī semper sē videant.

7. Id ubi dīxerat, aliquid vīnī bibit.

8. Hōc cum factum erat, bellum cum illīs gerēbant.

9. Cum manum eius tollit, sciunt eam velle aliquid rogāre.

10. Cum tantum meruerō quantum pater meus, eius similis erō.

VIII. CHANGE each of the following sentences into **oratio obliqua** introduced by the phrase in parentheses.

1. Cenābis bene apud mē. (dīcō)

2. Apud hunc philosophum litterās discet. (suō patrī dīxit) **NOTE** the future participle of **discō: discitūrus.**

3. Quaeritur an aliquis vēritātem dē morte sciat. (scrīpsērunt)
4. Vīnum quod tēcum attuleris bibēmus. (dīcō)
5. Virum quem timēbat interficiet. (ad suam fēminam scrībet)
6. Hīc reus furtī damnābitur. (omnēs vīdērunt)
7. Is poēmata scrībere sciet. (dīcit)
8. Dux fiet. (suō amīcō dīxit)
9. Amīcitiā huic sē iungent. (scrīpsērunt)
10. Laudābitur urbs illa quae perdita est. (audiunt)

IX. NOTE THE PATTERN in each of the following sentences and compose a translation of the English sentences using the same pattern.

1. Amīcī vitia sī ferās, faciās tua.

If you should speak, you would be heard.
If you should speak with him, you would learn much.
If he should die, no one would forget him.

2. Sapientis est nihil quod paenitēre possit facere. (paeniteō, -ēre "cause repentence")

(It is characteristic) of a leader to say everything that he wants to say.
It is characteristic of mothers to love every child that is born.

3. Quārē id faciam requiris.

He asks what kind of man the leader is.
They inquire (in) what manner the philosopher died.

4. Hīc aliquō mundus tempore nūllus erit.

In a few days this woman will become our leader.
At that time no one will be alive.

Piranesi, Pantheon, exterior

LESSON NINE

ABLATIVE ABSOLUTE, IMPERATIVE

Caesar, acceptīs litterīs, nuntium mittit.

PARTICIPLE. A participle is a verbal adjective. You have already learned the **perfect passive participle**, which is the fourth principal part of the verb (**vir beātus "a blessed man"**) and the **future active participle** (**vir futūrus "a man who is going to be"**) (see pages 88, 142). You have also learned an adjective like **sapiens, -ientis,** which is actually a **present active participle** of a verb **sapiō, -ere, -īvī,** meaning "to taste, have taste, be sensible."

These are the three participles that Latin has. You will notice that the system is not symmetrical. Latin does not have a **present passive participle** ("a man being loved"), although it does have a form, which you will learn later that functions like a **future passive participle**. Nor does Latin have a **past or perfect active participle** ("a man having loved").

The present active participle is formed by adding **-ns** (**-ntis**) to the verbal stem and it is declined like **sapiens,** an adjective of one termination in declension III.

PARADIGM 23
PRESENT ACTIVE PARTICIPLE

conj I	conj II	conj III	conj III i-stem	conj IV
amāns	docēns	regēns	cupiēns	audiēns
amantis	docentis	regentis	cupientis	audientis

ABLATIVE ABSOLUTE. You have already learned that the ablative can express manner (see page 68) with the preposition **cum**, which is commonly omitted when the noun is modified by an adjective.

Cum perīculō loquitur. **Magnō (cum) perīculō loquitur.**

When a verbal adjective (participle) is used in this way, the phrase similarly expresses the attendant circumstances or situation in which the action of the main verb occurs. This very common structure in Latin is called the **ablative absolute** because the ablative participle appears "absolute" or unrelated to the other words in the main sentence, although actually it is simply modifying an ablative noun of manner. **Cum** is never used in the ablative absolute structure. (The equivalent structure in English is a nominative absolute: "He being dead, I decided to marry again." This is very rare and formal in English and usually the Latin ablative absolute will be translated by a subordinate clause that will specify from the context what is left as a more vague indication of attendant circumstance in the Latin.)

Perīculō negātō loquitur. **"Since (when, if, although, after) the danger was denied, he speaks."**

Illō regente beātus sum. **"Since (while, if, etc.) he is ruling, I was blessed."**

NOTE that in the ablative absolute structure, the present participle (which is declined like a declension III i-stem) always has the singular ending in **-e** instead of **-ī**.

There is no present participle of *sum*. The missing participle, however, can be implied when the two ablatives obviously are in this ablative absolute structure.

Mē duce laudābuntur. — **"When I am leader, they will be praised."**

Since a participle "participates" in the functions of a verb as well as in those of an adjective, an ablative absolute can, of course, consist of more than just the basic two words of the absolute structure, with either the noun modified adjectivally or the participle modified adverbially by adverbs, accusatives, prepositional phrases, dependent clauses, etc.

Virō ēgregiō illam urbem cum amīcīs regente, laudābuntur. — **"With an illustrious man ruling that city with his friends, they will be praised."**

Mē rogātō num mors malum esset, omnēs clāmāvērunt. — **"When I was asked whether death was something bad, everybody shouted."**

IMPERATIVE MOOD. You have already learned to express commands in the mode of the **jussive subjunctive** (see pages 44–45 and 92). There is also a more direct emotive way of commanding the person to whom you are speaking (i.e., the second person only). This is the **imperative mood** (from **imperō, -āre** "command").

The imperative in the active voice is formed by the verbal stem alone for the singular and by the verbal stem plus **-te** for the plural. There is no distinction between conjugation III e-stems and i-stems, and both have **-i-** in the plural (just as they do in the indicative).

Mī fīlī, amā. — **"My son, love."**

Meī fīliī, amāte. — **"My sons, love."**

PARADIGM 24
IMPERATIVE CONJUGATION

	I	II	III	III i-stem	IV
singular	amā	docē	rege	cupe	audī
plural	amā-te	docē-te	regi-te	cupi-te	audī-te

In the passive, the imperative is identical with the indicative second person passive (using the alternative **-re** suffix for the singular, see page 56).

The verbs **ferre** and **esse** have **fer-** and **es-** for their stems (see page 132); hence their imperatives are **fer, fer-te** and **es, es-te.** Three other verbs imitate this "irregular" conjugation in the singular only: **dīc** (dīcere), **dūc** (dūcere), and **fac** (facere).

Negative commands are expressed either by the jussive subjunctive (negated by **nē**, see pages 45 and 92) or by the imperative of **nōlle "be unwilling"**, regularized into a fourth conjugation form.

Nōlī amāre.	**"Don't love." ("Be unwilling to love.")**
Nōlīte amāre.	**"Don't (you-all) love."**

RESULT CLAUSES. You have already seen that the jussive subjunctive when subordinated yielded the **purpose** clause (see page 59), and that the deliberative (jussive) subjunctive when subordinated yielded the **indirect question** (see page 59). Similarly, the potential subjunctive when subordinated into a relative clause yielded the **relative clause of generic characteristic** (see pages 121–22) and *cum* clauses (see page 145). You have also learned to use the subjunctive for **relative clauses in oratio obliqua** (see page 120). Another very common subordinated subjunctive clause, the result clause, is derived from the potential subjunctive.

Stultus est. Poēma longum scrībat.	**"He is stupid. He may write a long poem."**
Tam stultus est ut poēma longum scrībat.	**"He is so stupid that (as a result) he writes a long poem."**

Often the context for such a result clause is established by an adjective (**tantus, tālis, tot "so many"**) or adverb (**tam, ita "so," sīc "thus"**) expressing degree. This same context for a result clause can also be established by certain appropriate verbs.

Fierī potest ut poēma longum scrībat.	**"It is possible (to happen) that he write a long poem."**
Efficimus ut poēma longum scrībat.	**"We bring it about (i.e., make it happen) that he write a long poem."**
Fit ut poēma longum scrībat.	**"It happens that he writes a long poem."**

As with the potential subjunctive, the negative is **nōn** (see page 44). Distinguish between the negative result clause (**ut nōn**) and the negative purpose clause (**nē**).

Vir tantus est ut nōn stulta faciat.	**"He is so great a man that he doesn't do stupid things."**
Id facit nē stultus videātur.	**"He does it in order not to seem stupid."**

Since both the generic clauses of characteristic and the result clauses are really subordinated potentials, it is not surprising that a relative in an appropriate context can introduce subjunctive results.

Nēmō est tam stultus quī poēma longum scrībat.	**"Nobody is so stupid that he writes a long poem."**

As always, the pattern of sequence of tenses is observed (see page 145).

Tam stulta erat ut poēma longum scrīberet.	**"She was so stupid that she wrote a long poem."**
Tam pulchra erat quam omnēs amāvissent.	**"She was so beautiful that everybody loved her."**

ADVERBS. You have already learned several adverbs as indeclinable lexical entries (**umquam, cur, crās, hodiē, herī, dum, autem,** etc.). In addition to such adverbs, many adverbs are regularly formed from related adjectives and do not have to be separately learned. Since the accusative case of a noun (or adjective) is basically adverbial in function, it is not surprising that the neuter singular of many adjectives is often used simply as an adverb.

Multum tē amō.	**"I love you much."**
Tantum tē amābam ut alia nōn esset quācum vellem vīvere.	**"I loved you so much that there wasn't any other with whom I wanted to live."**
Dulce cecinit.	**"She sang sweetly."**

Adverbs can also be formed by replacing the ending of first and second declension adjectives with **-ē**.

Amīcē loquēbāmur.	**"We spoke in a friendly fashion."**

Adjectives of the third declension form adverbs by adding **-ter** to the stem.

Fortiter bellum gessit.	**"He waged war vigorously."**
Sapienter fēcit.	**"He acted wisely."**

Just as the first and second declension adjectives with **-ē** resemble the neuter singular forms of third declension adjective-adverbs (**amīcē, dulce**), the ending **-iter** is sometimes used for first and second declension adjective-adverbs: **amīciter**.

Still other adverbs are identical with ablative singular forms, either neuter or feminine (in agreement with the unexpressed **viā** **"way"**). This is not surprising since you have already learned that the ablative of manner gives precisely this sort of adverbial information with nouns.

Prīmō tē amābat.	**"In the beginning he loved you."**
Multō mālō scrībere.	**"I much prefer to write."**
Rectā ad tē veniet.	**"Directly he will come to you." (rectus, -a, -um "straight," from regō)**

Such easily recognized adverbs will not be glossed in this book.

REMEMBER

Latin has only three participles:

present active: amāns, -antis / docēns, -entis / regēns, -entis cupiēns, -entis / audiēns, -entis

perfect passive: amātus, -a, -um / doctus, -a, -um / rectus, -a, -um cupītus, -a, -um / audītus, -a, -um

future active: amātūrus, -a, -um / doctūrus, -a, -um / rectūrus, -a, -um cupītūrus, -a, -um / audītūrus, -a, -um

INDEX VERBORUM

(illa) anima, -ae	**wind, breath, soul**
(ille) animus, -ī	
(illud) caelum, -ī	**sky, heaven, the heavens**
(illa) cūra, -ae	**care, concern**
(illa) fidēs, -eī	**trust, fidelity**
(illud) foedus, -eris	**treaty**
(illa) mulier, -eris	**woman**
(ille) nuntius, -ī	**messenger**
(illud) opus, -eris	**work, labor, art, workmanship, any result of work / opus est +** ***abl.*** **"there is need of** (In this idiom **opus** means literally **"work, service,"** and the **ablative** functions as instrument.) Example: ***Rege opus est.*** **"There is need of a king, i.e., there is work for (with) him."**
(illa) ratio, -ōnis	**reckoning, account, a business transaction, regard, concern for, understanding, reason**
(illa) via, -ae	**road, way**

quisquam, quidquam	**someone, anyone** (declined like **quis, quid** with the suffix **-quam**). Corresponds to the adjective **ūllus, -a, -um:** used in negative contexts, whereas **aliquis, aliquid** and **aliquī, aliqua, aliquod** are used in positive contexts. Remember that the forms without **ali-** are used after **num, sī, nisī**, and **nē** (see page 146) Example: *Aliquis aliquem rogat num quis cui noceat nē quisquam ūllī hominī odiō sit.* **"Someone asks someone whether someone is hurting someone so that someone not be to any man as an object of hatred."**
cupidus, -a, -um	**longing, desiring, loving, greedy for**
fidēlis, -e	**trusty, faithful**
iūcundus, -a, -um	**agreeable, pleasant, delightful**
perpetuus, -a, -um	**continuous, perpetual**
sincērus, -a, -um	**genuine, sincere**
vērus, -a, -um	**true**
accipiō, -ere, -cēpī, -ceptus	**accept, take possession of, take by perception, take upon one's self**
capiō, -ere, cēpī, captus	**take, seize, capture**
efficiō, -ere, -fēcī, -fectus	**effect, work out**
hortor, -ārī, -ātus	**exhort**
imperō, -āre, -āvī, -ātus	**command**
legō, -ere, lēgī, lectus	**gather, pick out, survey with the eye, read**
licet, licuit, licitum est	**be at liberty, be allowed, be permitted** (3rd person singular only) + *dat.* Example: *Mihi licet amāre.* **"I am allowed to love."/** *Mihi licet ut amem.* **"I am allowed to love."/** *Hōc mihi licet.* **"This is allowed me."**
mālō, mālle, māluī	**prefer** (from *magis volō)* Conjugated like **nōlō** (see pages 132–33) Present indicative: **mālō, māvis, māvult, mālumus, māvultis, mālunt.** Present subjunctive: **mālim,** etc.

persuādeō, -ēre, -suāsī, -uāsus	**persuade +** ***dat.*** Example: ***Eī persuādeō nē veniat.*** **"I persuade him not to come."**
anteā	**before, earlier**
atque (ac)	**and, also**
diū	**for a long time**
ita	**so, in this way, in such a manner**
magis . . . quam	**more . . . than**
saepe	**often**
sīc	**so, thus in such a manner, in this (or that) way**
tam	**so, so much**
tam . . . quam	**as (much) . . . as**
tot	**so many, so great a number**
tot . . . quot	**so many . . . as**

EXERCITATIONES

I. MATCH the second phrase to the first by changing it into the same form. Some items will require more than one answer.

1. muliere fidēlī (hīc nuntius)
2. vultūs iūcundī (aliqua cūra)
3. ratiōnēs difficilēs (via recta)
4. opera ipsa (animus cupidus)
5. līber fidēlis (meus fīlius dīgnus)
6. duce captō (pānis ēsus)
7. foedere effectō (lex perpetua)
8. cuius caelī (imperāns rex)
9. togīs gestīs (fidēs sincēra)
10. reī vērae (nuntius legēns)
11. avis interfectae (quod speculum)
12. grātiīs actīs (cūra satiāta)
13. fortium manuum (nōmen appellātum)
14. tempus perditum (bonus fīlius)
15. invidiae similis (tōta nox)
16. diē veniente (breve tempus)
17. vīnō bibitō (dēformis mors)
18. operis acceptī (nūllus nāsus)
19. quālis fideī (quae timēns)
20. caela sempiterna (opus atrox)

II. MATCH the second verb to the first by changing it into the same form. Some items will require more than one answer.

1. hortārī (efficiō)
2. imperāte (nōlō)
3. legam (persuādeō)
4. licitum erit (capiō)
11. dīxissētis (vīvō)
12. scrībe (faciō)
13. es (ferō)
14. mālumus (oblīviscor)

5. imperāre (hortor)
6. nescientibus (cōgitō)
7. iunctum īrī (veniō)
8. dēbitūram esse (audiō)
9. crēdēbantur (aestimō)
10. interfēcēre (vīvō)
15. conspiciēmus (rogō)
16. noceat (laudō)
17. meminerātis (sum)
18. est (mālō)
19. ferte (beō)
20. fiat (volō)

III. TRANSLATE.

1. Mī amīce, tēcum volō iūcundē loquī. Amīcē loquāmur. Mēcum amīcē loquere. Mihi vidēris pār esse patrī tuō. Semper mihi vīsus es eī pār esse. Tē hortor ut semper īdem sīs. Nōlī quidquam facere quod dissimile eius sit. Is vir erat magnae virtūtis. Tam fortis erat ut ab omnibus laudārētur. Sīc vītam ēgit suam ut nēminī fuisset odiō. Fīēbat ut nōn nūllī eum amārent. Tū sōlus dīgnus es quī eī pār sīs. Es patre tuō dīgnus, tē hortor, amīce. Tam fortis sīs quam ille. Tot amīcōs habē ipse quot ille. Nisī tam fortis essēs quam ille vir magnae virtūtis, nōn dīcerem tē eī parem esse. Nōn imperārem ut similiter ac eōdem modō vīverēs. Fac semper sōlum quae eī placuerint. Tālibus factīs, iūcundē ac amīciter vīverēs. Cum eius similis sīs, iūcundē vīvēs. Tē dīcō sīc vīventem iūcundum futūrum esse. Tē dīcō ab omnibus laudātum īrī. Omnēs dīcō tē laudātūrōs esse. Nōmen tuum nōn moriētur, sed sempiternum erit. Perpetuum tē laudātō, puer dīgne, urbs nostra beāta erit. Perpetuō hanc urbem nostram omnēs, tē duce, laudābunt. Tē hanc urbem dūcente, laudābimur. Nōbīs laudātīs, tam ēgregius noster dux vidēbitur ut patre suō sit dīgnus.

2. Quam tē nēmō est quācum mālim loquī, mea puella. Nūllī mālō placēre quam tibi. Nēminem esse dīcō quam mālim amāre. Tēcum loquēns, tam plēnus fīō amōris ut mē crēdam parem deō esse. Mē tēcum loquente, omnēs invidiae plēnī fiunt. Tēcum locūtus, tam beātus fīō quam deus ipse. Tam pulchra es ut mē tēcum loquentem deum efficiās. Fit ut deus videar fierī cum tēcum loquar. Nēmō tam pulchra est quam tū, mea amāta. Magis tē amō quam vītam meam ipsam. Nisī tē amārem, rectā mallem morī. Sine tē nōn esset mihi vīta. Tē mortuā, nōllem ipse vīvere. Tantus meus tuī amor est ut sine tē nōlim vīvere. Nōnne mālīs morī quam sine mē vīvere? Num mālīs vīvere sine mē quam morī? Nōlī vīvere sine mē. Mēcum iūcundē vīve, puella mea.

IV. TRANSLATE. (Try to guess the meaning of new words on the basis of context and cognates before consulting the adjacent **reading notes.**)

1. CATULLUS 51 (adaptation of a poem by Sappho)

Ille **mī** pār esse deō vidētur,
ille, sī **fas** est, **superāre dīvōs,**
quī **sedēns adversus identidem** tē spectat et audit
dulce **rīdentem**, miserō **quod omnīs**
ēripit sensūs mihi: nam **simul** tē,
Lesbia, **aspexī**, nihil est **super** mī,
Lesbia, **vōcis.**
Lingua sed **torpet, tenuīs** sub **artūs**
flamma dēmānat, gemina teguntur
lūmina nocte.
Ōtium, Catulle, tibi **molestum** est:
ōtiō exultās nimiumque gestis:
ōtium et rēgēs prius et beātās
perdidit urbēs.

mī = mihi
(illud) fas *(indeclinable)* divine law, right, lawful, allowable
superō, -āre, -āvī, -ātus rise above, surpass
dīvus, -a, -um divine **dīvus = deus** Cf. divine
sedeō, -ēre, sēdī, sessus sit Cf. sedate
adversus (adversum) opposite, facing over against + *acc.* Cf. adverse
spectō, -āre, -āvī, -ātus look at Cf. spectator
rīdeō, -ēre, rīsī, rīsus laugh Cf. risible
quod *(the antecedent is the whole previous clause)*
omnīs = omnēs *(see page 38)*
ē-ripiō, -ere, -ipuī, -eptus snatch away Cf. rape
(ille) sensus, -ūs sense, faculty of feeling and perceiving
simul at the same time, as soon as Cf. simultaneous
a-spiciō, -ere, -spexī, -spectus = conspiciō
super above, beyond, in addition
(illa) vox, vōcis voice Cf. vocal **Nihil vōcis** is a partitive genitive phrase.
torpeō, -ēre be sluggish, torpid, dull
tenuis, -e thin, fine Cf. tenuous
(ille) artus, -ūs limb, joint Cf. articulate
(illa) flamma, -ae flame
dē-mānō, -āre, -āvī, -ātus flow down Cf. emanate
geminus, -a, -um twin Cf. the constellation Gemini
tegō, -ere, texī, tectus cover Cf. protect

(illud) lūmen, -minis light, light of life, eye Cf. luminous
molestus, -a, -um troublesome, annoying

2. CATULLUS 70

Nūllī sē dīcit mulier mea **nūbere** mālle
quam mihi, nōn sī sē **Iūppiter** ipse **petat.**
Dīcit: sed mulier cupidō quod dīcit amantī,
in **ventō** et **rapidā** scrībere oportet aquā.

nūbō, -ere, nupsī, nuptus marry, primarily of the bride: to veil herself for the bridegroom + *dat.;* but also of the bridegroom: to marry + *acc.*
(ille) Iūppiter, Iōvis Jupiter
petō, -ere, -ī(v)ī, -ītus attack, demand, seek, require Cf. petition
(ille) ventus, -ī wind Cf. ventilate
rapidus, -a, -um quick, rapid

3. CATULLUS 109

Iūcundum, mea vīta, mihi **prōpōnis** amōrem
hunc nostrum inter nōs perpetuumque **fore.**
Dī magnī, facite ut vērē **prōmittere** possit,
atque id sincērē dīcat et ex animō,
ut liceat nōbīs tōtā **perdūcere** vītā
aeternum hōc **sanctae foedus** amīcitiae.

prō-pōnō, -ere, -posuī, -positus propose
fore = futūrum esse *(from the obsolete fuō, which also supplies the perfect stem fuī)*
prō-mittō, -ere, -mīsī, -missus promise
per-dūcō, -ere, -dūxī, -ductus conduct, draw out, lengthen
aeternus, -a, -um = sempiternus
sanctus, -a, -um holy, saintly
(illud) foedus, -eris treaty

4. CICERO (Letter to Atticus 1.2, adapted)

L. Iūlio Caesāre C. Marciō Figulō **consulibus, fīliolō**

L. = Luciō (*nominative* **Lucius**)
C. = Gaiō (Caiō) (*nominative* **Gaius**)
(ille) consul, -ulis consul, one of the two highest Roman magistrates, chosen annually: hence it was customary to indicate the year by the names of that year's consuls, expressed as an ablative absolute. This was the year 64 BC.
(ille) fīliolus, -ī *diminutive of* **fīlius**

mē **auctum scītō, salvā Terentiā. Abs** tē tam diū nihil litterārum? Ego dē meīs ad tē ratiōnibus scrīpsī anteā **dīligenter.** Hōc tempore **Catilīnam, competītōrem** nostrum, **dēfendere** cōgitāmus; **iūdicēs** habēmus, quōs voluimus, **summā accusātōris**

augeō, -ēre, auxī, auctus increase, augment, furnish (someone *acc.* with something *abl.*)
scītō imperative of **sciō** In addition to the imperatives presented in this lesson, Latin also had a so-called **future imperative**, which is more formal in tone and is usually used only when the futurity or eternal application of the injunction is emphasized. Some verbs, however, have only this future imperative. The endings, added onto the verbal stem, are, for the active: **-tō/ -tōte**; and for the passive: **-tor/** lacking the plural. Examples: **amā-tō** "thou shalt love;" **scī-tōte** "ye shall know;" **rege-tor** "thou shalt be ruled;" etc.
salvus, -a, -um safe, unharmed, well, sound Cf. salvage
(illa) Terentia, -ae Cicero's wife
abs = ab
dīligens, -entis diligent **diligenter** *adverb*
(ille) Catilīna, -ae a Roman young man who attempted to lead an insurrection against the state, here considered as a potential client for Cicero, although eventually the object of his intense hatred when he as consul opposed the threatened coup d'etat.
(ille) competītor, -ōris rival, competitor (Catiline was Cicero's potential rival in the election for the consulship.)
dēfendō, -ere, -dī, -nsus defend
(ille) iūdex, -dicis judge
summus, -a, -um greatest, highest Cf. summit
(ille) accusātor, -ōris accuser, plaintiff (The plaintiff has apparently been bribed.)

voluntāte. Spērō, sī **absolūtus** erit, **coniunctiōrem** illum nōbīs fore in ratiōne **petītiōnis; sīn** aliter **accīderit, hūmāniter** ferēmus. Tuō **adventū** nōbīs opus est **mātūrō**; nam **prorsus** summa hominum est **opīnio** tuōs **familiārēs, nōbilēs** hominēs, **adversāriōs honōrī** nostrō fore: ut eōrum voluntas mihi **conciliētur, maximō** tē mihi **ūsuī** fore videō. Quā rē, **Iānuāriō mense, ut constituistī,**

(illa) **voluntas, -ātis** will, goodwill Cf. voluntary
spērō, -āre, -āvī, -ātus hope Cf. despair
ab-solvō, -ere, -vī, -lūtus absolve, acquit
coniunctior, -ōris more connected
(illa) **petītio, -ōnis** petition, campaign for election to office
sīn = sī-ne if on the contrary, if not
ac-cīdō, -ere, -cīdī fall upon, fall down, happen, occur Cf. accident
hūmānus, -a, -um human
(ille) **adventus, -ūs** arrival Cf. advent
mātūrus, -a, -um ripe, mature, timely, speedy
prorsus straight on, precisely
(illa) **opīnio, -iōnis** opinion
familāris, -e belonging to one's household or family, intimate, political associate. Cicero did not belong to the noble class; Atticus was of lower nobility, but his great wealth and intelligence had won him friends amongst the patricians, who ordinarily would tend to despise Cicero as nouveau riche.
nōbilis, -e noble
adversārius, -a, -um opposed Cf. adversary
(ille) **honor, -ōris** honor, public office
conciliō, -āre, -āvī, -ātus bring together, conciliate
maximus, -a, -um greatest, maximum
(ille) **ūsus, -ūs** use, usefulness (For structure, see double dative, page 69.)
Iānuārius, -a, -um belonging to Iānus, the two-faced god of entrances or January
(ille) **mensis, -is, -ium, (-um)** month
ut + *indicative* as
constituō, -ere, -uī, -ūtus establish, determine, agree upon Cf. constitution

cūrā ut **Rōmae** sīs.

cūrō, -āre, -āvī, -ātus take care
Rōmae at or in Rome

5. CICERO (Letter to his wife, written from exile 14.4)

Ego **minus** saepe dō ad vōs litterās quam possum, **propterеā quod** cum omnia mihi tempora sunt misera, **tum** vērō, cum aut scrībō ad vōs aut vestrās legō, **conficior lācrimīs** sīc, ut ferre nōn possim. **Quod** utinam minus vītae cupidī fuissēmus! **Certē** nihil aut nōn multum in vītā malī vīdissēmus.

minus less Cf. minus
propterеā quod because (**propter**)
tum then (temporal correlative with **cum**)
con-ficiō, -ere, -fēcī, -fectus make, compose, consume
(illa) lācrima, -ae tear (weeping) Cf. lacrimose
quod *(adverbial accusative)* = **quā rē**
certus, -a, -um certain

V. CHANGE each of the following sentences, replacing the subordinate clause with an ablative absolute.

Sī dux vester erō, haec urbs beāta erit.

Mē duce vestrō, haec urbs beāta erit.

Cum ille laudātus esset, nihil mihi invidiae erat.

Illō laudātō, nihil mihi invidiae erat.

Dum apud mē meī amīcī cēnant, rex interfectus est.

Meīs amīcīs apud mē cēnantibus, rex interfectus est.

NOTE that the ablative absolute is less precise than the various dependent clauses.

NOTE also that deponent verbs have present participles in the regular active form; hence: **loquēns, -entis (loquor)**.

1. Cum litterae tuae acceptae essent, rectā et vērā poteram loquī dē omnibus rēbus.

2. Cum fidēs accepta dataque erat, rēs inter rēgem urbemque nostram iūcundae erant.

3. Dum tēcum loquor, persuāsit aliīs ut pecūniam accipere māllent.

4. Dum dux noster servum hortātur ut vērum dīceret, nuntius advēnit quī dīceret urbem herī captam esse.

5. Sī dī favent, hanc rectam vītae viam ad aeternam glōriam nostrae ēgregiae urbis sequēmur.

6. Sī ratiōnēs meae cognitae essent, numquam fēcissēs quae facerēs.

7. Sī deus velit, mī fīlī, vir meī similis sīs.

8. Cum haec facta erant, dīcēbant sē bellum cum illīs gestūrōs esse.

9. Cum ea quae geruntur scīta erunt, nēmō erit quī illī crēdat.

10. Sī laudāta esset, vīta mihi iūcunda vidērētur.

VI. CHANGE each of the following sentences into directly expressed commands, using the imperative mood.

Hortor ut mē amēs.	**Amā mē.**
Vōs imperō nē mē amētis.	**Nōlīte mē amāre.**

1. Hortor ut sincērē dīcātis.

2 . Vōs hortor, fīliī meī, ut semper mihi fidēlēs sītis.

3. Tē imperō ut legere mālīs quam scrībere.

4. Vōs hortor nē mē sequāminī.

5. Tē hortor ut accipiās dēsque fidem.

6. Tē imperō ut rectā et vērā loquāris.

7. Tē hortor, puer dīgne, ut patris similis et eī pār sīs.

8. Tē imperō nē mihi persuādeās ut pecūniam accipiam.

9. Vōs hortor ut illī dēformī fēminae persuādeātis nē in speculō conspiciat.

10. Tē hortor nē quemquam interficiās.

VII. CHANGE each of the following sentences, replacing the ablative absolute with an equivalent dependent clause.

Mē duce, urbs nostra beāta erit.	**Cum dux sim, urbs nostra beāta erit.**

1. Deō volente, rectā ad tē veniam ut tēcum loquar dē hāc rē.

2. Hōc factō, nuntium ad eōs mīsit quī fidem acciperet.

3. Tē hortante ut foedus cum illīs facerem, erant nōn nūllī quī vellent bellum perpetuum gerere.

4. Fidē acceptā datāque, amīcī fidēlēs erimus.

5. Litterīs acceptīs, nuntium ad eōs mitterem quī dīceret mē foedus cum illīs factūrum esse.

6. Semper magnā cum cūrā loquēbar, tē audiente.

7. Hōc scītō, rectā viā dē meīs ad tē ratiōnibus scrīpsī.

8. Lēgibus et foederibus iunctīs, amīciter fidēliterque vītam ēgērunt.

9. Muliere audīre nōlente, nihil dē hāc rē dīcerem.

10. Fortūnā vītam regente, opus sapientibus est quī doceant quid nōs oporteat facere.

VIII. CHANGE each of the following paired sentences so that the second expresses the result of the action expressed in the first.

Tantā cum cūrā vītam ēgit. Numquam sibi perīculum fēcit.	**Tantā cum cūrā vītam ēgit ut numquam sibi perīculum faceret.**

1. Sīc id fēcistī. Cupidus pecūniae nōn vidēbāre.
2. Tam dēformis erat. Omnibus odiō erat.
3. Tot amīcōs habēbat. Nēmō erat quī quidquam malum dē eō dīceret.
4. Fierī potest. Mulierēs dēformēs amantur.
5. Vir tantae sapientiae erat. Nihil erat dē quō dīcere nōn posset.
6. Tam caecus sum. Nihil vidēre possum.
7. Nēmō tam stultus erat. Is morī mālēbat quam vīvere.
8. Tantum, mea puella, tē amō. Mea anima mihi es.
9. Tot opera et tam magna fac, mī fīlī. Meī similis vidēris esse.
10. Tam diū dīxit. Nēmō erat quī eī crēderet.

IX. NOTE THE PATTERN in each of the following sentences and compose a translation of the English sentences using the same pattern.

1. **Dī magnī, facite ut liceat nōbīs perdūcere hōc foedus amīcitiae.**
   My son, make (it happen) that it be allowed to you to be as wise as I.
   My soul, see (to it) that you be permitted to come to me.
2. **Nōn quod quisquam potest, id eī licet.**
   What everybody wants, that's not what is permitted him.
3. **Tuō adventū nōbīs opus est matūrō.**
   I need your great trust.
   We need his wisdom.
   He needed your friendship.

Piranesi, The Arch of Constantine

LESSON TEN

COMPARATIVES, SUPERLATIVES

Exēgī monumentum aere perennius.

DEGREE. The attribute expressed by an adjective or an adverb can be stated in three degrees of intensity: the simple statement of the attribute or **positive** degree ("wise/ wisely"); the **comparative** degree ("wiser/ more wisely"), in which the attribute is more intensely expressed; and the **superlative** degree ("wisest/ most wisely"), in which the attribute surpasses in intensity.

COMPARATIVE DEGREE. The comparative of adjectives is normally formed by adding the suffix **-ior** (**-ius** for neuter) to the adjective's stem (without its final vowel, for declensions I and II); the resulting form is an adjective of declension III.

iūcundus, -a, -um	**iūcundior, -ius (iūcundiōris)**
fortis, -e	**fortior, -ius (fortiōris)**

(Such comparatives are not declension III i-stems, although they may have **-ī**, instead of **-e** in the ablative singular: hence, **iūcundiōrum hominum; fortiōra animālia;** but **fortiōre (-ī) homine.)**

The comparative can also be formed as a compound expression with **magis** (**"more"**).

magis iūcundus, -a, -um

For adverbs, the comparative is simply the accusative neuter singular of the adjective in the comparative degree.

iūcundius	**"more pleasantly"**

SUPERLATIVE DEGREE. Most adjectives form the superlative by adding **-issimus (-a, -um)** to the stem (without the final vowel, for declensions I and II).

iūcundissimus, -a, -um

fortissimus, -a, -um

Six adjectives of the IIIrd declension ending in **-lis (-e)** form the superlative by doubling the **-l-** and adding **-imus (-a, -um)**.

difficilis, -e	**difficillimus, -a, -um**	**"most difficult"**
dissimilis, -e	**dissimillimus, -a, -um**	**"most dissimilar"**
facilis, -e	**facillimus, -a, -um**	**"most easy"**
gracilis, -e	**gracillimus, -a, -um**	**"most graceful"**
humilis, -e	**humillimus, -a, -um**	**"most humble"**
similis, -e	**simillimus, -a, -um**	**"most similar"**

Adjectives of the I-II declension ending in **-er (-era, -um)** form the superlative by doubling the **-r-** and adding **-imus (-a, -um)**.

miser, -era, -erum	**miserrimus, -a, -um**

The superlative can also be formed as a compound with **maximē** (**"most"**).

maximē iūcundus, -a, -um

For adverbs, the superlative is regularly formed from the superlative of the adjective by replacing the endings of the first and second declensions with **-ē** (see page 159).

iūcundissimē	**"most pleasantly"**
difficillimē	**"most difficultly"**
miserrimē	**"most miserably"**

IRREGULAR COMPARISON. As in English, some adjectives and adverbs have irregular forms for the comparative and superlative degrees, often entirely different words (compare: "good, better, best"). These must be learned as new lexical items. A few of the most common are listed below.

bonus, -a, -um	**melior, -ius (-iōris)**	**optimus, -a, -um**
malus, -a, -um	**peior, -ius (-iōris)**	**pessimus, -a, -um**
magnus, -a, -um	**maior, -ius (-iōris)**	**maximus, -a, -um**
parvus, -a, -um	**minor, -us (-ōris)**	**minimus, -a, -um**
multus, -a, -um	**plūs** (a neuter noun in the singular; in the plural, an adjective: **plūrēs, plūra**)	**plūrimus, -a, -um**

These irregular forms yield adverbs of the regular pattern: accusative neuter singular for comparative (**melius**, etc.); **-ē** for superlative (**optimē**, etc.).

Some adverbs, however, have irregular forms:

bene	**melius**	**optimē**
diū	**diūtius**	**diūtissimē**
magnopere (multum)	**magis**	**maximē**
saepe	**saepius**	**saepissimē**

REFERENTS FOR COMPARATIVES. The thing to which something is compared (in the comparative degree) can be indicated by the adverb **quam** (**"than"**), followed by the same case as the thing compared.

Ille maior est poēta quam pater suus.	**"He is a greater poet than his father."**
Dīxit sē maiōrem poētam esse quam patrem.	**"He said that he was a greater poet than his father."**

Such comparisons can also be expressed with the so-called **ablative of comparison**, in which the thing to which something is compared is considered as the starting point (hence ablative) or referent from which we reckon the greater attribute of the other.

Ille maior est poēta patre suō.	**"He is a greater poet, as compared from the reckoning point of his father."**

Dīxit sē maiōrem poētam esse patre suō. — **"He said that he is a greater poet than his father."**

For the superlative degree, the referent for the comparison is expressed as a **partitive genitive** (see page 36).

Ille maximus est poētārum. — **"He is the greatest of poets."**

For both the comparative and superlative degrees, an **instrumental ablative** (see page 68) can express the means or measurement by which one thing is compared to another. This is the so-called **ablative of degree of difference.**

Ille multō est maior poēta patre suō. — **"He is (by) much a greater poet than his father."**

Ille tantō est maximus poētārum. — **"He is (by) so much the greatest of poets."**

SUBJUNCTIVE CLAUSES OF FEARING. The subjunctive can be subordinated with verbs expressing fear. The subjunctive clause represents an exhortation, potential, or wish, but since the main clause expresses some fear that the subject has about the outcome, the implication is that the subjunctive clause may turn out opposite to the expressed possibility. Hence, **ut** introduces what the subject fears may **not** happen, and **nē** introduces what the subject fears **may** happen.

Timeō ut poēma scrībat. — **"I am afraid that he may not write a poem."** (The eventuality, exhortation, or wish is that he write a poem, but since I am expressing some misgiving about that, my fear is that he not write the poem.)

Timeō nē poēma scrībat. — **"I am afraid that he may write a poem."**

As usual, the pattern for sequence of tenses is observed (see page 145).

SUBJUNCTIVE OF INTEGRAL PART (ATTRACTION). Just as dependent clauses in oratio obliqua commonly have their verb in the subjunctive as an indication of subordination unless they are considered not to be an integral part of the quoted material (see page 120), so also are all other dependent clauses within a subjunctive clause expressed in the subjunctive if they form an integral part of the subjunctive clause.

Timeō nē poēma scrībat quod sit malum.	**"I am afraid that he may write a poem that may be bad."**

> REMEMBER
>
> Latin expresses what is compared as an ablative, like English *"different from me."*

INDEX VERBORUM

(illa) cīvitas, -ātis	**citizenship, the body-politic, the state**
(illud) consilium, -ī	**deliberation, counsel, council**
(illud) iter, itineris	**journey, way**
(illa) lībertās, -ātis	**liberty**
(illa) pax, pācis	**peace**
(ille) populus, -ī	**people**
(illa) potestas, -ātis	**political power**
(ille) status, -ūs	**posture, attitude, state, condition**

quīdam, quaedam, quoddam (as pronoun, **quiddam**)	**a certain (one), some(body)** (pronominal declension, see page 80), with -**n**- instead of -**m**- before -**d**-; Example: **quendam, quōrundam**)
commodus, -a, -um	**complete, perfect, of full measure, opportune, commodious, appropriate**
difficilis, -e	**difficult**
dissimilis, -e	**dissimilar**
facilis, -e	**easy**
fīnitimus, -a, -um	**adjoining, neighboring, related**
iustus, -a, -um	**just**
maior, -ōris / maximus, -a, -um	**greater / greatest (maiōrēs, -um adults, forefathers)**
melior, -ōris / optimus, -a, -um	**better / best**
minor, -ōris / minimus, -a, -um	**smaller / smallest**
optimas, -ātis	**belonging to the best or noblest, aristocratic**
paucus, -a, -um	**few**
peior, -ōris/ pessimus, -a, -um	**worse / worst**
plūs (plūrēs, plūra) / plūrimus, -a, -um	**more / most**
pūblicus, -a, -um	**public / (rēs pūblica republic)**

summus, -a, -um		**highest**		
duo, duae, duo		**two**		
		dual declension:		
	accusative	**duōs (duo)**	**duās**	**duo**
	genitive	**duōrum,**	**duārum**	**duōrum**
	dative	**duōbus**	**duābus**	**duōbus**
	ablative	**duōbus**	**duābus**	**duōbus**
trēs, tria		**three**		
		declension:		
	accusative	**trēs (trīs), tria**		
	genitive	**trium**		
	dative	**tribus**		
	ablative	**tribus**		
ūnus, -a, -um		**one** (pronominal declension)		
dē-ligo, -ere, -lēgī, -lectus		**select, choose out**		
eō, īre, ī(v)ī, ītus		**go** (for use, see EXERCITATIO VII)		
sinō, -ere, sīvī, situs		**allow, permit**		
soleō, -ēre, -uī, -itus		**be wont, be accustomed**		
vereor, -ērī, -itus		**fear, be afraid**		
vocō, -āre, -āvī, -ātus		**call, invite, summon, name**		

penes (+ *acc.*)	**in the possession or power of** (often follows its object)
per (+ *acc.*)	**through, through the midst of, throughout, on account of**
igitur	**therefore**
quīn	**but that** (introduces result clause, see pages 158–59, after a negative; Example: ***Nēmō est tam stultus quīn sciat.*** **"No one is so stupid but that he knows this (... so that he not know this)."**

EXERCITATIONES

I. MATCH the second phrase to the first by changing it into the same form. Some items will require more than one answer.

1. statūs maximī (cīvitas iusta)
2. duo ducēs (melior mulier)
3. optimātium foederum (homo dēlectus)
4. caelīs summīs (trēs puellae)
11. cuius imperātī (nūllus status)
12. fīnitimae urbis (optimas fidēs)
13. huic caelō (ūnum consilium)
14. dissimillima itinera (populus atrox)

5. lēgum quārundam (facillima opera)
6. fideī optimae (ūna cūra)
7. rērum pūblicārum (fortior quīdam)
8. tālis avis (dīgnus fīlius)
9. plūrimīs statibus (duae rēs)
10. paucōs poētās (facile opus)
15. pācī commodae (qua lībertās)
16. potestāte quādam (vir volēns)
17. maiōrum nostrōrum (iūcundior diēs)
18. ratiōnēs pessimae (hōc iter)
19. līberī servī (cupidus optimas)
20. puerī pessimī (haec urbs)

II. MATCH the second verb to the first by changing it into the same form. Some items will require more than one answer.

1. verēre (faciō)
2. sinat (volō)
3. dēlectūrōs esse (capiō)
4. vocātum īrī (efficiō)
5. es (legō)
6. dēligī (vocō)
7. imperāre (hortor)
8. cēpissētis (mālō)
9. dīc (ferō)
10. este (vereor)
11. sīverāmus (accipiō)
12. hortābāre (vereor)
13. bibere (cēnō)
14. vēnit (edō)
15. māvīs (nōlō)
16. fers (volō)
17. mīserint (ferō)
18. gesserō (sciō)
19. fīat (vereor)
20. māvultis (dēligō)

III. TRANSLATE.

1. Maximus ego poētārum sum. Multō maior omnibus poēta sum. Multō omnium aliōrum maximus poētārum sum. Melior tē poēta sum. Nam tū pessimus es poētārum. Tantō ego optimus poētārum sum, quantō tū pessimus. Nisī melior essem quam tū, carmina nōn canerem. Plūs carminum scrīpsistī quam ego et longiōra, sed omnia meīs peiōra. Utinam nihil scrīpsissēs. Nūllīs scrīptīs, nēmō esset quī scīret quantō tū pessimus poētārum essēs. Simillimus es patris tuī, stultissime hominum, quem omnēs dīxēre poētam malum esse. Vereor nē tū eius similis sīs. Vereor nē patre tuō dīgnissimus sīs. Tam stultus es ut nēmō quam tū stultior possit esse. Nēmō est tam stultus quīn sciat tē pessimum poētārum esse. Tē igitur hortor nē poēmata scrībās. Cum ā mē tibi persuādeātur nē poēmata scrībās, iūcundius vītam tuam agēs. Sapientior vidēbēre esse. Multō sapientiōrem omnēs dīcent tē esse. Nōn fierī potest quīn omnēs dīcant tē hominem meliōrem esse.

2. Tantō dēformissima illa erat puella, quantō mea pulcherrima. Illā dēformior fierī nōn potest, neque meā pulchrior. Sī sē in speculō saepius conspiceret, scīret quantō esset meā puellā dēformior. Scīret quantō omnium esset dēformissima. Neque eī quidquam sapientiae erat, sed stultissima fēminārum semper vidēbātur esse. Multō stultissimē dīcēbat dē omnibus rēbus. Nihil ratiōnis eī erat, nihil sapientiae. Sed dīxit haec fēmina sē pulchriōrem esse meā puellā, quam plūs

amābam vītā ipsā. Tantum meam amābam, quantum illa mihi odiō erat. Rogō num quis stultior fierī possit. Rogō num qua fēmina umquam stultius dīxerit. Nōn fierī potest quīn illa fēminārum stultissima fuerit. Tam dēformis eius status erat ut plūs vidērētur animal quoddam quam mulier esse. Vultus eius tam dēformis erat ut vererer nē morerer cum eam vidērem. Sī eam rectā in vultū conspicerem, fierī posset ut mē interficeret.

IV. TRANSLATE. (Try to guess the meaning of new words on the basis of context and cognates before consulting the adjacent **reading notes.**)

1. CICERO, Dē Rē Pūblicā

Saepissimē **dispūtāre** solent hominēs, quī sit optimus rērum pūblicārum status. Nam tria sunt genera rērum pūblicārum: cum penes ūnum est omnium summa rērum, rēgem illum vocāmus et **regnum** eius reī pūblicae statum; cum autem est penes dēlectōs, tum illa cīvitas optimātium consiliō regī dicitur; illa autem est cīvitas **populāris**, in quā in populō sunt omnia. Negārī nōn potest quīn sua habeant **singula** commoda. **Cāritāte** nōs capiunt rēgēs, consiliō optimātēs, lībertāte populī. Nūllum tamen est genus illārum rērum pūblicārum, quod nōn habeat iter ad fīnitimum quoddam malum **praeceps** ac **lūbricum.** Regnum iustissimī virī ac sapientissimī saepius in **importūnissimī tyrannī dēlābitur,** paucōrum **administrātio** in **factiōnem opulentōrum immutātur,** populī omnium rērum potestas ad **furōrem multitūdinis licentiam**que **convertitur.** Nūllum igitur eōrum ipsum per sē **sēparātum probō, antepōnō**que singulīs illud quod **conflātum** fuerit ex omnibus.

dis-pūtō, -āre, -āvī, -ātus dispute, discuss
(illud) regnum, -ī kingship
populāris, -e belonging to the people
singulus, -a, -um (usually plural) one to each, separate, single
(illa) cāritas, -ātis costliness, dearness, esteem, affection, love
praeceps, -cipitis headlong, precipitous
lūbricus, -a, -um smooth, slippery Cf. lubricate
importūnus, -a, -um unfit, distressing, savage Cf. importune
(ille) tyrannus, -ī tyrant
dē-lābor, -ī, -lāpsus fall down, slide or fall into Cf. collapse
(illa) administrātio, -iōnis administration
(illa) factio, -iōnis faction
opulentus, -a, -um wealthy, opulent
immutō, -āre, -āvī, -ātus transform, mutate
(ille) furor, -ōris madness, furor
(illa) multitūdo, -inis multitude
(illa) licentia, -ae license (licet)
convertō, -ere, -tī, -rsus turn toward, convert
sē-parō, -āre, -āvī, -ātus separate

probō, -āre, -āvī, -ātus test, examine, approve Cf. probate
ante-pōnō, -ere, -posuī, -positus place before, prefer Cf. position
con-flō, -āre, -āvī, -ātus flow together, conflate

2. HORATIUS (3.30)

Exēgī monumentum aere perennius
rēgālīque **sitū pȳramīdum altius,**
quod nōn **imber edax,** nōn **Aquilo**
impotens
possit **dīruere** aut **innumerābilis**
annōrum series et **fuga** temporum.
Nōn omnis moriar, multaque pars
meī
vītābit Libitīnam.

ex-igō, -ere, -ēgī, -actus drive (**agō**) out, exact, complete
(illud) monumentum, -ī monument
(illud) aes, aeris bronze or other alloyed metals, metal ore (except gold or silver), coinage
perennis, -e lasting through the year(s), perennial, enduring
rēgālis, -e regal
(ille) situs, -ūs site, construction
(illa) pȳramis, -īdis pyramid
altus, -a, -um high Cf. altitude
(ille) imber, -bris rain
edax, -ācis voracious, devouring (**edō**)
impotens, -entis impotent
(ille) Aquilo, -ōnis North Wind
dī-ruō, -ere, -ruī, -ūtus tear asunder, demolish, destroy
innumerābilis, -e innumerable
(ille) annus, -ī year Cf. annual
(illa) series, (-is, not attested) series
(illa) fuga, -ae flight, running away Cf. fugitive
vītō, -āre, -āvī, -ātus avoid, escape
(illa) Libitīna, -ae Goddess of corpses

3. CORNELIUS NEPOS 24 (Life of Cato)

In omnibus rēbus **singulārī** fuit **industriā**: nam **agricola sollers** et **perītus iūris consultus** et magnus **imperātor** et **probābilis ōrātor** et **cupidissimus** litterārum fuit. Quārum **studium etsī senior arripuerat**, tamen tantum **prōgressum** fēcit, ut nōn facile **reperīrī** possit neque dē Graecīs neque dē Ītalicīs rēbus quod eī fuerit **incognitum**. Ab **adulescentiā confēcit ōrātiōnēs. Senex historiās** scrībere **instituit.**

singulāris, -e singular, alone of its kind
(illa) **industria, -ae** industry, diligence (for structure, see pg. 67)
(ille) **agricola, -ae** farmer, husbandman, agriculturalist
sollers, -ertis skilled
perītus, -a, -um experienced
(illud) **iūs, iūris** law Cf. jury
(ille) **consultus, -ī** lawyer = **iūrisconsultus, -ī**
(ille) **imperātor, -ōris** general, commander Cf. emperor
probābilis, -e credible, believed, probable, good
(ille) **ōrātor, -ōris** orator
cupidus, -a, -um desirous of
(illud) **studium, -ī** study, application to something, inclination, devotion
etsī although, albeit (**et + sī**)
senior, senius (seniōris) older Cf. senior
ar-ripiō, -ere, -ripuī, -reptus lay hold of, take to one's self
(ille) **prōgressus, -ūs** progress
re-periō, -īre, -pperī, -pertus find, discover
incognitus, -a, -um unknown
(illa) **adulescentia, -ae** adolescence, the age from 15 to 30
con-ficiō, -ere, -fēcī, -fectus make, compose Cf. confection
(illa) **ōrātio, -ōnis** oration
senex, senis old Cf. senile
(illa) **historia, -ae** history
instituō, -ere, -uī, -ūtus institute, undertake

4. CATULLUS (49)

Disertissime Rōmulī nepōtum,
quot sunt quotque fuēre, **Marce Tullī,**
quotque **post** aliīs erunt in annīs,
grātiās tibi maximās Catullus
agit pessimus omnium poēta,
tantō pessimus omnium poēta,
quantō tū optimus omnium **patrōnus.**

disertus, -a, -um eloquent, fluent Cf. dissertation
(ille) **Rōmulus, -ī** mythical founder and first king of Rome
(ille aut illa) nepos, -ōtis descendant, nephew
Marcus Tullius (Cicero)
post afterwards
(ille) **patrōnus, -ī** patron, advocate, lawyer

5. PHAEDRUS (1.13)

Cum dē **fenestrā corvus raptum cāseum**
comēsse vellet, **celsā resīdēns** arbore
vulpes hunc vīdit, **deinde** sīc **coepit** loquī:
"Ō quī tuārum, corve, **pennārum** est **nitor**!
Quantum **decōris** corpore et vultū geris!
Sī **vōcem** habērēs, nūlla **prior āles foret.**"
At ille stultus, dum vult vōcem **ostendere,**

(illa) **fenestra, -ae** window
(ille) **corvus, -ī** raven
rapiō, -ere, -puī, -ptus snatch, steal Cf. rape
(ille) **cāseus, -ī** cheese
com-edō, -ere (-ēsse), -ēdī, -ēsus eat up (for form, see pg. 147)
celsus, -a, -um high Cf. excel, excellence
re-sīdō, -ere, -sēdī sit down Cf. reside
(illa) **vulpes, -is** fox
deinde thereupon, then
coepit (incipiō, -ere, -coepī, -ceptus)
(illa) **penna, -ae** feather Cf. pinnate, pen
(ille) **nitor, -ōris** splendor, lustre, sheen, beauty
(illud) decus, -cōris grace, splendor, decorum
(illa) **vox, vōcis** voice Cf. vocal
prior, -ius (-ōris) prior, better, superior
āles, -litis winged **(illa) āles = avis**
foret = futūra esset (for form, see pg. 165)
at = sed (at-que)
ostendō, -ere, -dī, -nsus display Cf. ostentation

ēmīsit ōre cāseum, quem **celeriter dolōsa** vulpes **avidīs** rapuit **dentibus.** Tum **dēmum ingemuit** corvī **dēceptus stupor.**

ē-mittō, -ere, -mīsī, -missus send forth
(illud) ōs, ōris mouth Cf. oral
celer, -eris, -ere swift **celeriter** *adverb*
dolōsus, -a, -um crafty
avidus, -a, -um avid, eager, greedy
(ille) dens, dentis tooth Cf. dental
dēmum at last, not until then
in-gemō, -ere, -uī groan, lament, bewail
dē-cipiō, -ere, -cēpī, -ceptus deceive, beguile Cf. deception
(ille) stupor, -ōris numbness, dulness, stupidity Cf. stupor

6. CICERO (Dē Inventiōnibus)

In itinere quīdam proficiscentem ad **mercātum** quendam et sēcum **aliquantum nummōrum** ferentem **est comitātus.** Cum hōc, **ut ferē** fit, in viā **sermōnem contulit**; ex quō factum est, ut illud iter **familiārius** facere vellent. Quā rē cum in eandem **tabernam dīvertissent, simul** cēnāre et in eōdem **locō somnum** capere voluērunt. Cēnātī **discubuērunt ibīdem. Caupo** autem (nam **ita**

(ille) mercātus, -ūs marketplace Cf. merchant
aliquantus, -a, -um some, considerable, not a little (Cf. **ali-quis**)
(ille) nummus, -ī coinage, money Cf. numismatics
comitor, -ārī, -ātus join one's self to another as an attendant, accompany Cf. count
ut + *indicative* as
ferē usually, generally
(ille) sermo, -ōnis conversation Cf. sermon
con-ferō, -ferre, -tulī, -llātus unite, join Cf. collate
familiāris, -e familiar, intimate
(illa) taberna, -ae inn Cf. tavern
dī-vertō, -ere, -tī, -sus turn out of the way, divert
simul together Cf. simultaneous
(ille) locus, -ī place Cf. local
(ille) somnus, -ī sleep Cf. somnulant
dis-cumbō, -ere, -cubuī, -cubitus recline at table to eat, lie down to sleep
ibī-dem in the same place
(ille) caupo, -ōnis innkeeper
ita thus

dīcitur **post inventum**, cum in aliō **maleficiō dēprehensus est**) cum illum **alterum, vidēlicet** quī nummōs habēret, animum **advertisset, noctū postquam** illōs **artius** iam, ut fit, ex **lassitūdine dormīre sensit, accessit** et alterīus eōrum, quī sine nummīs erat, gladium **propter appositum** ē **vāgīnā** ēdūxit et illum alterum **occidit,** nummōs **abstulit,** gladium **cruentum** in vāgīnam **recondidit,** ipse sē in suum **lectum recēpit.** Ille autem, cuius gladiō **occīsio** erat facta, multō ante **lūcem surrexit,**

post + *acc* after
in-veniō, -īre, -vēnī, -ventus discover Cf. invent
(illud) maleficium, -ī crime Cf. **malē faciō**
dē-prehendō, -ere, -dī, -nsus apprehend
alter, -tera, -terum other, another (pronominal declension)
vidēlicet clearly, it is allowed to see (contracted from **vidēre licet**)
ad-vertō, -ere, -tī, -rsus turn toward
animum advertere + *acc* notice
noctū in the night (**nox**)
postquam after (subordinating conjunction)
artus, -a, -um close **artius** firmly, soundly (comparative adverb)
(illa) lassitūdo, -inis fatigue Cf. lassitude
dormiō, -īre, -ī(v)ī, -ītus sleep Cf. dormitory
sentiō, -īre, -nsī, -nsus perceive, sense
ac-cēdō, -ere, -cessī, -cessus approach, go near Cf. accede
propter nearby
ap-pōnō, -ere, -posuī, -positus place near
(illa) vāgīna, -ae sheath
occīdō, -ere, -cīdī, -cīsus strike to the ground, kill
af-ferō, -ferre, abs-tulī, al-lātus bear away, steal
cruentus, -a, -um bloody, stained with blood
re-condō, -ere, -didī, -ditus put back, hide Cf. recondite
(ille) lectus, -ī bed
re-cipiō, -ere, -cēpī, -ceptus take back **sē recipere** betake one's self
(illa) occīsio, -ōnis murder
(illa) lux, lūcis light, daylight Cf. lucid

comitem illum suum **inclāmāvit semel** et saepius. Illum somnō **impedītum** nōn **rēspondēre existimāvit**; ipse gladium et cetera, quae sēcum attulerat **sustulit,** sōlus profectus est. Caupo nōn multō post **conclāmat** hominem esse occīsum et cum quibusdam **dīversōribus** illum, quī ante **exīerat,** consequitur in itinere. Hominem **comprehendit,** gladium eius ē vāgīnā ēdūcit, **reperit** cruentum. Homo in urbem ab illīs **dēdūcitur** ac reus fit.

surgō, -ere, surrexī, surrectus arise, get up Cf. insurrection
(ille aut illa) comes, -mitis companion Cf. committee
in-clāmō, -āre, -āvī, -ātus call upon, cry out to Cf. exclaim, acclamation
semel once, a single time
impediō, -īre, -ī(v)ī, -ītus hinder, impede
rē-spondeō, -ēre, -dī, -nsus respond
existimō, -āre, -āvī, -ātus think
suf-ferō, -ferre, sustulī, sublātus take upon one's self
con-clāmō, -āre, -āvī, -ātus call together, cry out loudly
(ille) dī-versor, -ōris guest at an inn
ex-eō, -īre, ī(v)ī, -ītus go away Cf. exit
com-prehendō, -ere, -dī, -nsus catch hold of something on all sides Cf. comprehend
re-periō, -īre, repperī, repertus find out, discover
dē-dūcō, -ere, -dūxī, -ductus bring or lead away Cf. deduce

V. **CHANGE** each of the following sentences, replacing the comparative phrases with **quam** with equivalent phrases of comparison with the ablative structure.

NOTE that **quam** can also be a relative pronoun or adjective. **Quam** can also be used with a superlative as an intensifying adverb: **quam saepissimē** "as often as possible;" **quam maximus** "as great as possible." **Quam** can also introduce indirect questions: **Sciō quam timidus sīs.** "I know how timid you are."

1. Tē, mea amātissima puella, quam omnēs quam maximē laudant, semper dīcam pulchriōrem esse quam illam quam stultissimam fēminam.

2. Nisī quam puellam quam tē meliōrem amārem, meus tuī amor quam maximus semper esset.

3. Aliquis forsitan quaerat num qua sit mulier quam vir quīdam, cuius nōmen nōn mē oportet dīcere, umquam amāverit quīn peior ab eō facta sit quam omnēs fēminae et caeca ad omnia sua vitia.

4. Sī tam sapiens esset quam pulchra, plūs pecūniae habēret neque tam saepe

vidērētur nescīre quō modō sē oporteat vītam suam agere, sed, ut vērē dīcam, numquam vīdī fēminam stultiōrem quam eam.

5. Nisī quid sapientiae sibi esset, peior quam pater suus esset, quī, ut scīs, vir erat iūcundus, sed numquam cognōvī quemquam stultiōrem quam eum.

6. Vereor nē qua sit mulier sapientior quam tē aut minus virtūtis cupida. Nam tē volō semper omnium sapientissimam vidērī et quam optimam fēminam, quam nōn possit fierī quīn aliae laudent.

7. Tē, mī quam dīgnissime fīlī, hortor nē quem sinās umquam meliōrem vidērī quam tē ipsum neque minus vitiōrum cupidum.

8. Hōc, quod tibi summae cūrae sit, tē hortor nē quam hominēs dīcant meliōrem quam tē aut fīliam tuam fuisse.

9. Sī quis quam amet, eam velit plūris aestimārī quam aliās et fēminam quam optimam vidērī.

10. Quaesītum est num quid sit peius quam mors.

VI. CHANGE each of the following statements of potential events into a statement of a fear that the event occur, using the verb in parentheses.

Poēma scrībat. (Timeō)	**"He may write a poem."**
Timeō nē poēma scrībat.	**"I am afraid that he may write a poem."**

1. Aliquis tē pulchrior sit. (Vereor)

2. Nōn fierī possit quīn plūris aestimētur patre eius. (Timeō)

3. In itinere quōdam aliquis quendam ad urbem quandam proficiscentem et cum eō aliquid pecūniae ferentem interficiat. (Verēmur)

4. Aliquae aliquā stultior sit aut minus pecūniae habeat. (Timēbat)

5. Illud genus rērum pūblicārum hōc peius sit. (Verēbātur)

6. Nōn quaerās num quis sit homo fidēlior eō aut tam fortis. (Timēbam)

7. Nōn dēligam ducem omnium optimum quī hanc cīvitātem in pāce regat. (Verēbar)

8. In potestāte rēgis tam atrōcis sīmus ut morī mālīmus quam diūtius in hāc cīvitāte vīvere. (Timēbāmus)

9. Nōn videātur sapientior hōc homine esse. (Hōc mihi summae cūrae erat)

10. Aliquibuscum aliquis dē rēbus quibusdam soleat loquī. (Hōc eī summae cūrae erat)

VII. CHANGE each of the following sentences into a dependent clause introduced by the phrase in parentheses. You will have to distinguish between the various structures required by the different types of introductory phrases.

NOTE that the verb **eō, īre, ī(v)ī, ītus** has an "irregular" conjugation (see pages 132–33). The stem of **eō** is **ei-** (**-i-** here is the consonant **-j-**) and like the other irregular verbs, the personal suffixes are added directly onto the stem without a connecting vowel. However, in certain situations, the **-j-**, which cannot be pronounced before another consonant, will shift to the vocalic **-i-**, and the initial **e-** was lost. When the **-j-** fell before a vowel, however, it was lost. The chart summarizes the conjugation.

PARADIGIM 25
Conjugation of *eō*

pres indic	*pres subj*	*imprf indic*	*imprf subj*	*future*	*present participle*
eō	eam	ībam	īrem	ībō	iēns, euntis
īs	eās	ībās	īrēs	ībis	*Other forms are*
it	eat	ībat	īret	ībit	*predictable from the*
īmus	eāmus	ībāmus	īrēmus	ībimus	*principal parts*
ītis	eātis	ībātis	īrētis	ībitis	*eō, īre, ī(v)ī, ītus*
eunt	eant	ībant	īrent	ībunt	

NOTE that the passive infinitive is used to form the future passive infinitive: **amātum īrī.**

NOTE that **eō** is often compounded: **ex-eō, ab-eō**, etc.

1. Quam saepissimē, mī fīlī amātissime, ad tē ībō. (Nōn fierī potest quīn)

2. Is tē amābit plūs quam vītam suam. (Dīxit)

3. Ex urbe ad tē exībāmus ut tē ad cēnam vocārēmus. (Ā nōbīs quaesīvit an)

4. Aliquis ad tē eat quī dīcat mē plūris aestimātum īrī ab homine quōdam quam tē. (Vereor)

5. Nēmō est eō fortior. (Tam fortis est ut)

6. Optimātēs penes, deō volente, cīvitātis potestātem oportet esse. (Rogābat an)

7. Alicui hōc summae cūrae est, nē quem dēligās eō peiōrem. (Rogō num)

8. Solēs cum eīsdem quam diūtissimē loquī. (Hortor ut)

9. Nōn est quisquam eō deformior. (Audīverat)

10. Ad eam adībō quae mihi vidētur quam illa pulchrior esse. (Dīxī)

VIII. NOTE THE PATTERN in each of the following sentences and compose a translation of the English sentences using the the same pattern.

1. **Exēgī monumentum aere perennius.**
   Somebody saw a woman more splendid than you.
   This is more difficult than that.

2. **Sī vōcem habērēs, nūlla prior āles foret.**
   If you had sent a letter to me, I would have received it from your servant.
   If you were as just as I, there would be no one so stupid but that he choose either you or me.

Piranesi, The Temple of Saturn

LESSON ELEVEN

GERUND, GERUNDIVE, SUPINE

Intellexī tē summā cupiditāte adfectum esse videndī meī.

VERBAL NOUNS. You have already learned that the infinitive (which is the form of the verb without limitation of personal suffix) can be used like a noun that is neuter in gender, and that although it cannot be declined, it can function as a nominative-accusative case as subject or object of a conjugated verb (see pages 7–8). You have also learned that certain nouns are related to verbal stems and name the action of that verbal idea; example: **(ille) amor, -ōris/ amō, -āre, -āvī, -ātus** (see page 37).

There are also two regularly formed verbal nouns in Latin that are common only in certain relatively rare grammatical structures. These verbal nouns are the **gerund** and the **supine**.

GERUND. The gerund is like the English verbal noun ending in **-ing** (example: loving). It occurs only in the singular oblique cases; it has no nominative, for which case, the infinitive is used.

The gerund is formed by adding **-nd-** to the present verbal stem. It is a neuter noun of declension II.

PARADIGM 26
GERUND

	conj I	*conj II*	*conj III*	*conj III i-stem*	*conj IV*
acc	ama**ndum**	doce**ndum**	rege**ndum**	incipie**ndum**	audie**ndum**
gen	ama**ndī**	doce**ndī**	rege**ndī**	incipie**ndī**	audie**ndī**
dat	ama**ndō**	doce**ndō**	rege**ndō**	incipie**ndō**	audie**ndō**
abl	ama**ndō**	doce**ndō**	rege**ndō**	incipie**ndō**	audie**ndō**

NOTE that the vowel of the declensional stem is **never long**, and that conjugation III i-stems and conjugation IV have **-ie-** before the gerund ending.

Since the gerund, like the participle, is a verbal form, it too can take various types of adverbal modification.

The following are typical gerund structures:

Ille cupidus est vīvendī. — **"He is desirous of living."**

Ille cupidus est bene vīvendī. — **"He is desirous of living well."**

Dīcendī grātiā vēnit. — **"He came for the sake of speaking."** **NOTE** that a phrase like this can be used to express purpose and is equivalent to a subjunctive purpose clause: **ut dīceret vēnit.**

Ad dīcendum vēnit. — **"He came to(ward) speak(ing)."** This too is equivalent to an expression of purpose.

Mē vocās ad scrībendum. — **"You summon me to write."**

Loquendō docet. — **"He teaches by speaking." (ablative)**

Diem dīxit loquendō. — **"He set the day for speaking." (dative)**

SUPINE. The supine is a masculine noun of declension IV. It is identical, except for its declension, to the fourth principal part of the verb (masculine past passive participle): participle **amātus, -ī/** supine **(ille) amātus, -ūs**. It occurs only in the accusative singular and the ablative singular.

PARADIGM 27
SUPINE

	conj I	*conj II*	*conj III*	*conj III i-stem*	*conj IV*
acc	amātum	doctum	rectum	inceptum	audītum
abl	amātū	doctū	rectū	inceptū	audītū

The supine is used in only two structures and hence is quite rare. Since it is a verbal form, it can be modified adverbially, although it is more common alone. It is common with the verb **eō**, and the accusative case in such contexts signifies the goal of the motion, never, however, clarified by the preposition **ad**. (The English infinitive is actually a derivation from the Latin supine: hence its use with the preposition "to" to express purpose.)

Dictum vēnit. — **"He came to speak."**

Locūtum it. — **"He goes to speak."**

Servum ad tē mīsī litterās rogātum. — **"I sent a servant to you to ask for a letter."**

NOTE that the supine with the passive infinitive of **eō** forms the future passive infinitive: **amātum īrī** "to be going to be loved , i.e., to be gone (or begone) toward love" (see page 142).

Eam dīxit amātum īrī. — **"He said that she was going to be loved."**

The ablative of the supine is common for only a few verbs and only in contexts with certain words. The ablative function is basically comitative (see pages 67–68) and expresses with what respect the statement is made.

Id difficile est dictū. — **"It is difficult to say, i.e., with respect to saying."**

Opus est vīsū. — **"There is need to see."**

Ea iūcunda est audītū. — **"She is pleasant to hear."**

GERUNDIVE. The gerundive is identical in form to the gerund, except that it is a participle or verbal adjective and hence has a full range of declensional forms, in all the cases and genders, both singular and plural. It is declined like adjectives such as **magnus, -a, -um.** It, however, has a different meaning from that of the gerund. The gerundive describes a future passive obligation or necessity, and hence it sometimes is called the **future passive participle.**

amandus, -a, -um	**"going to have to be loved, to be loved in the future as an obligation."**

This is the Latin form that gives us such words in English as **agenda** ("things to be done"), **addenda** ("things that have to be added"), and **memorandum** ("something to remember").

Carthāgo dēlenda est.	**"Carthage is going to have to be destroyed."** This is equivalent to other expressions of obligation such as: **Carthāginem oportet dēlērī**; or **Carthāgo dēlērī dēbet.**
Ille laudandus est.	**"He must be praised, is going to have to be praised, ought to be praised."**

When a gerund would normally have an accusative direct object, the gerundive instead is commonly (although not always) used.

Ille cupidus est vītae vīvendae.	**"He is desirous of life to be lived."** Compare: **Ille est cupidus vītam vīvendī.**
Vēritātis dīcendae grātiā vēnit.	**"He came for the sake of truth that had to be said."** Compare: **Vēritātem dīcendī grātiā vēnit.**
Ad multa dīcenda vēnit.	**"He came toward many things that had to be said, i.e., to say many things."**
Cupidus es meī videndī.	**"You are desirous of me who must be seen, i.e., of seeing me."**
Diem dīxit multīs loquendīs.	**"He set the day for many things that were going to have to be said."**

Although the gerundive in these expressions is future and passive, English would not normally express such ideas in this form, and a good translation would not usually imitate the Latin grammatical structure.

SUBJUNCTIVE CLAUSES. Grammarians often classify several more types of dependent subjunctive uses than you have learned. These additional types, however, are not really different from the basic uses that you already know, and the expected structures with particular introductory verbs are listed in most lexica. There is no need to learn these as new material. For example, the so-called **clauses of prevention** are nothing but negative result clauses introduced by certain (but not all) verbs expressing the idea of prohibition.

Mē dēterret quōminus dīcam. — **"He deters me from speaking, i.e., he deters me, whereby (quō) less (minus) as a result do I speak."** But a similar idea with a different verb might take an infinitive phrase as completion: **Mē prohibet dīcere. "He probits me from speaking."**

The so-called **clauses of proviso** are simply conjoined jussive subjunctives.

Vīvat dum taceat. — **"Let him live provided he keep silent, i.e., let him live, (the) while let him keep silent."**

The use of the subjunctive in certain **temporal clauses** is simply a natural development of the potential subjunctive.

Priusquam dīcerem, discessit. — **"Before I could speak, he went away."** Compare: **Priusquam dīxī, discessit. "Before I spoke, he went away."**

It is best to become familiar with such structures by using a lexicon as you read, since the particular introductory adverbs and the idiomatic uses will be given in the lexicon and often are even clear from the context alone.

IDIOMATIC EXPRESSIONS OF PLACE. With certain words, the ablative idea of place from which and the accusative idea of the goal or place toward which and the locative (dat.-abl.) idea of place in which are idiomatically expressed without the clarification of a preposition (**ab, ex/ ad/ in**). This is the idiomatic structure for the names of towns, small islands, and with the words **domus** ("home") and **rūs** ("country, as opposed to the city"). In this structure, an actual **locative case** (instead of ablative) is preserved. The locative for the singular of declensions I and II has the same form as the genitive; in the plural, it is identical to the ablative. For declension III, the locative is identical to either the dative or the ablative. There are no nouns of declensions IV and V for which this idiomatic structure occurs. The omission of the clarifying preposition is analogous to the English usage with **home**: e.g., I am going home.

Rōmā profectus est.	**"He set out from Rome."**
Domō abīit.	**"He left home."**
Rūre vēnit.	**"He came from the country."**
Athēnās vēnit.	**"He came to Athens."**
Domum īit.	**"He went home."**
Rūs ībit.	**"He will go to the country."**
Rōmae est.	**"He is in Rome."**
Domī est.	**"He is at home."**
Rūrī est.	**"He is in the country."**
Carthāginī est.	**"He is in Carthage."**
Athēnīs vēnit, nam Athēnīs vīvit.	**"He came from Athens, since he lives in Athens."**

REMEMBER

The supine is a fourth declension masculine noun and has only two cases, accusative and ablative singular (identical in form with the perfect passive participle).

The gerund is a second declension neuter noun and has only singular oblique cases.

The gerundive is an adjective of the first and second declensions and has all the cases, singular and plural, masculine, feminine, and neuter: it describes the action as a future obligation, and hence is sometimes called the 'future passive participle.'

INDEX VERBORUM

(illa) auris, -is (-ium)	**ear**
(illud) lūmen, -minis	**light, lamp, torch**
(illa) mens, -ntis	**the mind**
(ille) metus, -ūs	**fear, dread**
(ille) oculus, -ī	**eye**
(illud) rūs, rūris	**country** (as opposed to the city)
(ille) stilus, -ī	**stylus** (for writing on waxen tablets), **pen**
(illa) tenebra, -ae (usually plural)	**darkness, darkness of the underworld**

iste, ista, istud	**that (person or thing) near you (in place or thought), that of yours, that particular one** (pronominal declension, see page 80)
nesciō quis, nesciō quid	**I know not who/ what, someone, something** Examples: ***Hīc nesciō quis loquitur.*** **"This somebody or other is speaking."** ***Istam nescio quam sapientiam laudant.*** **"That wisdom of yours, whatever it is, they praise."** The phrase is treated like an indefinite pronoun, with **nesciō** immutable and the interrogative **quis / quid** declined, but not used to introduce an indirect question with the subjunctive. So also with other interrogatives: **Ille nesciō quō modō vīvit. "He lives by I don't know what means."** Compare: ***Nesciō quō modō ille vīvat.*** **"I don't know how he lives."**
quisque, quaeque, quodque/ quisque, quidque	**every(one)** (pronominal declension, see page 80, with **-que** immutable: **cuiusque,** etc.; generally does not stand first in a clause) Example: ***Suās quisque abeunt domōs*** . **"They go away, everyone to his own home. "**
bellus, -a, -um	**pretty, handsome, charming**
infāmis, -e	**ill spoken of, disreputable**
senex, senis	**old, aged**
ap-pellō, -ere, -pulī, -pulsus	**drive toward, direct toward**
arbitror, -ārī, -ātus	**give judgment, consider as, believe, think, suppose**
dē-leō, -ēre, -lēvī, -lētus	**delete, destroy, terminate**
dis-cēdō, -ere, -cessī, -cessus	**depart, go away**
dē-terreō, -ēre, -uī, -itus	**deter, frighten from**
fore	future infinitive of esse (= **futūrum esse**)
intellegō, -ere, -lexī, -lectus	**perceive, understand, know**
libet, libuit, libitum	**(it) is pleasing** Example: ***Id mihi libet.*** **"That pleases me, or I like that."**

moveō, -ēre, mōvī, mōtus	**move, set in motion, disturb**
red-eō, -īre, -iī, -ītus	**return** (compound of **eō**)
prohibeō, -ēre, -buī, -bitus	**prohibit**
taceō, -ēre, -cuī, -citus	**be silent, keep silent**

donec	**while, until, as long as** (+ ***indicative,*** for a factual occurrence, but ***subjunctive,*** for an intended occurrence, i.e., a purpose clause) Examples: ***Tacēbat donec dīcēbam.*** **"He was silent as long as I was speaking."** ***Tacēbat donec dīcerem.*** **"He was silent until I might say something."**
dummodo	**provided, as long as** (+ ***subjunctive,*** like **dum** in a clause of proviso, see page 193)
mox	**soon**
postquam (posteāquam)	**after** (+ ***indicative,*** because obviously always a factual occurrence) Example: ***Postquam dīxeram, tacēbat.*** **"After I had spoken, he kept silent."**
priusquam	**before** (+ ***indicative,*** for a factual occurrence, but + ***subjunctive*** for an intended occurrence) Examples: ***Priusquam dīxī, tacēbat.*** **"Before I spoke, he was silent."** ***Priusquam dīcerem, abīit.*** **"Before I might speak, he went away."** The comparative adverb **prius** can be separated from **quam:** ***Prius abīit quam dīcerem.***
quia	**because** (+ ***indicative,*** for factual occurrence, but + ***subjunctive*** for a potential occurrence) Examples: ***Tacēbam quia dīcēbās.*** **"I was silent because you were speaking."** ***Tacēbam quia dīcerēs.*** **"I was silent because (supposedly) you were speaking."**
quōminus (quō minus)	**whereby the less, from** (+ ***subjunctive,*** see page 193)
rursus (rursum)	**again, on the other hand**

EXERCITATIONES

I. MATCH the second phrase to the first by changing it into the same form.

1. urbis dēlendae (senex infāmis)
2. commodīs ratiōnibus (rēs pūblica)
3. intellegentī cuidam (haec pax)
4. itinera quaeque (ista potestas)
5. mentī timendae (sapiens nesciō quis)
6. vir docte (meus amātus fīlius)
7. bellō prohibitō (auris maior)
8. istīus metūs (aliquod rūs)
9. lūmen acceptum (arbitrāns senex)
10. tenebrārum infāmium (duo stilī)
11. illīus reī (ūnus quīdam)
12. statūs optimī (minus perīculum)
13. tōtīus itineris (aliqua mens)
14. nūllī metuī (vīnum bibendum)
15. longiōrem nāsum (manus iuncta)
16. oculī bellī (lūmen tollendum)
17. tenebrae adeuntēs (pānis bonus)
18. sāl candidus (nesciēns homo)
19. lēgibus tacendīs (hōc lūmen)
20. dōnō meritō (ūna auris)

II. MATCH the second verb to the first by changing it into the same form. Some items will require more than one answer.

1. prohibitum īrī (intellegō)
2. vīvendī (dēterreō)
3. fore (edō)
4. movēte (sum)
5. mōverint (proficiscor)
6. es (discēdō)
7. taceās (nōlō)
8. sequere (arbitror)
9. redeant (discēdō)
10. mōvēre (redeō)
11. adībō (agō)
12. vocandum (timeō)
13. vīsū (dīcō)
14. movērēminī (appellō)
15. audītum (loquor)
16. discēdente (scrībō)
17. sīvērunt (vereor)
18. dēlētūrōs esse (sum)
19. vēnerāmus (cēnō)
20. māvultis (eō)

III. TRANSLATE.

1. Mē appellat ad scrībendum. Ad librōs scrībendōs vir magnae sapientiae mē vocat. Ad poēmata scrībenda mē appellat. Eī dīxī mē librōs scrīptūrum esse. Dīxī librōs ā mē scrīptum īrī. Rūs ībō scrīptum. Domum ībō ut scrībam. Librōrum scrībendōrum causā Rōmā discēdam. Nam Rōmae scrībere nōn possum. Domī scrībam. Librī ā mē scrībendī sunt. Maximī aestimō librōs scrībere. Difficile est dictū quantō opere velim scrībere. Dum domī sum, scrībam. Dummodo domī sim, scrībam. Domī nihil mē dēterrēbit quōminus scrībam. Nihil iūcundius mihi erit quam librōs scrībere. Librōs scrībere mihi libēbit. Diem dīcam scrībendō. Librīs scrībendīs diem dīcam. Cupidissimus sum scrībendī. Poēmatum scrībendōrum cupidissimus sum. Iūcunda mihi vīta erit donec me scrībendō dabō. Iūcunda mihi vīta nōn erit donec mē scrībendō dem.

2. Ex tuīs litterīs, mī amīce, quās mihi dedit tuus fidēlissimus servus, intellexī quantō opere sīs cupidissimus meī videndī. Id etiam sine litterīs arbitrārer, nam saepissimē amīcitiae grātiā nostrae mē bene fēcistī et omnibus dīxistī tē plūris mē aestimāre quam nesciō quem amīcum. Tē hortor ut Rōmae sīs cum rūre vēnerō tēcum loquendī causā. Sī Rōmam īre nōn potes, faciam modō nesciō quō ut veniam ad tē videndum. Difficile mihi est dictū quō modō id faciam, quia multae sunt rēs quae mē dēterreant quōminus ad tē eam. Quā rē rursus tē hortor ut Rōmam eās meī videndī causā.

IV. TRANSLATE. (Try to guess the meaning of new words on the basis of context and cognates before consulting the adjacent **reading notes.**)

1. CATULLUS (2)

Passer, dēliciae meae puellae,
quīcum lūdēre, quem in **sinū tenēre**,
cui prīmum **digitum** dare **appetentī**
et acrīs solet **incitāre morsūs**,
cum dēsīderiō meō **nitentī**
cārum nesciō quid **lubet iōcārī**,

(ille) passer, -eris sparrow
(illa) dēlicia, -ae delight (usually plural) Cf. delicious
quīcum = quōcum (quī is used for both singular and plural ablative: **quō** and **quibus)**
lūdeō, -ēre, lūsī, lūsus play (a game)
lūdēre is complementary with **solet**
(ille) sinus, -ūs fold, particularly the fold of the upper part of the toga, hence, the bosom; also the lap
teneō, -ēre, -uī, tentus hold Cf. tenacious **tenēre** i.e., **tenēre solet**
(ille) digitus, -ī finger Cf. digit
dare i.e., **dare solet**
ap-petō, -ere, -ī(v)ī, -ītus strive after, seize Cf. appetite
in-citō, -āre, -āvī, -ātus incite
(ille) morsus, -ūs bite Cf. morsel
cum temporal, with **lubet**
(illud) dēsiderium, -ī desire, of a person as the object of longing
nitens, -entis shining bright and beautiful
cārus, -a, -um dear and precious
lubet = libet (for structure, see ***index verbōrum***)
iōcor, -ārī, -ātus joke

et **sōlāciolum** suī **dolōris,**
crēdō, ut **tum gravis acquiescat ardor:**
tēcum lūdēre **sīcut** ipsa possem
et **tristīs** animī **levāre cūrās!**

(illud) sōlāciolum, -ī (diminutive of **sōlācium**) comfort, consolation Cf. solace
(ille) dolor, -ōris pain, grief Cf. dolorous
tum then (temporal correlative with **cum**)
gravis, -e heavy, serious Cf. grave
ac-quiescō, -ere, -ēvī, -ētus become quiet Cf. acquiesce
(ille) ardor, -ōris flame, fire, heat, ardor
sīcut = sīc ut just as, thus as
tristis, -e sad Cf. triste **tristīs = tristēs**
levō, -āre, -āvī, -ātus lift up Cf. levitate

2. CATULLUS (3)

Lūgēte, ō **Venerēs Cupīdinēs**que,
et quantum est hominum
  venustiōrum:
passer mortuus est meae puellae,
passer, dēliciae meae puellae,
quem plūs illa oculīs suīs amābat.
Nam **mellītus** erat suamque **nōrat**
ipsam tam bene quam puella matrem,
nec **sēsē** ā **gremiō** illīus movēbat,
sed **circumsiliēns modo huc modo
  illuc**
ad sōlam **dominam pipiābat;**
quī nunc it per iter **tenebricōsum**
illud, **unde** negant **redīre** quemquam.
At vōbīs **male** sit, malae tenebrae

lūgeō, -ēre, -xī, -ctus lament, mourn Cf. lugubrious
(illa) Venus, -eris Venus, goddess of Love, Love as a force of Nature
(ille) Cupīdo, -inis Cupid, son of Venus, often pluralized into a group
venustus, -a, -um graceful, beautiful, elegant, Venus-like
mellītus, -a, -um honey-sweet, lovely Cf. miel
nōrat = (cog)nō(ve)rat
sēsē = sē
(illud) gremium, -ī lap, bosom
circum-siliō, -īre hop around
modo . . . modo (adverb, originally ablative of **modus**) sometimes . . . sometimes
huc to this place
illuc to that place
(ille/illa) dominus/domina, -ī /-ae master or mistress of a **domus**
pipiō, -āre pip, chirp
tenebricōsus, -a, -um shadowy, full of **tenebrae**
unde from which place
red-eō (compound of **eō**) return
male adverb from **malus / vōbīs male sit** a curse: May it be bad(ly) for you!

Orcī, quae omnia bella **dēvorātis:**
tam bellum mihi passerem
abstulistīs.
ō factum male! ō **miselle** passer!
Tuā nunc **operā** meae puellae
flendō turgidulī rubent ocellī.

(ille) Orcus, -ī god of the Lower World, the abode of the dead
dē-vorō, -āre, -āvī, -ātus devour Cf. voracious
abs-tulistīs compound of **ferō** (afferō)
misellus, -a, -um diminutive of **miser**
(illa) opera, -ae work, effort Cf. **opus**
fleō, -ēre, flēvī, flētus weep
turgidulus, -a, -um diminutive of **tugidus** swollen, turgid
rubeō, -ēre be red Cf. ruby
(ille) ocellus, -ī diminutive of **oculus**

3. HORATIUS (1.37)

Nunc est bibendum, nunc **pede**
līberō
pulsanda tellūs . . .

Written upon the news of Cleopatra's death
(ille) pēs, pedis foot Cf. pedestrian
pulsō, -āre, -āvī, -ātus strike, stamp Cf. pulse
(illa) tellūs, -ūris earth Cf. tellurian

4. CICERO (Epistulae ad familiārēs 5.21)

M. CICERO S. D. L. MESCINIO:

Grātae mihi tuae litterae fuērunt; ex quibus intellexī, quod etiam sine litterīs arbitrābar, tē summā **cupiditāte adfectum** esse videndī meī. Quod ego ita **libenter accipiō**, ut tamen tibi non **concēdam**; nam tēcum esse, ita mihi commoda omnia, quae optō, **contingant**, ut **vehementer** velim!

Marcus Cicero salūtem dīcit Luciō Mēscinō a typical heading for a letter
(illa) salūs, -ūtis health, a wish for one's welfare, a greeting Cf. salutary
grātus, -a, -um pleasing, grateful
(illa) cupiditas, -ātis desire
ad-ficiō, -ere, -fēcī, -fectus affect, influence
libenter willingly Cf. **libet**
ac-cipiō, -ere, -cēpī, -ceptus accept
con-cēdō, -ere, -cessī, -cessus concede
con-tingō, -ere, -tigī, -tactus touch, attain, arrive Cf. contingent
vehementer vehemently

5. PLINIUS (Epistulae 7.27.5)

Erat Athēnīs **spatiōsa** et **capax** domus, sed infāmis et **pestilens.** Per **silentium** noctis **sonus ferrī**, et, sī **attenderēs acrius, strepitus vinculōrum** longius prīmō, deinde ē **proximō reddēbātur;** mox **apparēbat īdōlon**, senex **maciē** et **squālōre confectus, promissā barbā, horrentī capillō: crūribus compedēs**, manibus **catēnās gerēbat quatiēbat**que.

spatiōsus, -a, -um spacious
capax, -ācis capacious
pestilens, -entis pestilentious, unwholesome
(illud) silentium, -ī silence, stillness
(ille) sonus, -ī sound, noise
(illud) ferrum, -ī iron, implement made of iron Cf. ferrous
at-tendō, -ere, -tentī, -tentus direct toward, attend to, direct the attention toward
acrius (adverb from **acer**)
(ille) strepitus, -ūs noise
(illud) vinc(u)lum, -ī fetter, chain
proximus, -a, -um superlative of **propior, -ius** nearer
red-dō, -ere, -uī, -itus give back, return
ap-pareō, -ēre, -uī, -itus appear, come in sight Cf. apparition
(illud) īdōlon (-um), -ī image, spectre, ghost Cf. idol
(illa) maciēs, -ēī leaness, thinness Cf. emaciation
(ille) squālor, -ōris squalor
con-ficiō, -ere, -fēcī, -fectus bring about, consume, destroy
pro-mittō, -ere, -mīsī, -missus send forth, let (hair) fall down
(illa) barba, -ae beard Cf. barber
horreō, -ēre, -uī stand on end, bristle Cf. horrible
(ille) capillus, -ī hair (of the head) Cf. capillary
(illud) crūs, crūris leg, shin
(illa) com-pēs, -pedis fetter, shackle
(illa) catēna, -ae chain, handcuffs
gerō, -ere, gessī, gestus wear (as clothing (see ***index verbōrum, Lesson 7***)
quatiō, -ere, quassī, quassus shake, quake

Inde inhabitantibus tristēs **dīraeque** noctēs per **metum vigilābantur: vigiliam morbus** et **crescente formīdine** mors sequēbātur. Nam **interdiū** quoque, quamquam **abscesserat imāgo**, memōria imāginis oculīs **inerrābat**, longiorque causīs **timōris** timor erat. **Dēserta** inde et **damnāta sōlitūdine** domus tōtaque illī **monstrō relicta; prōscrībēbātur** tamen, **seu** quis **emere**, seu quis **condūcere ignārus** tantī malī vellet. Vēnit Athēnās philosophus Athēnodōrus, legit **titulum**, audītō pretiō, quia **suspecta vīlitas**, **percunctātus**, omnia docētur ac nīhilō minus, **immo** tantō magis condūcit.

inde thenceforward
inhabitō, -āre, -āvī, -ātus inhabit
dīrus, -a, -um dire, fearful
(ille) metus, -ūs fear
vigilō, -āre, -āvī, -ātus spend the night awake Cf. vigil
(illa) vigilia, -ae wakefulness
(ille) morbus, -ī sickness Cf. morbidity
cresco, -ere, crēvī, crētus grow, increase Cf. crescendo
(illa) formīdo, -inis dread Cf. formidable
interdiū during the day, meanwhile
abs-cēdō, -ere, -cessī, -cessus depart
(illa) imāgo, -inis image, apparition
in-errō, -āre, -āvī, -ātus wander about
(illa) causa, -ae cause
(ille) timor, -ōris fear Cf. timorous
dē-serō, -ere, -ruī, -rtus desert, forsake
damnō, -āre, -āvī, -ātus condemn, damn
(illa) sōlitūdo, -inis solitude
(illud) monstrum, -ī monster
re-linquō, -ere, -līquī, -lictus relinquish, leave behind
prō-scrībō, -ere, -scrīpsī, -scrīptus publish by writing, advertise
seu...seu if...or if, whether...or
emō, -ere, ēmī, emptus buy Cf. emporium
con-dūcō, -ere, -dūxī, -ductus rent
ignārus, -a, -um ignorant, not knowing
(ille) titulus, -ī title, placard, sign, notice (that something is for sale)
suspiciō, -ere, -spexī, -spectus suspect
(illa) vīlitas, -ātis cheapness Cf. vile
percunctor, -ārī, -ātus investigate by inquiry, question thoroughly, hesitate
immo on the contrary, by no means

Ubi **coepit advesperascere, iubet sternī** sibi prīmā domūs parte, **poscit pugillārēs**, stilum, lūmen: suōs omnēs in **interiōra dīmittit**, ipse ad scrībendum animum, oculōs, manum **intendit**, nē **vacua mens** audīta **simulācra** et **inānēs** sibi metūs **fingeret. Initiō**, quāle **ubīque**, silentium noctis, **dein concutī** ferrum, vincula movērī: ille nōn **tollere** oculōs, nōn **remittere** stilum, sed **offirmāre** animum auribusque **praetendere:**

coepiō, -ere, coepī, coeptus = **incipiō**
ad-vesperascit, -ere, -āvit get to be evening Cf. vespers
iubeō, -ēre, iussī, iussus command Cf. jussive
sternō, -ere, strāvī, strātus spread out, unpack
poscō, -ere, poposcī demand, ask for
pugillāris, -e belonging to the fist or hand Cf. pugilist **pugillārēs (libellī)** writing tablets
interior, -ius inner Cf. interior
dī-mittō, -ere, -mīsī, -missus dismiss, send away
in-tendō, -ere, -dī, -tensus bend toward, direct Cf. intend
vacuus, -a, -um empty, vacant Cf. vacuum
(illa) mens, mentis mind Cf. mental
(illud) simulācrum, -ī likeness, semblance, phantom Cf. simulacrum
inānis, -e empty Cf. inane
fingō, -ere, finxī, fictus fashion, make up Cf. fiction
(illud) initium, -ī beginning Cf. initial
ubique everywhere Cf. ubiquitous
dein (= deinde) thereafter, then
con-cutiō, -ere, -cussī, -cussus strike together Cf. concussion
NOTE historical infinitives: infinitives in narration can be used instead of the imperfect indicative; the subjects are nominative
tollō, -ere, sustulī, sublātus lift up, raise Cf. sublate
re-mittō, -ere, -mīsī, -missus send back, put aside Cf. remit
offirmō, -āre, -āvī, -ātus render firm, hold fast to
prae-tendō, -ere, -tendī, -tentus stretch forth Cf. pretend

tum **crēbrescere fragor, adventāre**, et **iam ut** in **līmine, iam ut intrā** līmen audīrī: **rēspicit**, videt **agnoscit**que narrātam sibi **effigiem. Stābat innuēbat**que digitō, similis vocantī: hīc contrā ut **paulum exspectāret** manū **significat** rursusque **cērīs** et stilō **incumbit**: illa scrībentis capitī catēnīs **insonābat**: rēspicit rursus idem quod prius innuentem, nec **morātus** tollit lūmen et sequitur. Ībat illa **lentō gradū, quasi** gravis vinculīs: postquam **dēflexit** in **āream** domūs, **repentē dīlapsa** dēserit **comitem**:

crēbrescō, -ere, -buī become frequent
(ille) fragor, -ōris crashing (of something broken to pieces) Cf. fragile
adventō, -āre, -āvī, -ātus come continually nearer
iam... iam now... now
ut... ut as if... as if
(illud) līmen, -inis threshold Cf. liminal
intrā + *accusative* within
rē-spiciō, -ere, -spexī, -spectus look away, look up
agnoscō, -ere, -nōvī, -nōtus recognize
(illa) effigiēs, -ēī effigy, image, ghost
stō, -āre, stetī, status stand
in-nuō, -ere, -nuī, -ūtus nod, give a sign (with the head) Cf. innuendo
paulum for a while
exspectō, -āre, -āvī, -ātus wait Cf. expect
significō, -āre, -āvī, -ātus signify
(illa) cērna, -ae wax writing tablets
incumbō, -ere, -cubuī, -cubitus lay one's self upon, bend one's attention to Cf. incubus, incumbent
in-sonō, -āre, -uī make a noise on
moror, -ārī, -ātus delay, wait Cf. moratorium
lentus, -a, -um slow
(ille) gradus, -ūs step Cf. grade
quasi as if
dē-flectō, -ere, -flexī, -flectus deflect, turn aside
(illa) ārea, -ae piece of level ground, courtyard of a house Cf. area
repentē suddenly
dī-labor, -ārī, -lapsus collapse, melt away, dissolve
(ille) comes, -mitis comrade, companion

dēsertus **herbās** et **folia concerpta signum locō pōnit. Posterō** diē **adit magistrātūs, monet** ut illum locum **effodī** iubeant. **Inveniuntur ossa inserta** catēnīs et **implicita,** quae corpus **aevō** terrāque **putrefactum nūda** et **exēsa** relīquerat vinculīs: **collecta pūblicē sepeliuntur.** Domus **posteā rīte conditīs manibus caruit.**

(illa) **herba, -ae** grass, vegetation, herb
(illud) **folium, -ī** leaf Cf. foliage
con-cerpō, -ere, -psī, -ptus pluck
(illud) **signum, -ī** sign
(ille) **locus, -ī** place, spot, locale
pōnō, -ere, posuī, positus place Cf. position
posterus, -a, -um next
ad-eō (compound of **eō**) go to
(ille) **magistrātus, -ūs** magistrate, municipal official
moneō, -ēre, -uī, -itus warn, advise
ef-fodiō, -ere, -fōdī, -fossus dig up Cf. fossil
in-veniō, -īre, -vēnī, -ventus discover Cf. invention
(illud) **ossum, -ī** bone Cf. ossify
in-serō, -ere, -sēruī, -sertus insert
implicitus, -a, -um entangled Cf. implicate
(illud) **aevum, -ī** age, time Cf. eon
putrefaciō, -ere, -fēcī, -factus putrefy
nūdus, -a, -um nude, exposed
ex-edō, -ere, -ēdī, -ēsus consume Cf. edible
col-ligō, -ere, -lēgī, -lectus collect
pūblicē (adverb of **pūblicus**)
sepeliō, -īre, -pelī(v)ī, -pultus entomb Cf. sepulcre
posteā thereafter
rīte ritually
con-dō, -ere, -uī, -itus establish
(illī) **manēs, -ium** ghosts, deified spirits of the dead
careō, -ēre, -uī, -itus be without, be free from

V. CHANGE each of the following sentences so that the purpose is expressed by the supine instead of the subjunctive clause of purpose.

Vēnī ut dīcerem. **Vēnī dictum.**

1. Discēdam ut moriar.
2. Ut mē vidērent rediērunt.
3. Ībimus ut tēcum loquāmur.
4. Servum ad tē, mī amīce, mox mittam ut tibi nesciō quid prō amīcitiā nostrā dem.
5. Saepissimē Athēnās ībam ut Graecē loquerer.
6. Suās quisque abeunt domōs ut cēnent.
7. Iste infāmissimus senex semper rediit ut dīceret.
8. Aliquī miserrimus vīsū puer vēnit ut apud istam bellissimam puellam cēnāret.
9. Nōn nūllī semper mē domum sequuntur ut amīcitiae nostrae causā mēcum loquantur.
10. Admōvit aurēs ut melius audīret.

VI. CHANGE each of the following sentences so that the purpose is expressed by a gerund or gerundive phrase with **ad**, **causā**, or **grātiā**.

Vēnit ut dīceret. **Ad dīcendum vēnit.**
Dīcendī grātiā vēnit.
Dīcendī causā vēnit.

Vēnit ut vēritātem dīceret. **Vēnit ad vēritātem dīcendam.**
Vēnit vēritātis dīcendae grātiā.
Vēnit vēritātis dīcendae causā.

1. Mē vocāvit ut scrīberem.
2. Omnēs bonōs vocāvit ut istam infāmissimam urbem dēlērent.
3. Illam iūcundissimam audītū mulierem appellat ut poēmata canat.
4. Rūs mox ībō ut poēmata legam.
5. Aurēs admovēte, meī amīcī, ut melius vēritātem dē hāc rē audiātis.
6. Istī reī, mī amīce, mentem tuam dā ut metus oblīviscāris.
7. Athēnīs vīvit ut Graecē loquātur.
8. Venīte Rōmam ut mē videātis.
9. Domī erat rūrī ut dē rē pūblicā et metibus suī tacēret.
10. Rōmā proficiscere, mī fīlī, ut metum meum dē tuā salūte rēmoveās.

VII. CHANGE each of the following sentences so that the idea of obligation is expressed by the gerundive.

Ille laudārī dēbet.	**Ille laudandus est.**
Illum laudārī oportet.	**Ille laudandus est.**

1. Haec infāmissima urbs dēlērī dēbet.
2. Nōs oportuit dēterrērī ā scrībendō.
3. Laudārī dēbuit illa bellissima vīsū mulier.
4. Vīta ā fortūnā nōn dēbet regī.
5. Istum hominem oportet capitis damnārī.
6. Dē istā rē oportet ā nōbīs tacērī.
7. Illum atrōcissimum vīsū rēgem nōn oportuit ad bellum movērī.
8. Stultī dēbent ā dīcendō prohibērī.
9. Ūnus dēligī dēbet quī prō nōbīs dīcat.
10. Eī persuādērī oportet nē veniat.

VIII. CHANGE each of the following sentences so that the gerund is replaced by a gerundive.

Ille cupidus est vītam vīvendī.	**Ille cupidus est vītae vīvendae.**

1. Tam cupidissima est mea puella mē videndī ut nēmō est alius quōcum velit loquī.

2. Rōmam rediit iste bellissimus vīsū vir suam puellam amandī causā.

3. Omnēs dēterreāmus bonōs quōminus velint cīvitātem nostram dēlēre bellum cum fīnitimīs gerendī grātiā.

4. Vōs nōn oportuit dē rē pūblicā tacēre nōbīs placendī causā.

5. Vīvat iste cupidissimus nōs interficiendī senex dum Rōmā discēdat priusquam ad urbem redeam.

IX. NOTE THE PATTERN in each of the following sentences and compose a translation of the English sentences using the same pattern.

1. **Intellexī tē summā cupiditāte adfectum esse meī videndī.**
   He supposed that we were led by the most infamous desire for destroying the state.
   They soon saw that their own friends were desirous of killing them.

2. Priusquam dīcerem, abiit.

Before his enemies could destroy the republic, he returned to Rome.

Before he could have known that I was going to be in Rome, he had set out for the country.

NOUN DECLENSIONS

NOTE that the cases, as in the text, are presented in order of decreasing survivability, with the most moribund last.

DECLENSION ONE
Ā-STEM
NOUN

(mostly feminine nouns, but some masculine; no neuter)

vīta, **-ae** *fem.*

poēta, **-ae** *masc.*

case	*ending*	*feminine*	*masculine*
		SINGULAR	
nominative	(-a)	vīta	poēta
accusative	(-am)	vīt**am**	poēt**am**
genitive	(-ae)	vīt**ae**	poēt**ae**
dative	(-ae)	vīt**ae**	poēt**ae**
ablative	(-ā)	vīt**ā**	poēt**ā**
vocative	(-a)	vīta	poēta
		PLURAL	
nominative	(-ae)	vīt**ae**	poēt**ae**
accusative	(-ās)	vīt**ās**	poēt**ās**
genitive	(-ārum)	vīt**ārum**	poēt**ārum**
dative	(-īs)	vīt**īs**	poēt**īs**
ablative	(-īs)	vīt**īs**	poēt**īs**
vocative	(-ae)	vīt**ae**	poēt**ae**

ADJECTIVE

magnus, **-a**, -um

miser, misera, -um

Combines declensions II and I, and uses first declension for feminine.

DECLENSION TWO
O-STEM
NOUN

(mostly masculine and neuter, but some feminine: in particular the names of trees, countries, and small islands)

serv**us**, -ī *masc.*
liber, librī *masc.*
līber, līberī *masc.*
vir, virī *masc.*
fāg**us**, -ī *fem.* beech tree
bell**um**, -ī *neut.*

Masculine nouns may lack the **-us** of the nominative singular ending; and the stem is not predictable from the nominative in such nouns.

case	*ending*	*masculine*	*feminine*	*neuter*
		SINGULAR		
nominative	(-us/-um)	serv**us**	fāg**us**	bell**um**
accusative	(-um)	serv**um**	fāg**um**	bell**um**
genitive	(-ī)	servī	fāgī	bellī
dative	(-ō)	servō	fāgō	bellō
ablative	(-ō)	servō	fāgō	bellō
vocative	(-e) *only for masc. nouns in* ***-us***	serve	fāg**us**	bell**um**
		PLURAL		
nominative	(-ī/-a)	servī	fāgī	bella
accusative	(-ōs/-a)	serv**ōs**	fāg**ōs**	bella
genitive	(-ōrum)	serv**ōrum**	fāg**ōrum**	bell**ōrum**
dative	(-īs)	serv**īs**	fāg**īs**	bell**īs**
ablative	(-īs)	serv**īs**	fāg**īs**	bell**īs**
vocative	(-ī/-a)	servī	fāgī	bella

ADJECTIVE

magn**us**, -a, **-um**
miser, misera, miser**um**

Combines decl. I & II; uses decl. II for masculine and neuter.

DECLENSION THREE CONSONANT-STEM NOUN

(masculine, feminine, and neuter nouns)

rex, rē**gis** *masc.*
princeps, princip**is** *masc.*
lex, lē**gis** *fem.*
homo, homin**is** *masc.*
urbs, urb**is**, -b**ium** *fem.*
nōmen, nōminis *neut.*
animal, amimāl**is**, -l**ium**, *neut.*

The -**s** of the nominative singular may combine with the stem consonant (i.e., **g** + **s** = -**x**); or be lost; the stem cannot be predicted from the nominative singular. I-stems must be noted with the genitive plural. Some of these are true i-stems and will have -**ī** for ablative singular (and accusative plural and/or singular).

case	*ending*	*masc/fem*	*i-stem*	*true i-stem*	*neuter*	*neuter i-stem*
			SINGULAR			
nom	(-s/_)	rex	urbs	ignis	nōmen	animal
acc	(-em/_)	rēg**em**	urb**em**	ign**em**	nōmen	animal
gen	(-is)	rēg**is**	urb**is**	ign**is**	nōmin**is**	animāl**is**
dat	(-ī)	rēg**ī**	urb**ī**	ign**ī**	nōmin**ī**	animāl**ī**
abl	(-e/-ī)	rēg**e**	urb**e**	ign**ī/e**	nōmin**e**	animāl**ī**
voc	(-s/_)	rex	urbs	ignis	nōmen	animal
			PLURAL			
nom	(-ēs/a)	rēg**ēs**	urb**ēs**	ign**ēs**	nōmin**a**	animāl**ia**
acc	(-ēs/a)	rēg**ēs**	urb**ēs**	ign**īs/ēs**	nōmin**a**	animāl**ia**
gen	(-um)	rēg**um**	urb**ium**	ign**ium**	nōmin**um**	animāl**ium**
dat	(-ibus)	rēg**ibus**	urb**ibus**	ign**ibus**	nōmin**ibus**	animāl**ibus**
abl	(-ibus)	rēg**ibus**	urb**ibus**	ign**ibus**	nōmin**ibus**	animāl**ibus**
voc	(-ēs/a)	rēg**ēs**	urb**ēs**	ign**ēs**	nōmin**a**	animāl**ia**

ADJECTIVE

acer, acris, acre
brevis, breve
atro**x** (*gen* atrōcis)

Declined like **urbs** for masc-fem and **animal** for neuter

Called ***three***, ***two***, or ***one termination*** on the basis of the lexical entry, but all are declined similarly, with only one form for all cases:
except nominative singular (three termination has separate forms for feminine and neuter; two has separate forms for masc.-fem. and neuter).
All have separate forms for neuter pl. nom.-acc.
All are **i-stems** with -**ī** in abl. sing., but one termination may have -**e**.

DECLENSION FOUR
U-STEM
NOUN

(mostly masculine, but some feminine and only four neuter nouns; no adjectives)

lac**us**, -**ūs** *masc.*

man**us**, -**ūs** *fem.*

corn**ū**, -**ūs** *neut.*

case	*ending*	*masculine*	*feminine*	*neuter*
		SINGULAR		
nominative	(-us/ū)	lac**us**	man**us**	corn**ū**
accusative	(-um/ū)	lac**um**	man**um**	corn**ū**
genitive	(-ūs)	lac**ūs**	man**ūs**	corn**ūs**
dative	(-uī/ū) *Neuter nouns always use* -**ū**.	lac**uī/ū**	man**uī/ū**	corn**ū**
ablative	(-ū)	lac**ū**	man**ū**	corn**ū**
vocative	(-us/ū)	lac**us**	man**us**	corn**ū**
		PLURAL		
nominative	(-ūs/ua)	lac**ūs**	man**ūs**	corn**ua**
accusative	(-ūs/ua)	lac**ūs**	man**ūs**	corn**ua**
genitive	(-uum)	lac**uum**	man**uum**	corn**uum**
dative	(-ibus/-ubus) *usually* -ibus, *except lacus & a few others*	lac**ubus**	man**ibus**	corn**ibus**
ablative	(-ibus/-ubus) *usually* -ibus, *except lacus & a few others*	lac**ubus**	man**ibus**	corn**ibus**
vocative	(-ūs/ua)	lac**ūs**	man**ūs**	corn**ua**

NOTE

Domus has two stems: **domu-** and **domo-**; and hence can be declined either as second or fourth declension (although not all forms occur):

	nom	*acc*	*gen*	*dat*	*abl*
sing	dom**us**	dom**um**	dom**ūs/ī** (*locative* dom**ī**)	dom**uī/ō**	dom**ō/ū**
plur	dom**ūs**	dom**ōs/ūs**	dom**uum/ōrum**	dom**ibus**	dom**ibus**

DECLENSION FIVE
Ē-STEM
(feminine nouns only, except for ***diēs***, which is usually masculine; when feminine, it means *time* or *a fixed day;* and ***meridiēs***, *noon;* no adjectives)
rēs, -eī *fem.*
(only rēs and diēs occur in all forms)

SINGULAR			PLURAL	
	ending	*case*	*ending*	
rēs	-ēs	*nominative*	-ēs	rēs
rem	-em	*accusative*	-ēs	rēs
reī	-eī	*genitive*	-ērum	rē**rum**
reī diēī (diē)	-eī/ē	*dative*	-ēbus	rē**bus**
rē	-ē	*ablative*	-ēbus	rē**bus**
rēs	-ēs	*vocative*	-ēs	rēs

PRONOUNS

PERSONAL PRONOUNS
(The third person *he, she, it, they* is lacking in Latin.)
NOTE that the genitive is not used for possession; instead the possessive adjectives **meus, -a, -um; noster, -tra, -trum; tuus, -a, -um; vester, -tra, -trum** are used.

FIRST PERSON			SECOND PERSON	
singular	*plural*	*case*	*singular*	*plural*
ego	**nōs**	*nominative*	**tū**	**vōs**
mē	**nōs**	*accusative*	**tē**	**vōs**
meī	**nostrum** **nostrī**	*genitive*	**tuī**	**vestrum** **vestrī**
mihi (mī)	**nōbīs**	*dative*	**tibi**	**vōbīs**
mē	**nōbīs**	*ablative*	**tē**	**vōbīs**

DEMONSTRATIVE PRONOUNS

	HĪC			ILLE			IS		
				SINGULAR					
	masc	*fem*	*neut*	*masc*	*fem*	*neut*	*masc*	*fem*	*neut*
N	hīc	haec	hōc	ille	illa	illud	is	ea	id
A	hunc	hanc	hōc	illum	illam	illud	eum	eam	id
G	huius	huius	huius	illīus	illīus	illīus	eius	eius	eius
D	huic	huic	huic	illī	illī	illī	eī	eī	eī
A	hōc	hāc	hōc	illō	illā	illō	eō	eā	eō
				PLURAL					
N	hī	hae	haec	illī	illae	illa	eī iī ī	eae	ea
A	hōs	hās	haec	illōs	illās	illa	eōs	eās	ea
G	hōrum	hārum	hōrum	illōrum	illārum	illōrum	eōrum	eārum	eōrum
D	hīs	hīs	hīs	illīs	illīs	illīs	eīs iīs īs	eīs iīs īs	eīs iīs īs
A	hīs	hīs	hīs	illīs	illīs	illīs	eīs iīs īs	eīs iīs īs	eīs iīs īs

	INTENSIVE PRONOUN			IDENTIC PRONOUN ("same")		
			SINGULAR			
N	ipse	ipsa	ipsum	īdem	eadem	idem
A	ipsum	ipsam	ipsum	eundem	eandem	idem
G	ipsīus	ipsīus	ipsīus	eiusdem	eiusdem	eiusdem
D	ipsī	ipsī	ipsī	eīdem	eīdem	eīdem
A	ipsō	ipsā	ipsō	eōdem	eādem	eōdem
			PLURAL			
N	ipsī	ipsae	ipsa	īdem eīdem	eaedem	eadem
A	ipsōs	ipsās	ipsa	eōsdem	eāsdem	eadem
G	ipsōrum	ipsārum	ipsōrum	eōrundem	eārundem	eōrundem
D	ipsīs	ipsīs	ipsīs	eīsdem īsdem	eīsdem īsdem	eīsdem īsdem
A	ipsīs	ipsīs	ipsīs	eīsdem īsdem	eīsdem īsdem	eīsdem īsdem

RELATIVE PRONOUN
(the man) who

INTERROGATIVE PRONOUN
who? / what?
INDEFINITE PRONOUN
anybody / somebody

	SINGULAR					
	masc	*fem*	*neuter*	*masc-fem*		*neuter*
N	quī	quae	quod	quis		quid
A	quem	quam	quod	quem		quid
G	cuius	cuius	cuius	cuius		cuius
D	cui	cui	cui	cui		cui
A	quō	quā	quō	quō		quō
	PLURAL					
				masc	*fem*	*neuter*
N	quī	quae	quae	quī	quae	quae
A	quōs	quās	quae	quōs	quās	quae
G	quōrum	quārum	quōrum	quōrum	quārum	quōrum
D	quibus	quibus	quibus	quibus	quibus	quibus
A	quibus	quibus	quibus	quibus	quibus	quibus

INTERROGATIVE ADJECTIVE
what (man)?

INDEFINITE ADJECTIVE
some (man)

	SINGULAR					
N	quī	quae	quod	quī	**qua**	quod
A	quem	quam	quod	quem	quam	quod
G	cuius	cuius	cuius	cuius	cuius	cuius
D	cui	cui	cui	cui	cui	cui
A	quō	quā	quō	quō	quā	quō
	PLURAL					
N	quī	quae	quae	quī	quae	**qua**
A	quōs	quās	quae	quōs	quās	**qua**
G	quōrum	quārum	quōrum	quōrum	quārum	quōrum
D	quibus	quibus	quibus	quibus	quibus	quibus
A	quibus	quibus	quibus	quibus	quibus	quibus

(CONTUMELIOUS) DEMONSTRATIVE
that (man) probably of questionable worth

REFLEXIVE
third person

	masc	*fem*	*neuter*	*masc-fem-neut*
			SINGULAR	
N	iste	ista	istud	
A	istum	istam	istud	sē
G	istīus	istīus	istīus	suī
D	istī	istī	istī	sibi
A	istō	istā	istō	sē
			PLURAL	
N	istī	istae	ista	
A	istōs	istās	ista	sē
G	istōrum	istārum	istōrum	suī
D	istīs	istīs	istīs	sibi
A	istīs	istīs	istīs	sē

NOTE that the oblique cases of the first and second persons of the personal pronouns can also be used reflexively; to clarify the reflexive meaning they can be combined with the intensive **ipse**: for example, **mē ipsum**. Since the personal pronouns are not used in the genitive for possession, the reflexive meaning of the personal possessive adjectives can be clarified by adding the genitive of the pronoun **ipse: mea ipsīus vīta** "*my own life*;" **nostra ipsōrum vīta** "*our own life.*"

PRONOMINAL ADJECTIVES

Nine adjectives (of the first & second declensional type) are declined like pronouns in the **genitive** and **dative singular**.

alius, alia, aliud	**nūllus, nūlla, nūllum**	**ūllus, ūlla, ūllum**
alter, altera, alterum	**sōlus, sōla, sōlum**	**ūnus, ūna, ūnum**
neuter, neutra, neutrum	**tōtus, tōta, tōtum**	**uter, utra, utrum**

g **alīus**	**alterīus**	**neutrīus**	**nūllīus**	**sōlīus**	**tōtīus**	**ūllīus**	**ūnīus**	**utrīus**
d **aliī**	**alterī**	**neutrī**	**nūllī**	**sōlī**	**tōtī**	**ūllī**	**ūnī**	**utrī**

NUMBERS

Cardinal	Ordinal	Numeral	Adverbs
ūnus, ūna, ūnum	prīmus, -a, -um	I	semel "once"
duo, duae, duo	secundus, -a, -um	II	bis "twice"
trēs, tria	tertius, -a, -um	III	ter "thrice"
quattuor	quārtus, -a, -um	IIII or IV	quater
quīnque	quīntus, -a, -um	V	quīnquiē(n)s
sex	sextus, -a, -um	VI	sexiē(n)s
septem	septimus, -a, -um	VII	septiē(n)s
octō	octāvus, -a, -um	VIII	octiē(n)s
novem	nōnus, -a, -um	VIIII or IX	noviē(n)s
decem	decimus, -a, -um	X	deciē(n)s
ūndecim	ūndecimus, -a, -um	XI	ūndeciē(n)s
duodecim	duodecimus, -a, -um	XII	duodeciē(n)s
tredecim (decim trēs)	tertius, -a, -um decimus, -a, -um	XIII	terdeciē(n)s
quattuordecim	quārtus decimus	XIIII or XIV	quaterdeciē(n)s
quīndecim	quīntus decimus	XV	quīndeciē(n)s
sēdecim	sextus decimus	XVI	sēdeciē(n)s
septemdecim	septimus decimus	XVII	septiēsdeciē(n)s
duodēvīgintī octōdecim	duodēvīcēnsimus octāvus decimus	XVIII	duodēvīciē(n)s
ūndēvīgintī novemdecim	ūndēvīcēnsimus nōnus decimus	XIX	ūndēvīciē(n)s
vīgintī	vīcensimus vigēnsimus	XX	vīciē(n)s
vīgintī ūnus	vīcēnsimus prīmus	XXI	semel vīciē(n)s
trīgintā	trīcēnsimus	XXX	trīciē(n)s
quadrāgintā	quadrāgēnsimus	XXXX or XL	quadrāgiē(n)s
quīnquāgintā	quīnquāgēnsimus	L	quīnquāgiē(n)s
sexāgintā	sexāgēnsimus	LX	sexāgiē(n)s
septuāgintā	septuāgēnsimus	LXX	septuāgiē(n)s
octōgintā	octōgēnsimus	LXXX	octōgiē(n)s
nōnāgintā	nōnāgēnsimus	LXXXX or XC	nōnāgiē(n)s
centum	centēnsimus	C	centiē(n)s
centum ūnus	centēnsimus prīmus	CI	centiē(n)s semel
ducentī, -ae, -a	ducentēnsimus	CC	ducentiē(n)s
trecentī, -ae, -a	trecentēnsimus	CCC	trecentiē(n)s
quadrigentī, -ae, -a	quadringentēnsimus	CCCC	quadringentiē(n)s
quīngentī, -ae, -a	quīngentēnsimus	D	quīngentiē(n)s
sescentī, -ae, -a	sescentēnsimus	DC	sescentiē(n)s
septingentī, -ae, -a	septingentēnsimus	DCC	septingentiē(n)s
octingentī, -ae, -a	octingentēnsimus	DCCC	octingentiē(n)s
nōngentī, -ae, -a	nōngentēnsimus	DCCCC	nōngentiē(n)s
mīlle	mīllēnsimus	M	mīlliē(n)s

DECLENSION
ŪNUS

	masculine	*feminine*	*neuter*	PLURAL
nominative	ūnus	ūna	ūnum	with meaning "same, only"
accusative	ūnum	ūnam	ūnum	regular I&II decl.
genitive	ūnīus	ūnīus	ūnīus	Also as "one" with
dative	ūnī	ūnī	ūnī	plural nouns with singular
ablative	ūnō	ūnā	ūnō	meaning: ūna castra

DUO / TRĒS

	DUO *masculine*	DUO *feminine*	DUO *neuter*	TRĒS *masc-fem*	TRĒS *neuter*
nominative	duo	duae	duo	trēs	tria
accusative	duōs (duo)	duās	duo	trēs (trīs)	tria
genitive	duōrum	duārum	duōrum	trium	trium
dative	duōbus	duōbus	duōbus	tribus	tribus
ablative	duōbus	duōbus	duōbus	tribus	tribus

Ambō (**"both"**) is delcined like **duo**, except that its final **ō** is long.

Except for **ūnus, duo**, and **trēs**, the cardinal numbers up to and including **centum** are indeclinable. The hundreds above **centum** are declinable as regular I&II adjectives.

Mīlle in the singular is an indeclinable adjective; but declined as a declension III i-stem noun in the plural (**mīlia, -ium**) with a partitive genitive:

mīlle hominēs **duo mīlia hominum**

SYNCHRONOUS CHART: FIVE DECLENSIONS

	FIRST	SECOND		THIRD					FOURTH		FIFTH
	(masc)-fem	*masc-(fem)*	*neuter*	*masc-(fem)*	*i-stem*	*true i-stem*	*neuter*	*neuter i-stem*	*masc-(fem)*	*neuter*	*fem-(masc)*
nom.	vīta	servus	bellum	rex	urbs	ignis	nōmen	animal	lacus	cornū	rēs
acc.	vītam	servum	bellum	rēgem	urbem	ignem	nōmen	animal	lacum	cornū	rem
gen.	vītae	servī	bellī	rēgis	urbis	ignīs	nōminis	animālis	lacūs	cornūs	reī
dat.	vītae	servō	bellō	rēgī	urbī	ignī	nōminī	animālī	lacuī/ū	cornū	reī
abl.	vītā	servō	bellō	rēge	urbe	ignī/e	nōmine	animālī	lacū	cornū	rē
voc.	vīta	serve	bellum	rex	urbs	ignis	nōmen	animal	lacūs	cornū	rēs
nom.	vītae	servī	bella	rēgēs	urbēs	ignēs	nōmina	animālia	lacūs	cornua	rēs
acc.	vītās	servōs	bella	rēgēs	urbēs	ignīs/ēs	nōmina	animālia	lacūs	cornua	rēs
gen.	vītārum	servōrum	bellōrum	rēgum	urbium	ignium	nōminum	animālium	lacuum	cornuum	rērum
dat.	vītīs	servīs	bellīs	rēgibus	urbibus	ignibus	nōminibus	animālibus	lacubus manibus	cornibus	rēbus
abl.	vītīs	servīs	bellīs	rēgibus	urbibus	ignibus	nōminibus	animālibus	lacubus manibus	cornibus	rēbus
voc.	vītae	servī	bella	rēgēs	urbēs	ignēs	nōmina	animālia	lacūs	cornua	rēs

SYNCHRONOUS CHART: FIVE DECLENSIONS *continued*

	ADJECTIVE I and II			ADJECTIVE III		
	masc. II	fem. I	neut. II	masc. III	fem. III	neut. III
nom.	magnus	magna	magnum	**acer brevis atrox**	**acris brevis atrox**	**acre breve atrox**
acc.	magnum	magnam	magnum	acrem	acrem	acre
gen.	magnī	magnae	magnī	acris	acris	acris
dat.	magnō	magnae	magnō	acrī	acrī	acrī
abl.	magnō	magnā	magnō	acrī brevī atrōcī (-e)	acrī brevī atrōcī (-e)	acrī brevī atrōcī (-e)
voc.	magne	magna	magnum	acer brevis atrox	acris brevis atrox	acre breve atrox
nom.	magnī	magnae	magna	acrēs	acrēs	acria brevia atrōcia
acc.	magnōs	magnās	magna	acrēs	acrēs	acria brevia atrōcia
gen.	magnōrum	magnārum	magnōrum	acrium	acrium	acrium
dat.	magnīs	magnīs	magnīs	acribus	acribus	acribus
abl.	magnīs	magnīs	magnīs	acribus	acribus	acribus
voc.	magnī	magnae	magna	acrēs	acrēs	acria

brevis, breve & **atrox** same as **acer, acris, acre** unless indicated

SYNCHRONOUS CHART: FOUR VERB CONJUGATIONS

INDICATIVE MOOD (MODE)

	FIRST **ā-stem**	SECOND **ē-stem**	THIRD **e-stem**	THIRD **i-stem**	FOURTH **ī-stem**
			PRESENT ACTIVE INDICATIVE		
1	amō	doceō	regō	incipiō	audiō
2	amās	docēs	regis	incipis	audīs
3	amat	docet	regit	incipit	audit
1	amāmus	docēmus	regimus	incipimus	audīmus
2	amātis	docētis	regitis	incipitis	audītis
3	amant	docent	regunt	incipiunt	audiunt
			PRESENT PASSIVE INDICATIVE		
1	amor	doceor	regor	incipior	audior
2	amāris amāre	docēris docēre	regeris regere	inciperis incipere	audīris audīre
3	amātur	docētur	regitur	incipitur	audītur
1	amāmur	docēmur	regimur	incipimur	audīmur
2	amāminī	docēminī	regiminī	incipiminī	audīminī
3	amantur	docentur	reguntur	incipiuntur	audiuntur
			IMPERFECT ACTIVE INDICATIVE		
1	amābam	docēbam	regēbam	incipiēbam	audiēbam
2	amābās	docēbās	regēbās	incipiēbās	audiēbās
3	amābat	docēbat	regēbat	incipiēbat	audiēbat
1	amābāmus	docēbāmus	regēbāmus	incipiēbāmus	audiēbāmus
2	amābātis	docēbātis	regēbātis	incipiēbātis	audiēbātis
3	amābant	docēbant	regēbant	incipiēbant	audiēbant

SYNCHRONOUS CHART: FOUR VERB CONJUGATIONS
INDICATIVE MOOD (continued)

	FIRST ā-stem	SECOND ē-stem	THIRD e-stem	THIRD i-stem	FOURTH ī-stem
	IMPERFECT PASSIVE INDICATIVE				
1	amābar	docēbar	regēbar	incipiēbar	audiēbar
2	amābāris amābāre	docēbāris docēbāre	regēbāris regēbāre	incipiēbāris incipiēbāre	audiēbāris audiēbāre
3	amābātur	docēbātur	regēbātur	incipiēbātur	audiēbātur
1	amābāmur	docēbāmur	regēbāmur	incipiēbāmur	audiēbāmur
2	amābāminī	docēbāminī	regēbāminī	incipiēbāminī	audiēbāminī
3	amābantur	docēbantur	regēbantur	incipiēbantur	audiēbantur
	FUTURE ACTIVE INDICATIVE				
1	amābō	docēbō	regam	incipiam	audiam
2	amābis	docēbis	regēs	incipiēs	audiēs
3	amābit	docēbit	reget	incipiet	audiet
1	amābimus	docēbimus	regēmus	incipiēmus	audiēmus
2	amābitis	docēbitis	regētis	incipiētis	audiētis
3	amābunt	docēbunt	regent	incipient	audient
	FUTURE PASSIVE INDICATIVE				
1	amābor	docēbor	regar	incipiar	audiar
2	amāberis amābere	docēberis docēbere	regēris regēre	incipiēris incipiēre	audiēris audiēre
3	amābitur	docēbitur	regētur	incipiētur	audiētur
1	amābimur	docēbimur	regēmur	incipiēmur	audiēmur
2	amābiminī	docēbiminī	regēminī	incipiēminī	audiēminī
3	amābuntur	docēbuntur	regentur	incipientur	audientur

SYNCHRONOUS CHART: FOUR VERB CONJUGATIONS
INDICATIVE MOOD (continued)

	FIRST **ā-stem**	SECOND **ē-stem**	THIRD **e-stem**	THIRD **i-stem**	FOURTH **ī-stem**
			PRESENT PERFECT ACTIVE INDICATIVE		
1	amāvī	docuī	rēxī	incēpī	audīvī
2	amāvistī	docuistī	rēxistī	incēpistī	audīvistī
3	amāvit	docuit	rēxit	incēpit	audīvit
1	amāvimus	docuimus	rēximus	incēpimus	audīvimus
2	amāvistis	docuistis	rēxistis	incēpistis	audīvistis
3	amāvērunt amāvere	docuērunt docuēre	rēxērunt rēxēre	incēpērunt incēpēre	audīvērunt audīvēre
(**NOTE:** -v- between vowels can be lost and the adjacent vowels then contracted: **amāstis, audīstis.**)					
			PRESENT PERFECT PASSIVE INDICATIVE		
1	amātus -a -um sum	doctus -a -um sum	rectus -a -um sum	inceptus -a -um sum	audītus -a -um sum
2	amātus -a -um es	doctus -a -um es	rectus -a -um es	inceptus -a -um es	audītus -a -um es
3	amātus -a -um est	doctus -a -um est	rectus -a -um est	inceptus -a -um est	audītus -a -um est
1	amātī -ae -a sumus	doctī -ae -a sumus	rectī -ae -a sumus	inceptī -ae -a sumus	audītī -ae -a sumus
2	amātī -ae -a estis	doctī -ae -a estis	rectī -ae -a estis	inceptī -ae -a estis	audītī -ae -a estis
3	amātī -ae -a sunt	doctī -ae -a sunt	rectī -ae -a sunt	inceptī -ae -a sunt	audītī -ae -a sunt
			PAST PERFECT ACTIVE INDICATIVE		
1	amāveram	docueram	rēxeram	incēperam	audīveram
2	amāverās	docuerās	rēxerās	incēperās	audīverās
3	amāverat	docuerat	rēxerat	incēperat	audīverat
1	amāverāmus	docuerāmus	rēxerāmus	incēperāmus	audīverāmus
2	amāverātis	docuerātis	rēxerātis	incēperātis	audīverātis
3	amāverant	docuerant	rēxerant	incēperant	audīverant

SYNCHRONOUS CHART: FOUR VERB CONJUGATIONS
INDICATIVE MOOD (continued)

	FIRST ā-stem	SECOND ē-stem	THIRD e-stem	THIRD i-stem	FOURTH ī-stem
			PAST PERFECT PASSIVE INDICATIVE		
1	amātus -a -um eram	doctus -a -um eram	rectus -a -um eram	inceptus -a -um eram	audītus -a -um eram
2	amātus -a -um erās	doctus -a -um erās	rectus -a -um erās	inceptus -a -um erās	audītus -a -um erās
3	amātus -a -um erat	doctus -a -um erat	rectus -a -um erat	inceptus -a -um erat	audītus -a -um erat
1	amātī -ae -a erāmus	doctī -ae -a erāmus	rectī -ae -a erāmus	inceptī -ae -a erāmus	audītī -ae -a erāmus
2	amātī -ae -a erātis	doctī -ae -a erātis	rectī -ae -a erātis	inceptī -ae -a erātis	audītī -ae -a erātis
3	amātī -ae -a erant	doctī -ae -a erant	rectī -ae -a erant	inceptī -ae -a erant	audītī -ae -a erant
			FUTURE PERFECT ACTIVE INDICATIVE		
1	amāverō	docuerō	rēxerō	incēperō	audīverō
2	amāveris	docuēris	rēxeris	incēperis	audīveris
3	amāverit	docuērit	rēxerit	incēperit	audīverit
1	amāverimus	docuerimus	rēxerimus	incēperimus	audīverimus
2	amāveritis	docueritis	rēxeritis	incēperitis	audīveritis
3	amāverint	docuerint	rēxerint	incēperint	audīverint
			FUTURE PERFECT PASSIVE INDICATIVE		
1	amātus -a -um erō	doctus -a -um erō	rectus -a -um erō	inceptus -a -um erō	audītus -a -um erō
2	amātus -a -um eris	doctus -a -um eris	rectus -a -um eris	inceptus -a -um eris	audītus -a -um eris
3	amātus -a -um erit	doctus -a -um erit	rectus -a -um erit	inceptus -a -um erit	audītus -a -um erit
1	amātī -ae -a erimus	doctī -ae -a erimus	rectī -ae -a erimus	inceptī -ae -a erimus	audītī -a -a erimus
2	amātī -ae -a eritis	doctī -ae -a eritis	rectī -ae -a eritis	inceptī -ae -a eritis	audītī -a -a eritis
3	amātī -ae -a erunt	doctī -ae -a erunt	rectī -ae -a erunt	inceptī -ae -a erunt	audītī -a -a erunt

SYNCHRONOUS CHART: FOUR VERB CONJUGATIONS
SUBJUNCTIVE MOOD (MODE)

	FIRST ā-stem	SECOND ē-stem	THIRD e-stem	THIRD i-stem	FOURTH ī-stem
			PRESENT ACTIVE SUBJUNCTIVE		
1	amem	doceam	regam	incipiam	audiam
2	amēs	doceās	regās	incipiās	audiās
3	amet	doceat	regat	incipiat	audiat
1	amēmus	doceāmus	regāmus	incipiāmus	audiāmus
2	amētis	doceātis	regātis	incipiātis	audiātis
3	ament	doceant	regant	incipiant	audiant
			PRESENT PASSIVE SUBJUNCTIVE		
1	amer	docear	regar	incipiar	audiar
2	amēris amēre	doceāris doceāre	regāris regāre	incipiāris incipiāre	audiāris audiāre
3	amētur	doceātur	regātur	incipiātur	audiātur
1	amēmur	doceāmur	regāmur	incipiāmur	audiāmur
2	amēminī	doceāminī	regāminī	incipiāminī	audiāminī
3	amentur	doceantur	regantur	incipiantur	audiantur
			IMPERFECT ACTIVE SUBJUNCTIVE		
1	amārem	docērem	regerem	inciperem	audīrem
2	amārēs	docērēs	regerēs	inciperēs	audīrēs
3	amāret	docēret	regeret	inciperet	audīret
1	amārēmus	docērēmus	regerēmus	inciperēmus	audīrēmus
2	amārētis	docērētis	regerētis	inciperētis	audīrētis
3	amārent	docērent	regerent	inciperent	audīrent

SYNCHRONOUS CHART: FOUR VERB CONJUGATIONS
SUBJUNCTIVE MOOD (continued)

	FIRST **ā-stem**	SECOND **ē-stem**	THIRD **e-stem**	THIRD **i-stem**	FOURTH **ī-stem**
	IMPERFECT PASSIVE SUBJUNCTIVE				
1	amārer	docērer	regerer	inciperer	audīrer
2	amārēris amārēre	docērēris docērēre	regerēris regerēre	inciperēris inciperēre	audīrēris audīrēre
3	amārētur	docērētur	regerētur	inciperētur	audīrētur
1	amārēmur	docērēmur	regerēmur	inciperēmur	audīrēmur
2	amārēminī	docērēminī	regerēminī	inciperēminī	audīrēminī
3	amārentur	docērentur	regerentur	inciperentur	audīrentur
	PRESENT PERFECT ACTIVE SUBJUNCTIVE				
1	amāverim	docuerim	rēxerim	incēperim	audīverim
2	amāveris	docueris	rēxeris	incēperis	audīveris
3	amāverit	docuerit	rēxerit	incēperit	audīverit
1	amāverimus	docuerimus	rēxerimus	incēperimus	audīverimus
2	amāveritis	docueritis	rēxeritis	incēperitis	audīveritis
3	amāverint	docuerint	rēxerint	incēperint	audīverint
	PRESENT PERFECT PASSIVE SUBJUNCTIVE				
1	amātus -a -um sim	doctus -a -um sim	rectus -a -um sim	inceptus -a -um sim	audītus -a -um sim
2	amātus -a -um sīs	doctus -a -um sīs	rectus -a -um sīs	inceptus -a -um sīs	audītus -a -um sīs
3	amātus -a -um sit	doctus -a -um sit	rectus -a -um sit	inceptus -a -um sit	audītus -a -um sit
1	amātī -ae -a sīmus	doctī -ae -a sīmus	rectī -ae -a sīmus	inceptī -ae -a sīmus	audītī -ae -a sīmus
2	amātī -ae -a sītis	doctī -ae -a sītis	rectī -ae -a sītis	inceptī -ae -a sītis	audītī -ae -a sītis
3	amātī -ae -a sint	doctī -ae -a sint	rectī -ae -a sint	inceptī -ae -a sint	audītī -ae -a sint

SYNCHRONOUS CHART: FOUR VERB CONJUGATIONS
SUBJUNCTIVE MOOD (continued)

	FIRST **ā-stem**	SECOND **ē-stem**	THIRD **e-stem**	THIRD **i-stem**	FOURTH **ī-stem**
			PAST PERFECT ACTIVE SUBJUNCTIVE		
1	amāvissem	docuissem	rēxissem	incēpissem	audīvissem
2	amāvissēs	docuissēs	rēxissēs	incēpissēs	audīvissēs
3	amāvisset	docuisset	rēxisset	incēpisset	audīvisset
1	amāvissēmus	docuissēmus	rēxissēmus	incēpissēmus	audīvissēmus
2	amāvissētis	docuissētis	rēxissētis	incēpissētis	audīvissētis
3	amāvissent	docuissent	rēxissent	incēpissent	audīvissent
			PAST PERFECT PASSIVE SUBJUNCTIVE		
1	amātus -a -um essem	doctus -a -um essem	rectus -a -um essem	inceptus -a -um essem	audītus -a -um essem
2	amātus -a -um essēs	doctus -a -um essēs	rectus -a -um essēs	inceptus -a -um essēs	audītus -a -um essēs
3	amātus -a -um esset	doctus -a -um esset	rectus -a -um esset	inceptus -a -um esset	audītus -a -um esset
1	amātī -ae -a essēmus	doctī -ae -a essēmus	rectī -ae -a essēmus	inceptī -ae -a essēmus	audītī -ae -a essēmus
2	amātī -ae -a essētis	doctī -ae -a essētis	rectī -ae -a essētis	inceptī -ae -a essētis	audītī -ae -a essētis
3	amātī -ae -a essent	doctī -ae -a essent	rectī -ae -a essent	inceptī -ae -a essent	audītī -ae -a essent

SYNCHRONOUS CHART: FOUR VERB CONJUGATIONS

INFINITIVE MOOD (MODE)

	FIRST **ā-stem**	SECOND **ē-stem**	THIRD **e-stem**	THIRD **i-stem**	FOURTH **ī-stem**
pres act	amāre	docēre	regere	incipere	audīre
pres pass	amārī	docērī	regī	incipī	audīrī
perf act	amāvisse	docuisse	rēxisse	incēpisse	audīvisse
perf pass	amātum -am -um/ -ōs -ās -a esse	doctum -am -um/ -ōs -ās -a esse	rectum -am -um/ -ōs -ās -a esse	inceptum -am -um/ -ōs -ās -a esse	audītum -am -um/ -ōs -ās -a esse
fut act	amāturum -am -um/ -ōs -ās -a esse	doctūrum -am -um/ -ōs -ās -a esse	rectūrum -am -um/ -ōs -ās -a esse	inceptūrum -am -um/ -ōs -ās -a esse	audītūrum -am -um/ -ōs -ās -a esse
fut pass	amātum īrī	doctum īrī	rectum īrī	inceptum īrī	audītum īrī

PARTICIPLE MOOD (MODE)

pres act	amāns, amantis	docēns, docentis	regēns, regentis	incipiēns, -cipientis	audiēns, audientis
perf pass	amātus, -a, -um	doctus, -a, -um	rectus, -a, -um	inceptus, -a, -um	audītus, -a, -um
fut act	amātūrus, -a, -um	doctūrus, -a, -um	rectūrus, -a, -um	inceptūrus, -a, -um	audītūrus, -a, -um

GERUNDIVE

("future passive participle" with obligation implied)

fut pass participle	amandus, -a, -um	docendus, -a, -um	regendus, -a, -um	incipiendus, -a, -um	audiendus, -a, -um

SYNCHRONOUS CHART: FOUR VERB CONJUGATIONS

IMPERATIVE

active	amā / amāte	docē / docēte	rege / regite	incipe / incipite	audī / audīte
passive	amāre / amāminī	docēre / docēminī	regere / regiminī	incipere / incipiminī	audīre / audīminī

VERBAL NOUNS

gerund only oblique singular					
	(illud) amandum, -ī	(illud) docendum, -ī	(illud) regendum, -ī	(illud) incipiendum, -ī	(illud) audiendum, -ī
supine only acc & abl singular					
	(ille) amātus, -ūs	(ille) doctus, -ūs	(ille) rectus, -ūs	(ille) inceptus, -ūs	(ille) audītus, -ūs
In addition to the gerund and the supine, the (indeclinable) infinitive is also a verbal noun. All three are quite restricted in their uses. Often the verbal action can also be named with regular nouns.					
verbal noun					
	(ille) amor, -ōris	(illa) doctrīna, -ae	(illa) regio, -ōnis	(illa) inceptio, -ōnis	(illa) auditio, -ōnis
Such nouns may have both subjective and objective modification: **meus amor tuī** "my love for you"; **amor deī hominis** "god's love for man" or "man's love for god."					

IRREGULAR VERBS

	sum, esse, fuī, futūrus	possum, posse, potuī	volō, velle, voluī	nōlō, nōlle, nōluī	mālō, mālle, māluī	ferō, ferre, tulī, lātus	eō, īre, ī(v)ī, ītus	edō, edere (ēsse), ēdī, ēsus	fīō, fierī, factus
PRESENT INDICATIVE ACTIVE									
1	sum	possum	volō	nōlō	mālō	ferō	eō	edō	fīō
2	es	potes	vīs	nōn vīs	māvīs	fers	īs	edis (ēs)	fīs
3	est	potest	vult (volt)	nōn vult	māvult	fert	it	edit (ēst)	fit
1	sumus	possumus	volumus	nōlumus	mālumus	ferimus	īmus	edimus	fīmus
2	estis	potestis	vultis	nōn vultis	māvultis	fertis	ītis	editis (ēstis)	fītis
3	sunt	possunt	volunt	nōlunt	mālunt	ferunt	eunt	edunt	fīunt
PRESENT INDICATIVE PASSIVE									
1						feror		edor	
2						ferris (ferre)		ederis (edere)	
3						fertur		ēstur	
1						ferimur		edimur	
2						feriminī		ediminī	
3						feruntur		eduntur	
PRESENT SUBJUNCTIVE ACTIVE									
1	sim	possim	velim	nōlim	mālim	feram	eam	edam (edim)	fīam
2	sīs	possīs	velīs	nōlīs	mālīs	ferās	eās	edās (edīs)	fīās
3	sit	possit	velit	nōlit	mālit	ferat	eat	edat (edit)	fīat
1	sīmus	possīmus	velīmus	nōlīmus	mālīmus	ferāmus	eāmus	edāmus (edīmus)	fīāmus
2	sītis	possītis	velītis	nōlītis	mālītis	ferātis	eātis	edātis (edītis)	fīātis
3	sint	possint	velint	nōlint	mālint	ferant	eant	edant (edint)	fīant

IRREGULAR VERBS (continued)

	sum	possum	volō	nōlō	mālō	ferō	eō	edō	fīō
					PRESENT SUBJUNCTIVE PASSIVE				
1						ferar		edar	
2						ferāris (ferāre)		edāris (edāre)	
3						ferātur		edātur	
1						ferāmur		edāmur	
2						ferāminī		edāminī	
3						ferantur		edantur	
					IMPERFECT INDICATIVE ACTIVE				
1	eram	poteram	volēbam	nōlēbam	mālēbam	ferēbam	ībam	edēbam	fīēbam
2	erās	poterās	volēbās	nōlēbās	mālēbās	ferēbās	ībās	edēbās	fīēbās
3	erat	poterat	volēbat	nōlēbat	mālēbat	ferēbat	ībat	edēbat	fīēbat
1	erāmus	poterāmus	volēbāmus	nōlēbāmus	mālēbāmus	ferēbāmus	ībāmus	edēbāmus	fīēbāmus
2	erātis	poterātis	volēbātis	nōlēbātis	mālēbātis	ferēbātis	ībātis	edēbātis	fīēbātis
3	erant	poterant	volēbant	nōlēbant	mālēbant	ferēbant	ībant	edēbant	fīēbant
					IMPERFECT INDICATIVE PASSIVE				
1						ferēbar		edēbar	
2						ferēbāris (ferēbāre)		edēbāris (edēbāre)	
3						ferēbātur		edēbātur	
1						ferēbāmur		edēbāmur	
2						ferēbāminī		edēbāminī	
3						ferēbantur		edēbantur	

IRREGULAR VERBS (continued)

	sum	possum	volō	nōlō	mālō	ferō	eō	edō	fīō
				IMPERFECT SUBJUNCTIVE ACTIVE					
1	essem	possem	vellem	nōllem	māllem	ferrem	īrem	ederem	fierem
2	essēs	possēs	vellēs	nōllēs	māllēs	ferrēs	īrēs	ederēs (ēssēs)	fierēs
3	esset	posset	vellet	nōllet	māllet	ferret	īret	ederet (ēsset)	fieret
1	essēmus	possēmus	vellēmus	nōllēmus	māllēmus	ferrēmus	īrēmus	ederēmus	fierēmus
2	essētis	possētis	vellētis	nōllētis	māllētis	ferrētis	īrētis	ederētis (ēssētis)	fierētis
3	essent	possent	vellent	nōllent	māllent	ferrent	īrent	ederent (ēssent)	fierent
				IMPERFECT SUBJUNCTIVE PASSIVE					
1						ferrer		ederer	
2						ferrēris (ferrēre)		ederēris (ederēre)	
3						ferrētur		ederētur (ēssētur)	
1						ferrēmur		ederēmur	
2						ferrēminī		ederēminī	
3						ferrentur		ederentur	
				PRESENT INFINITIVE					
act.	esse	posse	velle	nōlle	mālle	ferre	īre	edere (ēsse)	fierī
passive						ferrī	īrī	edī	
				PRESENT IMPERATIVE					
active	es / este			nōlī / nōlīte		fer / ferte	ī / īte	ede (ēs) / edite (ēste)	fī / fīte
passive							ferre / feriminī		

IRREGULAR VERBS (continued)

	sum	possum	volō	nōlō	mālō	ferō	eō	edō	fīō
					PARTICIPLE				
present		potēns	volēns	nōlēns		ferēns	iēns, euntis	edēns	
perfect						lātus	ītus	ēsus	factus
future	futūrus					lātūrus	itūrus	ēsūrus	factūrus
gerundive						ferendus	eundum		faciendus

Other forms are predictable from the principal parts:

sum, esse, fore, fuī, futūrus
volō, velle, voluī
mālō, mālle, māluī
eō, īre, iī (īvī), ītus
possum, posse, potuī
nōlō, nōlle, nōluī
ferō, ferre, tulī, lātus
edō, edere (ēsse), ēdī, ēsus
fīō, fierī, factus

Piranesi, Architectural Fantasy: A Grouping of Steps

ANSWERS

LESSON ONE
NOMINATIVE AND ACCUSATIVE

I. CHANGE

1. fēminās
2. virī
3. fortūnae
4. hominēs
5. deōs
6. diēs
7. diēs
8. puerōs
9. manūs
10. lēgēs
11. puerī
12. fīliae
13. matrēs
14. puellae
15. hominēs
16. amōrēs
17. deī
18. virōs
19. patrēs
20. vītae

II. MATCH

1. virum
2. deī / dī / deōs
3. hominēs
4. diēs
5. virī / virōs
6. matrem
7. manus / manūs
8. puerī / puerōs
9. puellae / puellās
10. diem
11. lēgem
12. fēminās
13. amōrēs
14. sapientia / sapientiae / sapientiās
15. pater
16. virī
17. hominēs
18. diēs
19. manūs
20. virī / virōs

III. MATCH

1. vir / virī / virōs
2. amor / amōrēs
3. fēminae / fēminās
4. fīlius / fīliī / fīliōs
5. fortūna / fortūnae / fortūnās

IV. MATCH

1. audit
2. audiunt
3. regit
4. amant
5. docent
6. regunt
7. audiunt
8. cupit
9. amat
10. videt

V. TRANSLATE *(TRANSLATION conveys the meaning of the Latin, but different wordings in English that convey the same meaning are all correct.)*

1. Fortune / luck, not wisdom, always rules (or controls) life. It (wisdom) ought to rule life. Fortune ought not to rule life. Wisdom ought to rule life. Women want to control life. Men say that fortune always rules life. Men see that fortune rules life. The gods rule life; fortune doesn't. The gods rule life; they don't control fortune.

2. Love is a god; fortune isn't.

3. Sons and daughters love (their) father and mother. Sons and daughters ought always to love their father and mother. (The / a) mother sees that (her) daughter loves (her) son. (The / a) father says that (the / a) mother loves (her) daughter.

4. Law rules men / mankind, and so does god. Girls and boys see that law and god always rule men. Fortune ought not to rule life. God ought to, and law.

5. The gods teach men to love wisdom. Women hear that men don't love wisdom.

VI. TRANSLATE

1. (One) hand rubs (another) hand.
2. Money provokes a greedy man; it doesn't satisfy him.
3. A greedy man is always in need.
4. Fortune / luck aids the bold (man) and repels the timid / cowardly.
5. Love begets love.
6. Favor begets favors.
7. A wolf changes its pelt, not its mind (or personality).
8. A lawsuit engenders (another) lawsuit.
9. Eagles don't give birth to doves.
10. A wolf recognizes (another) wolf, and a thief, (another) thief.

VII. CHANGE

1. AUDIT / DICIT / VIDET vītam fortūn**am** reg**ere**. *(S-he HEARS / SAYS / SEES that fortune rules life.* But **NOTE** that in oratio obliqua you cannot tell (except from context) that this doesn't also mean: *S-he hears / says / sees that life controls fortune.* Similarly, for all the following answers.*)*

2. Audit semper vid**ēre** hominēs de**ōs**. *(He hears that the gods always see men / mankind.)*

3. Dīcit cup**ere** matr**em** puellam docēre. *(She says that the mother wants to teach her daughter.)*

4. Videt vir**ōs** lēgēs am**āre**. *(He sees that men love laws.)*

5. Audit fīliās doc**ēre** matrēs fīliōsque patrēs. *(She hears that mothers teach their daughters, and fathers, their sons.)*

6. Dīcit sapientiam vītam regere oport**ēre**. *(He says that wisdom ought to rule life.)*

7. Videt puer**um** patrem am**āre**. *(She sees that a son loves his father.)*

8. Audit de**ōs** virōs fēmināsque reg**ere**. *(He hears that the gods rule men and women.)*

9. Dīcit amōr**em** deōs reg**ere**. *(She says that love rules the gods.)*

10. Videt patr**em** fīlium lēgēs doc**ēre**. *(He sees that a father teaches his son laws.)*

VIII. CHANGE

1. Matr**em** puellam am**āre** et patr**em** puerum oportet. *(A mother ought to love her daughter and a father, his son. Or, for a mother to love her daughter and for a father to love his son is fitting, proper, and necessary. Or, it is proper for a mother to love her daughter, and a father, his son. Or, a mother should love her daughter, and a father, his son.)*

2. Oportet de**ōs** hominēs reg**ere**. *(The gods ought to rule men/mankind.)*

3. Sapienti**am** vītam reg**ere** oportet. *(Wisdom should rule life.)*

4. Oportet cup**ere** puer**um** sapientiam amāre. *(A boy ought to want to love wisdom.)*

5. Semper vid**ēre** de**ōs** fēminās virōsque oportet. *(The gods always ought to watch men and women.)*

IX. NOTE THE PATTERN

1. *Love begets love.*
   Homo videt hominem. / Vir videt virum.
   Fortūna regit vītam.
   Mater amat fīliam.

2. *Fortune rules life; wisdom doesn't.*
   Fīliōs docet pater, nōn mater.
   Hominēs / virōs regit lex, nōn dī.

3. *S-he says that men love god.*
   Dīcit matrem fīliam amāre.
   Vident matrem fīliōs amāre.
   Audit fēmina virum fīliōs fīliāsque docēre.

4. *One ought to love god.*
   Vītam regere oportet.
   Virōs fēmināsque fīliōs fīliāsque docēre oportet.

LESSON TWO
GENDER, ADJECTIVES, PRESENT CONJUGATION

I. IDENTIFY

acer	3rd, three terminations
amīcus	1st & 2nd
atrox	3rd, one termination
audax	3rd, one termination
avārus	1st & 2nd
brevis	3rd, two terminations
bonus	1st & 2nd
longus	1st & 2nd
miser	1st & 2nd
mūtābilis	3rd, two terminations
prīmus	1st & 2nd

sōlus	1st & 2nd
timidus	1st & 2nd
varius	1st & 2nd

II. MATCH

1. audācēs
2. acris / acrēs
3. mūtābilēs
4. miser
5. amīcī / amīcōs
6. atrox
7. acrēs
8. bonās
9. misera
10. brevia
11. miseram
12. bonōs
13. atrōcia
14. bonī / bonōs
15. brevis
16. acria
17. longī / longōs
18. bona / bonae / bonās
19. mūtābilēs
20. miserī

III. MATCH

1. fēminam acrem
2. matrēs timidās
3. poētās bonōs
4. poētae audācēs
5. carmen miserum
6. cornū acre
7. daemonēs atrōcēs
8. vītae brevēs
9. virī bonī / virōs bonōs
10. mūtābilem fēminam
11. matrēs audācēs
12. poēmata misera
13. artēs prīmae / artēs prīmās
14. puerōs timidōs
15. timidī sōlī / timidōs sōlōs
16. poēta miser / poētam miserum
17. rem brevem
18. fīliī sōlī
19. carmina brevia
20. rēs prīmae / rēs prīmās

IV. MATCH

1. vir bonus / virī bonī / virōs bonōs
2. lex atrox / lēgēs atrōcēs
3. amīcus mūtābilis / amīcī mūtābilēs / amīcōs mūtābilēs
4. patrēs avārī / patrēs avārōs
5. poētae timidī / poētās timidōs

V. MATCH

1. incipit
2. canunt
3. satiāmus
4. docet
5. amātis
6. incipiunt
7. amās
8. sumus

9. audiunt
10. satiātis
11. videt
12. es
13. regunt
14. docētis
15. incipimus
16. satiāre
17. audīs
18. incipere
19. audītis
20. docent

VI. TRANSLATE

1. The poet begins to sing a song first. The man is first, not the woman. He begins first, not she. She does sing. The woman doesn't begin to sing. He begins. He is a first(-rate) poet and first does he begin to sing. She isn't first. The poet ought to begin first. The woman ought not to begin first. The woman is a poet. She is not a first(-rate) poet. The poet and the woman sing.

2. Poets teach men / mankind not to love a long life. A short life is good, not a long one. The cowardly love a long life, not the good (and brave). Life is changeable. The good love a short life. Life is miserable. Miserable fortune / luck rules life, not good fortune / luck. Wisdom ought to rule life; luck shouldn't.

3. The greedy ought not always to love money. The wretched love money, not the good. A good man doesn't love money. He loves wisdom / knowledge. Good poets teach mankind not to love money. Only the greedy love money.

4. It is a good thing to write laws. Good men write laws. The first law / commandment is not to love a long life.

5. Variable and changeable is always that danger. It is miserable. The miserable man doesn't see the danger. The woman begins to see the danger first. The miserable woman doesn't see the first danger.

6. There are good men. There are good women. Men are good and women miserable. Men and women ought to be good.

7. Only the gods ought to rule life. Nor ought mutable, miserable men to rule life. Only the gods are good.

8. We poets teach the women to sing songs first, and not the men. Women ought to begin to sing first, and not the men. The women sing first.

9. Good men write laws. Good men write good laws. The cruel man writes cruel laws, and the good man, good laws.

10. The greedy always desire money. Money doesn't satisfy the greedy. A good life ought to satisfy mankind, money shouldn't.

VIII. TRANSLATE

1. A changeable and mutable thing is a woman always. Changeable and mutable always is that woman.

2. Indulgence produces friends; truth produces hatred.
3. To grieve is (a) bad (thing).
4. Fortune / luck does not change (one's) class.
5. To err is (a) human (thing).
6. Man alone / only man is either a god or a demon.
7. Hunger is not sought after.
8. A woman either loves or hates (you). There is no third (possibility).
9. Experience teaches.
10. The hours I do not count, except the serene / sunny (ones).
11. To err is (a) human (thing); human, however, is (it also) to forgive.
12. (It) is art to conceal art / artifice.
13. Fire is the proof for gold; misery, for brave / strong men.
14. To work is to pray.
15. (One) hand washes (the other) hand.
16. Prudence / caution first deserts the miserable (people).
17. Nature abhors a vacuum.
18. Friendship is (only a) word; (only an) empty word is trust.
19. (It) is a big matter to keep silent.
20. (It) is virtue to flee vice.
21. To be alive is to be thinking.
22. The gods have feet (shod with) woolen (slippers).

VIII. CHANGE

1. AUDIT / CANIT / DOCET / DICIT / SCRIBIT / VIDET diēs semper aut long**ōs** **esse** aut brevēs. *(S-he hears / sings / teaches / says / writes / sees that days always are either long or short.)*

2. Canit pecūni**am** avārōs sati**āre** sōl**am**. *(He sings that money alone satifies the greedy.)*

3. Mūtābile et varium semper **esse** fēmin**am** docet. Mūtābil**em** et vari**am** semper (**esse**) ill**am** fēmin**am** docet. *(She teaches that a woman is always a mutable and changeable thing. She teaches that that woman is always mutable and changeable.)*

4. Dīcit puell**ās** et puer**ōs** semper mūtābilēs vari**ōs**que **esse**. *(He says that girls and boys always are mutable and changeable.)*

5. Carmina audācia poēt**am** miser**um** scrīb**ere** scrībit. *(She writes that the unhappy poet writes audacious songs / poems.)*

6. Videt prīm**um** incip**ere** poēt**am** canere poēma longum. *(He sees that the poet begins to sing a long poem first.)*

7. Cornua acria aud**īre** timid**ōs** audit. *(She hears that the timid (men) hear the fierce (battle) horns.)*

8. Canit sapientiam oport**ēre** semper vītam bonam regere. *(He sings that wisdom ought always to rule the good life.)*

9. Homin**em** sōl**um** aut de**um** aut daemon**em** (**esse**) docet. *(She teaches that man alone is either a god or a demon.)*

10. Scrībit vīt**am** brev**em** **esse** art**em**que long**am**. *(He writes that life is short and art long.)*

IX. NOTE THE PATTERN

1. *A variable and changeable thing is woman always.*
   Miserum et avārum semper homo / vir.
   Bonī semper dī.

2. *To grieve is a bad thing/It is bad to grieve.*
   Canere bonum est.
   Amīcōs amāre prīmum est.

3. *The hours I don't count, except the serene/sunny ones.*
   Carmina nōn canō nisī bona.
   Amīcōs nōn videt nisī miserōs.
   Hominēs / virōs nōn amant dī nisī bonōs.

LESSON THREE
GENITIVE AND SUBJUNCTIVE

I. IDENTIFY

animal	3rd, i-stem
caput	3rd
cursus	4th
domus	4th & 2nd
furtum	2nd
genus	3rd
glōria	1st
ignis	3rd, i-stem
lignum	2nd
memoria	1st
miseria	1st
pars	3rd, i-stem
pretium	2nd
vīnum	2nd
glōriōsus	1st & 2nd
ligneus	1st & 2nd

magnus	1st & 2nd
paternus	1st & 2nd
pretiōsus	1st & 2nd
reus	1st & 2nd
sapiens	3rd, i-stem
sempiternus	1st & 2nd
stultus	1st & 2nd

II. MATCH

1. poētae stultī
2. amōrum avārōrum
3. prīmās fēminās
4. puerī reī / puerōs reōs
5. ignium sempiternōrum
6. animālis timidī / animālia timida
7. glōriae sempiternae / glōriās sempiternās
8. artium paternārum
9. perīculum prīmum
10. lacuum magnōrum
11. acrium puerōrum
12. daemonum atrōcium
13. diērum glōriōsōrum
14. manūs atrōcis
15. sapientēs matrēs
16. capita stulta
17. cornūs acris
18. partium prīmārum
19. animālium atrōcium
20. reī audācēs / reōs audācēs

III. MATCH

1. amet
2. incipiunt
3. admoneās
4. sītis
5. vidēmus
6. damnēmus
7. cupiās
8. satiāmus
9. satiāre
10. dīcit
11. incipiāmus
12. audiat
13. dēbētis
14. habeant
15. sīs
16. satiētis
17. docēre
18. amat
19. cupis
20. regunt

IV. TRANSLATE

1. We hear that that wise poet has a house of great value.
2. Let's always esteem (it) of great (value) to have wise friends.
3. Perhaps the wise man may condemn the stupid woman (for the crime) of theft.
4. You / one may say that atrocious and audacious men always are guilty of a capital punishment or (a fine) of money.
5. Is (it) a wise man's (role) to sing short songs?
6. Wise men do not put aside / forget the memory of (their) mothers' and fathers' lives.

7. May stupid men always esteem wisdom and glory (as something) of great (value)!
8. Does the greedy man have wooden vats of wine or a costly house of wood?
9. Granted he is / be a poet of great wisdom; nevertheless, he writes miserable and long poems.
10. Should we remind the good (men) of glory?

V. TRANSLATE

1. Let the buyer beware!
2. Infinite is the number of the stupid (men).
3. Let's live, my Lesbia, and let's love!
4. Let a parent neither have vices nor tolerate them!
5. The nature of men is greedy for novelty.
6. No abundance of money satisfies a greedy man.
7. Let reason lead me / (be my guide), not fortune!
8. All (things / posessions) of friends are common / held in common.
9. Grave / grievous always is the wrath of kings.
10. Love of praise motivates men.

VI. CHANGE

1. AUDIT / CANIT / DOCET / DICIT / SCRIBIT / VIDET ill**um** prīm**um** **esse** poētārum magnōrum. *(S-he hears / sings / teaches / says / writes / sees that that (man) is the first (out of the group) of great poets.)*

2. Partem sōlam vītae reg**ere** de**ōs** videt. *(S-he sees that the gods rule only a part (out of the totality) of life.)*

3. Docet sapientis **esse** deōs amāre. *(S-he teaches that it is a wise person's role to love the gods.)*

4. Poēt**ās** virōs admon**ēre** vītae glōriōsae dīcit. *(S-he says that poets remind men of a glorious life.)*

5. Dīcit ill**um** poēt**am** vir**um** **esse** magnae sapientiae. *(S-he says that that poet is a man of great wisdom.)*

VII. CHANGE

1. **NOTE** that modal auxiliary verbs like *dēbeō* can be used in the subjunctive: Virī dēbeant semper sapientēs esse. *Let men owe it always to be wise.* But what we are practicing in exercises like this, is to eliminate the modal auxiliary and to say something similar with the subjunctive, without a modal auxiliary. Virī semper sapientēs **sint**. *(Men ought always to be wise / Men should always be wise.)*

2. Stultumne damn**ēmus** furtī? *(Should we condemn the stupid man of theft?)*

3. Glōriae memoriam **nē** dēpōn**ās**. *(You/one shouldn't put aside the memory of glory.)*

4. Sapientiam(ne) magnī **nē** aestim**ēmus**? (Shouldn't we esteem wisdom as something of great value?)

5. Ille poēta scrīb**at** aut bona aut brevia carmina. *(That poet should write either good or short songs.)*

6. **NOTE** that the subjunctive of *oportet* would be *oporteat,* but we want to eliminate the modal auxiliary, which will incidentally do away with the whole original structure of an infinitive phrase as subject of the so-called impersonal verb *oportet.* Puerī patrēs matrēsque aestim**ent** magnī. *(Boys should esteem their fathers and mothers highly/as something of great value.)*

7. Dom**us** pretiōs**a** lignī **sit**. *(A costly house should be of wood.)*

8. Fēmin**ās**ne re**ās** capitis damn**ēmus**? *(Should we condemn the guilty women to death/of a capital offense?)*

9. Stultōs deōrum admone**āmus** sempiternōrum. *(We should remind the stupid people of the immortal gods.)*

10. Pecūnia avārōs **nē** sati**et**. *(Money shouldn't satisfy the greedy men.)*

VIII. CHANGE

1. **NOTE** that, as in the previous exercise, we want to replace the modal auxiliary, not change it into the subjunctive *possim.* (**Forsitan**) fēmina magnae sapientiae **sim**. *(I may/can be a woman of great wisdom.)*

2. (**Forsitan**) poētās admone**āmus** miseriae hominum. *(We may remind the poets of the misery of men.)*

3. (**Forsitan**) rea **sit** puella capitis. *(The girl may be guilty of a capital offense.)*

4. Nōn sapientia sapientium sempiternum **sit**. **NOTE** that the negative *nōn,* instead of *nē,* with a subjunctive is sufficient context to indicate that this is a negative potential, even without *forsitan,* instead of a jussive or optative subjunctive. *(The wisdom of the wise (people) may not be eternal.)*

5. (**Forsitan**) poēta carmina brevia can**at**. *(The poet may sing short songs.)*

6. (**Forsitan**) lignī domum hab**eās**. *(You may have a house of wood.)*

7. (**Forsitan**) magnī aestim**ētis** sapientiam fēminārum. *(You can esteem the wisdom of women highly/as something of great value.)*

8. Lēgēs vītam hominum stultōrum nōn reg**ant**. *(Laws can't rule the life of stupid men.)*

9. Ille timidus memoriam ignis magnī nōn dēpōn**eat**. *(That timid man can't put aside the memory of the great fire.)*

10. (**Forsitan**) mūtābile et varium homo **sit**. *(Man may be a changeable and variable creature/thing.)*

IX. CHANGE

1. **NOTE** that, as in the previous exercises, we don't want the subjunctive *optem*, but our task is to eliminate the modal auxiliary. (**Utinam**) vīt**a** avārī brev**is** miser**a**que **sit**. *(May the life of the greedy man be short and miserable.)*

2. (**Utinam**) curs**us** glōriae sempitern**us** **sit**. *(May the course of glory be eternal.)*

3. (**Utinam**) homo daemon **nē** **sit**. *(May man not be a demon.)*

4. (**Utinam**) prīmus poētārum **sim**. *(May I be the first of poets.)*

5. (**Utinam**) lacūs ligneōs hab**eāmus** vīnī. *(May we have wooden vats of wine.)*

6. (**Utinam**) **ars** sapientium long**a** **sit**. *(May the art of the wise people be long.)*

7. (**Utinam**) amīcōrum **sit** lēgēs scrībere. *(May it be the role of friends to write the laws.)*

8. (**Utinam**) atrōcēs stultīque vītam longam **nē** hab**eant**. *(May the atrocious and stupid people not have a long life.)*

9. (**Utinam**) timidōs admon**eam** perīculī. *(May I remind the timid of the danger.)*

10. (**Utinam**) cornua acria **nē** aud**iam**. *(May I not hear the fierce battle horns.)*

X. NOTE THE PATTERN

1. *The woman pities the man/the man's pitiableness disturbs the woman.*
   Miseret deōs hominum.
   Miseret patrem filiī.
   Miseret sapientēs stultōrum.
   Miseret amīcōs amīcōrum.

2. *Let the buyer beware.*
   Doceant sapientēs.
   Satiet pecūnia avārōs.
   Amet mater filiam.

3. *Let's listen and speak.*
   Audiāmus atque dīcāmus.

LESSON FOUR
PASSIVE, PURPOSE CLAUSE, INDIRECT QUESTIONS

I. MATCH

1. parēs partēs
2. vitiī paris
3. ovium caecārum
4. dōnōrum parvōrum
5. atrōcem virum
6. grātiārum omnium
7. vēritātēs sōlae / vēritātēs sōlās
8. philosophōrum sapientium
9. virtūs prīma
10. amīcī omnēs / amīcōs omnēs
11. aquae bonae / aquās bonās
12. matrēs caecae / matrēs caecās
13. parvōrum vitiōrum
14. magnī ignis
15. artēs omnēs
16. lacuum parvōrum
17. puerī miserī / puerōs miserōs
18. vītārum brevium
19. reī magnae
20. omne animal

II. MATCH

1. proficiscāmur (**NOTE**: match form, not meaning for deponent verbs)
2. quaeruntur
3. rogētur
4. docent
5. morī
6. negēs
7. dēs
8. amāris / amāre
9. audīrī
10. caniminī
11. scrībere / scrīberis
12. vīvātis
13. rogās
14. regāminī
15. quaerere / quaereris
16. aestimēris / aestimēre
17. damnantur
18. audior
19. amēre / amēris
20. damnēmur

III. CHANGE

1. incipere
2. dētur
3. quaerunt
4. scrībis
5. rogārī / rogās
6. doceāmus
7. audīre
8. videātis
9. canuntur
10. vīvuntur
11. videam
12. audīrī / audīs
13. regātur
14. audiar
15. dās
16. admoneor
17. damnētis
18. habet
19. repetī / repetis
20. satier

IV. TRANSLATE

1. It is questioned whether kings always are / be atrocious / cruel. Perhaps that king may not be atrocious. May he not be atrocious. Let that king not be cruel! Let him be good! Let all cruel kings always be condemned either (at the penalty) of a fine or their life / head! Do you deny (that) all cruel men ought to be comdemned to death? I say (that it) is a wise man's (role) to condemn all cruel people.

2. (Granted that it) is esteemed of great (value) to write songs; nevertheless, that poet always sings poems (that are) both long and glorious. He says (that) everyone can control a good life. We all ought to control our life. Let fortune not be king of all things! That poet questions whether death is / be eternal. Let him deny (that) death is / be (something) bad!

3. Let everyone / all pity the blind man! He is condemned to death, but guilty is he not of theft. Let us esteem that man of great (value) and let's say (that) he is good! Let's deny the man to be guilty! May it be questioned whether that blind man ought to be condemned to death. The man ought not to die. Let him not die! Let him live a long life! Let's not forget the poor man! Let him live! Let him not be miserable!

4. (Granted) she is a woman of great wisdom; nevertheless, she is guilty of theft. That wise woman ought not to forget all laws. Laws ought always to rule the life of men / people. Let it be asked whether that wise woman ought to be condemned for a fine or to death!

5. You / one may say (that) the course of life is glorious. Life ought to be glorious, but it isn't always glorious. It is said that fortune is blind and that she rules over the life of men. All men are not wise. A great part of mankind is stupid. May all people be philosophers so that they may rule a good life. Let fortune not be the king over mankind; but let virtue be the ruler. Let us all be rulers so that we not be ruled!

V. TRANSLATE

1. You ought to eat to live, not live to eat.
2. Water is the fountain of life.
3. The Lord pastures me / the Lord is my shepherd.
4. The heavens tell the glory of God, and the firmament announces the work of his hand.

VI. CHANGE

1. Quaeritur **num** omnēs sapientēs dēb**eant** magnī aestimārī. *(It is questioned / asked whether all wise men ought to be esteemed of great value.)*

2. Rogō **num** pars hominum sōla memoriam repet**at** grātiae. *(I ask whether only a part of mankind remembers a favor.)*

3. Negāmus philosoph**um** sapient**em** virtūtis oblīviscī. *(We deny that the wise philosopher is forgetful of virtue/we say that the wise philosopher doesn't forget virtue.)*

4. Quaeritur **num** fēmina furtī rea dēb**eat** pecūniae damnārī. *(It is questioned whether the woman guilty of theft ought to be condemned to pay a fine.)*

5. **Num** miser**eat** matrem filiae caecae rogās. *(You ask whether the mother pities her blind daughter.* **NOTE** that you don't have to place the main verb at the beginning of the sentence; similarly, for all the exercises of this type.*)*

6. Ōtium hab**ēre** semper stult**ōs** scrībit sapiens. *(The wise man writes that stupid people always have leisure time.)*

7. Dīcit philosophus fēmin**ās** virōrum parēs **posse** esse. *(The philospher says that women can be the equals of men.)*

8. Morī grāti**am** et odium vīv**ere** negant. *(They say that a favor doesn't die away and hatred live on.)*

9. Vidēmus ov**em** ovem semper sequī et caec**um** caecum. *(We see that sheep always follow sheep and the blind, the blind.)*

10. Vir**um** magnae sapientiae vitia nōn dēb**ēre** habēre audīmus. *(We hear that a man of great wisdom oughtn't have vices.)*

VII. CHANGE

1. Vēritātem dīcō **ut** damn**em** illum virum capitis. *(I say the truth in order to condemn that man to death.)*

2. Poēta incipit canere **ut** hominēs virtūtem doc**eat**. *(The poet begins to sing in order to teach men virtue.)*

3. **Ut** avārum sati**ēs** dōnum pecūniae dās. (*To satisfy the greedy man, you give him a gift of money*. **NOTE** that, as in the previous exercises, the main clause doesn't have to begin the sentence.)

4. Semper admonet hominēs glōriae **ut** magnī aestim**ētur**. *(He/she reminds mankind of glory in order to be highly esteemed/esteemed of great value.)*

5. Proficisciminī **ut** poētam magnum audi**ātis**. *(You-all start out on the journey to hear the great poet.)*

6. Omnēs amat illa fēmina stulta **ut** semper am**ētur**. *(That stupid woman loves everybody in order to be always loved herself.)*

7. Philosophum sapientem sequimur **nē** virtūtis oblīvisc**āmur**. *(We follow the wise philosopher in order not to be forgetful of virtue.)*

8. **Nē** vitia hab**eam** rēgem sapientem sequor. *(In order not to have vices, I follow the wise king.)*

9. Ovēs ovēs semper sequuntur **nē** mori**antur** sōlae. *(Sheep always follow sheep so as not to die alone.)*

10. **Ut** vītam bonam reg**am** sapiens cupiō esse. *(So as to rule over a good life, I want to be wise.)*

VIII. NOTE THE PATTERN

1. *You ought to eat to live, not live to eat.*
   Amāre oportet ut amēris, nōn amārī ut amēs.
   Dōna dare oportet ut magnī aestimēmur.
   Nōn vēritātis oblīviscī oportet ut sapiens videar.

   Amāre dēbēs ut amēris, nōn amārī ut amēs.
   Dōna dare dēbēmus ut magnī aestimēmur.
   Nōn vēritātis oblīviscī dēbeō ut sapiens videar.

   Amēs ut amēris, nē amēris ut amēs.
   Dōna dēmus ut magnī aestimēmur. *(The form* dēmus *by chance is unattested.)*
   Nē vēritātis oblīviscar ut sapiens videar.

2. *It is questioned whether death be a bad thing.*
   Quaeritur num vīta bonum sit.
   Rogāmur num avārus possit satiārī.
   Quaerunt num ovis ovem sequātur / Rogant num ovēs ovēs sequantur.

LESSON FIVE
ABLATIVE AND DATIVE

I. MATCH

1. dēformī fīliā
2. noctibus brevibus
3. mortium malārum
4. rēgī sapientī
5. urbium fortium
6. reī difficilī
7. vultū audācī / audāce
8. ovī stultae / ove (-ī) stultā
9. partibus dēformibus
10. nōminī dulcī / nōmine dulcī
11. atrōcēs reī / atrōcēs reōs
12. vēritāte sempiternā
13. virī fortēs / virōs fortēs
14. mūtābilibus fēminīs
15. pulchrī poētae
16. vīnī fortis / vīnō fortī / vīna fortia
17. stilīs longīs
18. fābulae dulcī / fābulā dulcī
19. matris pulchrae / matrēs pulchrae
20. mortium miserārum

II. MATCH

1. amantur
2. interficiam
3. satiāre / satiāris
4. habētur
5. audiāminī
6. amārī
7. perdere / perderis
8. cōgitet
9. placeam
10. canāmur
11. crēderis
12. dantur
13. audīs
14. cognōscat
15. dēris / dēre
16. vīvitis
17. amer
18. loquī
19. interficiam
20. rogēre / rogēris

III. TRANSLATE

1. In the city (there) is a great poet. (There) is a house of wood for the poet / the poet has a house of wood. A man is he of great virtue and wise. It pleases the poet to sing and always with great wisdom does he sing. Let him sing / may he sing always with great art. He is said by all to be wise and a man with a sweet tongue / voice. It is questioned by the poet in his poems whether fortune rules over the life of humans. Let / may the life of men not be ruled by fortune but by all the eternal gods! Fortune always is changeable, nor ought men to trust changeable fortune. Let us place our trust in the good gods! Everyone ought to hear that poet. Of great value by all wise people let / may that poet be esteemed! All ought to trust / believe the poet. Let / may all trust the wise poet. The poet's songs are wise / the poet has wise songs. May the stupid believe the poet. Perhaps the stupid may begin to think about the eternal gods. Let / may all the stupid people recognize the truth about all things! All day and all night long, poems does he write and with his friends he talks. Always at night he writes. He is said by his friends to write with great art, that man of great virtue. With all (our) friends, we set out on a journey to the poet's city to see the poet. With the poet we want to speak.

2. The king asks whether a cruel person in that city is condemned by all good men either for the penalty of a fine or death. The king says (that) every cruel person ought to be condemned by all wise people. (It is) a wise man's (role) always to condemn cruel persons either for a fine or to death. The king is a man of great virtue. With great virtue does he reign. Let / may that king reign forever! All good men thank the king / all good men give thanks to the king. All ought to thank the king. Either with (the instrument of) a rock or a sword ought the cruel guilty person to be killed. Let / may all good men kill the guilty person either with rock or sword!

3. Granted he is king; nevertheless, he is a man of great virtue. A brave man is he and with virtue is the city ruled by the brave king. All good men say (that) the

city is ruled with (the instrument of) laws by (the agency of) the king.

4. May (there) be wisdom for all men so that man not harm man, nor commit/ do stupid cruel (acts)! Let/may men not harm men! Man ought not to harm man. (It) pleases man to harm man. May man trust man. We recognize (that) man harms man. Man by man is killed. Man with rock or sword kills man. Man does not pity man.

5. Perhaps we cannot live without danger, but everybody ought not always to be cowardly. By fortune are we ruled, not by the eternal gods. From the great poet we ought to inquire whether death be something bad. By the poet in his sweet songs it is questioned whether a man of great wisdom can live without danger.

6. We do not forget the gods. Let us not be forgetful of the gods! It pleases men not to forget the gods. May we not forget the gods. Men ought not to forget the gods.

7. A long life is given by the gods to good men as a gift so that they live with great virtue. The gift of life do the gods give to men. Life do they give to men as a gift. Let/may the gods not give a short life to men as a gift! For men, a short life is (there) from the gods/Men have a short life from the gods. (It) is men's (lot) to have a short life from the gods.

8. All night long by the poet with his friends it is questioned whether poets ought to write short poems or long. At night, he asks whether a short poem is good/something good. (It) is a good (thing) to write poems about the virtue of men. About a brave man a poem is song by the poet. With (the instrument of) a stylus, a poem is written by the poet with (the manner of) great art. To his friends, a poem does he give as a gift.

9. We ought to forget all the arts and live without letters/literature. Can we live without the arts? I ask whether life without letters be death. With pen I write (that) life without letters is death. (It) is a good (thing) to have leisure with letters. (It) is a wise man's (role) to live with letters. Of slight value is esteemed a life without letters by all wise men. Wise men pity the stupid.

10. Wisdom is given to man as a danger by the gods. Wisdom to men as a danger do the gods always give. Philosophers recognize (that) wisdom is given to men as a danger. They inquire whether wisdom harms men.

IV. TRANSLATE

1. Difficult is (it) not to reveal a crime by your appearance.

2. Man to man is a wolf.

3. A thing said/a word to the wise is sufficient.

4. Let / may arms yield / give way to the toga; let / may the laurel (wreath of the victor) give way to the tongue (of political debate).

5. Concerning the dead, nothing but something good let us say.

6. Let kings yield to songs; and (so also) the triumphs of kings.

7. An art / trick (that has) various (aspects) is (there) for the fox; but (only) one for the hedgehog—the biggest / best.

8. Leisure without letters is death.

9. Virtue is (it) to flee vices.

10. They eat the bread of impiety, and the wine of iniquity do they drink. —Book of Proverbs of Solomon from the Sacred Bible (made into the) Common (language).

11. The first principle of wisdom is the fear of the Lord and the knowledge of holy things is prudence. —Same place.

12. Wise men hide (their) knowledge; the mouth of a stupid man, on the contrary, is the nearest to confusion. —Same place.

13. The law of a wise man is the fountain of life so that he turn away from the ruin of death. —Same place.

14. In the numerousness of (his) people is a king's dignity and in the paucity of (his) commoners is a prince's ignominy. —Same place.

15. Let your heart enter into learning, and your ears into the words of knowledge. —Same place.

V. CHANGE

1. Pecūnia nōn **est** avārī acr**is**. Pecūnia nōn **est** avār**ō** acr**ī**. *(The money is not the bitter greedy man's. There isn't money for the greedy bitter man to possess.)*

2. Matr**is** dēformis dēformēs **sunt** fīliī fīli**ae**que. Matr**ī** dēform**ī** dēformēs **sunt** fīliī fīli**ae**que. *(Ugly are the ugly mother's sons and daughters. For the ugly mother there are ugly sons and daughters.)*

3. Poēmata difficilia **sunt** sapient**is** poēt**ae**. Poēmata difficilia **sunt** sapientī poēt**ae**. *(The difficult poems are the the wise poet's. Difficult poems are there for the wise poet to possess.)*

4. Amīcī rēgum atrōc**is** **sunt** ovēs. Amīc**ō** rēgum atroc**ī** **sunt** ovēs. *(The sheep are the kings' cruel friend's. There are sheep for the cruel friend of the kings to possess.)*

5. Cornua longa acriaque **sunt** animāl**is**. Cornua longa acriaque **sunt** animāl**ī**. *(The long and sharp horns are the animal's. Long and sharp horns are there for the*

animal to use.)

6. Urb**is** rēgis bon**ae** **sunt** lēg**ēs**. Urb**ī** rēgis bon**ae** **sunt** lēg**ēs**. *(Good are the laws of the king's city. For the king's city there are good laws to use.)*

7. Nē **sit** stult**ōrum** sapienti**a**. Nē **sit** stult**īs** sapienti**a**. *(Let there not be any stupid people's wisdom. Let there not be any wisdom for stupid people to use.)*

8. Forsitan **sit** puer**ī** dēformis vīt**a** long**a**. Forsitan **sit** puer**ō** dēform**ī** vīt**a** long**a**. *(Perhaps the ugly boy's life may be long. Perhaps there may be a long life for the ugly boy.)*

9. Potestne fēmin**ae** magnae sapientis dom**us** lignī **esse**? Potestne fēmin**ae** magnae sapientis dom**us** lignī **esse**? *(Can the house of wood be the woman of great wisdom's? Can there be a house of wood for the woman of great wisdom?)*

10. Omn**ium** rē**rum** nōmina varia **sunt**. Omn**ibus** rē**bus** nōmina varia **sunt**. *(Various are the names of all things. There are various names for all things.)*

VI. CHANGE

(This exercise is like the second part of the previous exercise, but it will give you a chance to become familiar with the declension of pronouns and pronominal adjectives.)

1. Pecūni**a** nōn est **mihi**. *(I don't have money/there isn't any money for me.)*

2. Neque fīliī neque fīli**ae** **sunt** **nōbīs**. *(Neither sons nor daughters are there for us.)*

3. Illī magn**a** pars domūs **est** sōlī. *(A great part of the house is for her alone.* **NOTE** that you cannot distinguish, however, that it is hers, rather than his now, without further context.*)*

4. Forsitan cum omnibus bonīs **sit** mors glōriōs**a** **vōbīs**. *(Perhaps there may be a glorious death for you-all, along with all good men.)*

5. Utinam in illā urbe **sit tibi** omnibus cum amīcīs illīus rēgis magn**a** ex lignō dom**us**. *(May there be for you in that city, along with all the friends of that king, a great house made out of wood.)*

6. Illī animālī cornua illīus generis **sunt**. *(For that animal there are horns of that type.)*

7. Illī tēcum nōn **est** curs**us** vītae glōriōs**us**. *(For him, along with you, there is not a glorious course of life.)*

8. Lac**us** neque vīnī neque aquae **est tibi**. *(A vat neither of wine nor of water is there for you.)*

9. Utinam amīcī stultī avārīque nē **sint vōbīs** in illā urbe atrōcī. *(May there not be stupid and greedy friends for you in that cruel city.)*

10. Illī puell**ae** sapientī sōlī ex omnibus fēminīs vīt**a** miser**a** nōn **est**. *(For that wise girl alone out of all women there is not an unhappy life.)*

VII. CHANGE

1. Nōn reg**itur** vīt**a** **ab** homin**ibus** stultīs, sed **ā** sapient**ibus** sōl**īs**. *(Life is not ruled by stupid men, but only by the wise.)*

2. Capitis damn**antur** **ā** r**ēge** in illā urbe omnēs reī et interfic**iuntur** gladiō. *(To death are condemned by the king in that city all guilty men and they are killed with the sword.)*

3. Animal pulchrum illīus generis **ā** mat**re** puerīs dōnō d**atur**. *(An animal of that sort is given by the mother to her boys as a gift.)*

4. Magnī aestim**ātur** **ā** **tē** amīcōs sapientēs tēcum semper habēre, sed nōn **ā** **mē**. *(Of great value is it esteemed by you to have wise friends always with you, but not by me.)*

5. Nōbīscum vid**eātur** **ā** **vōbīs** in urbe **vir** magnae sapientiae. *(Along with us may / let the man of great wisdom be seen by you-all in the city.)*

6. Poēmata brevia sed magnā arte can**antur** **ab** **illō** **poētā** sapientī (-e). (*Let poems that are short but with great art be sung by that wise poet.)*

7. Vēritātis sempiternae admon**eātur** **ā** philosoph**ō** sapientī (**-e**) **rex** omn**is** atro**x** stult**us**que. *(Of the eternal truth let/may every cruel and stupid king be reminded by the wise philosopher.)*

8. Forsitan **ab** omn**ibus** vir**īs** bon**īs** damn**ētur** ill**e** **homo** auda**x** furtī. *(Perhaps by all good men that audacious man may be condemned of theft.)*

9. **Ā** poēt**īs** quaer**itur** num mors malum sit. *(By poets it is questioned whether death be something bad.)*

10. Pecūniam avārīs dōnō **ā** **mē** **darī** nōn cupiō. *(I don't want money to be given to greedy men as a gift by me.)*

VIII. CHANGE

1. Quaeritur ab illō **num** varium et mūtābile **sit** semper homo stultus. *(It is questioned by him whether a stupid man is always something variable and changeable.)*

2. Negant dēformēs fēminae illud vērit**ātem** **esse**. *(The ugly women deny that that is the truth.)*

3. Nōs rogātis **num** illī ex urbe nōbīscum nocte ad rēgem magnae virtūtis proficisc**antur**. *(You-all ask us whether they set out on the journey with us at night from the city toward the king of great virtue.)*

4. Mat**rem** rēgis, fēmin**am** dēform**em** sed magnae sapientiae, nostrī nōn oblīviscī vidēmus. *(We see that the king's mother, an ugly woman but one of great wisdom, isn't forgetful of us.* **REMEMBER** that the main introductory clause does not have to be first.*)*

5. **Num** interfici**antur** gladiō omnēs reī furtī in illā urbe ē rēge quaeris. *(You inquire from the king whether all people guilty of theft are killed with the sword in that city.)*

6. Negātur semper bona fac**ere** hominēs sapientēs. *(It is denied that wise men always do good things.)*

7. Illās rogō **num** poss**int** rēgēs atrōcēs cum perīculō omnibus cum amīcīs regere et urbem perdere. *(I ask those women whether cruel kings can with all their friends rule with danger/dangerously and destroy the city.)*

8. Aqu**am** mort**em** ignī, hominī vīt**am** (**esse**) dīcō. *(I say that water is death for a fire, but for man it is life.)*

9. Dē tē fābul**am** narr**ārī** audiō. *(I hear that about you a story is told.)*

10. Dīcō tēcum nōn **posse mē** vīvere neque sine tē. *(I say that with you I cannot live, nor without you.* **NOTE** that you must express the subject of the infinitive *posse* by the accusative pronoun *mē.)*

IX. CHANGE

1. Amīcus tibi pecūniam dōnō dat **ut** tibi plac**eat**. *(A friend gives you money as a gift to please you.)*

2. Mihi placēs **ut** mēcum semper vīv**ās**. *(You please me in order to live with me forever.)*

3. Ad illam urbem nocte omnibus cum amīcīs proficisciminī **ut** nōs vid**eātis**. *(You-all set out on a journey to that city with all your friends to see us.)*

4. Pecūniam nōbīs dōnō dās **ut** nōbīs grātiās ag**ās**. *(You give us money as a gift to thank us.)*

5. Vidēris amīcus rēgis atrōcis esse **nē** mor**iāris** neque ab illō interfic**iāris**. *(You seem to be a friend of the cruel king so as not to die nor be killed by him.)*

6. Sub urbe mihi domus est magna **ut** sine perīculō cum amīcīs vītam ag**am**. *(In the suburbs/down from the fortified walls of the city I have a great house so that free from danger with my friends I may live my life.)*

7. Amōris grātiā ad tē litterās dē illā rē difficilī scrībō **nē** tibi noc**eam**. (*For the*

sake of my love for you I am sending a letter to you about that difficult matter in order not to hurt you.)

8. Lēgēs scrībunt hominēs sapientēs **ut** sub manū rēgis sine perīculō vīv**ant** et ab illō sapientiā reg**antur**. *(Wise men write laws so that thay may live without danger under the control/hand of the king and be ruled by him with wisdom.)*

9. Dē dīs sempiternīs vēritas sōla ā poētā scrībitur **ut** hominēs doc**eat**. *(Concerning the eternal gods, only the truth is written by the poet to teach mankind.)*

10. Cupiō morī **ut** tuī oblīvisc**ar**. *(I want to die in order to forget you.)*

X. NOTE THE PATTERN

1. *Man to man is a wolf.*
   Fēmina fēminae amīca.
   Hominēs hominibus daemonēs.
2. *About the dead let us say nothing.*
   Dē rēbus deōrum nihil scrībāmus.
   Dē amīcīs nihil nisī bonum cōgitēmus.
3. *Let kings yield to songs, kings and the triumphs of kings.*
   Nē noceant hominēs hominibus neque hominum fīliī.
4. *It is hard not to reveal a crime by your appearance.*
   Bonum est poēmata scrībere arte.
   Malum est nōn regī lēgibus.

LESSON SIX
IMPERFECT, PRESENT PERFECT, PAST PERFECT

I. MATCH

1. animālibus fortibus
2. speculō dēformī
3. arborum similium
4. corporī parvō / corpore parvō
5. poētae sapientis
6. rēs magnae / rēs magnās
7. cornua acria
8. fēminīs fortibus
9. homo laudātus / hominem laudātum
10. invidiae similī / invidiā similī
11. arborēs pulchrās
12. puellārum omnium
13. sōlīus avis / sōlae avēs
14. atrōcī rēgī / atrōcī (-e) rēge
15. specula mala
16. illīus corporis
17. urbibus perditīs
18. carmen scrīptum
19. fēminārum doctārum
20. domūs aestimātae / domūs aestimātās

II. MATCH

1. nocuisset
2. moriēbātur
3. conspectae sint
4. amārī (**REMEMBER:** match form)
5. satiem
6. potuērunt
7. laudāveris
8. moriāre / moriāris
9. perditum erat
10. appellāvistī
11. audiēbās
12. fuit
13. dīcēbāminī
14. loquēbāre / loquēbāris
15. dedēre / dedērunt
16. beāverimus
17. damnent
18. peterent
19. loquī / loqueris / loquere
20. docuerātis

III. TRANSLATE

1. He always seemed to me to speak with wisdom about all matters. I used to always say to my friends that he was educated and a wise philosopher and worthy (when compared by means) of our ancestors and similar to them. A man of great virtue was he. He loved me without envy and alone (out) of my friends always he acted so that the king didn't hurt me. Might all of my friends have been of that sort. He ought always to have been praised by me. I should have thanked him, but I never did. Nothing about him good did I say. He has been condemned to (the penalty of) death by the king, and nothing about his virtue did I say. Perhaps he might not have recognized that I was his friend. If only he hadn't died / might he not have died. If only he hadn't been killed by that cruel king. But he is dead / he has died. He has been killed. I saw him be killed by the sword of that fierce king, and I said nothing. I don't pity him, but myself. I ought not to have ever been born. If only I might die, but the gods have given me a long life, and always I ought to remember him.

2. May you (lady) not forget me. Granted that I am ugly and you beautiful; but, nevertheless, I have always loved you and I wanted to live with you. If only you had been blind. Perhaps you might have loved me. If only you hadn't seen me. Always about you with my friends I used to speak, always I remembered you and always with myself I used to question whether I could please you. I esteemed you highly / of great (value), but you never loved me. Don't love me, but don't forget me. You shouldn't have said to your mother that you were not loved by me nor always had been loved by me, but you said that to her. I had money. A house in the suburbs was (there) for me (to possess) / I had a house in the suburbs. First (out) of the friends of the king was I. I would have given you all my (possessions) in order to please you / that I might please you. Your mother would have thanked me. She would have esteemed me of great value.

3. While I was setting out on a journey from the city with my friends to see my beloved (lady), a beautiful girl and (one) of great knowledge, I caught sight of a

timid bird in a tree. It was singing, that little bird, and about my (own) love did it seem to me to be singing. A blessed life did that animal seem to me to lead. If only I might be like / similar to that animal. If only a similar life I might lead, and about my girl friend might I sing (throughout) the entire night and all the day in a tree. Beneath that tree would I sing. Beneath that tree with my pen I began to write a short poem for my beloved girl to say that I love her. I asked her whether she loved me. You alone I said that I loved, (and) that you ought to be loved by only me. Perhaps I shouldn't have said that. If only I hadn't said that she ought to be loved by me alone. Don't remember that I said that. I may be greedy for love; granted without you I cannot live; nevertheless, I say that you can make love with every man. Don't love only me. Maybe I (too) may make love with every girl.

4. Of slight (value) to me always was love. Never was I greedy for love, but for money only. I hate everybody, and of everyone have I forgotten, of my father and mother and of my wife and of all my children, in order to lead my life alone with my money. Man to man is an evil demon, do I say. Let / may money alone please me. If only everybody might lead a life similar to mine. If only everybody would forget me. For me, a life of that sort seems to be blessed. By (means of) money alone is the greedy man satisfied, not by friends.

IV. TRANSLATE

1. Difficult, easy-going, pleasant, acerbic: (whatever you are) you're the same / it's all the same; neither with you can I live nor without you.

2. While Nature (is) / was in doubt whether she would make (you) a male or a girl, you were created, Oh pretty—almost girl—a boy.

3. In a meadow, once upon a time, a frog espied a cow, and touched with envy for such great magnitude, she inflated / blew up her wrinkled skin: then her children she asked whether (or not) she was bigger than the cow. They said no. Again she stretched her skin with greater effort and with similar manner / similarly , she asked who was bigger. They said the cow. Finally, angered, while she (is) / was wanting to blow herself up (still) more strongly, she lay (thrown down dead) with ruptured body *(ablative of manner: or ablative absolute* / after / since her body was ruptured: *see LESSON NINE).*

4. Every woman within her breast conceals a pestilential poison: sweet from their lips do they speak; (but) with a heart (that's) noxious do they live.

5. A raven from somewhere had stolen a (piece of) cheese and with it had flown from down below (up) into a tall tree. A vixen was striving (to have) that cheese, and the raven with blandishing words she addressed. First she praised the raven's figure and the lustre of his feathers. "By the god Pollux!" says she, "I would say you to be the king of the birds, but your song does not correspond to

your pulchritude." (**NOTE** *that the humor of animal fables is that the beasts use overly refined diction.)* Whereupon he, inflated by the vixen's (words of) praise, wanted to demonstrate the pulchritude of his song. Thus in truth from his opened beak was the cheese fallen down and the vixen seized it and devoured it.

6. I, (the courtesan) Lais, (now) a crone, do hereby dedicate (this) mirror to Venus. May (her) eternal (beautiful) figure have an eternal minister worthy of itself. But for me, there is no use in it: since to see myself such as I am, I do not want; (and) such as I used to be, I can't.

7. Leisure, Catullus, is troublesome for you: in leisure do you exult and too much revel. Leisure has destroyed both kings in previous times and their blessed cities.

8. (The nobody) Licinus lies (dead) with a marble tomb, but (the great) Cato with none, and (famous) Pompey, with a small one: do we believe that (there) are gods? —Song without name of author / anonymous.

9. That Fortune is insane and blind and brutish, the philosophers do describe; and that she stands on a rolling globe-like stone, they proclaim.

10. May you be equal to the virtue of your father, (but) unequal to his fortunes.

V. CHANGE

(**REMEBER** that the purpose of exercises like this is to replace the modal auxiliaries *dēbeō* and *oportet* with equivalent expressions using the subjunctive, and not to change the modal auxiliaries into subjunctives themselves, such as *dēbērēs* or *oportēret.*)

1. Patris similis ess**ē**s, sed nōn erās. *(You might have been / ought to have been your father's likeness / similar to your father, but you weren't.)*

2. **Pār** ess**ē**s patrī in omnibus rēbus, sed nōn erās. *(You ought to have been equal to your father, but you weren't.)*

3. Patre vestrō dīgnī ess**ē**tis, sed nōn erātis. *(You-all ought to have been worthy —by means of comparison with—of your father, but you-all weren't.)*

4. Carmen illīus generis similī modō **nē** can**erem**. Illud tamen cecinī. *(A song of that sort in a similar manner I shouldn't have sung. Nevertheless, I sang it.)*

5. Capitis damn**ārentur** ab omnibus bonīs illī reī, sed nōn damnātī sunt. *(Of a capital penalty ought to have been condemned those guilty people by all good men, but they haven't been condemned.)*

6. Magnī ill**a** dom**us** aestim**ārētur**, sed parvī aestimābātur. *(That house ought to have been assessed of great value, but it was assessed of small worth.)*

7. Tibi illud speculum dēforme dātum essēt dōnō, sed nōn datum est. *(That ugly mirror ought to have been given to you as a gift, but it hasn't been given.)*

8. **Nē** meī oblīvice**rēminī**, sed meī nōn meministis. *(You-all oughtn't to have forgotten me, but you didn't remember me.)*

9. Matris vid**ērētur** similis illa puella pulchra, sed nōn vidēbātur. *(That beautiful girl should have seemed like her mother, but she didn't.)*

10. Mē am**ārēs** / am**āvissēs**, sed semper mē ōderās. *(You ought to have loved me, but you always hated me.)*

VI. CHANGE

1. **Forsitan** illīus generis animālia hominibus noc**ērent**, sed nōn nocuērunt. *(Perhaps animals of that sort could have hurt men, but they didn't.)*

2. **Forsitan** illud animal rex avium ess**et**, sed nōn erat. *(Perhaps that animal could have been the king of the birds, but it wasn't.)*

3. **Forsitan** ille vid**ērētur** stultus, sed sapiens erat. *(Perhaps he might have seemed stupid, but he was wise.)*

4. **Forsitan** illa fēmina dēformis, invidiā recta, amīcīs noc**ēret**, sed numquam illīs nocuit. *(Perhaps that ugly woman, ruled by envy, could have hurt her friends, but she never has hurt them.)*

5. **Forsitan** ille puer more**rētur**, sed longam vītam ēgit neque mortuus est puer. *(Perhaps that boy could have died, but he lived a long life nor has he died (while still) a boy.)*

6. **Forsitan** tē in speculō conspice**rēs**, sed stulta erās neque vīdistī tē in illō speculō. *(You might have caught sight of yourself in the mirror, but you were a stupid woman nor have you ever looked at yourself in that mirror.)*

7. **Forsitan** meī memin**issētis**, sed oblitī estis et similī modō vestrī oblīviscī cupiō. *(Perhaps you-all might have remembered me, but you've forgotten me and similarly I want to forget you-all.)*

8. **Forsitan** magnā invidiā ad tē scrīb**erem** dē omnibus rēbus, sed cupīvī amīcus tuus vidērī et tēcum sub urbe vīvere. *(Perhaps I might have written to you with great envy about all things, but I wanted to seem your friend and to live with you in the suburbs.)*

9. **Forsitan** mihi speculum ess**et**, sed nōn cupīvī mē in speculō vidēre. *(Perhaps there might have been a mirror for me to use / I might have had a mirror, but I didn't want to see myself in a mirror.)*

10. **Forsitan** urbem illam beātam perd**erent**, sed ab omnibus bonīs laudārī illīs placuit. *(Perhaps they might have destroyed that blessed city, but it pleased them to be praised by all good men.)*

VII. CHANGE

1. **Utinam** matris patrisque similēs **essētis / fuissētis**, sed dissimilēs erātis. *(If only you-all might be—but you probably can't / couldn't have been—but that's impossible—similar to your mother and father, but you were dissimilar.)*

2. **Utinam** nostrī **nē** oblī**viscerēris / oblita essēs**, sed nostrī nōn meministī. *(If only you wouldn't / hadn't forgotten us, but you didn't remember us.)*

3. **Utinam** capitis ille **reus nē** ab omnibus damn**ārētur** / damn**ātus esset**, sed omnēs illum damnāvērunt. *(If only that guilty man might not / hadn't been condemned to death by everyone, but everyone has condemned him.)*

4. **Utinam** bon**us** amī**cus** ab omnī sapientī magnī aestim**ētur** (et illud potest esse). *(May a good friend be esteemed of great value by every wise person—and that can happen.)*

5. **Utinam** speculum mihi dōnō ā tē dar**ētur** / dat**um esset**, sed mihi illud nōn dedistī. *(If only a mirror might be given / had been given to me as a gift by you, but you haven't given me it.)*

VIII. CHANGE

(**NOTE** that the main purpose of this exercise is to become familiar with the pronominal declension.)

1. Pecūniam eī dōnō da**bāmus** ut ab eā am**ārēmur**. *(We gave her money as a gift in order to be loved by her.* Or, if the *eī* and the *eā* are not the same person: *We gave him money in order to be loved by her.)*

2. Quaesītum est / **erat** num haec fēmina sine eō et eius pecuniā pot**uisset** agere hanc vītam beātam. *(It has been questioned / was a question / had been questioned whether this woman without him and his money could live this blessed life.* **NOTE** that *quaesītum est* changes its meaning from *it is a question* to *it was / has been questioned* when it introduces a secondary sequence subjunctive.*)*

3. Is mēcum loqu**ēbātur** ut amīcus mihi vid**ērētur**. *(He used to speak with me in order to seem my friend.)*

4. Ā nūllō avārī hominēs cupi**ēbant** laudārī nē vid**ērentur** beātī esse. *(By no one did greedy men want to be praised in order not to seem to be blessed.)*

5. Eam rog**ābāmus** num vēritātem dē vītā eius hominis nōbīs dīcere po**sset**. *(We used to ask her whether she could tell us the truth about the life of that man.)*

6. Nūllī vōbīs dīcere cupi**ēbant** eum capitis damnātum esse. *(Nobody wanted to tell you-all that he had been condemned to death.)*

7. Nūllīus amīcus **eram** ut omnēs ōdisse po**ssem**. *(I was nobody's friend in order to be able to hate everybody.)*

8. Scrībēbās tē ā nūllīs laudārī. *(You wrote that you were praised by none.)*

9. Cum eīs proficiscē**bāmur** ut domum eōrum vidē**rēmus**. *(With them we set out to see their house.)*

10. Similī modō semper ab eīs quaerē**bātur** num dī hominibus nocē**ret** aut noc**uisset**. *(Similarly always by them it was questioned whether the gods hurt or had hurt men.)*

IX. CHANGE

1. Id aut **esse** aut **fuisse** huius generis **dīcō**. *(I say that it either is or was of this sort.)*

2. **Eum** carminibus ā poētīs aut laud**ātum esse** aut laud**ārī dīcēbat**. *(S-he said that he either had been praised or was being praised by poets in their songs.)*

3. **Scrīpsēre** sapientiam eius vēritātemque ab omnibus bonīs laudārī oport**ēre** aut oport**uisse**. *(They wrote/have written that his/her wisdom and truth ought to be praised or to have been praised by all good people.)*

4. **Hanc** matre dīgn**am fuisse** et **illum** similī modō patris par**em esse** vid**ēbāmus**. *(We saw/were seeing that this woman was/had been worthy of her mother and that man was/is similarly his father's equal.)*

5. Mēcum vīvere cum ōtiō magnōque amōre **eam** aut cup**īvisse** aut cup**ere** neg**āverant**. *(They had said that she either hadn't wanted or didn't want to live with me with leisure and great love.)*

6. **Dīxī** huius generis vīnum eī plac**uisse** aut plac**ēre**. *(I said/have said that a wine of this sort either pleased or pleases him/her.)*

7. Magnā invidiā speculum eī fēminae dēformī ab eō aut d**atum esse** aut d**arī** aud**īmus**. *(We hear that with great envy a mirror either was or is given by him to that ugly woman.)*

8. **Dīcis** ā nūllō cum vēritāte aut pot**uisse** aut posse **hunc** laudārī. *(You say that by no one truthfully either could or can this man be praised.)*

9. Eīs fortis vidērī **eum** aut cup**ere** aut nōn cup**ere audiēbam**. *(I heard that he either did or didn't want to seem brave to them.)*

10. E**am** huius oblīviscī et meī memin**isse dictum est**. *(It's said/has been said that she forgets/has fogotten him and remembers/remembered me.)*

X. CHANGE

(**NOTE** that this exercise is similar to the previous but requires you to distinguish between the patterns for indirect questions and statements, and clauses of purpose; and offers practice in using possessive adjectives.)

1. Magn**um esse** meu**m** am**ōrem** tuī tuōrumque amīcōrum **negāvī**. *(I denied/ have denied that my love for you and your friends is/was great.)*

2. **Hōc fēcimus ut** magna pars vestrum nostrī oblīvisc**ātur**/oblīvisc**erētur**. *(So that a great part of you-all forget us, we're the doers/have done this.)*

3. **Quaeritur ā vōbīs num** nōbīs **fuerit** domus vestra. *(It is questioned by you-all whether your house was ours/for us.)*

4. Me**um** pat**rem** tu**am**que mat**rem** nūllōs vestrum ōd**isse dīcēbam**. *(I said that my father and your mother hated none of you-all.)*

5. **Quaesītum est ab eīs num** patrī nostrō huius generis vīta semper plac**uerit**/ plac**uisset**. *(Whether this sort of life always pleased our father is a question/has been questioned by them.)*

6. **Nōbīs dīxistis** ā deō nostrō vest**rum** r**ēgem** nasc**ī**. *(You-all told us that your king was born from our god.)*

7. **Quaesīvī num** tua magna invidia meī vītam meam perdid**erit**/perdid**isset**. *(Whether your great envy of me destroyed my life, I'm the questioner/have questioned.)*

8. **Ad amīcum meum scrībō** nost**rōs** de**ōs** nūllōs vestrum vītā longā beāv**isse**. *(To my friend I write that our gods blessed none of you with a long life.)*

9. **Hōc fēcī ut** nūllī eōrum ā nostrō poētā **possint/possent** laudārī. *(I'm the doer/have done this in order that none of them can be/could be praised by our poet.)*

10. Sine invidiā vestrī **mē** loqu**ī** vōbīscum dē magnō amōre meō urbis vestrae beātae **dīxī**. *(I said that without envy for you-all I spoke with you about my great love for your blessed city.* **NOTE** that you must express the subject *mē* for the infinitive *loquī.)*

XI. NOTE THE PATTERN

1. *I would say that you are the king of the birds, but the song doesn't correspond to your pulchritude.*
   Mē dēformem esse vidērēs sed tuus amor meī tē fēcit caecum/caecam.
   Rex tuus/vester fuissem sed meus amor tuī/vestrī mē perdidit.

2. *While Nature was hesitating, you were made a boy.*
   Dum haec dē deīs dīcimus, illa urbs beāta perdēbātur.
   Dum hīc vir magnae sapientiae capitis damnātur, amīcī eius vēritātem dē eius vītā nōn dīxērunt.
   Dum loquī incipit illa, poēma meum eī dedī dōnō.

LESSON SEVEN
RELATIVE-INTERROGATIVE PRONOUNS, VOCATIVE

I. MATCH

1. cēnae ipsīus
2. mī fīlī
3. līberī hominis / līberī hominēs
4. eiusdem puerī
5. manibus atrōcibus
6. sapiens Lucilius / sapiens Lucilī
7. nēminī caecō
8. cui speculō
9. diēī beātī
10. cēna pretiōsa / cēnam pretiōsam
11. vir līber
12. nostrō rēgī / nostrō rēge
13. quae saxa / qua saxa
14. vultuum dēformium
15. philosophus magnus / philosophe magne
16. eārundem togārum
17. quī virī / quōs virōs
18. sōlīus carminis
19. lingua docta / linguam doctam
20. nūllīus fortis

II. MATCH

1. cōgitāvissent
2. canta sint
3. damner
4. cupiunt
5. audīvimus
6. sequī / sequeris / sequere
7. negārī
8. dēs
9. nascerētur
10. rogēminī
11. docēmur
12. dēbueris
13. cognitae erant
14. gererem
15. vīvantur
16. fēcēre / fēcērunt
17. laudāvērunt / laudāvēre
18. conspexit
19. possint
20. pōnitis

III. TRANSLATE

1. Nothing do I have (**NOTE** *that in a letter the tense is viewed from the time of its receipt, and not, as in English, from the moment of its being written.*) which (I might put to the purpose) to write to you about the affairs which had been enacted in the city. For nobody these days is in the city / none are there in the city who (are of the sort) to conduct business concerning the republic. Everybody has set out with the king to the war. Indeed, I would have written nothing, if nobody could have set out to you (**NOTE** *that a letter was entrusted to an intermediary to deliver.*), but I wanted to speak with you about other matters because of my great love for you. On account of which love this letter I gave to my slave / servant whom I've sent to you. You know him, a man informed about all my affairs (and) to whom I always tell everything. He alone is (there of the sort) to whom I (can) place my trust in these evil times. He deserves to be a free man / he

is a worthy person of the sort who (should) be free. There are others (of the sort) who (may) seem friends, but he alone is (of the sort) who never (would) hurt me. If only all people were like him / his similars. But, how are you (doing)? How / by what mode, my son, are you living? If I were with you at your place, I would say other things which I couldn't write in this letter. It would have pleased me if I could have written everything in this letter.

2. From your friend, whom I saw yesterday in the city, I've heard, my friend, that you have written fables which tell about the vices of animals so that we might recognize the same vices ourselves in our own life. I've always said that you are a man of great wisdom. You've written fables with great wisdom. Worthy are you (of the sort) to be praised by all and to be esteemed of great (value). If animals, in a similar mode, could write / were able to write books, they would narrate fables about the vices of men which (could be put to the purpose) to teach about the same affairs in their own life. If the lives of animals and men were not similar, we wouldn't be able to recognize ourselves and our vices in that mirror which is called a fable written about animals / animal fables. But there are (those) who (are of the sort that) don't recognize themselves in those fables which are narrated about animals. Why do they not recognize themselves? I ask why they don't recognize themselves. How / by what mode can't they recognize themselves? Aren't they not stupid / they're stupid—right? (Yes), they're stupid. Are they not blind to their own vices? (Yes), they're blind. They're not wise, are they? (No), they're not wise. If only everyone might see that (the story) is narrated about themselves and their own vices—but they don't see (it).

3. There is noboby (of the sort) who would love me. If there were anybody who would love me, he would love me. I ask whether there is anybody to love me. (There) isn't anybody to love me, (is there)? No, there's nobody. And there's nobody for me to love. If there were anybody for me to love, I would love him.

4. There are none for me to praise. None are there to be praised by me. If there were any for me to praise, I would praise them. I ask whether there are any for me to praise. Whom would I praise? There aren't (people) for me to praise, are there? (No), there aren't.

5. He is worthy for me to trust / worth my trusting. They are worthy for me to thank. She is worth my speaking to. (Those women) are worth my talking with. Aren't they worthy / worth it? (Yes), they're worth it. Who is a worthy woman? Which woman is worthy? That one is. I ask whether anyone is (a) worthy (woman). I ask whether any woman is worthy.

IV. TRANSLATE

1. Gaius Julius Caesar's Commentary about the Gallic War, (Book) the First. Gaul is in its entirety divided into three parts: of which one, the Belgians inhabit; another, the Aquitanians; the third, (people) who by their own language

are called Celts, (but) in ours, Gauls. These all differ amongst themselves in language, institutions, (and) laws. The Gauls from the Aquitanians, the river Garonne separates; (and) from the Belgians, the (rivers) Marne and Seine. Of all of these people, the bravest / fiercest are the the Belgians, since they are the farthest distant / away from the culture and civilization of Provence, and closest to the Germans, who dwell across the Rhine, with whom they constantly wage war. For which reason, the Swiss also surpass the other Gauls in (warfare) virtue, when they either exclude them from their own territories or wage war themselves in theirs.

2. Tomorrow let love who never has loved, and who has loved, let
that person, too, love:
Spring is fresh, Spring already now is singing, Spring is the earth's orb born
again;
In Spring love-contracts are agreed upon, in Spring the winged
creatures marry,
And the forest grove unties (her) hair for the nuptial rains.
Tomorrow let love who never has loved, and who has loved, let that
person, too, love. —The Night-long Vigil of Venus

3. To the same river had come a wolf and a lamb, by thirst compelled: up stream was standing the wolf, and far lower down, the lamb. Then, with wicked throat the thief, excited, introduced a reason for quarreling. "Why," says he, "have you made muddy for me the water which I am drinking?" The woolbearer in turn, timid: "How can I, I ask, do (that) which you complain about, Wolf? From you does the liquid flow down to my imbibings." Repulsed, he, by the forces of truth, "These six months ago, maliciously," says he, "did you speak against me." Replied the lamb: "I was not born / hadn't yet been born." "Your father, in the name of Hercules, in that case, maliciously spoke against me," and that way, the lamb, snatched up, does he tear to pieces, by unjustified murder. This fable is written / has been written on account of those people who oppress the innocent with ficticious reasons.

V. CHANGE

(**NOTE** that the object of this exercise is to practice the reflexive pronouns; the first translation is of the sentence as it appears in the exercise, before the changes.)

1. *Many books to **his, but not his own,** slave did he give as a gift so that he could teach **their sons** the Greek language.* Multōs librōs servō **suō** dōnō dedit ut fīliōs **suōs** docēret linguam Graecam. *(Many books he gave to **his own** slave as a gift to teach **his own** sons the Greek language.* The **suō** could also refer to **dōnō** now: *as **his own** gift.)*

2. *If they could write books, animals would tell fables about **them** so that they*

*would see **their** vices.* Sī librōs scrībere possent, dē **sē** animālia fābulās narrārent ut vitia **sua** vidērent. *(If they could write books, animals would tell fables about **themselves** in order to see **their own** vices.)*

3. *Few are there who recognize **their** children.* Paucī sunt quī nātōs **suōs** cognōscant. *(There are few who recognize **their own** children.)*

4. *They said that **the women** had led a life at **his place** in the the suburbs.* Dīxērunt **sē** vītam sub urbe apud **sē** ēgisse. *(They said that **they themselves** had led a life at **their own** place in the suburbs.)*

5. *He was the same person whom I myself said hurt **him / her**.* Īdem erat quem ipse dīxī **sibi** nocēre. *(He was the same person whom I myself said hurt **himself**.)*

6. *Always do they forget **them** and **their** city.* Semper **suī** oblīviscuntur et urbis **suae**. *(Always do they forget **themselves** and **their own** city.)*

7. *S-he asks **him** whether anyone sent **him** a letter about **his / her** life.* **Sē** rogat num quis litterās dē **suā** vītā ad **sē** mīserit. *(He asks **himself** whether anyone sent **himself, i.e., the person asking,** a letter about **his own** life* . The sentence could also mean: *She asks **herself** whether anyone sent **her** a letter about **her own** life.)*

8. *No poet was there in **his / her** city who was **his / her** equal or worthy of **his / her** father.* Nūllus erat in **suā** urbe poēta quī **sibi** pār esset aut patre **suō** dīgnus. *(No poet was there in **the poet's own** city who was **the poet's** equal or worthy of **the poet's own** father.)*

9. *A good and big dinner to **him / her** at **his** place did s-he give in order to be praised by **him** and seem to **him / her** to be blessed.* Bonam magnamque cēnam **sibi** apud **sē** dedit ut ā **sē** laudārētur et **sibi** beātus vidērētur esse. *(A good and big dinner to **himself** at **his own** place did he give in order to be praised by **himself** and seem to **himself** to be blessed.* **NOTE** that changing *beātus* to *beāta* would make the sentence mean: *A good and big dinner to **herself** at **her own** place did she give in order to be praised by **herself** and seem to **herself** to be blessed.)*

10. *On account of **his / her** great virtue always in all matters let him / her speak well of **him**.* Propter **suam** magnam virtūtem semper omnibus in rēbus **sē** bene dīcat. *(On account of **his own / her own** great virtue always in all matters let him / her speak well of **himself / herself**.)*

VI. CHANGE

1. Nēmō poēta omnium poētārum eius similis erat **quōcum** dī sempiternī loquēbantur. *(No poet out of all the poets was like him, with whom the eternal gods used to speak.)*

2. Nēmō eam ōdit **quae** dīxit sē omnēs amāre. *(No one hates her who said that she herself loved everybody / everybody loved her.)*

3. Nēminī omnium amīcōrum suōrum apud sē cēnam dedit **quī sibi** nocuer-

ant. *(S-he gave dinner at his/her own house to no one of his/her own friends who had hurt him/her.* **NOTE** that *eī* could be a different person from the subject of the first sentence: Nēminī omnium amīcōrum suōrum apud sē cēnam dedit **quī** eī nocuerant. ...*who had hurt some other person, male or female.)*

4. Nēmō tē amābat **quī** stultus erās et semper vir nūllīus sapientiae. *(Nobody loved you, who were stupid and always a man of no wisdom.)*

5. Fābulās dē sē narrābant hominēs nūllīus sapientiae **quās** illī scrīpserant ipsī. *(Men of no wisdom told stories about themselves which they had written themselves.)*

6. Dī vōs amant **quibus** omnia bona in vestrā vītā dedērunt. *(The gods love you-all to whom they have given all things good in your life.)*

7. Tuī oblitus sum **quae** matre dīgna numquam erās neque fēmina magnae virtūtis. *(I have forgotten you, who were never worthy of your mother nor were you a woman of great virtue.)*

8. Eum cum eīs ad eam mīsī **cui** togam pulchram dōnō dedī. *(I sent him with them to her, to whom I've given a beautiful toga as a gift.)*

9. Domus sub urbe eīs erat, in **quā** vītam beātam agēbant. *(They had a house in the suburbs, in which they lived a blessed life.)*

10. Capitis damnātae erant **quae** propter suum amōrem suī suam urbem perdiderant. *(The women had been condemned to death who had destroyed their own city on account of their own love for themselves.)*

VII. CHANGE

(**REMEMBER** that the point of the exercise is to replace the modal auxiliary, while becoming familiar with the conjugation of *volō, nōlō,* and *ferō*.)

1. Matre dīgna illa **sit**. *(May she be worthy of her mother.)*

2. **Vir** magnae sapientiae **essēs**, sed nōn erās. *(You should have been a man of great wisdom, but you weren't/Would that you were a man of great wisdom, but you weren't.)*

3. Illam fēminam **nē** amā**veris**. *(Don't love that woman.)*

4. Beātam vītam inter amīcōs nostrōs ag**āmus**. *(Let's lead a blessed life amongst our friends!)*

5. Tibi **nē** noc**ērem**, sed nocēbam. *(Would that I hadn't hurt you, but I did.)*

6. Speculum ad tē fer**ātur** ut tē videās. *(Let a mirror be brought to you to see yourself.)*

7. **Nē cecineris** carmen illīus generis. *(Don't sing a song of that type.)*

8. Nostrī memin**issēs**, sed nostrī oblita es. *(Would that you'd remembered us, but you-lady have forgotten us.)*

9. Pecūnia tibi **dētur** ut ad rēgem ferās. *(Let money be given to you to bring to the king.)*

10. Speculum **eī sit** ut **eum / eam** in speculō videat. *(Let there be a mirror for him / her to look at him / her in the mirror.)*

VIII. CHANGE

1. Vī**tam** mal**am** fu**isse** quam ēg**erit** / ēg**isset** servus miser **dīxit.** *(S-he's the sayer / has said that the life was bad that the unhappy slave led .)*

2. **Quaesītum est** vītamne reg**at** / reg**eret** fortūna an sapientia. *(It's questioned / has been questioned whether fortune or wisdom rules life.)*

3. **Dīcō** aliōs mihi ded**isse** pecūniam quae propter mea bene facta dēb**ita sit**. *(I say that others gave me the money which was owed me on account of my benefactions.)*

4. Cum invidiā semper ab omnibus vid**ērī** poēt**am** magnae virtūtis quī vītam beātam inter **eius** amīcōs **agat / ageret scrīpsit.** *(S-he's the writer / has written that the poet of great virtue who leads / led a blessed life amongst his friends is / was always viewed with envy by everybody.)*

5. **Dīxit sē** magnam bonamque cēnam ded**isse** suō amīcō quī carmen dē suā virtūte vol**uerit** / vol**uisset** scrībere. *(S-he's the sayer / has said that she herself / he himself gave a big and good dinner to her / his own friend who wanted to write a song about her / his own virtue.)*

6. Togam **nōs** nō**lle** gerere quī vītam sine perīculō hāc in urbe vel**īmus** agere **scrībimus**. *(We write that we who want to lead a life without danger in this city don't want to wear the toga.)*

7. **Dīcō eum / eam** avem timidam quae dē amōre **eius** cecin**erit** v**īdisse**. *(I say that s-he saw a timid bird which sang about his / her love.)*

8. Nōs oport**uisse** togam gerere quam līberī sōlī dēb**eant** gerere **dīcimus**. *(We say that we should have worn the toga which only free men ought to wear.)*

9. **Dīcit** magnō perīculō ā **sē** scrīptum **fuisse** illud poēma in quō dē **suā** vītā narr**et**. *(He says that with great danger had been written by himself that poem in which he tells about his own life.)*

10. **Scrīpsit** sē hodiē nōn **esse eundem** quī herī **fuerit / fuisset**. *(He's the writer / has written that he today is not the same person who yesterday he was.)*

IX. CHANGE

1. Sī qua fēminam bene **dīxisset**, nēmō crēdid**isset** eam cum vēritāte dē aliā dīcere. *(If any female had spoken well of another woman, no one would have believed her to be speaking with truth about the other.)*

2. Sī qua dōna pecūniae ab hōc avārō dēformī aliīs d**arēntur**, ā nōbīs omnibus laud**ārētur.** *(If any gifts of money were given to others by this ugly greedy man, he would be praised by us all.)*

3. Sī quis mihi crēdid**isset**, stultus fu**isset**. *(If anyone had trusted me, he would have been stupid.)*

4. Sī quae rēs dē bellō cum illīs atrōcibus ger**erentur**, omnēs cōgit**ārent** quid sē oportēret agere. *(If any matters were brought up concerning the war with those atrocious people, everyone would consider what they ought to do themselves.)*

5. Sī quibuscum vol**uissem** loquī, semper quaesī**vissem** num quī essent sapientēs in hāc urbe quī linguam Graecam mē possent docēre. *(If I had wanted to speak with anybody, I always would have asked whether there were any wise men in this city who could teach me the Greek language.)*

6. Sī magnum vīnī lacum ad meam cēnam fer**rēs**, mihi vid**ērēris** / vid**ērēre** sōlus dīgnus qui meus amīcus appellārēre. *(If you brought a great vat of wine to my dinner, you would seem alone worthy to be called my friend.)*

7. Sī quid bellum ger**eret**, semper ā stultīs laud**ārētur**. *(If he would wage any war, he would always be praised by the stupid people.)*

8. Sī mihi noc**ēret**, aliīs semper dīc**eret** sibi ā mē nocērī. *(If s-he hurt me, s-he would always tell others that s-he was hurt by me.)*

9. Sī mē am**āvissēs**, semper dīx**issēs** tē mē amāre. *(If you'd loved me, you would always have said that you loved me.)*

10. Sī fābulam aud**īvissētis**, vōs cognō**vissētis**. *(If you had heard the story, you would have recognized yourselves.)*

X. NOTE THE PATTERN

1. *Tomorrow let love who never has loved.*
   Dīcat quae numquam dīxit.
   Sit quod numquam fuit.

2. *How are you, my son?*
   Mī amīce, quis es?
   Philosophe, quem laudās?
   Vergilī, quod poēma scrībis?

LESSON EIGHT
FUTURE, FUTURE PERFECT

I. MATCH

1. salī candidō / sale candidō

2. aliquibus aquīs

3. ducis ēgregiī / ducī ēgregiō / ducēs ēgregiī
4. aliquae avēs
5. cuius arboris
6. tālium hominum
7. homo stulte
8. īdem līber
9. puellā līberā
10. cui cēnae / quae cēnae
11. hāc rē
12. partī parī
13. huic speculō
14. aliquam domum
15. vestrī ducēs / vestrōs ducēs
16. quibus ducibus
17. ūllum caput
18. fābulā narrātā
19. salibus tantīs
20. nostrō patrī / nostrō patre

II. MATCH

1. cēnābitis
2. velit
3. cēnem / cēnābō
4. ēsae erunt
5. fīēmus (*pass.*) / faciēmus (*act.*)
6. iunxerō
7. cōgitem / cōgitābō
8. agit
9. nōllēs
10. aestimābunt
11. fīant (**NOTE** that there is no passive form for *faciō*)
12. incipiēbam
13. appellāre / appellāris
14. biberint
15. sequī / sequeris / sequere
16. vīsūrās
17. fierēmus
18. perditum īrī
19. dabiminī
20. rogem / rogābō

III. TRANSLATE

1. If his own nose, which seems to everyone to be deformed and long, should not please him, never would he ought / never ought he to look at himself in a mirror. For why ought he to know what sort of person he always seems to others when they look at him? Let him see himself such as he wants to be seen. If ever he will have known what sort he seems to others, how will he be able to lead a life amongst others? Let that atrocious mirror be taken away which to him will tell the truth. By him let it be destroyed. There is no one who wants to see himself. Let him not know what sort he truthfully is. Let him be such as he wants to be. But perhaps this deformed nose he may have from his own father and from his father's father. These were men worth praising / worthy men of the sort that all might praise. Worthy were they to be praised by everyone. They had led illustrious lives of their own. All always had spoken well of them. If he were not similar to them, how could he himself be illustrious? In a similar mode he, too, will lead an illustrious life. If he will have led a life full of glory, everyone will praise his wisdom and virtue. He will be a man of great wisdom and great virtue, albeit / and the same with a long nose. He will be a man of such great glory himself as

were his ancestors. If only he were so great a man as his ancestors. A nose he has as great as his own ancestors had. If he will have wanted to be similar to his own ancestors, he will ask the gods in order that they make him all / total nose. Let him be called, by name, Nose. If he were made all nose, no one would be able to deny that he is like his ancestors. None will there be who might deny him to have been the son of his father.

2. I would give someone a big and good dinner at my place if anything were mine which we might eat or drink, but, that I may speak truthfully with you, there is nothing for me worthy to give. If you will have brought with you, my friend, the dinner for us to eat, you will dine well at my place. Don't come alone, but with you let there come some gorgeous girl for me to love. Don't come without some girl. Let's eat and drink and make love. Bread we will eat, and wine we will drink, and that dazzling girl we will love. In this manner I invite you to dinner at my place. For, money for me there is not much, but you out of all whom I know, well do I love, nor is there anyone else with whom I would want to converse. You alone are worthy for me to call by name friend. With great wit always do you converse with me, and on behalf of our love I would give you dinner if I could. If you will have come to dinner, wise friend, I will say to you how much is my love of you / how much love I have for you. How much is your love for me? I ask whether as much is your love of me as mine for you. When you will have come, not without wine and bread and that dazzling girl, I will sing a poem about our love, which poem, when you will have heard it, you will say was written by some illustrious poet. Since we are friends, why in this manner will we not dine well? Since it pleases me to speak with you, doesn't it behoove you / ought you not to come to dinner? Surely you don't hate me? If my love for you were not as great as yours for me, we wouldn't dine in this manner. There is no one else whom I would invite to dinner in this way. None is there about whom I'd have written the same poem. In this manner let's dine well. And my own girl (**NOTE** *mea ipsīus* : the first and second person reflexive adjectives, corresponding to *suus, -a, -um,* can be formed by adding the genitive of the intensive *ipse, ipsa, ipsum* to the possessive adjectives *meus, -a, -um; tuus, -a, -um; noster, nostra, nostrum; vester, vestra, vestrum*) whom well, these days, do I love, (and) who to me alone is my very life / my life itself—she will come to this dinner. To her the gods themselves have given a bit of wine, which when we will have drunk it, we will ask the gods that they make us total / entire a tongue. Of such quality there is not another such as this which to her by the gods themselves has been given.

IV. TRANSLATE

1. You will dine well, my Fabullus, at my place in a few days—if the gods favor you—if you will have brought with you a good and big dinner, not without a dazzling girl and wine and wit and all the jokings. These things if—say I—you will have brought, my / our elegant (friend), you will dine well; for your Catul-

lus's purse is full of cobwebs / spiders. But in return you will receive undiluted love(s), or whatever is more suave and elegant: for I will give you a perfume, which to my girlfriend the Venuses and Cupids have donated—which, when you will smell it, you will ask the gods that they make you entire, Fabullus, a Nose.

2. I hate and I love. Why do I do it, perhaps you ask? I don't know, but I sense that it is happening—and I am in torment.

3. No woman can say herself so much loved, in truth, as by me is Lesbia loved. No faith was there ever in any treaty so great as has been discovered on my part in your love.

4. A corporation had they formed, conjoined, the lion, the cow, the she-goat. and the sheep. The booty, however, which they had taken, into four equal portions had been divided. Then the lion, "The first," says he, "is mine; for this is owed to my preeminence. I will take / let me take also the second, which my robustness merits. The third, my illustrious labor claims as due for itself. The fourth, whoever will have wanted to arrogate to himself, let him know that he is going to have me as enemy for himself."

5. Edacious Time grazes upon everything, everything does it seize, everything from its settlement moves, nothing does it allow to be for long. Rivers become deficient, the beaches dry up the fleeing sea, mountains subside and their lofty ridges fall to ruins. Why such minor things should I mention? The most beautiful mass of heaven will burn suddenly entire, with its own flames. Everything does death demand. To perish—it's the Law, not a punishment. This universe, sometime, will be none.

V. CHANGE

(**NOTE** that the traditional translation of the future-less-vivid is: **should... would**; and of the future-more-vivid is: **shall... will**. This is archaic and confusing, since 'should' as a potential is easily confused in English with 'ought,' the jussive; and in formal usage, 'should / shall' is proper only with the first person (I, we), and 'would, will' with the second and third; unless special empasis is intended, in which case they are reversed. Although the translations presented for this exercise follow the tradition, the future-less-vivid is better understood as: **may / may have... may**, that is to say, as the potentials they truly are: 'IF I MAY HAVE DONE SOMETHING, I MAY DO SOMETHING.' Furthermore, since the present-perfect subjunctive is often identical in form with the future perfect indicative, you cannot tell which type of condition you have until you read the entire sentence. It is also possible that the main clause is not a potential, but an optative: 'IF I MAY / MAY HAVE DONE SOMETHING, MAY I DO SOMETHING.')

1. *If so much of glory **should** be for me as for you and your ancestors / if I **should have** as much glory as you etc., I **would** be an illustrious man.* Sī tantum glōriae mihi **fuerit** quantum tibi et patribus tuīs, vir ēgregius **erō**. *(If so much of glory **will have been** for me as for you and your ancestors, I **shall be** an illustrious man.)*

2. *If any bit of wine **should be** for us / if we **should have, we would give** some to another person to drink with us.* Sī quid vīnī nōbīs **fuerit**, aliquid aliī **dabimus** ut nōbīscum bibat. *(If any bit of wine **will have been** for us, **we will give** some to another person to drink with us.)*

3. *If **you should** not **have brought** with you-all some dinner, **we would have** nothing to eat at my place.* Nisī quam cēnam vōbīscum **attuleritis,** nihil **habēbimus** apud mē ut edāmus. *(If **you will** not **have brought** with you-all some dinner, **we shall have** nothing to eat at my place.)*

4. *Unless I **should have merited** that you love me well, I **would** not **be** the same person whom you always knew.* Nisī **meruerō** ut mē bene amēs, īdem nōn **erō** quem semper cognōveris. *(Unless I **shall have merited** that you love me well, I **will** not be the same person whom you always knew.)*

5. *If I **should** not **have learned** literature at his place, I **would** not **be able** to converse with great wisdom about all matters.* Nisī apud eum litterās **didicerō**, magnā sapientiā dē omnibus rēbus loquī nōn **poterō**. *(If I **shall** not **have learned** literature at his place, I **will** not **be able** to converse with great wisdom about all matters.)*

6. *If they **should fear** death, they **would** not **come** with me to tell our leader the truth about his friends.* Sī mortem **timēbunt / timuerint**, mēcum nōn **venient** ut ducī nostrō vēritātem dē eius amīcīs dīcam. *(If they **will fear** death, they **will** not **come** with me to tell / in order that I tell our leader the truth about his friends.)*

7. *If you **shouldn't know** that which I've done for you, somebody else—not I— **would / may tell** you it.* Sī **nesciēs / nescīveris** id quod pro tē fēcī, alius, nōn ego, id tibi **dīcet**. *(If you **won't know** that which I've done for you, somebody else—not I— **will tell** you it.)*

8. *Unless they **should have joined** themselves to someone in love, they **would die** alone without any friend to write what they've done in their life or how much merit they've earned.* Nisī cui sē in amōre **iunxerint**, sōlī **morientur** sine ūllō amīcō quī scrībat quid in vītā suā ēgerint aut quantum meritī sint. *(Unless they **will have joined** themselves to someone in love, they **will die** alone without any friend to write what they've done in their life or how much merit they've earned.)*

9. *If ever I **should have asked** you whether anyone spoke well of me, I **would learn** how much I am esteemed by him on behalf of my benefactions to him.* Sī umquam tē **rogāverō** num quis mē bene dīxerit, **discam** quantī ab eō pro meō eī bene factō aestimer. *(If ever I **will have asked** you whether anyone spoke well of me, I **will learn** how much I am esteemed by him on behalf of my benefactions to him.)*

10. *If any bird **should learn** to speak with the language of humans, it **would be made** the king of the birds.* Sī qua avis **discet** linguā hominum loquī, rex avium **fīet**. *(If any bird **will learn** to speak with the language of humans, it **will be made** the king of the birds.)*

VI. CHANGE

1. Sī tantum glōriae mihi **esset** quantum tibi et patribus tuīs, vir ēgregius **essem**. *(If there **were**, I **would be**.)*

2. Sī quid vīnī nōbīs **fuisset**, aliquid aliī **darēmus** ut nōbīscum **biberet**. *(If there **had been**, we **would give** some to another person to drink it with us.)*

3. Nisī quam cēnam vōbīscum **attulissētis**, nihil **habērēmus** apud mē ut **ēssēmus**. *(If you-all **had brought**, we **would have**.)*

4. Nisī **meruissem** ut mē bene **amārēs**, īdem nōn **essem** quem semper **cognōveris**. *(Unless I **had merited**, I **would not be**.)*

5. Nisī apud eum litterās **didicissem**, magnā sapientiā dē omnibus rēbus loquī nōn **possem**. *(If I **had not learned**, I **would not be able**.)*

6. Sī mortem **timērent**, mēcum nōn **venīrent** ut ducī nostrō vēritātem dē eius amīcīs **dīcerem**. *(If they **feared**, they **would not come**.)*

7. Sī **nescīrēs** id quod pro tē **fēcī**, alius, nōn ego, id tibi **dīceret**. *(If you **didn't know**, another **would say**.)*

8. Nisī cui sē in amōre **iunxissent**, sōlī **morerentur** sine ūllō amīcō quī **scrīberet** quid in vītā suā **ēgissent** aut quantum **meritī essent**. *(If they **had not joined**, they **would die**.)*

9. Sī umquam tē **rogāvissem** num quis mē bene **dīxisset**, **discerem** quantī ab eō pro meō eī bene factō **aestimārer**. *(If I **had asked**, I **would learn**.)*

10. Sī qua avis **disceret** linguā hominum loquī, rex avium **fieret**. *(If any bird **learned**, it **would be made**.)*

VII. CHANGE

1. ***When** I **shall have come** with danger to you, I **shall say** that which in this letter I was afraid to write about that atrocious leader.* Cum ad tē cum perīculō **vēnerim**, tibi dīcam id quod hīs in litterīs dē illō atrōcī duce timēbam scrībere. *(**Since/whenever/if ever/because/while/although** I **came**, I **shall be afraid**.* **NOTE**, however, that *dīcam* could be interpreted as a subjunctive; hence, in other contexts, the sentence could be future-less-vivid, that is to say, potential subjunctives: ***Since** I **may have come**, I **may be afraid**.*)

2. ***When** you **will have brought** dinner and a bit of wine with you, you **dined** well at my place.* Cum cēnam et aliquid vīnī tēcum **attulissēs**, bene apud mē

cēnāvistī. *(Since/etc. you **have brought**, you **dined**.* NOTE that the original sentence could also have been interpreted as already a *Cum* subjunctive clause with *cēnāvistī* in primary sequence: ***Whenever** you've come, you've dined.)*

3. ***When** they **have seen** you with your friends, you **have known** how much danger there was for you.* Cum tē tuīs cum amīcīs **vīdissent**, scīvistī quantum tibi esset perīculum. *(**Since** they **have seen**, you **have known**.* NOTE also: Cum tē cum amīcīs **vīderint**, scīvistī quantum tibi **sit** perīculum. ***Since** they've seen, you **are aware** how great the danger is for you.)*

4. ***When** I **was** myself **sending** to you this letter written by my own hand, I **was wanting** to learn from you whether there was any friend of yours to trust/in whom I might trust.* Cum hās litterās meā manū scrīptās ad tē ipse **mitterem**, volēbam ā tē discere an aliquī esset tibi amīcus cui crēderem. *(**Since** I **was sending**, I **was wanting**.)*

5. ***When** she **is** like her own mother, this **is** a woman of the sort that is praised by all.* Cum tālis **sit** quālis sua mater, haec est fēmina quae ab omnibus laudētur. *(**Since** she **is**, she **is**.)*

6. ***When** s-he **looks** at her/himself in a mirror, s-he **sees** her/himself such as others always see her/him.* Cum sē in speculō **conspiciat**, videt sē quālem aliī semper sē videant. *(**Whenever** s-he **looks**, s-he **sees**.)*

7. ***When** s-he **had said** this, s-he **drank** a bit of wine.* Id ubi **dīxisset**, aliquid vīnī bibit. *(**Whenever** s-he'**d say**/**since** s-he'**d said** this, s-he **drank**.* NOTE that *bibit* could also be primary sequence: Id ubi **dīxerit**, aliquid vīnī bibit.*)*

8. ***When** this **had been done**, they **waged** war with them.* Hōc cum **factum esset**, bellum cum illīs gerēbant. *(**Although**/**since** this **had been done**, they **waged**.)*

9. ***When** she **raises** her hand, they **know** that she wants to ask something.* Cum manum eius **tollat**, sciunt eam velle aliquid rogāre. *(**Whenever** she **raises** her hand, they **know**.)*

10. ***When** I **shall have merited** as much as my father, I **shall be** like him/his similar.* Cum tantum **meruerim** quantum pater meus, eius similis erō. *(**Whenever** I **have merited**, I **shall be**.)*

VIII. CHANGE

1. **Tē cēnātūrum/cēnātūram esse** bene apud mē **dīcō**. *(I say that you-boy/girl are going to dine well at my place.)*

2. **Sē** apud hunc philosophum litterās **discitūrum/discitūram esse suō patre dīxit**. *(S-he said to her/his own father that s-he was going to learn literature at this philosopher's school.)*

3. **Scrīpsērunt quaerī** an aliquis vēritātem dē morte **scīret**. *(They wrote that it was inquired whether anyone knew the truth about death.)*

4. **Nōs** vīnum quod tēcum **attuleris bibitūrōs / bibitūrās esse dīcō.** *(I say that we-guys / girls are going to drink the wine that you brought with you.* NOTE that *attuleris,* although identical in form, is now present perfect subjunctive, instead of future perfect indicative.*)*

5. **Ad suam fēminam scrībet sē virum** quem **timuerit interfectūrum esse.** *(He writes to his wife that he is going to kill the man whom s-he was afraid of.)*

6. **Omnēs vidērunt hunc reum** furtī **damnātum īrī.** *(Everybody saw that this man guilty of theft was going to be condemned.)*

7. **Eum** poēmata scrībere **scitūrum esse dīxit.** *(S-he said that he-some other was going to learn to write poems.)*

8. **Sē ducem factum īrī suō amīcō dīxit.** *(S-he said to her / his own friend that s-he was going to be made leader.)*

9. **Scrīpsērunt sē** huic amīcitiā sē **iunctūrōs / iunctūrās esse.** *(They-guys / girls wrote that they were going to unite themselves to him in friendship.)*

10. **Audiunt laudātum īrī urbem illam** quae perdita **sit.** *(They hear that that city which has been destroyed is going to be praised.)*

IX. NOTE THE PATTERN

1. *A friend's vices, if you should put up with them, you would make them your own.*
   Sī loquāris / dīcās, audiāris.
   Sī cum eō loquāris / dīcās / loquāminī / dīcātis, multa discās / discātis.
   Sī moriātur, nēmo eius oblīviscātur.

2. *It's a wise man's role to do nothing that (is of the sort that) can cause repentence.*
   Ducis est omnia dīcere quae dīcere velit.
   Matrum est omnēs nātōs amāre quī nascantur.

3. *Why do I do it, you ask.*
   Quālis dux sit rogat / quaerit / requīrit.
   Quō modō mortuus sit philosophus rogant / quaerunt / requirunt.

4. *This universe sometime will be nothing / none.*
   Haec paucīs fēmina diēbus dux nostra erit / fīet.
   Illō nēmo tempore vīvet.

LESSON NINE
ABLATIVE ABSOLUTE, IMPERATIVE

I. MATCH

1. hōc nuntiō

11. cuius speculī

2. alicuius cūrae / aliquae cūrae
3. viae rectae / viās rectās
4. animī cupidī / animōs cupidōs
5. meus fīlius dīgnus / mī fīlī dīgne
6. pāne ēsō
7. lēge perpetuā
8. imperantis rēgis
9. fidēbus sincērīs
10. nuntiī legentis / nuntiō legentī
12. cūrīs satiātīs
13. nōminum appellātōrum
14. bonus fīlius / bonum fīlium / bone fīlī
15. tōtīus noctis
16. brevī tempore
17. dēformī mortī / dēformī morte
18. nūllīus nāsī
19. cuius timentis
20 opera atrōcia

II. MATCH

1. efficī
2. nōlīte
3. persuādēbō / persuādeam
4. captum erit
5. hortārī / hortāre / hortāris
6. cōgitantibus
7. ventum īrī
8. audītūram esse
9. aestimābantur
10. vixēre / vixērunt
11. vixissētis
12. fac
13. fers / fer
14. oblīviscimur
15. rogābimus
16. laudet
17. fuerātis
18. māvult
19. beāte
20. velit

III. TRANSLATE

1. My friend, I want to speak with you pleasantly. Let's speak friendlily! Speak with me friendlily. You seem to me to be equal to your father. Always you have seemed to me to be equal to him. I exhort you to be always the same. Don't do anything (that is) different from him. He was a man of great virtue. So brave was he that (as a result) he was praised by everybody. In such a manner did he lead his life that for no one was he as an object of hatred / no one hated him. It happened that many loved him. You alone are worthy to be his equal. Be worthy of your father, I urge you, (my) friend. May you be as brave as he. Have as many friends yourself as (had) he. If you were not as brave as that man of great virtue, I would not say that you are his equal. I wouldn't command you to live / that you live similarly and in the same way. Do always only what would have pleased him. If / when / provided such things have been done / if you act in that way / with such things done, you would live pleasantly and friendlily. Whenever you are like him, you may live pleasantly. I say that you, living in that way, are going to be happy. I say that you are going to be praised by everybody. I say that everybody is going to praise you. Your name will not die. With you perpetually praised, worthy boy, our city will be blessed / will have been blest. With you as

leader, all will perpetually praise this city of ours / this our city. With you leading this city, we will be praised. With us praised / if we are praised, so outstanding will our leader seem that (as a result) he be worthy of his own father.

2. Than you there is no one with whom I would prefer to speak, my girl (friend). No one do I prefer to please (more) than you. I say that there is no one whom I prefer to love. When / if / while I am speaking with you, so full of love do I become that I believe that I am equal to a god. With me speaking to with you / when I am speaking to you, everybody becomes full of envy. Once I have spoken with you, I become as blessed as a god himself. So beautiful are you that you make me, as I speak with you, a god. It happens that I seem to become a god when I speak with you. No one is as beautiful as you, my beloved. More do I love you than my life itself. If I didn't love you, I would prefer straightway to die. Without you, there wouldn't be any life for me. If you were dead / with you dead, I wouldn't want to live myself. So great is my love for you that without you I wouldn't want to live. Wouldn't you prefer to die than to live without me? You don't prefer to live without me than to die, do you? Don't live without me. Live happily with me, my girl.

IV. TRANSLATE

1. He seems to me to be equal to a god, he—if it's all right (to say it)—(seems even) to surpass the deities, he, that man who sitting opposite (you) over and over again watches and hears you sweetly laughing: which (whole scene) snatches away from poor me all (my) senses: for as soon as I have seen you, Lesbia, there is nothing more for me of my voice / I have no more voice.

But my tongue gets sluggish; a burning flows beneath my weak limbs; my twinned lights / my eyes are covered with night.

Idleness, Catullus, is troublesome for you: in idle leisure too much do you exult and overreact: idleness has destroyed in previous times both kings and their blessed cities.

2. My woman says that she prefers to marry (as bride for) no one more than me, not if Jupiter himself should seek her. She says it: but that which a woman says to her desirous lover, (one) ought to write on the wind and rapid water.

3. You, my life, propose to me that this our love is going to be happy and perpetual between us. Oh you great gods, make (it) that she can promise truthfully and that she say this sincerely and from her soul: so that (it) be allowed to us to draw out for all our life this eternal treaty of sacred amicability.

4. (In the year with) Lucius Julius Caesar and Gaius Marcius Figulus (acting as) consuls, wilt thou know that I have been augmented by (the birth of) a little son, with (the mother) Terentia surviving and well. From you for so long not a bit of a letter. I wrote to you before diligently about my affairs. At this time, I am considering defending our opponent Catiline; we have the judges whom we've

wanted, with the highest collusion of the prosecutor. I hope, if he should be acquitted, that he will be more accommodating to us in the matter of our electoral campaign; but if it will have turned out otherwise, we will bear it gracefully. There is work for us with the use of your timely arrival / we need your timely arrival; for, to put it straight, the highest opinion of men / the common opinion is that your associates, the aristocrats, are going to be opposed to our candidacy: in order that their goodwill be reconciled with me, I see that you are going to be for me (something for) the greatest use / of the greatest use to me. For which reason, in the month (of) January, as you have agreed, take care to be in Rome.

5. I less often give / send a letter to you than I'm able, because, when / although all times are unhappy for me, (nevertheless) truely then, when I either write to you or read yours (to me), I am so overcome with tears that I cannot bear it. Wherefore, would that we had been less desirous of life! Certainly, nothing or not much of trouble in our life would we have seen.

V. CHANGE

1. *Since your letter had been received, straightway and truthfully I was able to speak about all matters.* **Litterīs tuīs acceptīs**, rectā et vērā poteram loquī dē omnibus rēbus. *(With your letter received...)*

2. *When (signs of) trust had been received and given / exchanged, affairs between the king and our city were pleasant.* **Fidē acceptā datāque**, rēs inter rēgem urbemque nostram iūcundae erant. *(With signs of trust received and given...)*

3. *While I was / am speaking with you, s-he persuaded the others to prefer to accept money / take a bribe.* **Mē** tēcum **loquente**, persuāsit aliīs ut pecūniam accipere māllent. *(With me in the process of speaking with you...)*

4. *While our leader was / is urging the slave to speak the truth, a messenger arrived to say that the city had been captured yesterday.* **Duce nostrō** servum **hortante** ut vērum dīceret, nuntius advēnit quī dīceret urbem herī captam esse. *(With our leader in the process of urging...)*

5. *If the gods are favorable, we will persue this straight way of life toward the eternal glory of our illustrious city.* **Dīs faventibus**, hanc rectam vītae viam ad aeternam glōriam nostrae ēgregiae urbis sequēmur. *(With the gods willing...)*

6. *If my reasons had been known, never would you have done what (things) you did.* **Ratiōnibus meīs cognitīs**, numquam fēcissēs quae facerēs. *(With my reasons known...)*

7. *If god should will it, my son, you may be / may you be a man like me / the similar of me.* **Deō volente**, mī fīlī, vir meī similis sīs. *(With god willing...)*

8. *When these things had been done, they said that they were going to wage war*

with them. **Hīs factīs**, dīcēbant sē bellum cum illīs gestūrōs esse. *(With these things done...)*

9. *When those things that are being done will have been known, there will be no one who trusts him/her.* **Eīs** quae geruntur **scītīs**, nēmō erit quī illī crēdat. *(With those things... known...)*

10. *If she had been praised, life would have seemed pleasant to me.* **Eā laudātā**, vīta mihi iūcunda vidērētur. *(With her praised...)*

VI. CHANGE

1. *I urge you-all to speak sincerely.* Sincērē **dīcite**. *(Speak sincerely.)*

2. *I urge you, my sons, always to be faithful to me.* Fīliī meī, semper mihi fidēlēs **este**. *(My sons, always be faithful to me.)*

3. *I command you to prefer to read than to write.* **Mālī** legere quam scrībere. *(Prefer to read than to write.)*

4. *I urge you-all not to follow me.* **Nōlīte** mē **sequī**. *(Don't follow me.)*

5. *I urge you to accept and receive/exchange (signs of) good faith.* **Accipe dāque** fidem. *(Exchange signs of good faith.)*

6. *I command you to speak straightway and truthfully.* **Loquere** rectā et vērā. *(Speak straightway and truthfully.)*

7. *I urge you, worthy boy, to be your father's likeness and equal to him.* **Es**, puer dīgne, patris similis et eī pār. *(Be, worthy boy, your father's likeness and equal to him.)*

8. *I command you not to persuade me to accept money/take a bribe.* **Nōlī** mihi **persuādēre** ut pecūniam accipiam. *(Don't persuade me to accept money.)*

9. *I urge you-all to persuade that ugly woman not to look in a mirror.* Illī dēformī fēminae **persuādēte** nē in speculō conspiciat. *(Persuade that ugly woman not to look in a mirror.)*

10. *I urge you not to kill anyone.* **Nōlī** quemquam **interficere**. *(Don't kill anyone.)*

VII. CHANGE

1. *God willing, I will/may come straightway to you to speak with you about this matter.* **Sī deus vult/velit/voluerit**, rectā... *(If god wills/should will/will have willed/should have willed...)*

2. *With this done, s-he sent a messenger to them to accept a sign of good faith.* **Cum hōc factum erat/esset**, nuntium... *(When this had been done/since this had been done...)*

3. *With you urging that I make a treaty with them, there were none who wanted to wage perpetual war.* **Dum hortāris / cum hortābāris / cum hortārēris / sī hortābāris** ut foedus cum illīs facerem... *(While you were urging/ when you were urging/ since you were urging/ if you were urging...)*

4. *With tokens of trust exchanged/ once tokens of trust have been exchanged, we will be faithful friends.* **Cum fidēs accepta dataque erit**, amīcī fidēlēs erimus. *(When tokens of trust will have been exchanged/ since tokens of trust will have been exchanged, we...)*

5. *With the letter received/ once the letter has been received, I would send a messenger to them to say that I was going to make a treaty with them.* **Sī litterae acceptae essent**, nuntium ad eōs mitterem quī dīceret mē foedus cum illīs factūrum esse. *(If the letter had been received, I...)* NOTE that *mitterem* suggests the implication of a contrary-to-fact condition.

6. *Always did I speak with great care, with you listening.* Semper magnā cum cūrā loquēbar **sī / cum / ubi audiēbās / cum audīrēs.** *(... if/ when you were listening/ since you were listening.)*

7. *Once this was known, straightway I wrote to you about my affairs.* **Cum hōc scītum erat / esset**, rectā viā dē meīs ad tē ratiōnibus scrīpsī. *When this had been known/ since this had been known, I...)* NOTE that primary sequence is also a possibility: **Cum hōc scītum sit**, rectā... *(Since this had been known, I ended up writing...)*

8. *With laws and treaties joined, friendlily and faithfully they conducted their life.* **Sī / cum / ubi lēgēs et foedera iuncta erant**, amīciter fidēliterque vītam ēgērunt. *(If/ when laws and treaties had been joined, friendlily...)*

9. *With the woman being unwilling to listen, I would say nothing about this matter.* **Sī mulier audīre nōllet**, nihil dē hāc rē dīcerem. *(If the woman were unwilling to listen, I would...)*

10. *With fortune ruling life, there is work for wise men/ wise men are needed to teach what we ought to do.* **Sī / cum fortūna vītam regit / cum... regat**, opus sapientibus est quī doceant quid nōs oporteat facere. *(If/ when fortune rules life, there... / since fortune rules life, there...)*

VIII. CHANGE

1. Sīc id fēcistī **ut** cupidus pecūniae nōn **vidērēris / videāris.** *(You did it so that, as a result, you didn't seem desirous of money. / You ended up having done this so...)* **REMEMBER** that primary sequence is always a possibility with a present perfect indicative.

2. Tam dēformis erat **ut** omnibus odiō **esset.** *(So ugly was s-he that s-he was for everyone somebody to hate / everybody hated her / him.)*

3. Tot amīcōs habēbat **ut** nēmō **esset** quī quidquam malum dē eō dīceret. *(So many friends did he have that there was no one who said anything bad about him.)*

4. Fierī potest **ut** mulierēs dēformēs **amentur**. *(It can happen that ugly women are / be loved.)*

5. Vir tantae sapientiae erat **ut** nihil **esset** dē quō dīcere nōn posset. *(A man of such great wisdom was he that there was nothing about which he couldn't speak.)*

6. Tam caecus sum **ut** nihil vidēre **possim**. *(I am so blind that I can see nothing.)*

7. Nēmō tam stultus erat **ut** morī **māllet** quam vīvere. *(No one was so stupid that he preferred to die than to live.)*

8. Tantum, mea puella, tē amō **ut** mea anima mihi **sīs**. *(So much, my girl, do I love you that you are for me my soul.)*

9. Tot opera et tam magna fac, mī fīlī, **ut** meī similis **videāris** esse. *(Do so many works and such great ones, my son, that you seem to be the likeness of me / like me.)*

10. Tam diū dīxit **ut** nēmō **esset** quī eī crēderet. *(So long did he speak that there was no one who trusted him.)*

IX. NOTE THE PATTERN

1. *Great gods, make it that it be permitted to us to lead out this treaty of amicability.*
   Mī fīlī, fac ut liceat tibi tam sapientem esse quam mē.
   Mea anima, vidē ut liceat tibi ad mē venīre.

2. *Not what anyone can do is permitted him / her to do.*
   Quod volunt omnēs nōn licet eīs velle.

3. *We need your timely arrival.*
   Tuā / vestrā magnā fidē mihi opus est.
   Eius sapientiā nōbīs opus est.
   Tuā / vestrā amīcitiā eī opus erat.

LESSON TEN
COMPARATIVES, SUPERLATIVES

I. MATCH

1. cīvitātis iustae / cīvitātēs iustae
2. meliōres mulierēs
3. hominum dēlectōrum
4. tribus puellīs
5. facillimōrum operum
11. nūllīus statūs
12. optimātis fideī
13. ūnī consiliō
14. populī atrōcēs / populōs atrōcēs
15. cui lībertātī

6. ūnīus cūrae / ūnī cūrae
7. fortiōrum quōrundam
8. dīgnus fīlius / dīgnī fīliī / dīgne fīlī
9. duābus rēbus
10. facilia opera
16. virō volente (-ī)
17. iūcundiōrum diērum
18. haec itinera
19. cupidī optimātis / cupidī optimātēs
20. huius urbis / hae urbēs

II. MATCH

1. fīs
2. velit
3. captūrōs esse
4. effectum īrī
5. legis / lege
6. vocārī
7. hortārī / hortāre / hortāris
8. māluissētis
9. fer
10. verēminī
11. accēperāmus
12. verēbāre / verēbāris
13. cēnāre / cēnāris
14. ēdit
15. nōn vīs
16. vīs
17. tulerint
18. scīverō
19. vereātur
20. dēligitis

III. TRANSLATE

1. The greatest of poets am I. By much a greater poet than all am I. By much the greatest of all other poets am I. A better poet than you am I. For you are the worst of poets. By so much the best of poets am I, by (just) as much as you are the worst. If I were not a better poet than you, I wouldn't sing songs. You have written more (of) poems than I and longer (ones), but all worse than mine. Would that you had written nothing. With none written / if you had written none, there would be no one to know / who would know by how much are you the worst of poets. Most the likeness of your father / most similar to your father are you, you most stupid of men, (your father), whom everybody said was a bad poet. I'm afraid that you are his similar / like him. I'm afraid that you are most worthy (by comparison with) / of your father. So stupid are you that no one than you can be more stupid. No one is so stupid but that he know / so that he not know that you are the worst of poets. Therefore, I urge you not to write poems. If by me you should be persuaded not to write poems / if it should be persuaded to you by me that you not write poems, more pleasantly will you conduct your life. You will seem to be wiser. By much wiser will everybody say you to be / that you are. It cannot happen but that everybody say that you are a better man.

2. By so much was that girl the ugliest, by as much as mine was the prettiest. Than she an uglier cannot be / happen, nor than mine, a prettier. If she were to look at herself more often in a mirror, she would know by how much she is uglier than my girl friend. Would that she knew by how much she is the ugliest

of all. Nor was there for her any bit of wisdom, but the stupidest of women always did she seem to be. By much the most stupidly did she speak about all things. No bit of reason was there for her, nothing of knowledge. But this woman said that she was prettier than my girl, whom more did I love than life itself. So much did I love my girl, by as much as I hated that one / as that one was for me an object of hatred. I ask whether anyone can be / happen to be stupider. I ask whether any woman ever said anything stupider. It cannot happen but that that one was the stupidest of women. So ugly was her posture / stature that more she seemed to be some animal than a woman. Her face so ugly was (it) that I was afraid that I would die when I saw her. If I were to look at her straight in the face, it could have happened that she kill me.

IV. TRANSLATE

1. Most often are men accustomed to dispute which is the best state / establishment of republic / government. For there are three types of republic: when in the hands of one / in one man's power is the supreme (control) of all matters, a king (is what) we call him, and a kingdom is his state of republic; when, however, in the hands of selected men, then that body-politic is said to be ruled by the council of the best men; that body-politic, however, is the popular (one), in which all matters are (invested) in the people. It cannot be denied but that each single one (of these three) has its advantages. Kings captivate us with their charisma; the aristocrats, with their (intelligent) counsel; popular democracy / the people, with its freedom. There is, however, no type of those republics that does not have a certain way (of its own) toward ultimate evil, a precipitous and slippery (itinerary). The kingship of the most just man—and the wisest—more often collapses into (one) of the most savage tyrant; the administration of the (oligarchical) few mutates into the faction / party of the wealthy; the people's power over all matters is concerted into the furor and license of the multitude. None, therefore, of them itself for itself in isolation do I approve, and I prefer, instead of any one of them alone. that which (is of the sort) that has been conflated (out of elements) from all (three).

2. I have erected a monument more enduring than bronze
and higher than the regal site of the pyramids,
which not the edacious rain, not Aquilo, the powerless,
(is of the sort) that can demolish (it)—or the innumerable
sequence of years and the flight of time(s).
Not entire(ly) shall I die, and a great part of me
will avoid Libitina.

3. In all matters he was (a man) with singular industry; for (he) was a skilled agriculturalist (farmer) and an experienced juridic consultant and a great general and a convincing orator and a most passionate (devotee) of literature / letters. The study of which, even though he had taken up (only) as an older man, never-

theless, so much progress did he make that not easily could be found, neither concerning Greek nor Italian matters, that which to him was unknown. From adolescence (on) he composed orations. As an old man, he undertook to write histories.

4. Most eloquent of the descendants of Romulus,
as many as there (now) are and as many as there have been, you Marcus Tullius,
and as many as in later years there will be,
the greatest thanks to you does Catullus
offer, (I), the worst poet of all,
by so much the worst poet of all,
as you (are) the best advocate of all.

5. Although a raven wanted to eat the cheese (he'd) snatched from a windowsill, sitting (as he was) in a high tree, a fox saw him; then thus began to speak: "Oh, what luster, Raven, (there) is of your feathers! How much of gracefulness do you bear with your body and your face! If (only) you had a voice, no winged (creature) would be going to be ahead of you." And he, stupid, while he wanted to show off his voice, sent forth / emitted from his mouth the cheese—which swiftly the crafty fox snatched up with greedy teeth. Then, not 'til then, did the deceived stupidity of the raven lament (what had happened).

6. On a journey, a certain person joined up with another certain person, one setting out to market and carrying with himself some amount of coinage. With this person, as usually happens, he took up a conversation on the way; from which it happened that they wanted to make that journey (of theirs) more familiar / together. For which reason, since they had turned aside into the same inn, they wanted to dine together / simultaneously and to take (their) sleep in the same place. (After they had) dined / been given their dinner, they went to bed in the same place. The innkeeper, however (for thus it is said, after it was found out, when he was apprehended in another crime)—since he had noticed / turned his attention to that other (guy, I mean) clearly the one who had the cash—(well, this innkeeper) at night, after he sensed that those (two) were sleeping deeply already, as happens, because of (their) tiredness, (he) approached them, and of the one of the two, the one who was without cash, that one's sword, (which was) placed nearby, he drew from its sheath, and the other (guy) he killed, took away the cash, replaced the bloody sword in the sheath, (and) he himself betook himself back to his own bed. He, however, with whose sword the murder had been committed, much before dawn arose, called (to waken) his companion once and (then) several times more often. He decided that he didn't respond (because he was) impeded by sleep; he himself took up the sword and the rest (of the stuff) which he had brought with him, (and) alone set out (on his journey). The innkeeper not much later (begins) shouting that a man has been murdered and with certain (of the) guests follows (after) the one who had gone out before. He apprehends the man, withdraws his sword from the sheath, (and)

finds it bloody. The man is arraigned in the city by them and is made / found guilty.

V. CHANGE

(The point of this exercise is to notice the various possible meanings of *quam*; it is, of course, unlikely that so many would be found in a single sentence.)

1. Tē, mea amātissima puella, quam omnēs quam maximē laudant, semper dīcam pulchriōrem esse **illā** quam **stultissimā fēminā**. *(You, my most beloved girl, whom everybody praises as greatly as possible—always will / may I say that you are prettier than that superlatively stupid woman.)*

2. Nisī quam puellam **tē** meliōrem amārem, meus tuī amor quam maximus semper esset. *(If I didn't love any girl better than you, my love for you would always be the superlatively greatest.)*

3. Aliquis forsitan quaerat num qua sit mulier quam vir quīdam, cuius nōmen nōn mē oportet dīcere, umquam amāverit quīn peior ab eō facta sit **omnibus fēminīs** et caeca ad omnia sua vitia. *(Someone perhaps may inquire whether there be any woman whom a certain man, whose name I ought not to say, ever loved but that she was made worse by him than all women and blind to all her own vices.)*

4. Sī tam sapiens esset quam pulchra, plūs pecūniae habēret neque tam saepe vidērētur nescīre quō modō sē oporteat vītam suam agere, sed, ut vērē dīcam, numquam vīdī fēminam **eā** stultiōrem. *(If she were as wise as she is beautiful, she would have more money nor would she seem so often not to know how she ought to conduct her own life, but, to speak truthfully, never have I seen a woman stupider than her.)*

5. Nisī quid sapientiae sibi esset, peior **patre suō** esset, quī, ut scīs, vir erat iūcundus, sed numquam cognōvī quemquam **eō** stultiōrem. *(If he didn't have a modicum of wisdom / if there were not some bit of wisdom for him to use, he would be worse than his own father, who, as you know, was a happy man, but never have I known anyone stupider than him.)*

6. Vereor nē qua sit mulier sapientior **tē** aut minus virtūtis cupida. Nam tē volō semper omnium sapientissimam vidērī et quam optimam fēminam, quam nōn possit fierī quīn aliae laudent. *(I'm afraid that some woman may be wiser than you or less desirous of virtue. For I always want you to seem the wisest of all and the superlatively best woman, whom it cannot but happen that other women praise.)*

7. Tē, mī quam dīgnissime fīlī, hortor nē quem sinās umquam meliōrem vidērī **tē ipsō** neque minus vitiōrum cupidum. *(You, my superlatively worthy son, do I urge that you not allow anyone ever to seem better that yourself nor less desirous of vices.)*

8. Hōc, quod tibi summae cūrae sit, tē hortor nē quam hominēs dīcant meliōrem **tē** aut **fīliā tuā** fuisse. *(This—which let be for you something for the highest concern—do I exhort you: that men not say any female was better than you or your daughter.)*

9. Sī quis quam amet, eam velit plūris aestimārī **aliīs** et fēminam quam optimam vidērī. *(If any man should love some woman, he would want her to be esteemed of greater worth than other women and to seem the superlatively best woman.)*

10. Quaesītum est num quid sit peius **morte**. *(It is a question whether anything be worse than death.)*

VI. CHANGE

1. **Vereor nē quis** tē pulchrior sit. *(I'm afraid that someone may be prettier than you.)*

2. **Timeō ut** fierī possit quīn plūris aestimētur patre eius. *(I fear it cannot but happen that he be esteemed of more worth than his father.)*

3. **Verēmur nē** in itinere quōdam **quis** quendam ad urbem quandam proficiscentem et cum eō **quid** pecūniae ferentem interficiat. *(We fear that on a certain journey someone may kill a certain person traveling to a certain city and carrying with him some bit of money.)*

4. **Timēbat nē quae quā** stultior **esset** aut minus pecūniae **habēret**. *(S-he was afraid that some woman be/was stupider than some other or have less of money.)*

5. **Verēbātur nē** illud genus rērum pūblicārum hōc peius esset. *(S-he was afraid that that type of republic be/was worse than this type.)*

6. **Timēbam ut quaererēs** num quis **esset** homo fidēlior eō aut tam fortis. *(I was afraid that you wouldn't inquire whether anyone was a more faithful man than he or so brave.)*

7. **Verēbar ut dēligerem** ducem omnium optimum quī hanc cīvitātem in pāce **regeret**. *(I was afraid that I wouldn't choose the best leader of all to rule this city in peace.)*

8. **Timēbāmus nē** in potestāte rēgis tam atrōcis **essēmus** ut morī **māllēmus** quam diūtius in hāc cīvitāte vīvere. *(We were afraid that we be/were in the power of a king so cruel that we would prefer to die rather than to live longer in this city.)*

9. **Hōc mihi summae cūrae erat ut vidērētur** sapientior hōc homine esse. *(This was for the highest concern for me that s-he not seem to be wiser than this man.)*

10. **Hōc eī summae cūrae erat nē quibuscum quis** dē rēbus quibusdam **solēret**

loquī. *(This was of the highest concern to him/her lest anyone be accustomed to speak with anybody about certain matters.)*

VII. CHANGE

(The purpose of this exercise is to review the different types of subordinate clauses, while becoming familiar with the conjugation of the verb *eō*; be careful to distinguish it from the declension of the demonstrative *is, ea, id.*)

1. **Nōn fierī potest quīn** quam saepissimē, mī fīlī, ad tē **eam**. *(It cannot but happen that as often as possible I come to you, my son.)* Negative result / primary sequence.

2. **Dīxit eum** tē **amātūrum esse** plūs quam vītam eius. *(S-he said that he was going to love you more than his life.)* **Dīxit sē** tē **amātūrum esse** plūs quam vītam **suam.** *(He said that he, himself, was going to love you more than his own life.)* Oratio obliqua.

3. Ā **nōbīs quaesīvit an** ex urbe ad tē **īrēmus** ut tē ad cēnam vōcārēmus. *(From us s-he inquired whether we were going from the city to you to invite you to dinner.)* Indirect question / secondary sequence.

4. **Vereor nē quis** ad tē eat quī dīcat mē plūris aestimātum īrī ab homine quōdam quam tē. *(I fear that someone may go to you to say that I am going to be esteemed of greater value by a certain man than you.)* Clause of fearing / primary sequence. **NOTE** that *eat* is already subjunctive: the original sentence said: *someone may go....*

5. **Tam fortis est ut** nēmō **sit sē** fortior. *(So brave/strong is he that no one is braver/stronger than he.)* Positive result / primary sequence.

6. **Rogābat an** optimātēs penes, deō volente, cīvitātis potestātem **oportēret** esse. *(S-he asked whether, god willing, the power of the state ought to be in the hands of the oligarchs.)* Indirect question / secondary sequence.

7. **Rogō num cui** hōc summae cūrae **sit**, nē quem dēligās eō peiōrem. *(I ask whether this is something for the highest concern to anyone, namely, that you may deligate/choose someone worse than him.)* Indirect question / primary sequence.

8. **Hortor ut soleās** cum eīsdem quam diūtissimē loquī. *(I exhort you to be accustomed to speak as long as possible with the same people.)* Positive command / primary sequence.

9. **Audīverat** nōn **esse quemquam** eō **dēformiōrem.** *(S-he had heard that there wasn't anyone uglier than he.)* Oratio obliqua.

10. **Dīxī** ad eam **mē itūrum esse** quae mihi **vidērētur** quam illa pulchrior esse. *(I said that I was going to her who seemed prettier than that woman.)* Oratio obliqua / relative clause in oratio obliqua. **NOTE** that the first person speaker could be feminine: **dīxī** ad eam **mē itūram esse**... Also, *dīxī* could be primary sequence: ...quae mihi **videātur**....

VIII. NOTE THE PATTERN

1. *I have erected a monument more lasting than bronze.*
   Aliquis fēminam vīdit tē candidiōrem / ēgregiōrem / pulchriōrem.
   Hōc illō difficilius est.

2. *If you had a voice, no bird would be going to be ahead of you.*
   Sī ad mē litterās mitterēs / mīsissēs, eās acciperem / accēpissem ē servō tuō.
   Sī tam iustus / iusta essēs quam mē, nēmō tam stultus esset quīn aut mē aut tē dēligeret.

LESSON ELEVEN
GERUND, GERUNDIVE, SUPINE

I. MATCH

1. senis infāmis
2. rēbus pūblicīs
3. huic pācī
4. istae potestātēs / istās potestātēs
5. sapientī nesciō cui
6. mī amāte fīlī
7. aurī maiōrī / aure maiōre (-ī)
8. alicuius rūris
9. arbitrāns senex / arbitrantem senem
10. duōrum stilōrum
11. ūnīus cuiusdam
12. minōris perīculī / minōra perīcula
13. alicuius mentis
14. vīnō bibendō
15. manum iunctam
16. lūminis tollendī / lūmina tollenda
17. pānēs bonī
18. nesciens homo
19. hīs lūminibus
20. ūnī aurī / ūnā aure

II. MATCH

1. intellectum īrī
2. dēterrendī
3. ēsūrum -am -um / -ōs, -ās, -a esse
4. este
5. profectī erunt / profectī sint / profectae erunt / profectae sint / profecta erunt / profecta sint
6. discēdis / discēde
7. nōlīs
8. arbitrāre / arbitrāris
9. discēdant
10. redīre / rediērunt / rediēre / redīris
11. agam
12. timendum
13. dictū
14. appellārēminī / appellerēminī
15. locūtum erunt
16. scrībente
17. veritī sunt / veritae sunt / verita sunt
18. futūrōs esse / fore
19. cēnāverāmus
20. ītis

III. TRANSLATE

1. He summons me to write. The man of great wisdom summons me to write books. He summons me to write poems. I told him that I was going to write books. I said that books were going to be written by me. I shall go to the country to write. I shall go home to write. For the sake of writing books I shall / let me / I may leave Rome. For in Rome I cannot write. At home I shall / let me / I may write. Books have to be written by me. I esteem it of the greatest value to write books. Difficult is (it) to say how much I want to write. While I am at home, I shall / let me / I may write. Provided I'm at home, I shall write. At home nothing will deter me / keep me from writing / whereby the less I write. Nothing will be more pleasant for me than writing books. (It) will be pleasing to me to write books. I shall / let me / I may set the day for writing. I shall / let me / I may set the day for writing books. I am most desirious of writing. I am most desirous of writing poems. Happy will my life be for me as long as I (shall) devote myself to writing. My life will not be happy for me until I devote myself to writing.

2. From your letter, my friend, which your most trustworthy slave / servant gave to me, I learned / am aware how much you are most desirous of seeing me. That even without the letter I would have thought, for most often for the sake of our friendship you have done me well and you have said to everybody that you esteem me of more value than I know not what friend / any friend. I urge you to be in Rome when I will have come from the country for the sake of talking with you. If you cannot come to Rome, I shall do it, I know not how, that I come to see you / I shall bring it about somehow to see you. Difficult is (it) for me to say how I'll do it since many are the affairs that keep me from coming to you / deter me whereby the less I come to you. For which reason again I urge you to come to Rome for the sake of seeing me.

IV. TRANSLATE

1. **NOTE** that birds are a common metaphor for the *membrum virile.*

Oh (you) sparrow, my girl (friend)'s delight, with which she is accustomed to play, (and) which (she is accustomed) to hold in her lap, (and) to which (she is accustomed) to give her first finger (as it is) seeking (it) and to incite its fierce bites when it pleases (her) my shining object of desire / (it) my shining urgent need to jest I know not what sweet (jest) and solace for her / its grief—I do believe—so that then her / its grave ardor may calm down: would that I might play with you (myself) just as she does and alleviate my soul's sad cares!

2. Weep, oh you Venuses and Cupids, and as much of mankind as is more prone to Love: dead is / has died the sparrow of my girl friend, the sparrow, my girl's delight, whom more she loved than her own eyes. For he was honey sweet and had known her herself as well as a girl her mother, nor did he used to move

himself from her lap, but hopping now here now there, he used to chirp to his mistress alone; which (sparrow) now goes upon that shadowy journey from which they deny that anyone returns / say that no one returns. Indeed, may it be bad for you, you evil shades of Orcus, who have devoured all (that is) beautiful: so beautiful a sparrow of mine / to my disadvantage have you taken away. Oh, evil deed! Oh poor little sparrow! Because of your act my girl's eyes grow red, swollen from weeping.

3. Now must one drink, now the ground should be struck with a (dancing) foot (that's) free.

4. Marcus Cicero says greetings to Lucius Mescinius: Welcome to me was your letter; from which I learned—what even without the letter I would have thought—that you were affected with the highest desire for seeing me. Which (news) I so willingly accept that, nevertheless, I cannot express it to you. For may everything appropriate that I hope for come about in such a way that I may want vehemently to be with you.

5. There was in Athens a spacious and capacious house, but infamous and pestilential. Throughout the silence of the night, the sound of iron, and—if you were to attend more consciously—the noise of chains, at first further away, then from most nearby used to reecho back and forth; soon there used to show up a spectre, an old man overcome with emaciation and squalor, with a falling beard, with bristling hair: on his legs fetters and on his hands manacles he wore and shook. From that point on, for the inhabitants sad and dire nights were spent awake through fear. Sickness followed upon the vigil and, with increasing dread, death. For in the day also, although the ghost had departed, the memory of the apparition used to wander in upon the eyes, and longer than the causes of the fear was the fear itself. Deserted, hence on, and condemned with solitude was the house and relinquished entire to that monster; it was advertised, however, whether any might want to buy or anyone to rent it, ignorant of such a great evil. (There) came to Athens the philosopher Athenodorus; he read the ad; when the price was heard, since its cheapness was suspect, he investigated thoroughly; he learns everything and nonetheless, indeed, by so much the more, he rents it. When it begins to be evening, he orders (it / his belongings) to be spread out / unpacked for him in the front part of the house; he requests writing tablets, a pen, a light / lamp; he dismisses all his household into the interior: he himself concentrates his attention, his eyes, (and) his hand to writing, so that a vacant mind not construct heard simulacra / phantoms and empty fears for himself. At first, just as everywhere, the silence of the night; then iron—clanked together; chains—moved: he—not to raise his eyes, not to put down his pen, but to hold fast his concentration and strain with his ears: then more frequent the noise; approach, and already as on the threshold, now as beyond the doorway being heard. He looks up, sees and recognizes the ghost (that had been) told about to him. It was standing and motioning with its finger, like to a person calling. He,

in return, signifies with his hand that it wait a bit, and back to his wax (tablets) and his pen, he bends (his attention). It was making noises with its chains at the head of the writer. He sees again, the same as before, the (creature) motioning, and without delay / not having waited he picks up his lantern and follows. It went with slow step, as if heavy with the chains: after it turned aside into the courtyard, suddenly, melted away it deserted its companion. He, deserted, places grasses and gathered leaves as a marker on the spot. On the next day, he goes to the magistrates, (and) advises that they order that place to be dug up. Bones are found, entangled and interwound with chains, (bones) which a body rotten with age and earth had left bare and eaten away to the chains. Collected together, (the bones) are publicly entombed. The house thereafter, with the ghost(s) ritually put to rest, had none.

V. CHANGE

1. Discēdam **mortuum**. *(I shall / let me / I may go away to die.)*

2. Mē **vīsum** rediērunt. *(They returned to see me.)*

3. Tēcum **locūtum** ībimus. *(We will go to speak with you.)*

4. Servum ad tē, mī amīce, mox mittam tibi nesciō quid prō amīcitiā nostrā **datum**. *(My slave / servant to you, my friend, soon I shall / let me / I may send to give you some little something / I know not what on behalf of our friendship.)*

5. Saepissimē Athēnās ībam Graecē **locūtum**. *(Most often I used to go to Athens to speak Greek / Greekly.)*

6. Suās quisque abeunt domōs **cēnātum**. *(They go away, each to their own houses / each to his own house to dine.)*

7. Iste infāmissimus senex semper rediit **dictum**. *(That most infamous old man always returned to speak.)*

8. Aliquī miserrimus vīsū puer vēnit apud istam bellissimam puellam **cēnātum**. *(Some most miserable to see boy came to dine at that most beautiful girl's place.)*

9. Nōn nūllī semper mē domum sequuntur amīcitiae nostrae causā mēcum **locūtum**. *(Not none / many people always follow me home because of our friendship to speak with me.)*

10. Admōvit aurēs melius **audītum**. *(S-he perked her / his ears to hear better.)*

VI. CHANGE

1. Mē vocāvit **ad scrībendum / scrībendī causā / grātiā**. *(S-he summoned me toward writing / because, for the sake of writing.)*

2. Omnēs bonōs vocāvit **ad istam infāmissimam urbem dēlendam / istīus**

infāmissae urbis dēlendae causā / grātiā. *(S-he summoned all good men to destroy that most infamous city.)*

3. Illam iūcundissiman audītū mulierem appellat **ad poēmata canenda / poēmatum canendōrum causā / grātiā.** *(S-he summons that most pleasant to hear woman to sing poems.)*

4. Rūs mox ībō **ad poēmata legenda / poēmatum legendōrum causā / grātiā.** *(I shall soon go to the country to read poems.)*

5. Aurēs admovēte, meī amīcī, **ad vēritātem audiendam / vēritātis audiendae causā / grātiā** melius dē hāc rē. *(Perk up your ears, my friends, to hear the truth about this affair better.)*

6. Istī reī, mī amīce, mentem tuam dā **ad metum oblīviscendum / metūs oblīviscendī causā / grātiā.** *(Devote your mind, my friend, to that affair to forget your fear.)*

7. Athēnīs vīvit **ad (linguam) Graecam loquendam / (linguae) Graecae loquendae causā / grātiā.** *(S-he lived in Athens to speak Greek.)*

8. Venīte Rōmam **ad mē videndum / ad mē videndam / meī videndī / videndae causā / grātiā.** *(Come to Rome to see me.)*

9. Domī erat rūrī dē rē pūblicā et metibus suī **ad tacendum / tacendī causā / grātia.** *(S-he was home in the country to keep silent about the republic and the fears for her / himself.)*

10. Rōmā proficiscere, mī fīlī, **ad metum meum** dē tuā salūte **rēmovendum / metūs meī** dē tuā salūte **rēmovendī causā / grātiā.** *(Set out from Rome, my son, to remove my fear for your safety.)*

VII. CHANGE

1. Haec infāmissima urbs **dēlenda est.** *(This most infamous city must be destroyed / is under a future obligation of being destroyed.)*

2. **Dēterrendī / dēterrendae fuimus** ā scrībendō. *(We-guys / girls had to be deterred from writing.)*

3. **Laudanda fuit** illa bellissima vīsū mulier. *(That most beautiful woman to see was to be praised.)*

4. Vīta ā fortūnā nōn **regenda est.** *(Life is not to be / must not be ruled by fortune.)*

5. **Iste homo** capitis **damnandus est.** *(That man is to be / must be condemned to death.)*

6. Dē istā rē ā nōbīs **est tacendum.** *(About that matter it is to be / must be kept silent by us.)*

7. **Ille atrōcissimus** vīsū **rex** nōn **fuit** ad bellum **movendus**. *(That most atrocious to see king was not to be provoked to war.)*

8. **Stultī** ā dīcendō **sunt prohibendī**. *(Stupid people are to be/must be prohibited from speaking.)*

9. Ūnus **dēligendus est** quī prō nōbīs dīcat. *(One man is to be chosen to speak for us.)*

10. Eī **persuādendum est** nē veniat. *(It must be persuaded to him/her not to come.)*

VIII. CHANGE

1. Tam cupidissima est mea puella **meī videndī** ut nēmō est alius quōcum velit loquī. *(So extremely desirous is my girl for seeing me that there is no one other with whom she wants to speak.)*

2. Rōmam rediit iste bellissimus vīsū vir **suae puellae amandae** causā. *(That most handsome to see man returned to Rome for the sake of loving his girl.)*

3. Omnēs dēterreāmus bonōs quōminus velint cīvitātem nostram dēlēre **bellī** cum fīnitimīs **gerendī** grātiā. *(Let's deter all good men from wanting to destroy our state for the sake of waging war with our neighbors.)*

4. Vōs nōn oportuit dē rē pūblicā tacēre **nostrī placendōrum** causā. *(You-all shouldn't have been silent about the republic for the sake of pleasing us.)*

5. Vīvat iste cupidissimus **nostrī interficiendōrum** senex dum Rōmā discēdat priusquam ad urbem redeam. *(Let that old man who is so extremely desirous of killing us live, provided he leave Rome before I return.)*

IX. NOTE THE PATTERN

1. *I have learned that you were affected with the highest desire for seeing me.*
   Arbitrābātur / arbitrātus est nōs infāmissimā cupiditāte adficī / adfectōs esse cīvitātis dēlendae.
   Mox vidēbant / vīdērunt amīcōs suōs cupidōs esse suī interficiendōrum.

2. *Before I could speak, s-he went away.*
   Priusquam inimīcī suī rem pūblicam dēlērent, Rōmam rediit.
   Priusquam intellexisset mē Rōmae futūrum / futūram esse, rūs profectus erat.

GLOSSARY

Numbers in parentheses indicate the lesson in which the word first appeared in the **INDEX VERBORUM.**

ā, ab: (away) from, by (agent) (+ abl.) (5)
abhorreō, -ēre: abhor, shrink away from
abscēdō, -ere, -cessī, -cessus: depart
abscondō, -ere, -condī, -conditus: conceal, hide
absolvō, -ere, -vī, -lūtus: absolve, acquit
absum, -esse, āfuī, āfutūrus: be away, be absent
ac = atque
accēdō, -ere, -cessī, -cessus: approach, go near
accidō, -ere, -cidī: fall upon, fall down, happen, occur
accipiō, -ere, -cēpī, -ceptus: accept, receive, take, take possession of, take by perception, understand, take upon one's self (9)
accūsātor, -ōris (ille): accuser, plaintiff
acer, acris, acre: sharp, acute, vehement, ardent, fierce (2)
acerbus, -a, -um: bitter, disagreeable
acquiescō, -ere, -quēvi, -ētus: become quiet
ad: toward, to (+ acc.) (5)
adeō (compound of **eō**): go to
adficiō, -ere, -fēcī, -fectus: affect, influence
administrātio, -ōnis (illa): administration
admoneō, -ēre, -monuī, -monītus: remind, admonish
adnuntiō, -āre, -āvī, -ātus: announce
adorior, -īrī, -ortus: rise up to address, accost
adulescentia, -ae (illa): youth, adolescence, the age from 15 to 30
adventō, -āre, -āvī -ātus: come continually nearer
adventus, -ūs (ille): arrival
adversārius, -a, -um: opposed
adversus (adversum) (adv. and prep.): opposite, facing over against (+ acc.)
advertō, -ere, -tī, -rsus: turn toward; **animum advertere** (+ acc.): notice
advesperascit, -ere, -āvit: get to be evening
aequālis, -e: equal
aes, aeris (illud): bronze or other alloyed metals, metal ore (except gold or silver), coinage
aestimō, -āre, -āvī, -ātus: value, appraise (3)
aeternus, -a, -um = sempiternus, -a, -um: eternal, immorta l
aevum, -ī (illud): age, time
afferō (ad-ferō), afferre, attulī, allātus: bring (to a place)
agnoscō, -ere, -nōvī, -nōtus: recognize
agō, -ere, ēgī, actus: do, drive, conduct, impel; **grātiās agere**: thank, give thanks (5)
agricola, -ae (ille): farmer
ait = dīcit
āles, ālitis: winged (= **avis**)
alicunde (adv.): from somewhere
aliquantus, -a, -um: some, considerable, not a little
aliquī, aliqua, aliquod: indefinite adjective: some, any
after **nē, nisī, num, sī: quī, qua, quod**; see also page 119 (8)
aliquis, aliquid: indefinite pronoun: someone, something, anyone, anything
after **nē, nisī, num, sī: quis, quid**; see also page 119 (8)
alius, alia, aliud: other, another (7)
alter, -tera, -terum: other, another (pronominal declension)
altus, -a, -um: high
ambitiōsus, -a, -um: fawning, vain
amīcitia, -ae (illa): friendship (4)
amīcus, -a, -um: friendly (2)
amō, -āre, -āvī, -ātus: love (1)
amor, amōris (ille): love (1)
an: whether, or (7)
anima, -ae (illa): wind, breath, soul (9)

animal, -ālis, -ium (illud): animate creature, animal, beast (3)
animus, -ī (ille): soul, mind, heart, courage (9)
annus, -ī (ille): year
ante (adv. and prep. + acc.): before
anteā before, earlier (9)
antepōnō, -ere, -posuī, -positus: place before, prefer
anus, -ūs (illa): old woman
aperiō, -īre, aperuī, apertus: open, uncover, reveal
appareō, -ēre, -uī, -itus: appear, come in sight
appellō, -āre, -āvī, -ātus: call, implore, address
appellō, -ere, -pulī, -pulsus: drive toward, direct toward (11)
appetō, -ere, -īvī,-ītus: strive after, try to get
appōnō, -ere, -posuī, -positus: place near
apud: at the house of (+ acc.) (7)
aqua, -ae (illa): water (4)
aquila, -ae (illa): eagle
aquilo, -ōnis (ille): north wind
arānea, -ae (illa): spider
arbitror, -ārī, -ātus: give judgment, consider as, believe, think, suppose (11)
arbor, -oris (illa): tree (6)
ardeō, -ēre, arsī, arsus: be on fire, burn
ardor, -ōris (ille): flame, fire, heat, ardor
ārea, -ae (illa): piece of level ground, courtyard of a house
arma, -ōrum (illa) n. pl.: arms (armor, weapons)
arripiō (adripiō), -ere, -ripuī, -reptus: snatch, seize, lay hold of, take to oneself
arrogō, -āre, -āvī, -ātus: claim as one's own, arrogate
ars, artis, (-ium) (illa): art, skill, profession (2)
artus, -a, -um: close, sound (sleep)
artus, -ūs (ille): limb, joint
aspiciō, -ere, -spexī, -spectus = conspiciō
at (ast): but (moreover)
Athēnae, -ārum (illae): Athens
atque: and, and also
atrox, -rōcis: savage, atrocious, cruel (2)
attendō, -ere, -tendī, -tentus: direct toward, attend to, direct the attention toward
audax, audācis: bold, audacious (1)
audiō, -īre, -īvī, -ītus: hear (1)
augeō, -ēre, auxī, auctus: increase, augment, furnish (someone *acc.* with something *abl.*)
auris, -is (-ium) (illa): ear (11)
aurum, -ī (illud): gold
auferō, auferre, abstulī, ablātus: bear away, steal
aut: or; **aut...aut**: either...or (2)
autem: however, on the other hand, moreover (5)
avārus, -a, -um: greedy, covetous, avaricious (2)
avidus, -a, -um: avid, eager, greedy
avis, -is (-ium) (illa): bird (6)

Belgae, -ārum (illī): Belgians
bellum, -ī (illud): war (7)
bellus, -a, -um: pretty, handsome, charming (11)
bene: well (7)
beō, -āre, -āvī, -ātus: make happy, bless (6)
bibō, -ere, bibī, bibitus: drink (8)
blandus, -a, -um: flattering, fawning
bonus, -a, -um: (morally) good; masc. pl. **bonī**: upper class people; neut. pl. **bona**: goods (2)
bōs, bovis (ille, illa): bull, cow
brevis, -e: short, small (2)
brūtus, -a, -um: irrational, unreasonable

cachinnus, -ī (ille): loud laughter
caecus, -a, -um: blind (4)
caelum, -ī (illud): sky, heaven, the heavens (9)
candidus, -a, -um: dazzling white, beautiful, clear (8)
canō, -ere, cecinī, cantus: sing, celebrate by song, recite (poetry) (2)
canōrus, -a, -um: melodious, harmonious

cantus, -ūs (ille): singing
capax, -ācis: roomy, spacious, capacious
capillus, -ī (ille): hair (of the head)
capiō, -ere, cēpī, captus: take, seize, capture (9)
capra, -ae (illa): she-goat
caput, -itis (illud): head (3)
caritas, -ātis (illa): costliness, dearness, esteem, affection, love
carmen, carminis (illud): song, poem (2)
carpō, -ere, carpsī, carptus: pluck, snatch
carus, -a, -um: dear and precious
cāseus, -ī (ille): cheese
catēna, -ae (illa): chain (used as a fetter)
caupo, -ōnis (ille): innkeeper
causa, -ae (illa): cause, reason
caveō, -ēre, cavī, cautus: beware, be on one's guard
cēdō, -ere, cessī, cessus: go, go away from, yield
celer, -eris, -ere: swift
celsus, -a, -um: high, lofty
Celtae, -ārum (illī): Celts
cēnō, -āre, -āvī, -ātus: take a meal, dine, eat (8)
cēra, -ae (illa): wax, wax writing-tablet
cernō, -ere, crēvī, crētus: discern, distinguish
certus, -a, -um: certain
circumsiliō, -īre: hop around
cīvitās, -ātis (illa): citizenship, the body-politic, the state (10)
clāmō, -āre, -āvī, -ātus: shout
coepiō, -ere, coepī, coeptus: (= **incipiō**) begin
cōgitō, -āre, -āvī, -ātus: pursue something in the mind, reflect, think (5)
cognōscō, -ere, cognōvī, cognitus: learn (by inquiring), recognize, know (5)
colligō, -ere, -lēgī, -lectus: collect
columba, -ae (illa): dove
coma, -ae (illa): hair of the head
comedō, -ēsse, -ēdī, -ēsus: eat up, consume
comes, -mitis (ille, illa): companion, comrade
comitor, -ārī, -ātus: join one's self to another as an attendant, accompany
commodus, -a, -um: complete, perfect, of full measure, opportune, commodious, appropriate (10)
commūnis, -e: common
compellō, -ere, -pulī, -pulsus: drive together, compel
compēs, -pedis (illa): fetter, shackle (for the feet)
competītor, -ōris (ille): rival, competitor
comprehendō, -ere, -dī, -nsus: catch hold of something on all sides, apprehend, comprehend
concēdō, -ere, -cessī, -cessus: yield along with, give up, relinquish, cede
concerpō, -ere, -psī, -ptus: pluck
conciliō, -āre, -āvī, -ātus: bring together, conciliate
conclāmō, -āre, -āvī, -ātus: call together, cry out loudly
concordō, -āre, -āvī, -ātus: agree together, become concordant
concutiō, -ere, -cussī, -cussus: strike together
condūcō, -ere, -dūxī, -ductus: rent
conferō, -ferre, -tulī, collātus: unite, join
conficiō, -ere, -fēcī, -fectus: make, compose; bring about, effect; consume, destroy
conflō, -āre, -āvī, -ātus: blow together, conflate
confūsio, -ōnis (illa): confusion
coniunctior, -ius: more connected
consilium, -ī (illud): deliberation, counsel, council (10)
conspiciō, -ere, -spexī, -spectus: look at attentively, catch sight of, perceive (6)
constituō, -ere, -uī, -tūtus: establish, determine, agree upon
consul, -ulis (ille): consul, one of the two highest Roman magistrates, chosen annually
consultus, -ī (ille): lawyer (= **iūrisconsultus**)
continenter: continually
contrā: in opposition, in return, opposite
convertō, -ere, -vertī, -versus: turn toward, convert
cōpia, -ae (illa): abundance

cor, cordis (-ium) (illud): heart
cornū, -ūs (illud): horn (2)
corpus, -oris (illud): body (6)
corripiō, -ere, -ripuī, -reptus: seize upon, snatch up
corvus, -ī (ille): raven
crās: tomorrow
crēbescō, -ere, -bruī: become frequent
crēdō, -ere, crēdidī, crēditus: entrust, confide to, believe (5)
crescō, -ere, crēvī, crētus: grow, increase
crīmen, -inis (illud): crime
cruentus, -a, -um: bloody, stained with blood
crūs, crūris (illud): leg, shin
cultus, -ūs (ille): culture
cum (quom): when: *generalized:* since, because, although, while (8)
cum: with (+ abl.) (5)
cupidissimus, -a, -um: most desirous of
cupiditās, -ātis (illa): desire
Cupīdo, -īdinis (ille): Cupid, son of Venus
cupidus, -a, -um: longing, desiring, loving, greedy for (9)
cupiō, -ere, -īvī, -ītus: desire, want (1)
cūr: why? (8)
cūra, -ae (illa): care, concern (9)
cūrō, -āre, -āvī, -ātus: take care
cursus, -ūs (ille): course, way, journey
cutis, -is (-ium) (illa): skin

daemon, -onis (ille): spirit, demon, god (2)
damnō, -āre, -āvī, -ātus: sentence, condemn (3)
dē: (down) from, concerning (+ abl.) (5)
dēbeō, -ēre, dēbuī, dēbitus: owe, be bound in duty (3)
dēcipiō, -ere, -cēpī, -ceptus: deceive, beguile
dēclīnō, -āre, -āvī, -ātus: turn away
dēcurrō, -ere, -cucurrī: run down, flow
decus, -oris (illud): grace, splendor
dēdūcō, -ere, -dūxī, -ductus: bring or lead away
dēfendō, -ere, -dī, -nsus: defend
dēficiō, -ere, -fēcī, -fectus: fail, cease
dēflectō, -ere, -flexī, -flectus: turn aside
dēformis, -e: ugly, misshapen (5)
deinde (dein): thereupon, then, thereafter
dēlabor, -ī, -lapsus: fall down, slide or fall into
dēleō, -ēre, -lēvī, -lētus: delete, destroy, terminate (11)
dēlicia, -ae (illa): (usually plural) delight
dēligō, -ere, -lēgī, -lectus: select, choose out (10)
dēmānō, -āre, -āvī, -ātus: flow down
dēmonstrō, -āre, -āvī, -ātus: show, demonstrate
dēmum: at last, not until then
dens, dentis (-ium) (ille): tooth
dēpascō, -ere, -pāvī, -pastus (also **dēpascor, -ī**): = **edō**
dēpōnō, -ere, -posuī, -positus: put aside (3)
dēprehendō, -ere, -dī, -nsus: apprehend
dēserō, -ere, -ruī, -rtus: forsake, desert
dēsiderium, -ī (illud): desire
dēterreō, -ēre, -uī, -itus: deter, frighten from (11)
deus, -ī (ille): god
dēvorō, -āre, -āvī, -ātus: swallow, devour
dīcō, -ere, dīxī, dictus: say, tell, speak (1)
dictum, -ī (illud): word, thing said
diēs, -ēī (ille, illa): day (1)
differō, differre, distulī, dīlātus: differ
difficilis, -e: difficult (5)
digitus, -ī (ille): finger
dignitas, -ātis (illa): dignity, worth, merit
dīgnus, -a, -um: deserving, worthy (+ abl.) (6)
dīlābor, -ī, -lapsus: melt away, dissolve
dīligens, -entis: diligent
dīmittō, -ere, -mīsī, -misus: send away, dismiss
dīruō, -ere, -ruī, -rutus: tear asunder, demolish, destroy
dīrus, -a, -um: fearful, horrible, dire
discēdō, -ere, -cessī, -cessus: depart, go away (11)
discō, -ere, didicī, discitūrus: learn (8)
discumbō, -ere, -cubuī, -cubitus: recline at table to eat, lie down to sleep

disertus, -a, -um: eloquent, fluent
dispār, -paris: different, unequal
disputō, -āre, -āvī, -ātus: dispute, discuss
dissimilis, -e: dissimilar (10)
diū: for a long time
diversor (dēversor), -ōris (ille): guest at an inn
dīvertō, -ere, -tī, -sus: turn out of the way
dīvidō, -ere, -vīsī, -vīsus: divide
dīvus, -a, -um: divine; **dīvus, -ī (ille)**: = **deus**
dō, -are, dedī, datus: give (4)
doceō, -ēre, docuī, doctus: teach (1)
doctrīna, -ae (illa): learning
doleō, -ēre, doluī, -itus: feel pain, grieve
dolor, -ōris (ille): pain, grief
dolōsus, -a, -um: crafty
domina, -ae (illa): mistress, royal lady
dominus, -ī (ille): lord, master
domus, -ūs or **-ī (illa)**: house (3)
donec: while, until, as long as (11)
dōnō, -āre, -āvī, -ātus: give
dōnum, -ī (illud): gift (4)
dormiō, -īre, -ī(v)ī, -ītus: sleep
dubitō, -āre, -āvī, -ātus: be in doubt, be uncertain
dūcō, -ere, dūxī, ductus: lead
dulcis, -e: sweet, pleasant (5)
dum: while (6)
dummodo: provided, as long as (11)
duo, duae, duo: two (11)
dux, ducis (ille, illa): leader, commander-in-chief (8)

ē, ex: (out) from (+ abl.) (5)
echīnus, -ī (ille): hedgehog, sea-urchin
edax, -ācis: voracious, devouring
edō, -ere (or **ēsse**), **ēdī, ēsus**: eat (8)
ēdūcō, -ere, -dūxī, -ductus: lead out, withdraw
efficiō, -ere, -fēcī, -fectus: effect, work out, bring about (9)
effigiēs, -ēī (illa): effigy, image, ghost
effodiō, -ere, -fōdī, -fossus: dig up
egeō, -ēre, -uī, -itūrus: be in need
ego: I (5)
ēgregius, -a, -um: distinguished, eminent, excellent (8)
ēlegantior, -ius: more elegant
ēmittō, -ere, -mīsī, -missus: send forth
emō, -ere, emī, emptus: buy
emptor, -ōris (ille): buyer
ēnarrō, -āre, -āvī, -ātus: explain in detail, describe
enim: indeed, of course (7)
eō, īre, -ī(v)ī, ītus: go (10)
equidem: truly, indeed
ēripiō, -ere, -ipuī, -eptus: snatch away
errō, -āre, -āvī, -ātus: wander, make a mistake
et: and (1)
etsī: although, albeit
excruciō, -āre, -āvī, -ātus: torment
exedo, -ēsse, -ēdī, -ēsus: consume
exeō, -īre, -ī(v)ī, -ītus: go away
exigō, -ere, -ēgī, -actus: drive out, exact, complete
existimō, -āre, -āvī, -ātus: think
experientia, -ae (illa): experience
exsultō, -āre, -āvī, -ātus: leap up, exult

fābula, -ae (illa): story (4)
facilis, -e: easy (10)
faciō, -ere, fēcī, factus: do, make (4)
factio, -ōnis (illa): faction
fames, -is (illa): hunger
familiāris, -e: belonging to one's household or family, intimate, familiar, political associate
fās (illud) (indeclinable): divine law, right, lawful, allowable
faux, faucis (-ium) (illa): throat, gullet (usually plural)
faveō, -ēre, fāvī, fautus: favor, be favorable to (+ dat.)
fēmina, -ae (illa): woman (1)
fenestra, -ae (illa): window
ferē: usually, generally
ferō, ferre, tulī, lātus: bring, carry, endure (7)
ferrum, -ī (illud): iron, implement of iron
fictus, -a, -um: fictitious

fidēlis, -e: trusty, faithful (9)
fidēs, -eī (illa): trust, fidelity, faith (9)
fīlia, -ae (illa): daughter (1)
fīliolus, -ī (ille): diminutive of **fīlius**
fīlius, -ī (ille): son (1)
fingō, -ere, finxī, fictus: form, fashion
fīnis, -is (-ium) (illa): boundary; pl.: territory, country (also masc. **ille**)
fīnitimus, -a, -um: adjoining, neighboring, related (10)
fīō, fierī, factus: be made, become (8)
firmāmentum, -ī (illud): a strengthening support, the heavens fixed above the earth, the firmament
flamma, -ae (illa): flame
fleō, -ēre, flēvī, flētus: weep
flūmen, -inis (illud): river, flowing water, flood
foedus, -eris (illud): treaty (9)
folium, -ī (illud): leaf
fons, fontis (-ium) (ille): spring, fountain, well
fore (= **futūrum esse**): future infinitive of **sum, esse** (11)
forma, -ae (illa): figure, shape, appearance, beauty
formīdo, -inis (illa): dread
forsitan: perhaps (3)
fortasse: = **forsitan**
fortis, -e: strong, courageous (5)
fortissimus, -a, -um: most brave (**fortis**), most powerful
fortūna, -ae (illa): fortune, luck (1)
fragor, -ōris (ille): crashing (of something broken to pieces)
fricō, -āre, -cuī, -ctum: rub
fuga, -ae (illa): flight, running away
fugiō, -ere, fūgī, fugitus: flee, shun
fūr, fūris (ille, illa): thief
furor, -ōris (ille): madness, furor
furtum, -ī (illud): theft (3)

Gallia, -ae (illa): Gaul, France
Gallus, -ī (ille): a Gaul
geminus, -a, -um: twin
generō, -āre, -āvī, -ātus: beget, produce
genus, generis (illud): birth, origin, class, descent, race (3)
Germānus, -ī (ille): a German
gerō, -ere, gessī, gestus: conduct, manage, wage (war); wear (as clothing) (7)
gestiō, -īre, -īvī, -ītus: gesticulate, exult
gignō, -ere, genuī, genitus: beget, produce
gladius, -ī (ille): sword (5)
globōsus, -a, -um: spherical
glōria, -ae (illa): glory (3)
glōriōsus, -a, -um: glorious (3)
gradus, -ūs (ille): step
grātia, -ae (illa): favor, friendship, grace, loveliness; **grātiās agere**: thank, give thanks; *abl.* **grātiā**: on account of, for the sake of (4, 5)
grātus, -a, -um: pleasing, agreeable
gravis, -e: heavy, grave, serious
gremium, -ī (illud): lap, bosom

habeō, -ēre, habuī, habitus: have (3)
haustus, -ūs (ille): drinking, swallowing
Helvētius, -ī (ille): a Swiss
herba, -ae (illa): grass, vegetation, herb
Hercle: an oath on the name of Hercules
herī: yesterday (7)
hīc, haec, hōc: this (6)
historia, -ae (illa): history
hodiē: today (7)
homo, hominis (ille): human being, man (1)
honor, -ōris (ille): honor, public office
hōra, -ae (illa): hour
horreō, -ēre, -uī: stand on end, bristle
hortor, -ārī, -ātus: exhort (9)
hūc: to this place
hūmānitās, -ātis (illa): humanity, civilization
hūmānus, -a, -um: human

iaceō, -ēre, -uī: lie, lie down, lie ill, lie dead
iam: now, already
iam ... iam...: now ... now ..., at one time ... at another time ...
Iānuārius, -a, -um: belonging to Janus or January

ibī: there, in that case
ibīdem: in that very same place
īdem, eadem, idem: (the) same (7)
identidem: habitually, often
īdōlon (-um), -ī (illud): image, spectre, ghost
igitur: therefore (10)
ignārus, -a, -um: not knowing, ignorant
ignis, -is (-ium) (ille): fire (3)
ignōminia, -ae (illa): dishonor, ignomy
ignōscō, -ere, -nōvī, -nōtus: forgive
ille, illa, illud: that; he, she, it (5)
illūc: to that place
imāgo, -inis (illa): image, apparition
imber, -bris (ille): rain, rainstorm
immō: on the contrary, by no means
immūtō, -āre, -āvī, -ātus: transform
impediō, -īre, -ī(v)ī, -ītus: hinder, impede
imperātor, -ōris (ille): general, commander
imperō, -āre, -āvī, -ātus: command (9)
impietās, -ātis (illa): impiety
implicitus, -a, -um: entangled
importūnus, -a, -um: unfit, distressing, savage
impotens, -entis: impotent
improbus, -a, -um: wicked, bad, violent
in: in, on, among (+ abl.); into (+ acc.) (5)
inānis, -e: empty
incipiō, -ere, -cēpī, -ceptus: begin (2)
incitō, -āre, -āvī, -ātus: set in rapid motion, incite
inclāmō, -āre, -āvī, -ātus: call upon, cry out to
incognitus, -a, -um: unknown
incolō, -ere, -uī: inhabit
incumbō, -ere, -cubuī, -cubitus: lay one's self upon, bend one's attention to
inde: thenceforward
indignor, -ārī, -ātus: be angry, be displeased
industria, -ae (illa): industry, diligence
inerrō, -āre, -āvī, -ātus: wander about
infāmis, -e: ill spoken of, disreputable, infamous, notorious (11)
inferior, -ius: lower
inferō, -ferre, -tulī, -lātus: carry in, introduce
infīnītus, -a, -um: boundless, unlimited
inflō, -āre, -āvī, -ātus: inflate
ingemō, -ere, -uī: groan, lament, bewail
ingredior, -ī, -gressus: enter in
inhabitō, -āre, -āvī, -ātus: inhabit
inimīcus, -a, -um: inimical
inīquitas, -ātis (illa): iniquity, inequality
initium, -ī (illud): beginning
iniustus, -a, -um: unjust
innocens, -entis: innocent
innumerābilis, -e: innumerable
innuō, -ere, -nuī, -nūtus: nod, give a sign (with the head)
inquam: = **dīcō**
inquit: he/ she/ it says (used only for direct quotation)
insānus, -a, -um: insane
inserō, -ere, -seruī, -sertus: introduce into, insert
insonō, -āre, -uī: make a noise on/ in
instituō, -ere, -uī, -ūtus: institute, undertake
institūtum, -ī (illud): institution
instō, -āre, -stetī, -status: stand upon
intellegō, -ere, -lexī, -lectus: perceive, understand
intendō, -ere, -tendī, -tensus (also **intentus**): stretch out, bend toward, direct
inter: between, among, amongst (+ acc.) (7)
interdiū: during the day
interficiō, -ere, -fēcī, -fectus: kill, murder (5)
interior, -ius: inner
interrogō, -āre, -āvī, -ātus: ask
intrā (adv. and prep. + acc.): inside, within
inveniō, -īre, -vēnī, -ventus: come upon, discover
invidia, -ae (illa): envy, ill will (6)
iocor, -ārī, -ātus: joke
ipse, ipsa, ipsum: very self (intensive) (7)
īra, -ae (illa): anger
irrītō, -āre, -āvī, -ātus: provoke, exasperate
is, ea, id: this/ that (6)
iste, ista, istud: that (person or thing) near you, that of yours, that particular one (11)

ita: so, thus, in this way, in such a manner (9)
iter, itineris (illud): way, journey (10)
iubeō, -ēre, iūssī, iūssus: command, order
iūcundus, -a, -um: pleasant, agreeable, delightful (9)
iūdex, -dicis (ille): judge
iugum, -ī (illud): yoke, ridge or summit of a mountain
iungō, -ere, iūnxī, iūnctus: join (8)
Iūppiter, Iōvis (ille): Jupiter
iurgium, -ī (illud): quarrel
iūs, iūris (illud): law
iustus, -a, -um: just (10)
iuvenca, -ae (illa): cow
iuvō, -āre, iuvī, iutus: aid, help

labor, -ōris (ille): labor
labōrō, -āre, -āvī, -ātus: labor
labrum, -ī (illud): lip
lacerō, -āre, -āvī, -ātus: tear to pieces, lacerate
lacrima, -ae (illa): tear (of weeping)
lacus, -ūs (ille): tub, vat, lake, cistern (2)
lāneus, -a, -um: woolen, soft
lāniger, -gera, -gerum: wool-bearing, wooly, fleecy
lassitūdo, -inis (illa): fatigue
lātior, lātius (gen. **lātiōris**): broader
laudō, -āre, -āvī, -ātus: praise (6)
laurea, -ae (illa): laurel branch carried as a sign of triumph
laus, laudis (illa): praise
lavō, -āre, lāvī, lautus (lavātus, lotus): wash
lectus, -ī (ille): bed
legō, -ere, lēgī, lectus: gather, pick out, survey with the eye, read (9)
lentus, -a, -um: slow
leo, -ōnis (ille): lion
levō, -āre, -āvī, -ātus: lift up
lex, lēgis (illa): law
līber, -bera, -berum: free (7)
liber, -brī (ille): book, scroll (7)
lībertās, -ātis (illa): liberty (10)
libet, (libēre), libuit, libitum: (it) is pleasing (11)
Libitīna, -ae (illa): Libitina, goddess of corpses
licentia, -ae (illa): license
licet, (licēre), licuit, licitum: be at liberty, be allowed, be permitted (9)
ligneus, -a, -um: wooden (3)
lignum, -ī (illud): wood (3)
līmen, -inis (illud): threshold
lingua, -ae (illa): tongue, language, dialect (5)
liquor, -ōris (ille): liquid, water
līs, lītis (illa): quarrel, law trial
littera, -ae (illa): letter (of the alphabet), mark; pl.: epistle, letters (as scholarship), literature (5)
lītus, -toris (illud): seashore, beach
locus, -ī (ille): place, spot
longē (adv.): far, long, at a distance
longissimē (adv.): farthest (**longus, -a, -um**)
loquor, -ī, locūtus: speak, talk, say (5)
lubet: = **libet**
lūbricus, -a, -um: smooth, slippery
lūdō, -ere, lūsī, lūsus: play
lūgeō, -ēre, luxī, (luctus): lament, mourn
lūmen, -inis (illud): light, lamp, light of life, eye, torch (11)
lupus, -ī (ille): wolf
lux, lūcis (illa): light, daylight

maciēs, -ēī (illa): leanness, thinness
magis . . . quam . . .: more . . . than . . . (9)
magistrātus, -ūs (ille): magistracy, municipal administration
magnitūdo, -dinis (illa): magnitude
magnus, -a, -um: big, great (3)
maior, maius (-ōris): greater; **maiōrēs, -um (illī)**: adults, forefathers (10)
male: badly
maleficium, -ī (illud): crime
mālō, mālle, māluī: prefer (9)
malus, -a, -um: bad, evil (4)
manus, -ūs (illa): hand (1)
mare, -ris (-ium/ -um) (illud): sea
marītus, -a, -um: nuptial, conjugal, marital
marmoreus, -a, -um: marble
mās, maris (-ium): male

mater, matris (illa): mother (1)
Mātrona, -ae (ille): the Marne River
mātūrus, -a, -um: ripe, mature, timely, speedy
maximus, -a, -um: greatest, biggest, maximum (10)
mē: me
melior, melius (-iōris): better (10)
mellītus, -a, -um: honey-sweet, lovely
meminī, -isse: remember, be mindful of (6)
memoria, -ae (illa): memory (3)
mens, mentis (illa): the mind (11)
mensis, -is (-ium) (ille): month
mercātus, -ūs (ille): marketplace
mereō, -ēre, -uī, -itus (also **mereor, -ērī, meritus**): deserve, merit, be worthy of (8)
merus, -a, -um: unmixed with anything to dilute it
metus, -ūs (ille): fear, dread (11)
meus, -a, -um: my (6)
mī: = **mihi**
minimus, -a, -um: smallest (10)
ministerium, -ī (illud): office, ministry, employment
minor, minus (-ōris): smaller, less (10)
misellus, -a, -um: diminutive of **miser**
miser, -era, -erum: miserable, wretched (2)
misereō, -ēre, miseruī, -itus (also **misereor, -ērī**): feel pity (3)
miserescō, -ere: pity
miseria, -ae (illa): misfortune, misery, wretchedness (3)
mittō, -ere, mīsī, missus: send (7)
modo ...modo ...: sometimes ... sometimes ...
modus, -ī (ille): a measure, mode, manner (6)
mōles, -is (-ium) (illa): a shapeless, huge, heavy mass
molestus, -a, -um: troublesome, annoying
moneō, -ēre, monuī, monitus: call to mind, remind, advise, warn
mons, montis (ille): mountain
monstrum, -ī (illud): monster
monumentum, -ī (illud): monument
morbus, -ī (ille): sickness
morior, -ī, mortuus: die (4)
moror, -ārī, -ātus: delay, wait
mors, mortis (-ium) (illa): death (4)
morsus, -ūs (ille): bite
mortuus, -a, -um: dead
moveō, -ēre, mōvī, mōtus: move, set in motion, disturb (11)
mox: soon (11)
mulier, -eris (illa): woman, female, wife (9)
multitūdo, -inis (illa): multitude
multus, -a, -um: much, many (7)
mundus, -ī (ille): world

nam: for, because (7)
narrō, -āre, -āvī, -ātus: narrate, tell (4)
nāscor, -ī, nātus: be born (5)
nāsus, -ī (ille): nose (8)
nātūra, -ae (illa): nature
-ne: interrogative suffix (3)
nē: not (emotive negative) (3)
nec (neque): and not, nor (2)
negō, -āre, -āvī, -ātus: deny
nēmō, -minis: no one (7)
nemus, nemoris (illud): grove, glade, meadow
nepos, -ōtis (ille): grandson, descendant, nephew
neque, (nec): and not, nor (2)
nequeō, -īre, -ī(v)ī, -ītus: be unable
nesciō quis, nesciō quid: I know not who/ what; someone, something (11)
nesciō, -īre, -īvī, -ītus: not know, be ignorant of
nex, necis (illa): violent death, murder
nihil (indeclinable neuter): nothing (5)
nīl: = **nihil**
nimium (adverb): too much
nisī: unless, if not, except (8)
nīsus, -ūs (illa): exertion, effort
nitens, -entis: shining bright and beautiful
nitor, -ōris (ille): lustre, sheen, sleekness, splendor, beauty
nōbilis, -e: noble
noceō, -ēre, nocuī, nocitus: hurt, be harmful (5)

noctū: in the night
nōlō, nōlle, nōluī: be unwilling (7)
nōmen, nōminis (illud): name, noun, word, renown (5)
nōn: not (1)
nōnne: negative adverb in direct question, anticipates the answer "yes": "Is it not...?" "It is... isn't it?" (7)
noster, -tra, -trum: our (6)
novissimē (adverb): finally
novitās, -ātis (illa): novelty
novus, -a, -um: new, fresh, young
nox, noctis (-ium) (illa): night (5)
noxius, -a, -um: harmful
nūbō, -ere, nupsī, nuptus: veil oneself for the bridegroom, primarily of the bride (+ dat.); but also of the bridgroom (+ acc.); marry
nūdus, -a, -um: nude, exposed
nūllus, -a, -um: no one, none (6)
num: negative adverb in direct question, anticipates the answer "no": "It is not ...is it?" (7)
num: whether (4)
numerō, -āre, -āvī, -ātus: count
numerus, -ī (ille): number
nummus, -ī (ille): coinage, money
numquam: never (6)
nunc: now
nuntius, -ī (ille): messenger (9)

oblīviscor, -ī, oblitus: forget (4)
obsequium, -ī (illud): indulgence
occīdō, -ere, -cīdī, -cīsus: strike to the ground, kill
occīsio, -ōnis (illa): murder
ocellus, -ī (ille): diminutive of **oculus**
oculus, -ī (ille): eye (11)
ōdī, -isse: hate (6)
odium, -i (illud): hatred (4)
offirmō, -āre, -āvī, -ātus: render firm, hold fast to
olfaciō, -ere, -fēcī, -factus: smell
omnis, -e: all, every (4)
opera, -ae (illa): work, effort
opīnio, -ōnis (illa): opinion
oportet, -ēre, oportuit: it is necessary, right, proper (one ought, should, must) (1)
opprimō, -ere, -pressī, -pressus: overpower, oppress
optimās, -ātis: belonging to the best or noblest, aristocratic (10)
optimus, -a, -um: best (10)
opulentus, -a, -um: opulent
opus, -eris (illud): work, labor, art, workmanship, any result of work; **opus est** (+ abl.): there is need of (9)
ōrātio, -ōnis (illa): oration
ōrātor, -ōris (ille): orator
orbis, -is (-ium) (ille): orb (of the earth)
Orcus, -ī (ille): Orcus, god of the Lower World; the abode of the dead
ōrō, -āre, -āvī, -ātus: pray
ōs, ōris (illud): mouth
os, ossis (illud): bone
ostendō, -ere, -dī, -nsus: display
ōtium, -ī (illud): leisure (4)
ovis, -is (-ium) (illa): sheep (4)

paene (adverb): almost
pānis, -is (-ium) (ille): bread (8)
pār, paris: equal (4)
parens, -entis (ille, illa): parent
pariō, -ere, peperī, paritus (partus): beget, produce
pars, partis (-ium) (illa): part (3)
parvus, -a, -um: small (4)
pascō, -ere, pāvī, pastus: drive to pasture, shepherd
passer, -eris (ille): sparrow
pater, patris (ille): father (1)
paternus, -a, -um: paternal (3)
patrōnus, -ī (ille): patron, advocate, lawyer
paucitās, -ātis (illa): paucity, scarcity
paucus, -a, -um: few, little (7)
pax, pācis (illa): peace (10)
pectus, -oris (illud): breast
pecūnia, -ae (illa): money, wealth, property (2)
peior, peius (-ōris): worse (10)

pellis, -is (-ium) (illa): skin, hide
penes (+ acc.): in the possession or power of
penna, -ae (illa): feather
per (+ acc.): through, through the midst of, on account of (10)
percunctor, -ārī, -cunctātus: investigate by inquiry, question thoroughly
perdō, -ere, perdidī, perditus: destroy, lose (5)
perdūcō, -ere, -dūxī, -ductus: conduct, draw out, lengthen
perennis, -e: lasting through the year, perennial, enduring
pereō, -īre, -ī(v)ī: pass away, die
perhibeō, -ēre, -buī, -itus: call, name
perīculum, -ī (illud): attempt, hazard, danger (2)
perītus, -a, -um: experienced
perpetuus, -a, -um: continuous, perpetual (9)
persuādeō, -ēre, -suāsī, -suāsus: persuade (+ dat.) (9)
pēs, pedis (ille): foot
pessimus, -a, -um: worst (10)
pestilens, -entis: pestilential, unwholesome
petītio, -ōnis (illa): petition, campaign for election to office
petō, -ere, -ī(v)ī, -ītus: make for, head for, look for, attack, demand, seek, require
philosophus, -ī (ille): philosopher (4)
pilus, -ī (ille): hair, fur
pipiō, -āre: pip, chirp
placeō, -ēre, placuī, placitus: please, be pleasing (5)
plebs, -bis (illa): common people, plebians
plēnus, -a, -um: full, filled (8)
plūrimus, -a, -um: most (10)
plūs (plūres, plūra): more (10)
poēma, -atis (illud): poem (2)
poena, -ae (illa): punishment, penalty
poēta, -ae (ille): poet (2)
pol: (interjection) by Pollux! by god!
pōnō, -ere, posuī, positus: put, place, put down
populāris, -e: belonging to the people
populus, -i (ille): people (10)
poscō, -ere, poposcī: demand, desire, beg for, ask for
possum, posse, potuī: be able (3)
post: after (+ acc.); afterwards
posteā: thereafter
posterus, -a, -um: next
postquam (posteāquam): after (11)
potestās, -ātis (illa): political power (10)
praecēdō, -ere, -cessī, -cessus: go before, precede, surpass
praeceps, -cipitis: headlong
praeda, -ae (illa): booty, plunder
praedicō, -āre, -āvī, -ātus: proclaim
praestantia, -ae (illa): preeminence, superiority
praetendō, -ere, -tendī, -tensus (-tentus): stretch forth
prātum, -ī (illud): meadow
pretiōsus, -a, -um: expensive, precious (3)
pretium, -ī (illud): price (3)
prīmus, -a, -um: first, chief (2)
princeps, -cipis: first, in front, foremost; **ille princeps, -cipis:** leader, chief, prince
principium, -ī (illud): beginning, first element
prior, -ius (-ōris): prior, better, superior
prius: (adverb) before
priusquam: (conjunction) before (11)
pro: in front of, on behalf of, instead of (+ abl.) (8)
probābilis, -e: credible, believed, probable, good
probō, -āre, -āvī, -ātus: test, examine, prove, approve
prōdō, -ere, -didī, -ditus: give over, betray
proficiscor, -ī, -fectus: set forth, travel, start out (4)
profugus, -a, -um: fugitive
progressus, -ūs (ille): progress
prohibeō, -ēre, -uī, -itus: prohibit, hold back (11)
prōmittō, -ere, -mīsī, -misus: send forth, let grow (hair), let fall down, foretell, promise

prō-pōnō, -ere, -posuī, -positus: propose, purpose
propter: (preposition) on account of, because of (+ acc.); (adverb) nearby (7)
propterea (quod): because (of which)
prorsus: straight on, precisely
proscrībō, -ere, -scrīpsī, -scrīptus: publish by writing, advertise
prōvincia, -ae (illa): province, a territory outside of Italy that was conquered and brought under Roman rule
proximus, -a, -um: nearest to, closest (+ dat.)
prūdentia, -ae (ille): intelligence, prudence
pūblicē: publicly
pūblicus, -a, -um: public; **rēs pūblica:** republic
puella, -ae (illa): girl (1)
puer, puerī (ille): boy (1)
pugillāris, -e: belonging to the fist or hand; **pugillārēs, -ium (illī):** writing-tablets
pulcher, -chra, -chrum: beautiful (4)
pulcherrimus, -a, -um: most beautiful
pulchritūdo, -inis (illa): beauty
pulsō, -āre, -āvi, -ātus: strike, stamp
putrefaciō, -ere, -fēcī, -factus: putrefy
pȳramis, -īdis (illa): pyramid

quaerō, -ere, quaesīvī, quaesītus: seek to learn, investigate, question (4)
quam: than
quārē (quā rē): why, for which reason (8)
quartus, -a, -um: fourth
quasi: as if, as it were
quatiō, -ere, quassī, quassus: shake
quattuor: four
-que: and (1)
queror, -ī, questus: complain
quī, quae, quod: relative pronoun-adjective: who, that; interrogative adjective: which, what, what kind of; indefinite adjective: any (7)
quia: because (11)
quīdam, quaedam, quiddam (pronoun): a certain one, a certain person/ thing, somebody, something (10)
quīn: but that (10)
quis, quid: interrogative pronoun: who, what? (7)
quisquam, quidquam: someone, anyone (in negative contexts, see page 161) (9)
quisque, quaeque, quodque (pronoun): each one, every one, everybody (11)
quod (adverbial accusative): = **quā rē:** because
quom: = **cum**
quōminus: whereby the less, from (11)
quoque: also

rāna, -ae (illa): frog
rapidus, -a, -um: quick, rapid
rapiō, -ere, -puī, -ptus: snatch, steal, seize
ratio, -ōnis (illa): calculation, reckoning, account, a business transaction, regard, concern for, understanding, reason (9)
re-cipiō, -ere, -cēpī, -ceptus: take, betake oneself
re-condō, -ere, -didī, -ditus: put back, hide
red-dō, -ere, -didī, -ditus: give back, return
red-eō, -īre, -iī, -ītus: return (11)
rēgālis, -e: regal
regnum, -ī (illud): kingship
regō, -ere, rēxī, rectus: rule, direct, administer (1)
relinquō, -ere, -līquī, -lictus: leave, leave behind, relinquish
reliquus, -a, -um: remaining, that which is left
re-mittō, -ere, -mīsī, -missus: send back, put aside
re-nāscor, -ī, -nātus: be born again
re-pellō, -ere, -ppulī, -pulsus: repulse, drive back
repente: suddenly
reperiō, -īre, repperī, repertus: find again, find out, discover
re-petō, -ere, -īvī, -ītus: seek again (3)
requīrō, -ere, -quīsī(v)ī, -quīsītus: seek to know, ask
rēs, reī (illa): affair, thing, property, cause, lawsuit, event (2)

resīdō, -ere, -sēdī: sit down
re-solvō, -ere, -solvī, -solūtus: untie, loosen
rēspiciō, -ere, -spexī, -spectus: look away, look up, look back
rēspondeō, -ēre, -spondī, -sponsus: answer, respond, present in return
reus, -a, -um: guilty
rex, rēgis (ille): king (4)
Rhēnus, -ī (ille): the Rhine River
rīdeō, -ēre, rīsī, rīsus: laugh
rīte: ritually, according to ritual observances
rīvus, -ī (ille): stream, brook
rōbur, -oris (illud): strength
rogō, -āre, -āvī, -ātus: ask (4)
Rōmae: at Rome
Rōmulus, -ī (ille): Romulus, the mythical founder and first king of Rome
rostrum, -ī (illud): beak, snout, muzzle, prow of a ship, rostrum
rubeō, -ēre: be red
rūgōsus, -a, -um: wrinkled
ruīna, -ae (illa): downfall, ruin
rumpō, -ere, rūpī, ruptus: burst
ruō, -ere, ruī, rutus: fall down, go to ruin
rursus (adverb): again, on the other hand (11)
rūs, rūris (illud): the country (as opposed to the city), countryside (11)

sacculus, -ī (ille): little sack, purse
saepe: often (9)
sāl, salis (ille): salt, wit, sarcasm (8)
salus, -ūtis (illa): health, a wish for one's welfare, greeting
salvus, -a, -um: safe, unharmed, well, sound
sanctus, -a, -um: holy, sacred
sapiens, -ientis (-ium): wise (3)
sapientia, -ae (illa): wisdom (1)
sapiō, -ere, -īvī: taste, have taste, be sensible
satiō, -āre, -āvī, -ātus: satisfy, satiate (2)
satis (sat) (indeclinable): enough (5)
saxum, -ī (illud): rock, stone (5)
scientia, -ae (illa): knowledge
sciō, -īre, -īvī, -ītus: know (8)
scītō: imperative of **sciō**
scrībō, -ere, scrīpsī, scrīptus: write, draw, compose in writing (2)
sē (sēsē) (gen.: **suī**; dat.: **sibi**; abl.: **sē**): reflexive pronoun: himself, herself, itself, themselves; one another (7)
secundus, -a, -um: second
sed: but (4)
sedeō, -ēre, sēdī, sessus: sit
sēdēs, -is (illa): seat, foundation
semel: once, a single time
semper: always, forever (1)
sempiternus, -a, -um: eternal (3)
senex, senis: old, aged (11)
senior, senius (seniōris): older
sensus, -ūs (ille): sense, faculty of feeling and perceiving
sentiō, -īre, sensī, sensus: perceive, sense
sēparō, -āre, -āvī, -ātus: separate
sepeliō, -īre, -pelī(v)ī, -pultus: entomb
Sēquana, -ae (illa): the Seine River
sequor, sequī, secūtus: follow (4)
serēnus, -a, -um: serene
seriēs, (**illa**; genitive not found; accusative: **-em**): series
sermo, -ōnis (ille): conversation
servus, -ī (ille): slave, servant (7)
sēsē: = **sē**
seu: = **aut, sive:** or (if)
seu... seu...: if... or if, whether... or...
sex: six
sī: if (7)
sīc: so, thus, in such a manner, in this (or that) way (9)
siccō, -āre, -āvī, -ātus: dry up
sīcut (sīc ut): just as, (thus as)
significō, -āre, -āvī, -ātus: give a sign, signify
signum, -ī (illud): sign
silentium, -ī (illud): silence, stillness
similis, -e: similar (+ gen. or dat.) (6)
simul: at the same time as, as soon as; together
simulācrum, -ī (illud): likeness, semblance, phantom
sīn: = **sī nē:** if on the contrary
sincērus, -a, -um: sincere, genuine (9)

sine: without (+ abl.)
singulāris, -e: singular, alone of its kind
singulus, -a, -um: (usually plural) one to each, separate, single
sinō, -ere, sīvī, situs: allow, permit (10)
sinus, -ūs (ille): fold, particularly the fold of the upper part of the toga, hence, the bosom; also the lap
sitis, -is (-ium) (illa): thirst
situs, -ūs (ille): site, construction
societās, -ātis (illa): society, association, union
sōlāciolum, -i (illud): diminutive of **sōlācium**: comfort, consolation
soleō, -ēre, -uī, -itus: be wont, be accustomed (10)
sōlitūdo, -inis (illa): solitude
sollers, -ertis: skilled
sōlus, -a, -um: alone, only, lonely (2)
somnus, -ī (ille): sleep
sonus, -ī (ille): sound, noise
spatiōsus, -a, -um: spacious
spectō, -āre, -āvī, -ātus: look at
speculum, -ī (illud): mirror (6)
spērō, -āre, -āvī, -ātus: hope
squālor, -ōris (ille): squalor
status, -ūs (ille): posture, attitude, state, condition (10)
sternō, -ere, strāvī, strātus: spread out
stilus, -ī (ille): stylus (pointed iron pen used for writing on wax tablets), style (5)
stō, -āre, stetī, status: stand
strepitus, -ūs (ille): noise
studium, -ī (illud): study, application to something, inclination, devotion
stultus, -a, -um: stupid (3)
stupor, -ōris (ille): numbness, dullness, stupidity
suāvior, -ius (-ōris): more delightful, more agreeable
sub: under (+ acc.); (within) under (+ abl.); near (+ abl.); at the outskirts of (e.g., a city); at the base of (e.g., a mountain) (5)
sub-sīdō, -ere, -sēdī, -sessus: sink down, subside
sub-volō, -āre, -āvī: fly up (from beneath)
suf-ferō, -ferre, sustulī, sublātus: take upon one's self
sum, esse, fuī, (futūrus): be, exist (2)
summus, -a, -um: greatest, highest, the top of (10)
super: above, beyond, in addition
superior, -ius (-ōris): higher
superō, -āre, -āvī, -ātus: rise above, surpass
surgō, -ere, surrexī, surrectus: arise, get up
suspiciō, -ere, -spexī, -spectus: suspect
suus, -a, -um: one's own, his/her/its/their own (7)

taberna, -ae (illa): inn
taceō, -ēre, -cuī, -citus: be silent, keep silent (11)
tālis, -e: such, of such a quality (8)
tam . . . quam . . .: as (much) . . . as . . . (9)
tam: so, so much (9)
tamen: nevertheless (3)
tangō, -ere, tetigī, tactus: touch, impress, affect
tantus, -a, -um: so great, so much (8)
tegō, -ere, texī, tectus: cover
tellus, -ūris (illa): earth
tempus, -oris (illud): time (6)
tenebra, -ae (illa) (usually plural): darkness, darkness of the underworld, haunts (11)
tenebricōsus, -a, -um: full of darkness
teneō, -ēre, tenuī, tentus: hold
tenuis, -e: thin, fine
tertius, -a, -um: third
timeō, -ēre, -uī: fear, be afraid of (8)
timidus, -a, -um: timid, afraid, cowardly (2)
timor, -ōris (ille): fear
titulus, -ī (ille): title, placard, sign, notice
toga, -ae (illa): toga (outer garment of male clothing, usually worn in times of peace and to conduct public affairs) (5)
tolerō, -āre, -āvī, -ātus (toleror, -ārī, -ātus): tolerate
tollō, -ere, sustulī, sublātus: lift up, take

up, raise (8)
torpeō, -ēre: be sluggish, torpid, dull
tot: so many, so great a number (9)
tot…quot…: so many…as…(9)
tōtus, -a, -um: whole, entire (6)
trahō, -ere, traxī, tractus: draw, drag
trans: beyond, across (+ acc.)
trēs, tria: three (10)
tristis, -e: sad
triumphus, -ī (ille): triumphal procession
tū: you (5)
tum (adverb): then, thereupon
tum deinde: then, next, thereupon
tumulus, -ī (ille): sepulchral mound
tunc: then
turbulentus, -a, -um: turbulent, turbid, muddy
turgidulus, -a, -um: diminutive of **turgidus:** swollen
tuus, -a, -um: your (singular) (6)
tyrannus, -ī (ille): tyrant

ubī: where, when (8)
ubīque: everywhere
ūllus, -a, -um: any (8)
umquam: ever (8)
unde: from which place
unguentum, -ī (illud): perfume, perfumed unguent
ūnus, -a, -um: one (10)
urbs, urbis (-ium) (illa): city (5)
usque: all the way
ūsus, -ūs (ille): use, usefulness, employment
ut + indicative: as
ut: (in order) that (4)
ut…ut…: as if…as if…
utinam: O that, if only (optative adverb) (3)

vacuus, -a, -um: empty, vacant
vāgīna, -ae (illa): sheath
validius (adverb): more strongly
varius, -a, -um: changing, various, diverse (2)
-ve: = **aut**
veniō, -īre, vēnī, ventus: come (8)
Venus, -neris (illa): Venus, goddess of love; love as a force of nature
venustus, -a, -um: lovely, graceful, elegant, beautiful
vēr, vēris (illud): spring
verbum, -ī (illud): word
vērē: truthfully
vereor, -ērī, -itus: fear, be afraid (10)
vēritas, -ātis (illa): truth (4)
vērō (adverb): in truth
vērus, -a, -um: true (9)
vester, -stra, -strum: your (plural)
via, -ae (illa): way, road (9)
vidēlicet: clearly, it is allowed to see
videō, -ēre, vīdī, vīsus: see (1)
vigilia, -ae (illa): wakefulness
vigilō, -āre, -āvī, -ātus: spend the night awake
vīlitās, -ātis (illa): cheapness
vinc(u)lum, -ī (illud): fetter, chain
vindicō, -āre, -āvī, -ātus: lay legal claim to as one's own
vīnum, -ī (illud): wine (3)
vir, virī (ille): man (1)
virtūs, -ūtis (illa): manliness, virtue, courage (4)
vīrus, -ī (illud): poisonous liquid, slime
vīs, vis (illa), plural: **vīrēs, -ium:** force, strength
vīta, -ae (illa): life (1)
vītālis, -e: of life, vital
vitium, -ī (illud): fault, vice (4)
vītō, -āre, -āvī, -ātus: avoid, escape
vīvō, -ere, vīxī, victus: live (4)
vocō, -āre, -āvī, -ātus: call, invite, summon, name(10)
volō, velle, voluī: be willing (7)
volūbilis, -e: rolling
voluntās, -ātis (illa): will, goodwill
vox, vōcis (illa): voice
vulpēcula, -ae (illa): diminutive of **vulpēs:** little fox
vulpēs, -is (-ium) (illa): fox
vultus, -ūs (ille): visage, countenance, face (5)

GLOSSARY FOR NOTE THE PATTERN EXERCISES

Numbers in parentheses indicate the lesson in which the word first appeared in the **index verborum**.

affair: **(illa) rēs, reī** (2)
always: **semper** (1)
art: **(illa) ars, artis, -ium** (2)
as . . . as . . . : **tam . . . quam . . .** (9)
ask: **rogō, -āre, -āvī, -ātus** (4)
avaricious: **avārus, -a, -um** (2)

bad: **malus, -a, -um** (4)
be: **sum, esse, fuī, (futūrus)** (2)
be alive: **vīvō, -ere, vīxī, victus** (4)
be allowed: **licet, -ēre, licuit, licitum est** (9)
be harmful: **noceō, -ēre, nocuī, nocitus** (5)
be permitted: **licet, -ēre, licuit, licitum est** (9)
become: **fīō, fierī, factus** (8)
before: **priusquam** (11)
begin: **incipiō, -ere, -cēpī, -ceptus**
behoove: **oportet, -ēre, oportuit** (1)
blessed: **beātus, -a, -um** (6)
blind: **caecus, -a, -um** (4)
born: **nāscor, -ī, nātus** (5)
but that: **quīn** (10)

can: **possum, posse, potuī** (3)
chief: **prīmus, -a, -um** (2)
child: **nātus, -a, -um** (5)
choose: **dēligo, -ere, -lēgī, -lectus** (10)
city: **(illa) urbs, urbis, -ium** (5)
come: **veniō, -īre, vēnī, ventus** (8)
concerning: **dē** (+ abl.) (5)
condemn: **damnō, -āre, -āvī, -ātus** (3)
condemn to death: **capitis damnāre** (3)
countryside: **(illud) rūs, rūris** (11)

daughter: **(illa) fīlia, -ae** (1)
day: **(ille, illa) diēs, diēī** (1)
death: **(illa) mors, mortis, -ium** (5)
desire: **(ille) amor, -ōris** (1); **(illa) cupiditās, -ātis**
desirous: **cupidus, -a, -um** (9)
destroy: **perdō, -ere, perdidī, perditus** (5)
devil: **(ille) daemon, -onis** (2)
die: **morior, -ī, mortuus** (4)
difficult: **difficilis, -e** (5)

either . . . or . . . : **aut . . . aut . . .** (2)
enemy: **inimīcus, -a, -um**
esteem: **aestimō, -āre, -āvī, -ātus** (3)
every(body): **omnis, -(e)** (4)
every(thing): **(omnis), -e** (4)

father: **(ille) pater, -tris** (1)
few: **paucus, -a, -um** (7)
forget: **oblīviscor, -ī, -blitus** (4)
follow: **sequor, -ī, secūtus** (4)
friend(ly): **amīcus, -a, -um** (2)
friendship: **(illa) amīcitia, -ae** (4)
from: **ā, ab** (+ abl.) (5)

gift: **(illud) dōnum, -ī** (4)
give: **dō, -are, dedī, datus** (4)
god: **(ille) deus, -ī** (1)
good: **bonus, -a, -um** (2)
great: **magnus, -a, -um** (3)

hear: **audiō, -īre, -īvī, -ītus** (1)
her: **(ea) / eam / eius / eī / eā** (6)
him: **(is) / eum / eius / eī / eō** (6)
his (own): **suus, -a, -um** (7)

if: **sī** (7)
infamous: **infāmis, -e** (11)
inquire: **quaerō, -ere, quaesī(v)ī, quaesītus** (4); **requirō, -ere, -quīsī(v)ī, -quisītus; rogō, -āre, -āvī, -ātus** (4)

just: **iustus, -a, -um** (10)

kill: **interficiō, -ere, -fēcī, -fectus** (5)
king: **(ille) rex, rēgis** (5)
know: **intellegō, -ere, -lexī, -lectus** (11)

law: (illa) **lex, lēgis** (1)
lead: **dūcō, -ere, dūxī, ductus**
leader: (ille, illa) **dux, ducis** (8)
letter: (illae) **litterae, -ārum** (5)
life: (illa) **vīta, -ae** (1)
listen: **audiō, -īre, -īvī, -ītus** (1)
love: **amō, -āre, -āvī, -ātus** (1); (ille) **amor, -ōris**

make: **faciō, -ere, fēcī, factus** (4)
man: (ille) **homo, -inis** (1); (ille) **vir, virī** (1)
manner: (ille) **modus, -ī** (6)
me: (**ego**) / **mē** / **meī** / **mihi** / **mē** (5)
money: (illa) **pecūnia, -ae** (2)
mother: (illa) **mater, -tris** (1)
much: **multus, -a, -um** (7)

need: **opus est** (+ abl.) (9)
never: **numquam** (6)
no one: **nēmō, -minis** (7); **nūllus, -a, -um** (6)
not: **nōn** (1)

only: **sōlus, -a, -um** (2)
ought: **oportet, -ēre, oportuit** (1)
our: **noster, -stra, -strum** (6)

philosopher: (ille) **philosophus, -ī** (4)
pity: **miseret, -ēre, miseruit** (3)
poem: (illud) **poēma, -atis** (2)
praise: **laudō, -āre, -āvī, -ātus** (6)

question: **quaerō, -ere, quaesīvī, quaesītus** (4)

receive: **accipiō, -ere, -cēpī, -ceptus** (9)
republic: (illa) **rēs pūblica, reī pūblicae** (10)
return: **redeō, -īre, -iī, -ītus** (11)
rule: **regō, -ere, rēxī, rectus** (1)

satisfy: **satiō, -āre, -āvī, -ātus** (2)
say: **dīcō,-ere, dīxī, dictus** (1)
see: **videō, -ēre, vīdī, vīsus** (1)
seem: passive of **videō** (4)
servant: (ille, illa) **servus / serva, -ī / -ae** (7)
set out: **proficiscor, -ī, -fectus** (4)
sheep: (illa) **ovis,-is, -ium** (4)
sing: **canō, -ere, cecinī, cantus** (2)
so... but that: introduces a result clause after a negative: **tam... quīn** (10)
so that (purpose): **ut** / negative: **nē** (4)
somebody: **aliquis, (aliquid)** (8), see also page 119
son: (ille) **fīlius, -ī** (1)
song: (illud) **carmen, -minis** (2) / (illud) **poēma, -atis** (2)
soon: **mox** (11)
soul: (ille) **animus, -ī** / (illa) **anima, -ae** (9)
speak: **dīcō, -ere, dīxī, dictus** (1) / **loquor, -ī, locūtus** (5)
splendid: **bellus, -a, -um** (11) / **candidus, -a, -um** (8) / **ēgregius, -a, -um** (8) / **pulcher, -chra, -chrum** (4)
state: (illa) **cīvitas, -ātis** (10) / (illa) **rēs pūblica, reī pūblicae** (10)
stupid: **stultus, -a, -um** (3)
suppose: **arbitror, -ārī, -ātus** (11)

teach: **doceō, -ēre, docuī, doctus** (1)
that (demonstrative): **ille illa, illud** (5) / **is, ea, id** (6) / **iste, ista, istud** (11)
that: (relative): **quī, quae, quod** (7)
their (own): **suus, -a, -um** (7)
them: (**eī, eae**) / **eōs, eās** / **eōrum, eārum** / **eīs** / **eīs** (6)
think: **arbitror, -ārī, -ātus** (11) / **cōgitō, -āre, -āvī, -ātus** (5)
this: **hīc, haec, hōc** (6) / **is, ea, id** (6)
time: (illud) **tempus, -oris** (6)
to: **ad** (+ acc.) (5)
trust: (illa) **fidēs, -eī** (9)
truth: (illa) **vēritas, -ātis** (4)

unhappy: **miser, -era, -erum** (2): *see* wretched
unless: **nisī** (8)
us: (**nōs**) / **nōs** / **nostrum, nostrī** / **nōbīs** / **nōbīs** (5)

want: **volō, velle, voluī** (7)
what: (interrogative): (**quis**), **quid** (7) / (relative): (**quī**), (**quae**), **quod** (7)

what kind: **quālis, -e** (8)
whether: **num** (4)
who: (interrogative): **quis, (quid)** / (relative): **quī, quae, (quod)** (7)
wisdom: **(illa) sapientia, -ae** (1)
wise: **sapiens, -ientis, -ium** (3)
with: **cum** (+ abl.) (5)
while: **dum** (6)
woman: **(illa) fēmina, -ae** (1)
wretched: **miser, -era, -erum** (2)
write: **scrībō, -ere, scrīpsī, scrīptus** (2)

you: singular: **tu / tē / tuī / tibi / tē**; plural: **vōs / vōs / vestrum, vestrī / vōbīs / vōbīs** (5)
your: singular: **tuus, -a, -um**; plural: **vester, -stra, -strum** (6)

INDEX